MW00628136

SERVICE ORIENTED ENTERPRISES

SERVICE ORIENTED ENTERPRISES

Setrag Khoshafian

Auerbach Publications is an imprint of the
Taylor & Francis Group, an informa business

Auerbach Publications
Taylor & Francis Group
6000 Broken Sound Parkway NW, Suite 300
Boca Raton, FL 33487-2742

Printed in the United States of America on acid-free paper
10 9 8 7 6 5 4 3 2 1

International Standard Book Number-10: 0-8493-5360-2 (Hardcover)
International Standard Book Number-13: 978-0-8493-5360-4 (Hardcover)

Library of Congress Cataloging-in-Publication Data

Khoshafian, Setrag.
Service Oriented Enterprises / Setrag Khoshafian.
p. cm.
Includes bibliographical references and index.
ISBN 0-8493-5360-2 (alk. paper)
1. Management information systems. 2. Business--Data processing. I. Title.

HD30.213.K455 2007
658--dc22 2006017155

Visit the Taylor & Francis Web site at
http://www.taylorandfrancis.com

and the Auerbach Web site at
http://www.auerbach-publications.com

Contents

Foreword

Ideas achieve their potential only if the context is appropriately understood. Without proper context even great ideas are underserved, markets are missed, and leaders of industry fall. This book provides a novel case for the business context in which to apply the important technical idea of *service orientation* and moves it from being an interesting tool for engineers to a vehicle for business managers to fundamentally improve their businesses.

This is a critical time for such an idea to be properly applied. An accelerating competitive drum demands that businesses change at a pace that was inconceivable a decade ago. Business must respond with ever faster continuous improvement of existing operations and the constant introduction of new products, and only companies that master the required rhythm of change will persevere and prosper. Businesses that learn to build in a capacity for rapid change are becoming the fiercest and boldest competitors.

Service orientation starts as a powerful technical idea to operationalize the goal of rapid enterprise change by allowing business processes to negotiate diverse systems. This offers a technical advantage as it becomes easier to integrate systems and to reposition existing capabilities for new purposes. Silos of technology that were hidden in arcane interfaces become reusable components that are accessible through transparent standards.

But an organization that only adopts service orientation as a technical architecture is missing the true potential of the concept. The service orientation revolution will fully empower organizations that apply it to both their technology and their culture. The proper context for service orientation extends beyond the technical architecture to the very philosophy of how a business should operate.

Applying a service oriented approach to the management of business performance will change the fundamental dynamics of a business. Interactions are understood in terms of results and quality. False boundaries melt—

boundaries between corporate silos, between business and information technology (IT), between a company and its customers. Establishing fluidity across boundaries provides agility, transparency, and fundamental competitive advantage.

Communications engineers use a measure called *quality of service* (QoS) in describing how networks should be tuned to optimize for different throughput needs and priorities. Service oriented enterprises (SOEs) can apply this concept to the full fabric of interactions in the business. Service level rules put prioritization and compliance into each interaction. Process monitoring is inherent in all transactions, ensuring objective assessments of responsiveness and quality. Much as QoS provides a basis for understanding and calibrating a messaging infrastructure, the broad application of service orientation creates transparency across all elements of a business.

Thus, understanding the technical aspects of service orientation is just a starting point. Applying its lessons to technical interoperability will yield an improved technical foundation. However, an outstanding foundation is insufficient in a world that demands the whole enterprise change at accelerating rates. Applying service orientation precepts to the overall philosophy of a company creates a new way of doing business—one that leverages the technical foundation into the very way the business is measured and managed.

In this important book, Setrag Khoshafian starts with the technological underpinnings of service orientation to show its value as a technical architecture. But he goes on to show that the optimal context for service orientation is in creating a service culture: a radical change that goes beyond the technology to the underlying dynamics of how business operates. As every layer of the business is transformed by these principles, the entire service oriented enterprise becomes agile and extraordinary.

Current enthusiasm about the technically appealing enterprise service bus (ESB) has obscured views of how this fits into the full needs of dynamic enterprises. Though this is an important technical foundation, there are three layers to the required enterprise architecture. Sitting above the enterprise service bus must be an organizational commitment to business process management (BPM) and enterprise performance management (EPM).

Service oriented enterprises understand that these relationships need to progress far beyond the technical. All constituencies need service-based relationships—spanning and integrating customers, partners, shareholders, employees, the government, and the community at large. The need to rapidly respond to these constituents is increasing as technology flattens our world, as enterprises globalize, and as competition intensifies. Treating these demands by only adopting the technical plumbing of interoperability will not provide the agility needed across the enterprise. Success requires that business executives drive a cultural transformation to achieve the service oriented enterprise. Bringing this service message out of the basement and into the corridors of the business will empower performance across the full continuum of technology and people.

Thus, the proper context for service orientation is in adopting the service oriented enterprise, where the business managers and technologists achieve breakthroughs in business integration. Here the technical principles are complemented and extended to how the business sets goals, measures progress, and evolves. The result is a powerful interoperability and true competitive advantage. This book will show you how a three-tier architecture of performance management, business process automation, and a strong service architecture supports the top priorities of twenty-first-century enterprises: innovation, productivity, and compliance.

I have had the pleasure of working closely with Setrag in recent years as we have developed an innovative technical architecture that lets businesses use agility as a competitive weapon. This book captures the context in which organizations should think about how service principles can enable rapid change throughout their businesses. Companies that master the message and drive service orientation across both technology and culture will find the agility and benefits to become best in class.

Alan Trefler
CEO and Chairman
Pegasystems Inc.

Preface

Service orientation has had quite a ride. In almost every trade magazine that covers enterprise computing can be found a service oriented "something." This is reminiscent of the object-oriented hype that swept the IT industry two decades ago. There were object-oriented languages, object-oriented analysis, object-oriented programming, object-oriented databases, ad infinitum. It was necessary to be object oriented then. Now, it is necessary to be service oriented.

But exactly what is service orientation, and, more important, why should business owners, IT managers, and programmers care? Is service orientation just a fad? Not quite.

This book will cover the core concepts of service orientation. But more than concepts of service orientation, the book is about service oriented enterprises (SOEs). SOEs are not just about technology or a framework for building systems. Technology is important and necessary. But the book is also about the service oriented culture. To fully realize the potential of service orientation, enterprises need to develop the corporate culture of service. Service oriented enterprises leverage technology to service and to serve many communities. It is this culture of serving and focusing on the needs of others that will best leverage the infrastructures of service orientation.

Therefore, the service oriented enterprise is a new standards-based integration paradigm. It is a new way of building enterprises that are extended, virtual, real-time, and resilient. It is a new way of thinking about applications, partnerships, and outsourcing. Service oriented enterprises provide a framework that narrows the chasm between IT and business owners. Finally, the elusive business–technical rapprochement becomes a reality under the umbrella of a service culture.

Service oriented enterprises are a new approach in professional dealings—in business. Each party or participant in service orientation sees herself as a service provider as well as a service consumer, in an increasingly

well-connected global economy. Actually there is nothing new here. Businesses have been serving their clientele (well, at least claiming to do so) since time immemorial. But service orientation is different in two essential ways. First, culturally organizations are realizing the best productivity could be achieved if they focus on serving the needs of the parties with whom they interact and serve: their customers, yes—but also their employees, trading partners, shareholders, government, and communities. This is often characterized as *servant leadership,* and without this essential cultural shift much of what goes under the banner of service orientation is hollow. The cultural shift to focus on and to serve the various target communities of the SOE helps the enterprise realize the full potential of the underlying service oriented infrastructures and technologies.

The second change, of course, is the emergence of service orientation as a new enabling technological trend. Building primarily on the success of the Internet as well as on a much better understanding of how business policies and processes could be automated, today we are witnessing the emergence of robust service oriented platforms. These platforms are reflected in three essential layers: an enterprise performance layer (also called business performance management and corporate performance management), a business process management layer, and the underlying service oriented architecture infrastructure.

The enterprise performance management layer focuses on specifying the strategic key performance indicators of the service enterprise and tying

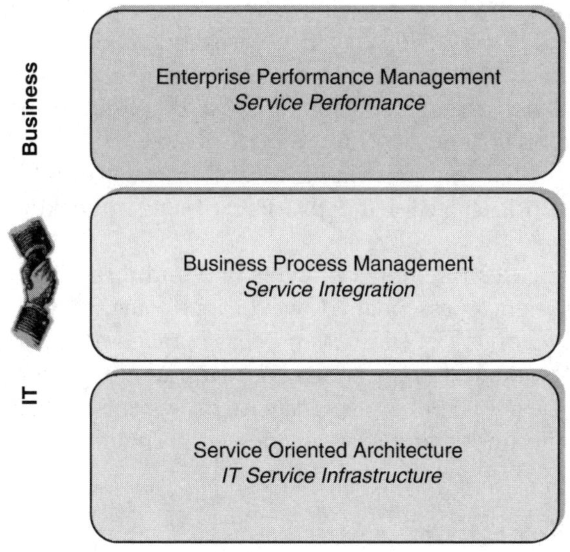

these to underlying business processes and policies, or business rules. Business processes in turn utilize the infrastructure services provided by the service oriented architecture. A key component here is the enterprise service bus (ESB). The ESB provides a common standards services-based brokering container. In its traditional role, the focus of IT is the underlying infrastructure and its reliability. New technologies such as ESBs have emerged to enhance, to extend, and to improve IT deployments. However, at their core the focus of these service technologies is on low-level infrastructure. In contrast, business stakeholders focus on performance management, strategies, and key performance indicators of the business. At this layer IT infrastructure is viewed as an enabler. Business process management systems—the middle layer—bring IT and businesses together and narrow, and sometimes eliminate, the IT–business divide. Business process management systems allow enterprises to separate their business processes and business rules to model and to manage them independently of applications. This is key. Business processes and policies become assets. Modeling, executing, and continuously improving the business processes and business policies become the common language between business and IT. The business processes include human participants; back-end applications, such as enterprise resource planning or human resources legacy applications; and trading partners. The business policies capture and digitize both strategic and tactical business objectives. In fact, business rules control and drive the business policies. With this middle BPM layer, the service enterprise is both collecting and maintaining processes and policies as enterprise assets while at the same time executing processes and continuously monitoring their performance. The managed processes and business rules are agile; they can easily be modified. In some cases processes can correct themselves to achieve the mission critical goals of the enterprise. In other cases management cockpits allow business owners to continuously monitor and control the performance of their processes. One of the most essential requirements is to drill down, to understand, and to improve the performance of the processes behind the key performance measures.

This book focuses primarily on layers two and three. Enterprise performance management is essential. However, performance will be discussed especially in the context of business process management and the management of service oriented applications. The overall emphasis of the book is the emerging business process management systems integrating services supported by the underlying service oriented architectures.

Service Orientation

Service orientation provides the ability to loosely couple applications, trading partners, and organizations and to invoke them via service calls. The coupling is often achieved through discovery. Furthermore, independent services can be composed in processes to provide even greater value than the sum of component services. Service orientation enables internal applications as well as external trading partners to participate in straight-through processing involving internal as well as partner procedures, policies, and applications.

Let's expand upon the terms in this very basic definition. One is *loose coupling*. This means the service can be used and integrated within an application while at the same time being isolated from the details of the service's implementation language, platform, location, or status. Services provide programmatic interfaces to Web sites or applications. There are a number of operations. Each operation has input and output messages. This collection of operations constitutes the programmatic interface to the service. The implementation details, the implementation platform, and the implementation language are all hidden.

The other term that characterizes service orientation is *discovery*. The famous triangle illustration is often used to depict the registration–discovery–exchange cycle in service orientation. The ultimate goal is to have dynamic discovery of services on the fly.

The enterprise service bus is a key layer used in the service discovery, management, and request–response brokering. The third term used in the description of service orientation is *process*. Business process management extends and leverages the service bus. A process provides the information as well as controls sequencing between services. Processes

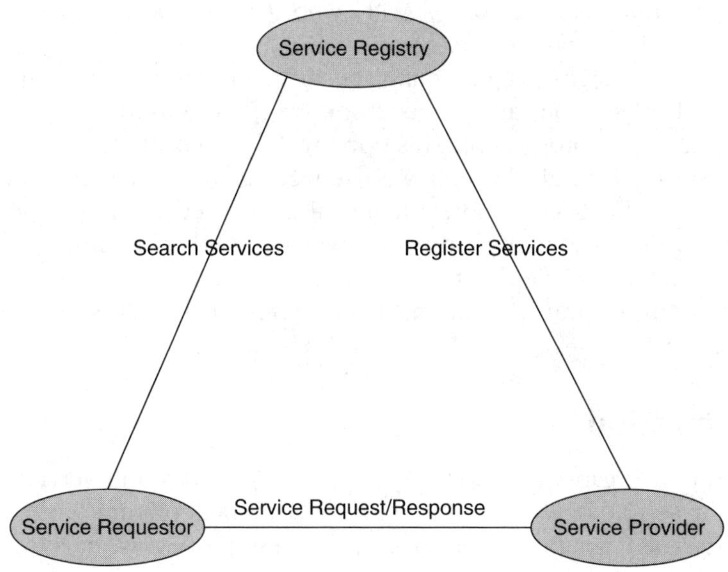

also involve human participants. More importantly, processes include simple as well as complex decision making. Business rules guide and control the processes.

The fourth term, *agreed upon,* pertains to agreements between service participants, which include internal participants and trading partners. To guarantee the required quality of service (e.g., performance, reliability, security, compliance), enterprises need to enact service level agreements, which involve response-time constraints. But they can also involve much more complex constraints (e.g., handling exceptions or faults) on the exchanges between the internal applications or trading partners.

Each of the terms in this very basic definition of service orientation contributes to the productivity and agility of the service oriented enterprise. In other words, service oriented enterprises use service orientation throughout their enterprise architectures. This helps the organization produce and consume services through a uniform paradigm.

Service Oriented Enterprises with Web Services

It should be noted that service orientation has been described here without getting mired in Web service jargon or technology details. Indeed, service orientation can occur through many types of technologies. However, as it turns out, the most popular mechanism for implementing service oriented architectures is through Web services. This book concentrates on service oriented enterprises with Web services as a key technology enabler. As stated earlier, service orientation is a new paradigm that spans analysis and design, programming, business process and rules management, and integration, as well as monitoring, measurement, and control for continuous improvement. This book will demonstrate how these capabilities are realized all through Web services technologies and solutions. Will other technologies and strategies also be used in conjunction with Web services? Absolutely. And they will be used in almost all service oriented enterprise deployment architectures. Enterprise service buses support transport transformations across different standards, not just Web services.

Organization

This book is organized as follows. Chapter 1 provides an overview of the emerging service oriented enterprises. SOEs are built on three components: enterprise performance management, business process management, and a core underlying service oriented IT architecture, especially the enterprise service bus. This chapter also shows that SOE is a culture. It is the culture of services where not only systems but also human participants view themselves as servants to various communities.

Chapter 2 covers one of the most important concepts in service orientation: namely, service oriented methodologies, including service oriented analysis and design. The chapter contrasts traditional waterfall and iterative methodologies. The chapter covers the core Unified Modeling Language notations that could be used in service oriented solution development. This chapter also covers the SOE maturity models, which provide a robust discipline with practices and principles to help SOE development achieve maturity in their software development processes.

Chapter 3 provides an overview of service description, discovery, and deployment techniques. This is the foundation for service oriented architectures. Descriptions indicate the protocols that are supported by the service provider. The chapter provides an overview of the three fundamental standards of Web services: Web Services Description Language (WSDL) + Universal Description, Discovery, and Integration (UDDI) + Simple Object Access Protocol (SOAP).

Chapter 4 delves deeper into service oriented concepts. This chapter elucidates all the key components of the enterprise service bus. The ESB acts as the core backbone for integration, providing standards-based integration capabilities together with support for synchronous and asynchronous messaging, message transformations, publish and subscribe interactions, and content-based routing rules. A large portion of IT budgets is spent on overall distributed infrastructures—both for hardware and software. This chapter explains how service orientation fits into existing and emerging IT infrastructures—important information that will help you spend wisely and prepare for upcoming developments in service orientation. This chapter sets the stage for the following topics on service orientation.

Chapter 5 focuses on the bridge aligning business and IT. It is the layer that is utilizing technology to realize service oriented enterprise objectives. Business process management (BPM) suites are emerging as the key central component in the SOE architecture. This chapter provides a primer on BPM, providing an explanation of all the key concepts. In a business process it is necessary to model the process data (information model), the flows, the business rules, the organizational model, and the integration. BPM involves humans as well as systems. SOE is about a serving culture; the communities who are served can become active participants in business processes and can control the business rules or policies that drive these processes. Individual services are building blocks in business processes. BPM orchestrates these service invocations. Chapter 5 expands on the ESB infrastructure through business processes and business rules. A business process represents a collection of activities that together achieve a business goal. This chapter discusses the central theme of the SOE three-layer architecture.

Quality of service (QoS) for services deals with production quality reliability, security, and performance (Chapter 6). A number of alternatives and solutions can be found for QoS, some of which are offered by application server vendors and ESB platforms. Chapter 6 also provides an overview of a number of standards that have now been ratified for reliable and secure exchanges of messages between services. Service implementations are complex, and an end-to-end invocation of a service invokes many different components. The chapter discusses performance-related issues as well as benchmarking of all these essential components that get involved in a service's journey from invocation to response. It also discusses system management of services. Once service oriented applications are in production, they need to be continually monitored, measured, and revised with enhancements.

The last chapter of the book is Chapter 7, which summarizes the essence of service oriented enterprises and focuses on enterprise performance management. This is the most important chapter of the book, in which everything is put together. It is like an orchestra with different instruments. The service oriented savvy knowledge worker is the conductor. The previous six chapters provide the various instruments involved in this wonderful orchestra. Care should be taken that the music is harmonious and not cacophonous. Chapter 7 is about the service oriented enterprise. This is an enterprise that has adopted a service coupling strategy. It publishes. It consumes services. It loosely couples its applications. It relies on standards to achieve connectivity. Chapter 7 expands on these concepts and also delves into some more interesting societal and behavioral aspects of the service oriented enterprise. Instead of choosing to have a summary or conclusion chapter, Chapter 7 serves as the crescendo.

Acknowledgments

First and foremost I would like to thank God for orchestrating the experiences, events, people, and vision that brought forth this book. I have been working on this book for about four years. I would like to thank my better half, Silva, who had to put up with yet another book project. I am grateful for her as well as my boys' patience as I spent long hours and sometimes time away from them writing and editing the book. Thank you Nishan, Jonathan, Shahan, and Nareg. You have been such a blessing and encouragement to me.

As I started this project I was teaching advanced SOA in a number of universities. I have participated in numerous successful customer deployments using underlying SOA and BPM infrastructures. I am grateful to all those who were involved in these projects. My interactions with analysts, thought leaders, customers, colleagues, and even some of my students have had a strong impact on my vision of *Service Oriented Enterprises*. These were tremendously helpful in shaping especially the technical foundation of this book. Thank you.

I would like to thank all those who graciously provided endorsements and quotes for the book: Jim Sinur of Gartner, Bill Chambers of Doculabs, Ken Vollmer of Forrester, Gregg Rock of BPM Institute, and Bob Thomas of *Business Integration Journal*.

I am grateful for the incredible talent that we have at Pegasystems. Many people at Pega were directly or indirectly contributors to this book and I would like to express my gratitude. I would like to thank Alan Trefler who graciously provided the Foreword of the book. Alan has been a source of inspiration and encouragement for me. I would like to thank our IT organization under the leadership of Jo Hoppe, our development team under the leadership of Mike Pyle, and our marketing organization under the leadership of Jay Sherry for many constructive interactions, inputs, and exchanges that were instrumental for this book. I would like to thank

Kerim Akgonul, Douglas Kim, and Russell Keziere for their support. I also would like to thank Eric Dietert, Ben Frenkel, and Bernie Getzoyan for their many helpful comments. I would like to thank Steve Hoffman of Forestay and Partha Nageswaran of Trans-World Resources for their perspectives and comments on component and service architectures.

Finally, last but definitely not least, I would like to thank several people from Taylor & Francis for their hard work and contributions. They include, among others, John Wyzalek, Takisha Jackson, and Heidi Rocke.

The Author

Dr. Setrag Khoshafian is one of the earliest pioneers and recognized experts in business process management (BPM). Currently, he is vice president of BPM Technology at Pegasystems Inc. He is the strategic BPM technology and thought leader at Pega. Khoshafian is involved in numerous initiatives, including BPM technology directions, enterprise content management and BPM, business performance management, and service oriented architecture infrastructures. He also leads Pega's Six Sigma initiative. He is a frequent speaker and presenter at international conferences.

Previously, Khoshafian was the senior vice president of technology at Savvion, Inc. He invented and designed a powerful process metamodel and led the implementation for one of the earliest distributed Web-centric BPM systems, involving human as well as system participants, through Common Object Request Broker Architecture (CORBA) components.

He has been a senior executive for the past 15 years. In addition to BPM, Khoshafian has done extensive research and implementations of Groupware and Advanced Database Management Systems. He was the inventor of the Intelligent SQL object-relational database. He also led the architecture, design, and implementation of one of the earliest distributed object-oriented database systems while working at MCC.

Khoshafian is the lead author of eight books and has numerous publications in business and technical periodicals. He has given seminars and presentations at conferences for technical and business communities. Khoshafian has also been a professor for the past 20 years. He has taught graduate and undergraduate courses in several universities around the world, providing his students a unique combination of academic depth and industry experience. He earned a Ph.D. in computer science from the University of Wisconsin–Madison.

Chapter 1

Introduction

> It is not simply about how governments, businesses, and people communicate, not just about how organizations interact, but is about the emergence of complete new social, political, and business models.
>
> **Thomas L. Friedman**

1.1 Overview

We are at an exciting crossroads, bringing technology and business together as never before. Global collaboration and emerging corporate cultures are creating a new type of innovative enterprise: one based on services. Service orientation is about culture, a new service-focused approach of doing business as the modus operandi. Service orientation is also about technology, a standard and effective way of connecting businesses. Enterprises can be empowered to live up to the potential of becoming dynamic, agile, and real-time. Service orientation is emerging from the amalgamation of a number of key business, technology, and cultural developments. Three essential trends in particular are coming together to create a new revolutionary breed of enterprise, the service oriented enterprise (SOE): (1) advances in the standards-based service oriented infrastructures; (2) the emergence of business process management (BPM); and (3) the continuous performance management of the enterprise.

This book focuses on this emerging three-layered architecture that builds on a service oriented information technology (IT) architecture framework, with

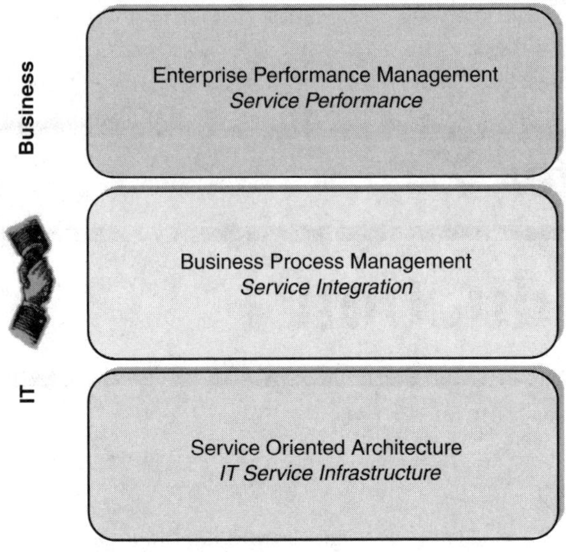

Figure 1.1 Three layers of service oriented enterprises

a process layer that brings technology and business together, and a corporate performance layer that continually monitors and improves the performance indicators of global enterprises (see Figure 1.1).

Service oriented architectures (SOAs) are providing unparalleled integration within and between enterprises. Performance monitoring and management are delivering incredible visibility to business practices. But what is even more exciting is the bridge between technology and business through automated business processes. IT and businesses are involved in continuous improvement feedback loops. Automated business processes can improve that feedback mechanism and thus can keep the IT and business goals better in sync. So sandwiched between the technical service oriented architectures and the business-focused performance management solution trends are the emerging business process management platforms, which are automating business policies and procedures and are supporting better business–IT alignment with continuous improvement of business process implementations.

1.1.1 IT and Business Focus

The emerging rapprochement between IT and business is essential in SOEs. In discussing service orientation there is the temptation to focus too much on technology. Technology is important and necessary. It serves as the foundation. IT is not only relevant; it is essential. Emerging services standards, services networks, business process management, and enterprise service buses (ESBs) are some of the building blocks discussed throughout this book. Effective service oriented enterprises cannot be achieved without technology.

Technology should be the catalyst for innovation to improve business performance. Performance management is essential. The past decade was turbulent. The much-anticipated recovery from the dot-com meltdown is still that: an optimistic yet elusive anticipation. Organizations are faced with pressures to innovate, to survive, to grow, to cut back, and to deal with governmental compliance. Performance improvement and serious gaps in implementations indicated there was and continues to be a serious gap between strategy and execution. Enterprises know what they want to achieve; they sometime even have a feel as to how to prioritize their objectives and milestones. But perhaps more than any other time in history, strategies fall short on execution. It is a common problem in the commercial as well as governmental circles. Identifying problems, charting them, and having lofty strategic or tactical objectives are not enough. Organizations need to execute measurably on these objectives. Enterprise corporate measurement is providing the mechanism to continuously monitor and to gauge corporate performance. It is allowing decision makers to respond to real-time events. Corporate performance management is also supporting analysis of historic corporate data to predictively identify trends and to introduce strategic changes to achieve corporate performance goals. The objective is to allow employees and managers at different levels to easily navigate from corporate objective measures down to executing processes, implemented on solid service oriented infrastructures.

This leads to the process-oriented culture. The heart and core of the service oriented enterprise is the business process management layer. This is where it all comes together.

In service oriented enterprises products are processes.

These processes need to be modeled, executed, monitored, and improved continuously. Processes in service oriented enterprises capture both the policies and procedures that could potentially span continents. The service oriented enterprise needs to respond to constant pressures to innovate for growth. The SOE also needs to enact productivity improvements to control costs. As if the pressures for growth and productivity were not enough, increasingly SOEs are facing complex regulatory compliance requirements. Adding to that the need to respond to constantly changing conditions, globalization, and insatiable demands by a finicky customer base leads to a conundrum: produce competitive and customizable products at an increasingly rapid pace while competing with emerging global enterprises.

With this wide scope of pressures on businesses and the rapid pace of change, IT backlogs can no longer be afforded. The business and IT cultures need to be aligned around processes, with business process management systems integrating employees, systems, and trading partners and driving automated enterprise processes to completion. Business process management is where the human participants, enterprise information systems, and trading partners come together.

Service oriented enterprises are all about streamlining business processes. They are also about being aware of change. The very nature of change in the 21st century implies that innovation needs to be introduced quickly in all domains: finance, customer, product, service, partner, and human resources. This culture of innovation needs a solid connectivity and plumbing infrastructure. Furthermore, it needs streamlined and digitized processes and business rules. It also needs continuous monitoring and management of the enterprise as a whole, linking performance measures to executing processes on top of the service architecture.

The service enterprise architecture is a compelling architecture with three distinct yet interdependent layers: guided by enterprise performance management, driven by business process management, and founded on service oriented IT architecture.

This book is about this new emerging enterprise philosophy. It defines, characterizes, and demonstrates how service orientation is affecting both infrastructure and organizational cultures in ways not seen since the dawn of the Internet age. This is the next wave of the technologies and communication revolution, which builds on and extends what was spurred by the success of the Internet.

Use cases and solution descriptions for SOEs: Throughout the book are examples of use cases and solutions using the three tiers of service oriented enterprises. In some cases the specific enterprise that has deployed the solution is mentioned. Other solution descriptions are examples of potential solutions for enterprises in specific industries.

1.1.2 It Is More Than Technology

> The convergence of high-performance computing, global high-speed communications, and advanced sensing and data analysis is driving the next information technology inflection point.
>
> **Intel**

Will technologies, solutions, and companies based on service orientation lead to the next bubble? It is not difficult to remember how bubbles occurred during the dot-com era. An initial stock increase in an Internet-based company resulted in investors having pseudo-confidence, which drove the price higher and, again, caused the initial price to rise and continue to rise, having the effect of increased demand. These rounds of increases continued to spiral for many dot-com companies. As higher prices were established, investor confidence was boosted, causing even more investing with inflated prices. In equity markets, such behavior could be considered irrational because investing decisions were based on unjustifiable reasons. Will emerging SOEs result in another bubble as investment increases without a firm foundation as to why? Perhaps. But more caution is taken now, and some would argue that service oriented architectures have not delivered—at least so far. But equating service oriented enterprises with service oriented architectures—especially Web services—misses the point. It is only a small part of the story; in actuality two trends can be found. In addition to the SOA and Web services trend, the emergence of the business process automation and management technologies can be seen as the core component of enterprise architecture frameworks. In fact, more than any other type of solution, BPM is showing continuous and tangible returns on investments emanating from automation in policies, procedures, tighter involvement of business stakeholders, and changes in IT development practices.

JetBlue, founded in 1999 by David Neelman, is a very successful low-cost airline. It illustrates a textbook case where information technology and straight-through processing is used in conjunction with an entrenched service culture. JetBlue leverages creative strategies in serving customers at low cost and high availability. JetBlue, like most other service oriented enterprises, maintains close contact with the customers. Set on two pillars of efficiency and service, JetBlue is a key example of how an enterprise can know and execute exactly what the consumer wants. The airline's strategy is to meet the needs of price and convenience sensitive passengers. Quality in customer service, operational efficiency, innovation, and responsiveness to customers is one of the ways the airline is able to gain market and mindshare with travelers. Also, JetBlue aspired to be the first completely paperless airline, streamlining all information technologies from operations to ticketing.

Service orientation takes a holistic approach to enterprise computing. Consider a skyscraper hosting offices. The lower-level IT-focused service oriented architecture deals with the plumbing—it is especially important that it not fail. Continuing with the analogy, the focus is on the work environment, especially the people who are the tenants. The center of attention needs to be the motivation and productivity of the office workers. It is important that not only the people but also the various processes carried out in the skyscraper are performing efficiently, minimizing waste. The work milieu and the interoffice relationships as well as the management styles are much more feasible and critical to productivity and innovation than the plumbing. In fact, the skyscraper is connected to other skyscrapers within its neighborhood as well as halfway across the globe. The communication again relies on reliable and secure networking. But once again, even more important are the end-to-end processes that span departmental and organizational boundaries. It is not just about the data or the bits that get communicated across the globe; it is about the knowledge and content of these bits. More importantly, it is about the communities: customers, shareholders, partners, and employees that are served across the extended network. It is about processes that span and integrate all these communities (Figure 1.2).

In terms of enabling technologies, what is emerging today is a three-tier architecture. At the top are business strategies, business models, business analytics, and business performance management. At the bottom are service oriented IT architectures with essential components such as enterprise service buses, application servers, legacy integration, and business-to-business (B2B)

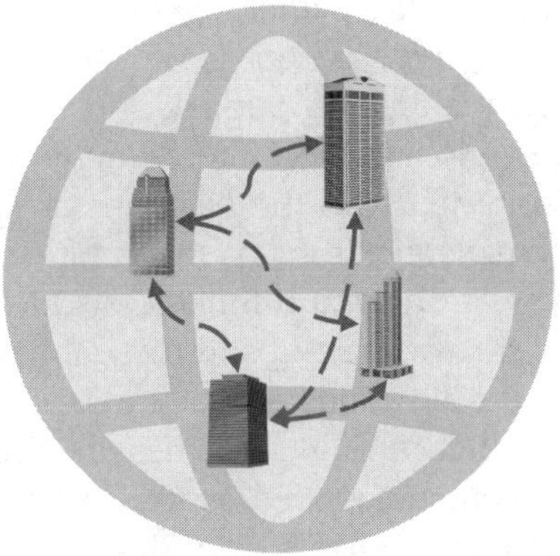

Figure 1.2 Global connectivity

services integration. The core component, however, is the middle tier: the service oriented business process integration layer that allows organizations to digitize and automate their business practices, policies, and procedures.

Dell is another example of a customer-focused company. Dell provides extensive customer support, primarily through outsourcing. It is an interesting example of how agility, the flat world, and a focus on service orientation come together to deliver success for the enterprise and its customers. Through its efficient end-to-end supply chain integration, the customer decides and controls the inventory and assembly as well as supply chain process. As Dick Hunter, the supply-chain manager at Dell, puts it, "We are not experts in the technology we buy; we are experts in the technology of integration."

1.1.3 Globalization

The skyscraper example alluded to a global connectivity and a global organization. No one put it more elegantly than Thomas Friedman in his seminal work *The World Is Flat: A Brief History of the Twenty-First Century*:[1] "... what the flattening of the world means is that we are now connecting all the knowledge centers on the planet together in a single global network, which—if politics and terrorism do not get in the way—could usher in an amazing era of prosperity and innovation."

What makes the new globalization interesting is that the bottom-up creative entrepreneurial spirit that was the hallmark of the U.S. software revolution is increasingly emanating from young creative engineers, especially in the emerging markets of China and India. Outsourcing for cheap labor is being augmented with creative start-ups in these emerging economies. This challenge to the U.S. software industry[2] is intrinsically different, and just as the other traditional manufacturing industries in almost every sector are being replaced by goods manufactured especially in China, this next wave could well become the creative force behind innovative software solutions and products. Friedman identifies ten forces that are flattening the world:

1. The fall of communism (or 11/9/89, the day the Berlin Wall fell): This opened up free markets and entrepreneurial ventures in the ex-Soviet empire.
2. The emergence of the Internet, especially Web, age (or 8/9/95, when Netscape went public): Observed was the emergence of standard protocols such as Hypertext Transfer Protocol (HTTP), File Transfer Protocol (FTP), Standard Mail Transfer Protocol Secure Sockets Layer (SMTP SSL), and Transmission Control Protocol/Internet Protocol (TCP/IP). HTTP and Hypertext Markup Language (HTML), the standard used by browsers, were critical in the emergence of the World Wide Web.
3. Workflow software: Here workflow implies system-to-system and trading partner connectivity. Soon after the emergence of Web-based connectivity, the Web became a conduit of business, and connectivity standards—especially eXtensible Markup Language (XML) and SOAP—emerged.
4. Open sourcing: Here Friedman explains several reasons where potentially free open-source software is preferred over costly enterprise software. Some of the reasons include the flexibility in trying new scientific ideas, the ability to have fresh innovations, as well as the investment of high-tech companies on some solutions such as Linux.
5. Outsourcing: Countries such as India, with their focus and excellence in education, are creating horizontal value to Western enterprises, especially in the United States. Other Asian countries such as Pakistan and Malaysia are also providing value-added extension to U.S. and other Western companies through outsourcing. The outsourced talent, combined with fast Internet and computing technologies such as the personal computer (PC), are providing a tremendous resource to Western companies.

6. Off-shoring: Here entire factories are off-shored to emerging markets such as China. The merchandise is built off shore and sold in Western countries such as the United States or the European Union. China joined the World Trade Organization in 2001, which made it even more attractive to off-shore to China. It also caused havoc on a number of industries, such as the textile industries in the West.
7. Supply chain: Major outlet chains such as Wal-Mart rely heavily on off-shored goods from China. There is still debate within the United States as to whether Wal-Mart is good or bad for the U.S. economy; it has created one of the world's largest supply chains, from manufacturing outlets in China to distribution to its retail outlets to customers.
8. Insourcing: This is equivalent to horizontal value creation. To explain the concept and potential of insourcing, Friedman uses the United Parcel Service as a textbook example. UPS has become the supply-chain manager; it is not only moving goods but is also providing value. More specifically, Friedman shows how Toshiba, for example, uses UPS stores not only to have its customers drop off broken computers but also to have them fixed—by UPS no less.
9. Informing: The poster child example here is Google. Throughout the ages it was the rich and the famous who had access to information that empowered and elevated them from the less privileged masses, but no longer. Now through search engines and portals such as Google, MSN, and Yahoo!, the world's knowledge can be searched and accessed—all with the ability to discover and connect as never before.
10. Steroids: They strengthen and accelerate the other flatteners to achieve more flattening. This is accelerated through digital representation of any type of media. Digitization means it can be sent over wired and wireless networks—over the Internet. The new types of devices are Internet enabled and multi-functional. People are perpetually on the Internet accessing any type of multimedia information.

These are excellent examples, or forces as Friedman calls them, of trends and technologies that are flattening the world and also of enablers for service oriented enterprises. These forces illustrate the increasing digital and global connectivity and the emergence of a new economy and flattened world.

What is being witnessed, especially in the Western world, is the emergence of global competitors, especially with India and China taking increasing leadership roles through outsourcing and offshore manufacturing of cheaper goods or services. The United States and Western Europe are facing unparalleled challenges, especially from Asia Pacific. Globalization has taken on a completely new meaning. The luxury no longer exists to conduct business as usual, and changing pressures should be responded to very quickly and efficiently.

So what about service oriented enterprises? Globalization not only facilitates but in a very real sense also drives SOEs. The communities that are being served are global. Both outsource providers and procurers need to be engaged in service level agreements. Globalization entails end-to-end global business processes that execute choreographies, potentially spanning continents. Behind the exchanges in these choreographies are internal orchestrations of services. The underlying BPM and ESB components should allow the SOE to easily specialize its policies, processes, and overall interface to specific target communities on a global scale. Specialization can take the form of policies and rules that pertain to specific countries or cultures or the form of agile localized interfaces for specific languages. The SOE can respond to the flattening world forces and can provide a dynamic infrastructure that responds to constantly changing requirements, emerging innovations, and market pressures.

What about the European Union? Europe has its own challenges. Today's European Union is faced with competition not only from the ex-Soviet block countries—especially Russia—but from a well-educated, motivated, young, and dynamic Asia. The European Union is successful especially in business, travel, and monetary unifications. However, Europe is seeing a new type of curtain that divides the ancient Europe from the Nouveaux Europe that consists of more dynamic and creative ex-Soviet-era Eastern European countries. There is more enthusiasm and a hard-working entrepreneurial spirit in Central and Eastern Europe. An energy and optimism can be observed in these new European countries, who want to catch up to (maybe even leap frog) Western Europe's economic successes and better themselves following especially American lifestyles and entrepreneurial trends. There are fears, though, and some protectionism from the Western European allies. The year 2005 showed two important referendums from two founding members of the European Union rejecting the European constitution and taking a more nationalistic stance. The implications of these votes will be discussed and felt for many years to come. Meanwhile, many more Eastern countries want to join the European Union, and the new Europe will emerge as a cohesive, growing, and exciting economic force responding to competition and challenges both from the United States and Asia Pacific.

1.1.4 Extended, Virtual, Real-Time, and Resilient

> In a virtual enterprise (VE), a company assembles a temporary consortium of partners and services for a certain purpose. This purpose could be a temporary special request, an ongoing goal to fulfill orders, or an attempt to take advantage of a new resource or market niche.
>
> **Charles Petrie and Christoph Bussler**

Enterprises have been associated with several adjectives, for instance, *extended* and *virtual*—sometimes used synonymously. Service oriented enterprises are also extended as well as virtual enterprises but in addition to all the attributes of the former, SOEs provide essentially a service oriented focus. It will help to delve a bit deeper into these terms that help clarify the taxonomy of service oriented enterprises.

The extended enterprise dimension connotes the notion of *integration* and *aggregation*. Aggregation implies that the enterprise extends beyond the narrower scope of its direct beneficiaries—such as its shareholders, employees, and managers—but also includes its partners, suppliers, customers, and the community. A service oriented enterprise is a special case extended of an enterprise. Integration is used to connect service providers and consumers. The focus is on integration technology that is used to access services in the context of end-to-end processes that provide business value to providers and consumers.

Before delving into the service oriented specific attributes of SOEs, an overview of the extended, virtual, real-time, and resilent features of service oriented enterprises is provided.

> *Extended:* The key feature here is that the various applications, repositories, and even roles or organizations appear to be well aggregated and integrated while staying loosely coupled and independent. The Internet has connected us in ways we have not imagined before. The services that are executing over the Internet will launch a new dawn for connecting and aggregating organizations. For instance, a production or development effort could involve many applications and different groups from potentially geographically distributed organizations. The applications need to be invoked in a particular sequence or process flow. The output of one application, such as the blueprint of a product component, needs to be the input of another application, such as an automated manufacturing plant. The data type exchanges among the various applications need to be consistent. Similarly, the different groups involved in the ultimate objective need to be part of the same production, testing, certification, and manufacturing

calendar. This end-to-end integration through services is an example of the value or supply chain so typical in flat organizations, which rely on services or products offered by other organizations. So the enterprise is extended: It includes parts and services obtained sometimes from organizations that are thousands of miles away from the corporate headquarters. Business involved in supply or value chains have specific message and information exchange orchestration with specific policies. The exchanges define not only the structure of the various messages exchanged but also the business rules, timing constraints, security requirements, and process flow logic of these exchanges. Figure 1.3 illustrates a simple example involving a step that carries out conference registration and then, depending on the

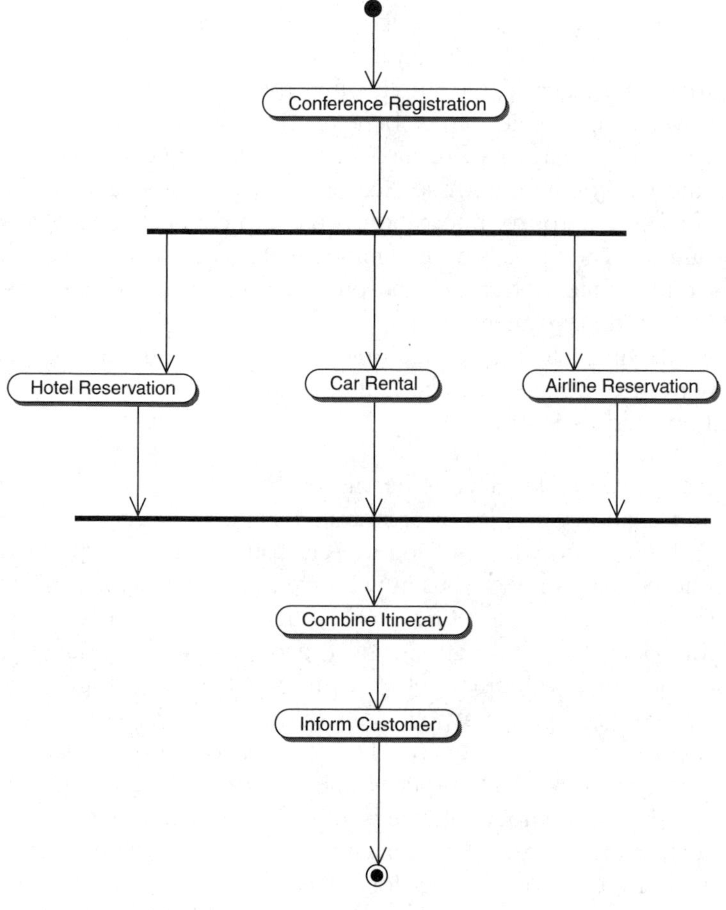

Figure 1.3 A process in an extended enterprise

customer request, can further process the request for hotel and airline reservations as well as car rental services. The process then aggregates the responses and subsequently provides the customer with an itinerary that includes the confirmation numbers. Each of the reservation or rental steps could be handled by an entirely different organization and the process flow by yet a fourth brokering organization.

Virtual: Often the terms *virtual* and *extended* are used interchangeably, as they are complementary concepts with a lot in common. Being virtual means the organization can come together whenever needed. Different organizations can expose different services. The hotel reservation, car rental, and airline reservation services illustrated in Figure 1.3 are carried out by different organizations. These organizations are brought together to "create" another organization—a virtual one that takes care of conference reservations. The customer of the virtual organization deals with this one entity. The virtual organization can come together for a single event or for a series of similar events. It is dynamic and flexible.[3] The various facets of virtuality can be described as follows:

- *Almost real:* Virtual reality and many popular video games best capture this category. The interaction of actors or consumers is very dynamic. With information technologies a virtual organization will act as a real organization for the external actor or consumer.
- *Virtual worlds*: Concepts such as virtual exhibitions, virtual shopping malls, or virtual schools capture this dimension of virtuality. These worlds do not physically exist but are created and accessed typically through Web browsers. In some ways portals that are completely customized are moving in this direction. The current virtual worlds are more sophisticated than portals.
- *Virtual presence*: Another common meaning is this notion of a virtual presence. Virtual offices are perhaps the most common example. The individuals, the various roles, the various organizational, and the various applications appear to be virtually present.
- *Virtually cohesive and well aggregated*: This concept is extremely important for the topic at hand. Subsequent sections expand more on this approach. The key feature of virtuality here is that the various applications, repositories, and even roles or organizations appear to be well aggregated and integrated.
- *Virtual existence*: This means the organization can come together whenever needed as described above.
- *Dynamic and temporal*: One of the big advantages of a virtual organization is the fact that it is dynamic. Partners, interfaces, and exchange choreographies could all change—which brings us to the real-time enterprise.

The real-time enterprise is a customer-driven organization that executes and adapts its mission-critical business processes using a sense and respond infrastructure that spans people, companies, and computers to provide information timely enough to make effective decisions and to act and where a late answer is a wrong answer.

Peter Fingar

Real-time: One of the big advantages of a service oriented enterprise is the fact that it is dynamic: Situations, requirements, and market conditions, customer demographics, and partners could all change. Just about the only constant is change. With SOEs the focus is on the objectives: what the organization is trying to achieve. For instance, the objective could be a financial transaction involving financial institutions, custodians, brokers, contractors, legal entities, and clearing. The particular selection of a financial institution that provides a product or a service or the selection of the service itself could be dynamic. It could depend on price, availability, or benefits. Thus, financial processes such as purchasing securities could involve different organizations depending on the parameters or requirements of the transaction. Interfaces could also change. For instance, if a particular XML vocabulary is used for the process, the vocabulary could undergo iterations and changes—that is, various versions. Exchange choreographies could also change. The agility required to adapt to these changes dynamically is part of the very nature of the real-time enterprise.

Resilient: After the September 11, 2001, tragedy we realized that in addition to the irreplaceable loss of human life, our tangible and intangible assets are more vulnerable than ever before. Resiliency addresses this core problem of disruptions in enterprises, emanating from natural or man-made disasters. A resilient enterprise has established policies, detection mechanisms, practices, and redundancies that enable it to recover from disruptions and restore the business. Resiliency and disaster recovery is often an afterthought. Disastrous disruptions are rare. But when they occur, they have the potential of wiping out the short-term revenue or worse, the long-term viability of the enterprise. Resiliency means the enterprise is able to respond to the disaster in real-time. If an earthquake disrupts a supplier, the enterprise has predetermined alternative supply channels; if a disaster hits an information center, the enterprise has built-in mirroring of data and applications, and can recover immediately. This whole notion of "agility" is put to the ultimate test. The protection and recovery processes have to be preplanned and put into effect and tested. When disasters hit, the recovery processes need to be enacted in real-time.

Enterprises can ill afford to interrupt business operations given the intensity of the competition and the cost pressures they are under. A resilient company is not only better able to endure the vagaries of global trading, it can actually gain competitive advantage by being one step ahead of the competition when a disruption hits. A fast recovery is crucial.

Yossi Sheffi

These four interrelated features of service enterprises make it possible for organizations to deliver on the promise of service orientation with tangible results. Skeptics will point to similar promises by other organizational, reengineering, or technology trends. We have seen too many *panacea du jour* principles and are perhaps somewhat disillusioned. Nevertheless, these four features are powerful trends that are already showing promising results.

1.1.5 Narrowing the Gap between IT and Business

In the new process-centric world of IT, software architecture aligns more readily with business activity—even across business boundaries. Processes can be expressed in any level of detail right down to fine-grained computational components, making it much easier for businesses to modify, redesign, and evolve business processes. Best of all, top-down process design activity can be driven directly by organizational objectives such as time, cost, and best practices.

Howard Smith and Peter Fingar

The previous section described the four fundamental dimensions of service oriented enterprise: extended, virtual, real-time, and resilient. Business and IT need to come together to focus on common goals such as the following:

- *Faster turnaround times for IT projects:* This has plagued the IT and business relationships for decades. It is sometimes identified as the *execution gap.* The beginning of projects typically brings a lot of excitement and promising handshakes and congratulations. Often, however, projects are marred by execution delays that could last months and sometimes even years with serious cost overruns. In most cases IT is unable to deliver on its promises or expectations. Many lower-level engineers and managers in IT are often not surprised. Promises are face saving. When it comes to schedules, reality is something else. In software being late is the norm.

- The emerging demand and fashionable trend is *agility*, which deals with responding very quickly to change. It also implies maneuvering dangerous terrains and moving rapidly. Organizations need to be agile. They need to be able to respond quickly to customer demands, increased competition, internal challenges, or globalization pressures. IT can help realize and implement this agility. The agility of IT is not sufficient—the entire enterprise in its production, marketing, sales, and operations needs to be agile. But the agility of the IT organization is necessary. It is the foundation.

- *Staying on budget:* Remember the cost overruns of the Federal Bureau of Investigation's virtual folder project?[4] It was a $170 million project gone awry. Unfortunately, the software industry is full of similar failings—especially those associated with large projects. This is of course related to the previous point. Cost overruns are also the norm, not only from turnaround time considerations but also because of poor planning: budgeting for all the necessary hardware and software to bring the project to a successful production.
- *Cost savings:* Software outsourcing industry has taken off—both in IT outsourcing and business process outsourcing.[5] Enterprises are eager to cut costs, often relying on less expensive talents offshore. This is one way to achieve cost savings, but frankly, there are a number of challenges when it comes to outsourcing. It is definitely working, but it is not a panacea.[6] Cost savings needs to also include technologies that automate and streamline the IT as well as manufacturing, services, and support processes within an organization.
- *Customer retention:* Businesses are very much interested in customer retention. The reputation of the business is critical. In fact, the Six Sigma quality assurance methodology often targets precisely this problem. There is a very direct and immediate relationship between customer retention and quality of the services and the products. But quality assurance is only part of the story. Customer retention is also beginning to imply process transparency and connectivity—through straight-through processing. This means for example a sale in a retail-store touch point could propagate demand for manufacturing units across the globe. It means that the manufacturing and production

value chains are connected and streamlined. Different organizations around the globe are involved in the production and distribution of goods and services with as little human interference as possible. This enhances inventory management and customer rentention. Customer retention is also directly related to the ability of the enterprise to quickly produce customized goods or services. In almost every industry customers are demanding customized solutions and products. Dell perhaps is the best example of this for PCs. The old models of rigid manufacturing and production plants are obsolete. Componentization and agility in producing very quickly customized goods and services are now taken for granted.

- *Innovate and create new products:* Innovation is always on the top-five list of priorities and goals for most companies. To sustain their competitive advantage, companies need to go beyond customer retention and need to quickly create new markets through new innovative products. An organization needs to liberate its knowledge worker so that the creativity can flow in all the departments—especially its product engineering departments. The creation of new products has other dimensions as well.

- *Coopetition:* One interesting area that is emerging here is the whole notion of *coopetition,* where organizations that typically compete can come together to cooperate in situations that are mutually beneficial for both. This has worked in some situations: For example, software companies involved with both software and services sometimes have situations where the services organization uses and builds an application using the software of its competitor, as in IBM global services for example building an Oracle application. In other situations this has not worked very well.

It is beyond the scope of this book, but it is interesting to note that most organizations in the West—and, alas, in the East also—though agreeing on these trends, continue to conduct business as usual. The traditional separation between IT and businesses has proven to be devastating for enterprises. More than any other time in the history and evolution of corporate America, the chief information officer (CIO) needs now to understand, to relate, and to respond to business needs. IT is becoming a service organization. We also are witnessing the emergence of new C-level roles, such as chief process officer and chief service oriented architect. Enterprises are starting to create business process and service oriented centers of excellence. Business stakeholders are promoting the emergence of service organizations—supporting IT and involving IT in innovation. The service culture is essential. When an enterprise sees itself as dynamic aggregation of services where IT and business come together to implement business processes, it can then radiate its service culture to its trading partners and can create dynamic enterprises: real-time, virtual, and extended.

1.2 Reengineering Business Process Reengineering: Changing the Nature of Change

> Business process reengineering is the key to transforming how people work.
>
> **Peter Carter**

Are the emerging rapprochements between business and IT the reincarnation of business process reengineering (BPR) that made quite a splash in the 1980s and 1990s? Not quite. As we shall see, BPR was about reorganizing the business workflows. The roots of workflow automation go back to Frederick Taylor's scientific management approach that started in late 19th century. The approach is appealing and scientifically sound. Everyone is guided by work rules and laws. Work is divided into well-defined individual units. The goal is to get the maximum quality output from each worker. Work is divided into specific discrete actions and performed by trained workers. So with this approach there is the potential of having less knowledgeable workers with focused tasks, especially in manufacturing plants, along with the opportunity to measure and to improve productivity. Workers and managers can become part of a large well-oiled machine whose performance is constantly measured, monitored, and improved. Systematic approaches to quality improvement such as Total Quality Management were based on Taylor's philosophy.

As with most management approaches, there were problems with Taylor's philosophy. For one thing, it was too mechanical and impersonal. To address some of the challenges that enterprises in manufacturing as well as other vertical sectors started to face in the late 1980s, Michael Hammer and James Champy introduced the revolutionary concept of *business process reengineering*. Reengineering in the context of business processes implies that the existing processes and organizations used to run a business are challenged and replaced by qualitatively more efficient processes and organizations. Improvements in productivity and revenue are achieved by throwing out well-established but rigid structures and by adopting more efficient and flexible principles, responding to ever-changing competitive market realities. A key characteristic of this changing world is customization and the flexibility to respond quickly to changing customer demands. Amplifying this trend is the emergence of giants such as China and India and an increasingly flattend world.

The challenges are enormous: Those who do not adapt to changes quickly, those who do not respond to customization fast enough, those who do not produce high-quality products and services at increasingly shorter develop cycles simply will not survive. The whole notion of reengineering was based on these premises. These goals were relevant in the late 1980s and early 1990s but are even more relevant today. However, the approach and the nature of addressing change are also changing: BPR is being revisited and reengineered.

The conventional reengineering approach from Hammer and Champy had several salient features that could be summarized as follows:

- Empowered workers: One of the most important characteristics of restructuring is empowering workers to make decisions. This enables field employees to make higher-quality decisions and also helps with the morale and motivation of workers. In fact, the current trends in increased availability of information, especially through Web services as well as the emergence of digitization of processes and business rules, indicate that technology can be used to support the empowerment of workers and their decision-making processes. This is enhancing and improving the performance of workers.
- Reduced checks and controls: Since employees are empowered, the checks and controls could be reduced. Through digitized business processes tracking the performance of workers, checks and controls can be automated and less intrusive. The presence of rule-based work processing can potentially remediate automatically worker performance and work quality.
- Eliminating redundant jobs and combining several jobs into one: This point is perhaps the most controversial, since the implications are obvious. When jobs consist of several component tasks that can be combined into more meaningful roles, it means some people will have to be either retrained or, worse, lose their jobs. Note that a similar transition happened during the Industrial Revolution. Many manual jobs were lost in favor of much more affordable automated factories.
- Top-down reengineering: In some cases—and at least in perception—business process redesign means top-level management redesigns and attempts to impose radical change in business processes through changing the organization and the way things are done (i.e., the processes) throughout the organization.

As these bullet points illustrate, the overall approach and philosophy of reengineering is not that bad—well, except the last one. In fact, current practices and trends confirm and validate the main premises of business process reengineering. However, the track record of reengineering is not that good. It focused on radical and organizational change. The estimates are that BPR has a success rate of between 20 and 30 percent, which is not something to write home about. However, the nature of building for change is changing. There are problems with process reengineering.

Recognizing these challenges, Champy came up with the next generation of reengineering, which he called *X-engineering*. The X stands for crossing various organizational and enterprise boundaries. Elucidating on the changes in engineering enterprises, Champy characterizes the evolution as follows:

> Today … I see the reengineering of the last decade as only a beginning. In this decade, the nature of work will change even more dramatically. And the corporation, once a closed enterprise, will become part of a much larger network of customers, suppliers, and collaborators, all working in concert to perform their work at new levels of efficiency. Companies like Dell, Intel, and Cisco have been leading the way, fundamentally changing how they do business with their customers and suppliers.[7]

The changes mentioned by Champy at their core reflect the agility of these service oriented enterprises. There are two fundamental and interrelated changes in achieving agility.

1. Long-phased and radical approaches are abandoned in favor of continuous and incremental improvements: Here the contrast is between traditional approaches in introducing change, which were marred by long requirement and analysis phases. There is typically a subsequent decoupling from the day-to-day operations or development. An initial dust-gathering analysis is soon abandoned to deal with the tyranny of the next crisis. The long-phased approach is being replaced with incremental approaches involving continuous improvements.
2. Focus on operations and results, not restructuring: This is perhaps even more important and radical than the first point. Reengineering focused too much on restructuring the organization—not that it is not important to restructure archaic organizations. Some—many—organizations need a long overdue radical makeover. But due to the ensuing resistance to the change, entire reengineering programs have failed with catastrophic results. And, yes, the baby is also thrown out with the bathwater, ignoring the many benefits and advantages of reengineering.

There is the perception that reengineering means downsizing and hence losing jobs. Business process reengineering had the right goals, but the approach did not work as expected. Perhaps the most serious mistake was the emphasis on restructuring and reorganization. Human nature being what it is, people resist change if they have not bought in to its benefits and if they perceive that it might cost them their jobs. On the other hand, no one will resist being efficient and having the underlying digitized platforms take on most of the mundane work and truly assist the productivity of the workers. Also, no one will resist help that could be rendered in dealing with backlogs and increased productivity, and innovation for products and services. So now it is taken for granted that change is necessary for survival and that organizational agility is a must.

1.2.1 Built to Change

> The benefit of aligning processes with goals is primarily to enable change within an on-demand paradigm rather than a push. This actually offers better distribution of the change management liability across the IT ecosystem.
>
> **Russell Keziere**

Service oriented architectures are often touted as being the ideal technology or approach for change. But one should be careful since what goes under the banner of SOA is often primarily plumbing technology. This is necessary but not sufficient. So how one should build to change, and how does service orientation help?

The build to change help comes from the second major layer of service oriented enterprises: service oriented business process integration. Chapter 5 goes deep into business process management for service oriented enterprises. Here a summary is provided of the build for change salient features that are crucial for SOEs.

- Focus on the end-to-end processes, not the organization: This is critical. What is the enterprise attempting to achieve? Everything from internal human resource operations to B2B interactions could be automated using various components of service oriented technologies. The build to change starts with the key strategies and key performance indicators for the organization. The enterprise should then be able to drill down from these key performance indicators all the way to automated and digitized processes.
- Analyze, build, and continuously improve the business processes: Rather than focusing on eliminating jobs from the beginning or introducing organizational change, the focus is on incrementally and iteratively improving the business processes, in which iteration is key. Many organizations that have successfully deployed process automation often started with few less-ambitious projects and demonstrated quick wins or achievements with tangible results, which opened the door for more opportunities of process automation. So rather than dramatically changing the way people are used to doing their jobs or their roles, change is introduced incrementally and continuously—with the same goals of empowering workers, as noted previously.

- Treat your processes and business rules as assets: About 30 years ago, the introduction of the relational database model and relational database management systems (RDBMS) was revolutionary. Dr. E. F. Codd introduced the concept through his classic work, "A Relational Model of Data for Large Shared Databanks."[8] His work provided a solid foundation for the emerging RDBMS industry where relational databases addressed key issues such as dependence on physical implementation of the database, problems in redundancy of the data, no clear separation between conceptual and physical representation, and the use of application code to handle integrity. The main point is that it was evident the data had to be separated from application code—that had embedded in it the logic of data integrity, physical data manipulation, and other DBMS-related features. The main reason for the emergence of the business process management is this idea of separating the operations, or processes, also from the application code. However, going back to the relational model, the reason RDBMSs are so critical is that databases are important assets in the organization that need to be managed, concurrently shared, and maintained independent of any application. They are separate. The same separation principle applies to processes as well as practices. Process and practice rules are different yet intertwined. A process needs rules for its execution and decision making. Processes provide the context of practice rules. Rules support, activate, and track processes. Just as in relational databases the integrity constraints had to be stored and managed in the DBMS, in the emerging BPM systems the rules and processes need to be managed together. More important, they need to be managed, maintained, and deployed as corporate assets. In the 1980s and 1990s databases were realized as assets that need to be managed separately. Today process flows as well as policy and practice rules are recognized as assets that need be managed separately; furthermore, process and practice rules are seen as intertwined (Figure 1.4).
- Support for specialization and application of the appropriate business rule or service or process, depending on the situation: Customization is a requirement—customized interfaces, special promotions depending on the customer category or time (e.g., sales), or location. So an environment is needed that supports not only creation of services and the easy discovery and deployment of these services but also the ability to define specialization of services, processes, or business rules along a number of important dimensions—temporal, customer category, geographical location, security, or circumstance, to name a few.

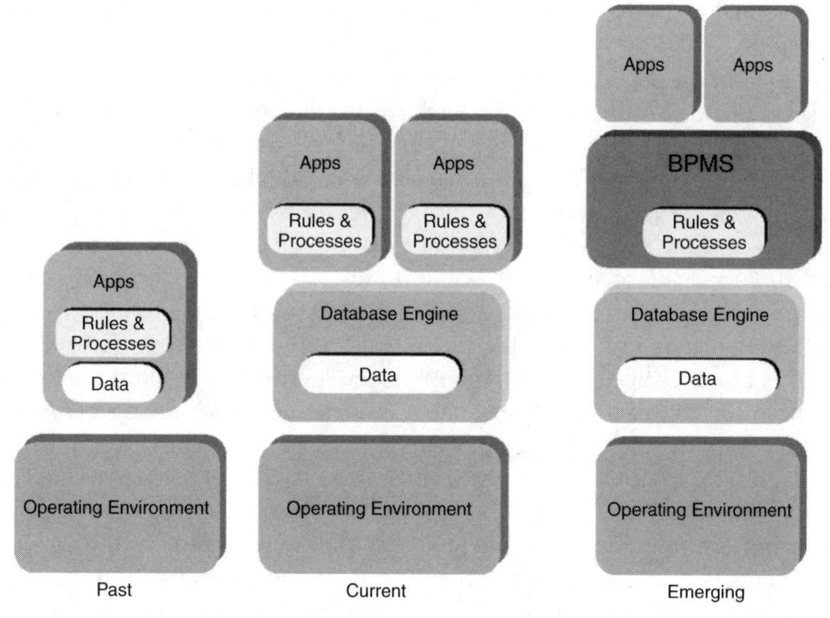

Figure 1.4 Separation of processes and rules from the application

1.2.2 *The Servant Leader*

> Servant Leaders: devote themselves to serving the needs of organization members; focus on meeting the needs of those they lead; develop employees to bring out the best in them; coach others and encourage their self expression; facilitate personal growth in all who work with them; listen and build a sense of community.
>
> **www.leadersdirect.com**

So far most of the focus here has been on the layers and architecture of service oriented enterprises. SOE is also about cultural changes within a technological context. Make no mistake: There will be plenty of technological discussions. And it is important for IT and business owners to speak the same language as much as possible. This book attempts to explain sometimes difficult and confusing concepts through simplified examples. But an explanation of the importance of a service culture is also necessary. And it starts from the top. There is an old proverb that says, "The fish stinks from the head." If there is a desire to bring about true change and to realize the potential of the service oriented enterprise, it is necessary to start with the leaders.

In their book *Beyond Workplace 2000,* Joseph Boyett and Jimmie Boyett[9] consider a renewed focus in leadership for change: servant leadership. A servant leader should be a servant to his or her customers and employees. The pyramid is reversed. It is an upside-down model of interactions. Unfortunately, this is easier said than done. For reasons beyond the scope of this book, leaders tend to demand having their way and insisting on their own agendas—on their own way of doing things.

James Hunter, in his book *The Servant,* provides an illustration of an upside-down pyramid where the first are last and the chief executive officer (CEO) is at the bottom of the pyramid[8] (see Figure. 1.5). As illustrated here, it is not only the executive power that is increased when going down the hierarchy but also the importance of serving and empowering the employees. It is interesting to note that almost invariably most C-level leaders will accept the fact that they are a service organization. This is true of any type of leadership, including in government. Officials are elected to serve their people. Managers and C-level executives serve their customers the best they can. But the service culture will be only a facade and a pretense if it does not permeate the very essence of governance and the very core objectives of its leaders.

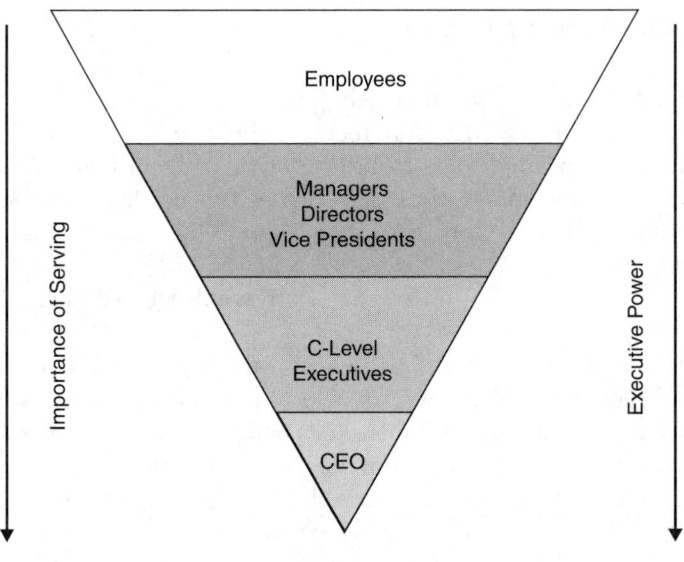

Figure 1.5 The inverted hierarchy in ideal service oriented enterprises

Becoming a service level organization is not about making the numbers or becoming a leader in a market sector or being lean and mean. These are important of course, but they should not be the core objective of a service oriented enterprise. The focus rather should be to serve with a genuine focus on those being served. There are commercials where the organization attempts to communicate about its care. But is it real? And can it be real if the C-level executives and below are not truly servant leaders? It is about really caring about the customers, employees, investors, partners, suppliers, and community where they function.

Service orientation as a cultural or personal trait is not a sign of weakness—on the contrary. For leaders it means the focus is on the organization or people being served. It also means trying to bring the best out of people. In his interesting and controversial book *Everything You've Heard Is Wrong,* Dr. Tony Campolo describes this new type of leadership as follows: "What we need in the business world today are managers and leaders who are bigger on the inside than they are on the outside. We need people whose inner qualities make them into people who elicit loyalty and commitment from their workers. We need leaders who inspire all of those around them with their vision and energy."[11] In other words, servant leaders are needed who will elevate themselves from the petty quick-material-win or power-trip mentalities and will strive to inspire through being a good role model with high integrity. The focus should be on the community being served to empower it and to help it realize its full potential. This is especially true of employees, but it is true of other communities that are served such as customers and partners. The CEO and other C-level as well as mid-tier managers need to provide both service governance and an environment where employees can innovate. Constant employee reinforcement and encouragement should be the norm.

This culture and servant leadership should also be translated to the other communities that are served. For instance, servant leadership in sales implies that the focus should be on helping and elevating customers so that they achieve success through the products or services procured through an organization. I have seen many situations where the customers were completely turned off by aggressive sales executives whose only focus was to make their own quotas. The better approach is to establish relationships, to understand the true needs of the community being served, and to accordingly provide the best solution that fits the requirements.

Only when leaders at all levels understand the importance of servant leadership and appropriate it in their leadership goals will the emergence of service oriented enterprises be observed. Technology and the platform categories that are helping to integrate, to create dynamic value chains, and to innovate are tools—important tools, for sure, but only tools. To use them in their full potential it is necessary to start with service orientation in the leadership at all levels.

1.3 Service Oriented Enterprise

> Today's reality of intense global competition is creating a need for increased operational efficiency, global collaboration, and workforce mobilization. While becoming more efficient, they must also become more agile and responsive, and find more ways to use information to create new customer value.
>
> **Intel**

These are exciting and yet dangerous times. Organizations are facing incredible challenges. Since the 1990s, mergers, acquisitions, turbulence, and unprecedented global changes have affected and will continue to affect almost every single business sector. In fact, today organizations—and especially CEOs—are concerned about three top priorities.

1. Growth: Revenue growth has become a top priority for CEOs. This is an important shift that means the focus is more on gaining market share and increasing revenue than on cutting cost. Innovation is essential for growth. Organizations need to be able to introduce new products at an increasingly accelerated rate. This innovation can be achieved when the entire life cycle of business process management is automated and when strategies are linked to digitized process and business rules. The three layers of a service oriented enterprise are critical in achieving this.
2. Productivity: To meet the challenges of the 21st century, even though the IT market has been soft for several years in a row, there is still demand and concern for specialized skilled workers. The requirement for productivity of employees, customers, and partners remains high.
3. Compliance: 2005 saw the emergence of the first Sarbanes–Oxley compliance prosecution trial.[12] In fact, compliance is a top priority in finance as well as IT governance, and companies are investing heavily in various types of systems—especially business process management, financial, and content management—to realize transparency.

These are not the only priorities of CEOs and large organizations, but they remain key factors in allocating resources, in striking new partnerships, and in considering new technology investments. These are definitely uncertain times. The United States in particular has emerged from the burst of the e-bubble with its confidence shaken, its corporate accountability exposed, and an unprecedented uncertainty about the future.

This book is not about a magical technological wand organizations must have to stay afloat. Far from it—service orientation is not even new. It has

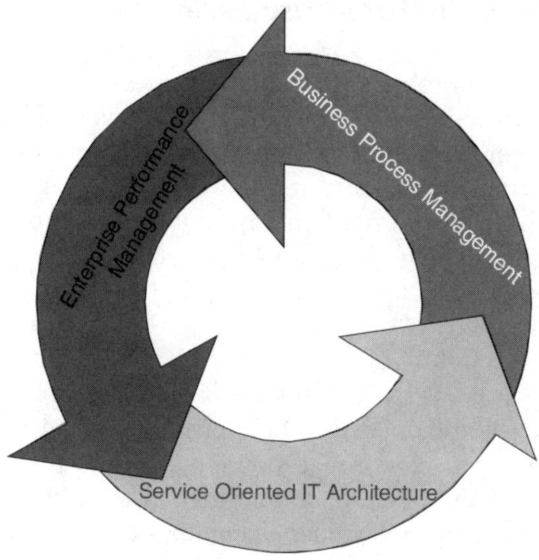

Figure 1.6 The continuous interdependencies among the three components of SOEs

taken several decades to emerge in ever-increasing clarity as the de facto modus operandi for enterprises. The seeds and elements of service orientation have been around for decades and even centuries. Even though most of the focus of this book is on technologies and bridging the gap between business and IT, the service oriented culture is much deeper than that. A service oriented enterprise has its focus first and foremost on its customers. But the employees, partners, suppliers, investors, and the community at large are also entities that need to be served. Service orientation is first and foremost a culture and a mindset. It sees every individual or organization as a VIP that needs to be served in the best way possible. When a service helps a customer readily obtain the latest information about a product, that is service orientation in action. When a customized product or service is produced within budget and on time, that is also service orientation in action. These are examples of customer-to-business exchanges and perhaps are the most visible and in some sense the most important aspect of service orientation. However, a service oriented enterprise also needs to serve its employees, trading partners, investors, and the community as a whole. So when an employee can readily find out or be informed about changes in his or her 401(k) plan, that is service orientation, too. When a trading partner can readily receive the information on the process status of the parts they order, that too is service orientation in action.

1.3.1 Governed by Enterprise Performance Management

> The two biggest problems in today's businesses are unmotivated workers and consumers. Routine types of work environments and consumer environments result in both employee as well as customer turnover. Making routine employees and customers experience fun can turn around an organization's performance. It can act as important differentiator in creating an edge over the competitors.
>
> **Atanu Adihari**

Many times organizations have high-level objectives and then come up with strategies to realize these objectives. Enterprises often realize the information they needed to avoid a crisis or to respond to a trend was always there either in the databases of their enterprise information systems or in the process data of their business process management applications. Often there are too much data stored in different databases. The challenge is to analyze, to summarize, and to provide the essential identifications of patterns, outliers, or trends. Many organizations have adopted or are about to adopt enterprise performance management (EPM) initiatives. Enterprise performance management systems help organizations formulate, implement, and monitor their strategies. According to Gartner, EPM is "an umbrella term that describes all of the processes, methodologies, metrics and systems needed to measure and manage the performance of an organization."

What are strategies? Executives come with the top-level strategies of the organization. Michael Coveney[13] defines mission, objectives, strategies, tactics, and key performance indicators (KPIs) as follows.

- Mission: A concise statement of the organization's reason for existing
- Objectives: Broad statements describing the targeted direction
- Goals: Quantifications of objectives for a designated period of time
- Strategies: Statements of how objectives will be achieved and the major methods to be used
- Tactics: Specific action steps that map out how each strategy will be implemented
- KPIs:[14] Measures of performance that show progress of each tactic in reaching the goals

Enterprise strategies are communicated to all operational levels. There are several essential elements in an EPM. Through EPM tools, real-time as well as historic data can be monitored and analyzed. In service oriented enterprises the data sourcing is achieved through feeding business process data to the measurement tools. BPM systems keep track of all process activities,

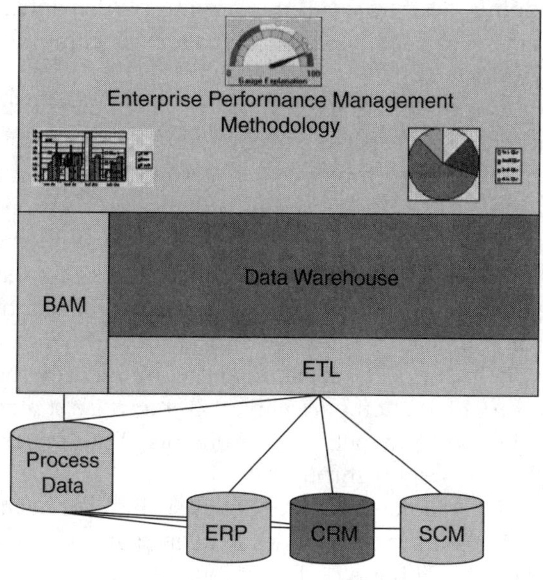

Figure 1.7 Enterprise performance management components

participants, and process events as well as the status and performance of the processes as a whole, which are monitored and measured. Process event data can be tracked and correlated, allowing managers to run real-time reports on the process data. An analysis of historic data can be performed through extracting process data in data warehouses. Through online analytical cubes, the data can be sliced and diced to discover trends pertaining to process workloads, human participation, and overall process application performance.

The historic data can be a day old or a month old or a year old. The source data is extracted from various processes or enterprise applications and is mapped onto historic data warehouses for analysis. Historic data analysis is a powerful business intelligence and mining tool to identify trends in the process data gathered by the underlying systems, especially the BPM system. The real-time monitoring, on the other hand, can enable the managers as well as the BPM system itself to take remediation or corrective actions in real-time to influence executing processes as it happens.

From business activity monitoring (BAM) measurement tools, reports, and front ends, managers can drill down to the individual processes and can proactively analyze potential performance bottlenecks. Managers can also rectify poorly performing processes through, for instance, raising alerts or reassigning tasks to weak-performing participants. The graphical monitoring interface can become the manager's cockpit, allowing him or her to analyze and to act.

It is not easy to translate strategies into practical and sustainable executions. Service oriented enterprises serve many communities: their customers, partners, shareholders, employees, government, and the community as a whole. SOEs need to be aware of performance to be more successful in translating strategy goals into executions that could be dynamically monitored and sustained. There are mid-tier departments or organizations that attempt to implement the strategic plans. In successful organizations, there is continuous communication between various departments and the overall IT solutions that help support, measure, and communicate the health of the business. At its core, EPM attempts to link the enterprise strategies to process execution through performance measurements. Enterprises develop and communicate their strategies through EPM.

This is where management methodologies such as the balanced scorecard or Six Sigma can be used to systematically align performance objectives and execution. The key contribution of the balanced scorecard is that it is a holistic and balanced approach to measuring the overall performance of the enterprise compared to traditional measures such as revenue, share value, or earning per share. More importantly, balanced scorecards with their focus on customers and employees as well as shareholders provide a very service oriented approach to measuring performance. The organization can view itself as a service oriented enterprise attempting to serve various communities through measurable results. Balanced scorecards identify four areas for organizational performance monitoring and measurements: financial, customer, internal business processes, and learning and growth for employees.

Six Sigma, on the other hand, is a rigorous approach to identifying key process characteristics as defined by the customer, discovering the process input or inputs that most influence that characteristic, and the implementation of process improvements designed to deliver the process characteristic to the customer. Six Sigma attempts to reduce the variances in process performance. Six Sigma is a framework that prescribes tasks, tools, and analytic methods to be used in different phases of the overall process improvement life cycle. Six Sigma methodology includes five phases: define, measure, analyze, improve, and control. It is a quality-focused, continuous-improvement methodology that attempts to reduce and eliminate variations in process performance.

Figure 1.8 illustrates the relationships between balanced scorecards and Six Sigma and the measurements that feed into the KPIs from real-time business activity monitoring as well as historic data. Once an improvement area—a KPI—is identified in the balanced scorecard, it can then be delegated to the Six Sigma methodology to achieve the desired objectives. Six Sigma uses the underlying BPM to automate the improved processes. Then through the BAM or online analytical processing (OLAP) measurements, the results can be fed back to the balanced scorecard monitoring cockpit, and the performance loop continues with the next iteration.

1.3.2 Driven by Business Process Management

> There is common consensus that a modern business … must put in place efficient systems for management of its processes. It seems to go almost without saying that the solution lies in computer systems for Business Process Management.
>
> **Keith Harrison-Broninski**

The enterprise performance measures capture key performance indicators from a number of disciplines. Almost every type of work carried out within

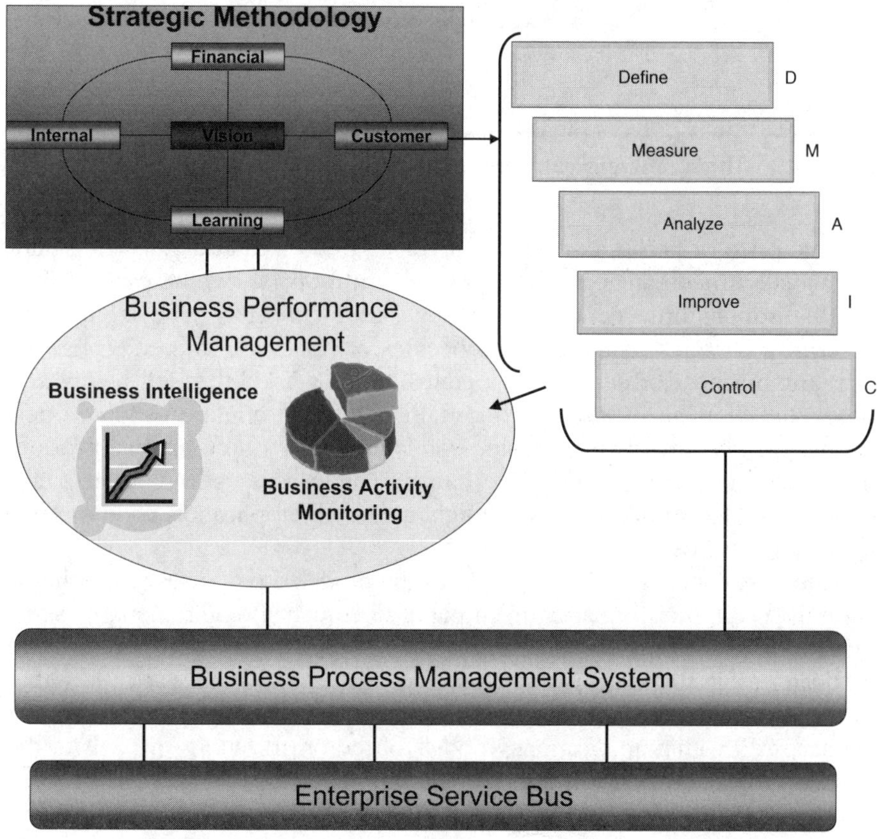

Figure 1.8 BSC and Six Sigma for business performance management

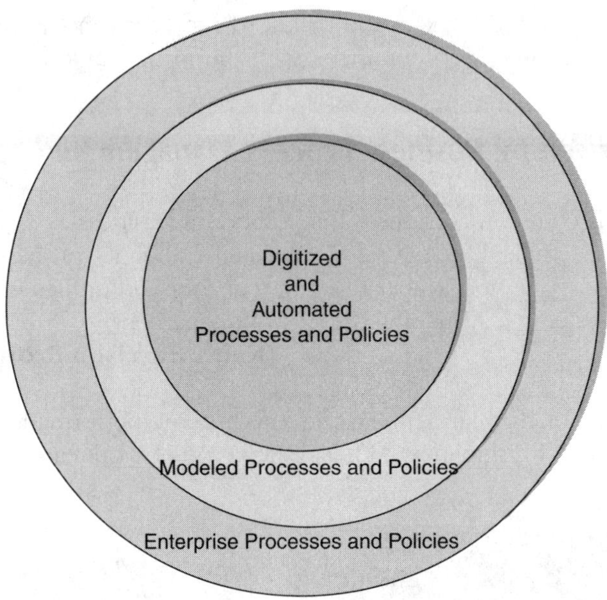

Figure 1.9 Three different categories of processes

an enterprise or across enterprises involves processes and policies. There are actually three categories of processes and policies, which can be illustrated through three concentric circles (see Figure 1.9). The largest and outermost circle contains all the processes or policies in the enterprise. In fact, any business or enterprise operates and is guided through policy and procedure manuals. These could pertain to internal human resource operations, finance, marketing, business relationships, procurement, production, customer service, and governance. The processes and policies are typically written in documents or might also be in application code or even in people's heads.

The next concentric circle represents the modeled processes and policies. Here there is a transformation from paper documents, requirement, or specification phases to more concrete policy and process maps, or models. Here modeling tools such as Visio are used to capture the process flows. Other modeling artifacts are produced in this phase: models of the information that get accessed within applications, models of the organizations, models of the business rules and policies, and models of the service interactions.

Modeling is important, but it is not sufficient to manage change and to improve the service oriented enterprise's performance goals. It is necessary to have automation: The processes and the business rules that drive them must execute in the business process management systems. This is the focus of the innermost circle. The main purpose and focus of automation is to enlarge the presence and scope of this innermost circle, providing increasing automation. As service oriented enterprises move in this direction, they are also realizing that the gap between modeling artifacts and execution needs to be eliminated. When a process executes, each step of a task assignment is recorded and saved in a work or process instance database. More specifically, the time a process instance is created, the assignment of a task to a user, the invocation of a service at a particular step, the time a particular task is completed, who completed it, and where you are in a particular process are all available for monitoring. A manager might decide to escalate a task, reject an approval, and have the task re-executed, and so on. You can also have business rules that can enact exception handling processes or tasks when, for instance, certain performance constraints are violated. The key element here is this notion of "execution." Execution goes beyond documentation and mere models (flowcharts) of the processes. The BPMS with the process engine and the associated rule engine "walk" through the process diagram and control the execution of the process. Managers can then view the status of executing processes and potentially effect the run-time execution of the process instances. The real-time performance monitoring helps organizations correct processes while in flight.

The amalgamation of human workflow, enterprise application integration, B2B integration, business rules management, and process monitoring have resulted in the emergence of holistic end-to-end BPM suites (see Figure 1.11). BPM suites always include the active participation of human beings. Work can be routed to people based on their roles (e.g., administrators) and skills (e.g., knowledge of Windows networking). When the people are employees, they will be organized in various organizational units and groups. Today's BPM suites should be able to handle various models of work assignments, including assignments to work baskets, or queues, and work lists. Human participation was typically the forte of earlier document-centric workflow systems, and it continues to be important, especially in complex BPM applications. This is the workflow capability of BPM suites.

In addition, BPM includes the active participation of enterprise systems. These systems could be databases, ERP applications, legacy applications, document management systems, or any enterprise application required to complete the work. System participation was the forte of earlier enterprise application integration products. The participation of these internal systems, updating them transactionally, and providing an overall flow-based integration all continue to be important requirements in many BPM solutions. This is the enterprise application integration capability of BPM suites.

In addition to human and back-end system applications, BPM includes trading partners as participants. Here the process is no longer an internal one; it involves extended trading partners in streamlined flows. The most important technological development in this area is the emergence of Web

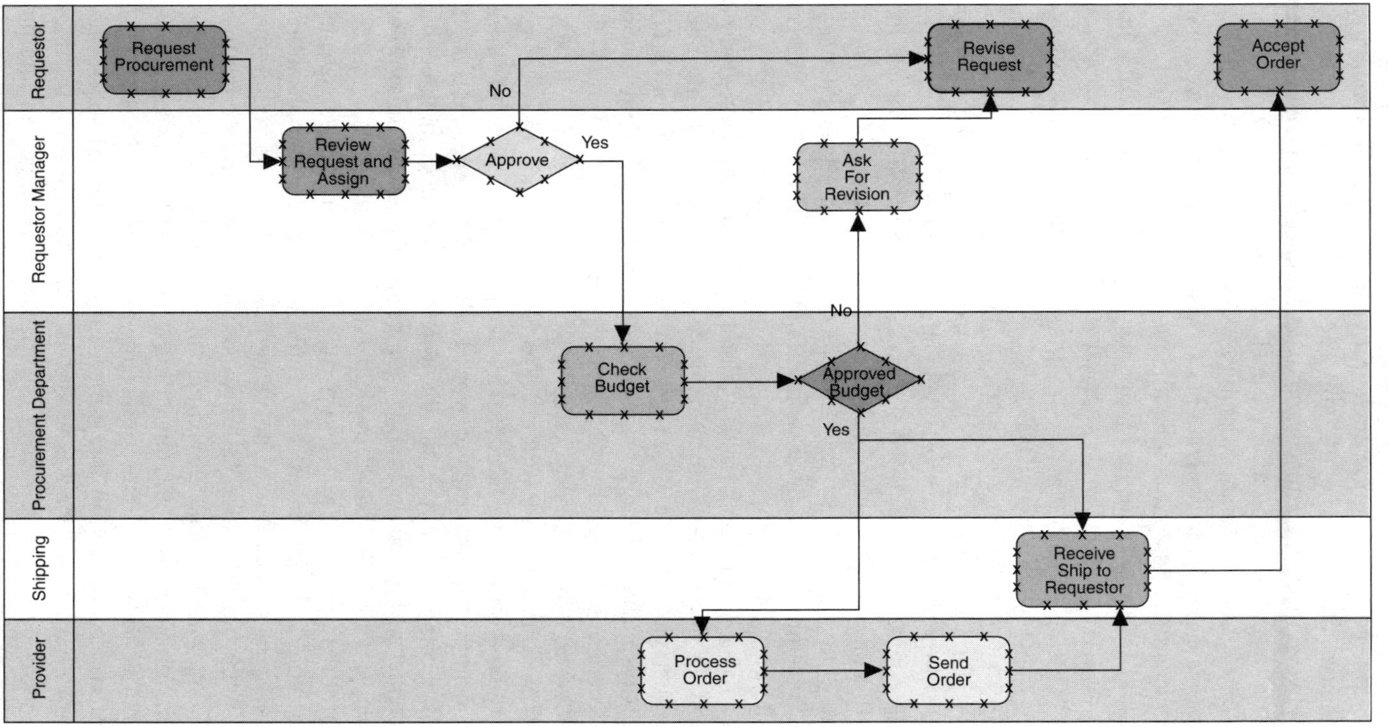

Figure 1.10 Example of a modeled process

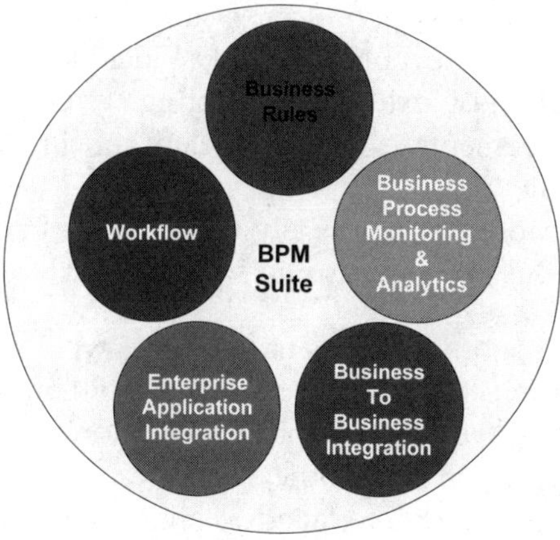

Figure 1.11 BPM suites

services-based SOAs. In short, these SOAs allow trading partners programmatic or browserless access to Web sites via the Internet, within the context of processes that often link internal activities with external trading partner requests. B2B vendors started to offer such extended enterprise connectivity, but now this is becoming a hallmark of all BPM products.

In addition to the various types of participants (human, system, trading partner), there is the business rule support in BPM suites. A business is a collection of policies (rules) and procedures (flows). The two are inseparable. Modern-day BPM suites cohesively integrate business rules. These rules can include decision-making criteria, evaluation of conformance, risk assessments, time constraints, task reassignment decisions, or decisions on quality. These business rules need to be captured and executed in the context of process flows, creating smart processes. The two are inseparable and actually feed on one another: Rules influence the flow control, and the flow map determines which rules are involved in the process. Behind every decision, service level, and task assignment there can be rules.

There are several categories of business rules.

- *Decisioning* rules can be used in various decisioning steps within processes (the famous diamond shape for decisions); decision trees, decision maps, and decision tables are all examples of production rules within processes.
- *Inferential* rules can be used to evaluate properties and to capture complex computational dependencies between properties. The evaluations are done automatically whenever a property value changes.

- *Event correlation and action* rules can be used to fire actions upon the occurrence of events; examples include temporal events or events published by external monitoring systems. For example, service level agreements can be modeled and implemented as event correlation rules.
- *Constraints* capture semantically valid states of process objects and raise exceptions when constraints are violated.

These are few of the major categories of rule types within a BPM suite. These rules together with the process flows are assets within an organization.

BPM suites support "intelligent" processing along a number of dimensions. Intelligent integration means the system can go to back-end systems or can invoke trading partner interfaces on an as-needed basis—as it needs information from external systems. Intelligent task assignment means the smart BPM system assigns and reassigns tasks based on skills, roles, workload, and work performance. And intelligent interfacing means the smart BPM systems generate and allocate the appropriate interface to the user based on the profile of the user, the geographical location, and the time of the invocation.

More importantly, rules can be applied situationally by selecting the appropriate decision, integration, document, or action based on where, by whom, when, or why an action is taken.

Finally, BPM suites include business process analysis and activity monitoring. This deals primarily with the B (business) and M (management) of BPM suites. Businesses are defined through KPIs, goals, objectives, policies, processes, practices, and priorities. The analysis component allows for modeling, simulating, and analyzing the performance of the processes. The analysis of historic data is key in identifying potential bottlenecks in the processes or the participants—human, trading partner, or back-end applications—of the process activities. BPM also provides real-time monitoring and measurement, allowing managers or monitoring agents to be proactive in taking actions to improve processes on the fly.

1.3.3 Founded on the Service Oriented Architecture

> Many of the concepts for Web services come from a conceptual architecture called service oriented architecture (SOA). SOA configures entities (services, registries, contracts, and proxies) to maximize loose coupling and reuse.
>
> **Michael Stevens**

So how can companies thrive in this milieu of unparalleled competitive trends, with pressures to increase productivity, sustain double-digit growth and at the same time maintain compliance with governmental standards? Through becoming service oriented enterprises. Technology is neither a panacea nor an anathema; it is a tool. And with an increasingly service oriented mentality, a number of trends have emerged that are starting to provide the foundation for service oriented enterprises. Not surprisingly, these are culminating in service oriented architectures. SOAs do not constitute a product category: Technologies can be purchased that support service orientation and service oriented architectures, but SOA is more a framework and organization of concepts than a product category. A basic definition follows.

A service oriented architecture is a framework that supports the discovery, message exchange, and integration between loosely coupled services using industry standards. Each party complies with agreed on protocols and carries out its part in the overall execution of processes involving services from diverse organizations.

Each of the terms in this SOA framework definition is important. *Loose coupling* means being able to use the service and to integrate it within the application while at the same time being isolated from the details of the service's implementation language, platform, location, or status. Web services provide programmatic interfaces to Web sites or applications. There are a number of operations, and each one has input and output messages. This collection of operations constitutes the programmatic interface to the service. The implementation detail, the platform, and the implementation language are all hidden. A core component of the SOA is the ESB. There are some ESB products today. ESB is also an architecture concept or pattern. In either case, there are some essential and key elements or features of ESBs, as illustrated in Figure 1.12, including the following.

- Transport protocol translation: ESBs support service brokering for a plethora of standard transport protocols, including SOAP over HTTP (the most popular one for Web services), Java Message Service (JMS), and SMTP (e-mail protocol). The key advantage of the ESB is to provide the mechanism for translating between protocols. This means a service requestor can communicate via SOAP over HTTP through the ESB; then the ESB can turn around and invoke the service through, for instance, a JMS protocol.

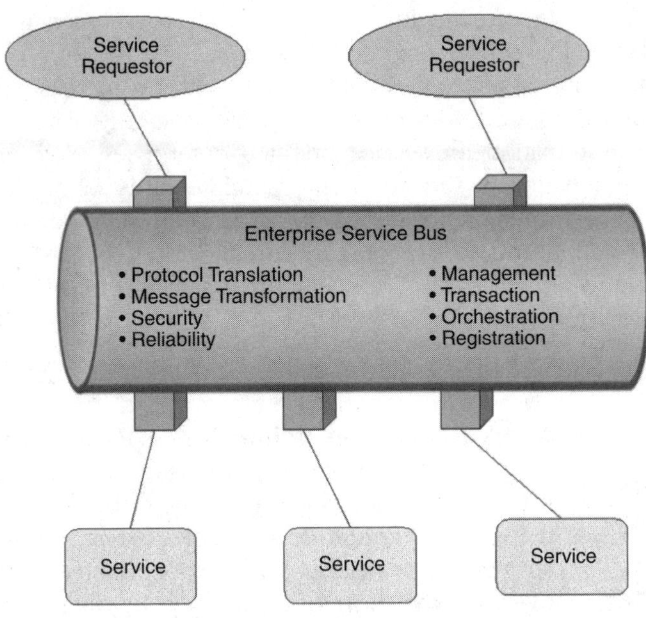

Figure 1.12 The enterprise service bus

- Message transformation: ESBs also provide the capabilities to transform messages while connecting service requestors and providers. These transformations pertain to the content of the message. For example, a service requestor might have one representation for, say, a customer, and a service provider might have another.
- Security: ESBs also support the authentication and authorization of services. Message exchanges can be encrypted and digitally signed. Service requests and responses require credential exchanges as well as message exchange confidentiality and integrity. In addition to core secure transmissions of service requests and responses, ESBs support the privileged accesses to specific service operations. Security includes provisioning and include authentication with third-party security services.
- Reliability: The quality of the service is an essential requirement in service oriented enterprise applications. It is not possible to solve many business problems if the participants cannot be sure of the completion of message exchanges. Handling a service request requires the reliable communication (e.g., once and only once) of the transmission of the requestor to the provider and the reliable transmission of the responses. In clustered distributed deployments, reliability also means handling failovers when resources handling service executions fail.

- Management: Service management supports the installation, versioning, and deprecation of services. Management also includes monitoring and measurements of service performance. Through management dashboards, service architects can view the system performance parameters. They can also define rules that can correlate and act on exception events. The service level agreements between service producers and consumers will also be monitored and managed through the ESB.
- Transaction: Transactional consistency in updating and requesting services from various enterprise applications is essential. Service requests could cause modifications on a number of information systems, which need to be propagated consistently. There are different types of transactions. The most important category of transactions are those that guarantee consistency while allowing concurrent access and updates through services.
- Orchestration of services: The previous section mentioned business process management as the second major layer in an overall enterprise architecture of service oriented enterprises. BPM includes human participants as well as back-end systems and trading partners. Services can be composed and orchestrated in microflows that can in turn be published as services. Thus, BPM processes can invoke subprocesses that are orchestrations of services.

As service invocations cross enterprise boundaries, federations of enterprise service buses will become increasingly popular. The federated ESBs will manage invocation of services from one enterprise to services in another enterprise (Figure 1.13). External service invocation can already be found today, as organizations such as Google, Amazon, and eBay expose interfaces to their sites through service calls. With federated ESBs, the opportunity will

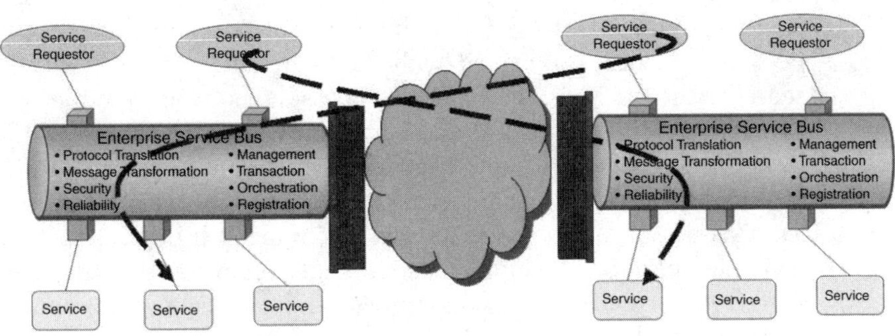

Figure 1.13 Federated enterprise service buses

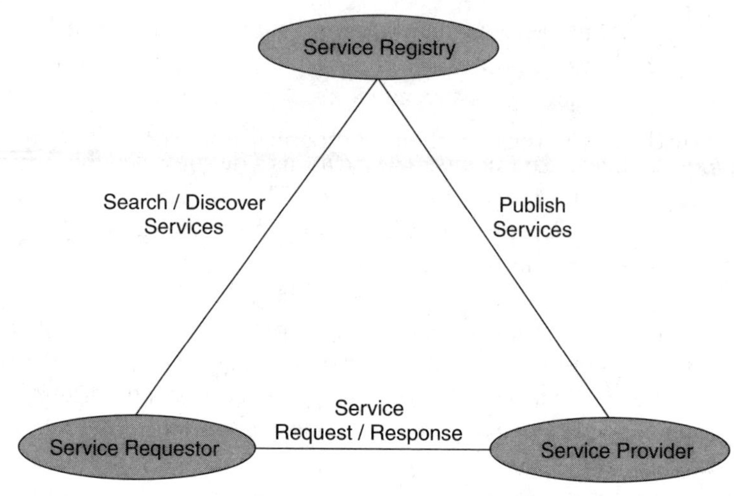

Figure 1.14 Registration, discovery, and exchange of service request and responses

arise to realize streamlined straight-through processing of service invocations while marshaling the service calls and implementing robust, secure, and high-performance orchestration of services.

Another term that characterizes service orientation is *discovery*. The famous triangle illustration (Figure 1.14) is often used to depict the registration-discovery-exchange cycle in service orientation.

There are three essential elements for service interaction: (1) registering the service to a registry; (2) locating the service; and (3) making service calls and message exchanges.

- Registries: One of the most popular activities over the Web is searching, which is why search engines such as Google or Yahoo! or MSN are so popular. However, search engines have some drawbacks. People are often unsatisfied with the search results because web searches are ad hoc. The engine is guessing as to what is the best hit for a particular search. There is another type of search that should be quite familiar: the Yellow Pages search. Here different categories of products and services are provided, in which someone can look for a particular listing based on ads or company listings. This is an example of a more structured search. Registries provide a structured search for services, where companies can be categorized based on industries and then for each category the organizations and their services can be listed, thus providing a much better categorization of what a person is searching for than ad hoc searching. So a registry is really an online database of registered companies and services, which can be accessed either through Web interfaces or application programming interfaces—in most cases Web services. Thus, service providers will register their companies and services. Companies looking for services will search the registry. The search is much more targeted since the companies and their services are categorized in the registry. The service provider will describe specific invocation details and protocols to help requestors use the service.

- Service request/response exchanges: Once a service requestor knows how to invoke a service, the service requestor and service provider can start communicating and conducting e-business transactions. There are many variations for this. It could be as simple as searching for the price of an item to actual long duration transactions involving several exchanges. One of the key features of service orientation is loose coupling because the service provider and service consumer are decoupled and independent. This is taken for granted in other business channels: distributors, online, or retail. Someone can search the Yellow Pages and can call a company he or she has never called before. A person can walk into a store in a retail mall and conduct business on the fly. What is revolutionary with service orientation is that now due to the support of standards, organizations and the services that were developed independently can be integrated in complete solutions with automated, or programmatic, access to the services via their published interfaces. This sounds like a mouthful, but it is essential. In fact, the concept of electronic business where companies exchange structured electronic documents for business transactions is not new. Standards such as electronic data interchange (EDI) have been around for quite some time. But EDI used expensive proprietary solutions and systems; only very large companies could afford it. In contrast, service orientation allows organizations to exchange electronic documents over the Internet and to invoke each other electronically through programs, using standard and affordable technologies.

The third term used in the description of service orientation is *process*. There are two categories of processes. Service processes, also called microflows or microprocesses, are relatively shorter-duration processes that involve service orchestration and execute within the ESB, where the short-duration and reliable transaction support is provided. The other category of processes is business processes, which is the layer above the service oriented IT architecture involving human participants as well as back-end services and trading partners. In the context of the service bus, processes control the service call sequences: the orchestration of the services. More importantly, processes include simple as well as complex decision making in constructs such as decision switches or loops. Business rules guide and control the business as well as the service processes.

The fourth term, *agreed on,* pertains to agreements between trading partners. To guarantee the required quality of service—such as performance, reliability, security, or compliance—enterprises need to enact service level agreements, which involve response-time constraints. But they can also involve much more complex constraints (e.g., handling exceptions or faults) on the exchanges between the trading partners. Once again, for service level agreements to be effective, the underlying process engine needs to use business rules to handle the complex relationship between the trading partners. Each of the terms defining service orientation contributes to the productivity and agility of the service oriented enterprise.

Notice that an SOA is a framework. Many technologies are used in supporting SOAs, such as application servers, enterprise service buses, and security servers, to name a few. Similar to other creative architectures in other domains, there are also many options when building a service oriented architecture. SOA is not a one-size-fits-all or static framework.

1.4 Can We Dream?

> When you wholeheartedly adopt a "with all your heart" attitude and go all out with the positive principle, you can do incredible things.
>
> **Norman Vincent Peale**

The history of computer science is truly amazing. In fact, no other technological achievement has had such a rapid evolution. It is reminiscent of science fiction movies where the aging process is suddenly accelerated. A new field of science was created with unprecedented accomplishments and intractable progress in digital automation.

The history outlined here is primarily technological, but there is a much more important history regarding the manner in which computers are changing lives. Andy Rooney once said on *60 Minutes*, "Computers make it easier to do a lot of things, but most of the things they make it easier to do don't need to be done." Computers have become a must have without always having a clear analysis as to why they are necessary. The one place where the impact of the computers is clearly evident is the Internet, which is now culminating with Web services and service oriented architectures.

Computer science started not too long ago. In 1946 the first digital computer emerged, with punched cards that could carry out programmable mathematical calculations—a beastly machine to say the least. The electronic

Figure 1.15 The ENIAC—the first computer (U.S. Army photo)

numerical integrator and computer (ENIAC) had 18,000 vacuum cubes and took over 1,800 square feet—practically the size of a small apartment (Figure 1.15). And that was only 60 years ago.

From these humble beginnings of the mid-1940s has come the emergence of a modern-day miracle, a new field of science: computer science. In the melee of computational models, programming paradigms, and computing disciplines now can be witnessed the emergence of perhaps the greatest computer yet. Sun Microsystems trademarked the phrase "The Network is the Computer." Today that vision, involving many computational services cooperating over completely interconnected networks, is becoming a reality through the service oriented enterprise.

Think about the day when a business owner can create new products on the fly through assembling existing components—very much like business owners assemble PowerPoint shapes today and create new presentations. And imagine the assembled product becomes instantly available. Imagine also if that business owner can now measure how well the product is doing and can decide whether it should be continued. The notion of easy-to-use graphical interfaces controlling and running large multi-billion-dollar organizations has been around for quite some time. Reality of this dream has been elusive. We are not there yet. Service orientation is only part of the solution, but it is an essential one. However, there is and continues to be some confusion in the industry as to exactly what *service orientation* is.

From a technology perspective, service orientation, although not exclusive to Web services, has really taken off as the next phase in the evolution of service oriented enterprise architectures precisely because of the success and permeation of Web services technologies. In fact, the notion of composing or orchestrating Web services and producing new services has often been identified as the distinctive characteristic of service orientation. These services can be obtained from a plethora of sources. The service providers might not even know they are participating in an overall service oriented solution.

Each service could be supported by an entirely different organization that has its own underlying implementation technology—completely independent or different from the other service providers participating in the overall service offering. This in essence is at the heart of loose coupling. Different services from completely different organizations can participate in the same overall composite service solution. Furthermore, the integration of loosely coupled components or technologies is facilitated through the use of standards, which make it easy for organizations to publish, to discover, and to interact with published services. It's easy to know what protocols can be used for discovery. It's easy to know what protocols to use to send and receive messages or otherwise invoke remote services. You are ready for integration and interaction out of the box. The approach is similar to "plug and play" with computer peripherals. For instance, a mouse or a printer could be plugged into a USB port and, assuming the drivers are available, used instantaneously. Web services bring this "plug and play" capability to remote service accesses through standard interfaces. The service providers or consumers could potentially be halfway across the globe. As long as the service provider and service consumer use the same protocols for exchanging service exchanges, they could interact through standardized service calls.

The focus of this book is on service oriented enterprises. As discussed in Section 1.1, service orientation is also about organizational culture—not just technology. But technology is important and often goes hand in hand with technology. In fact, both parties—business owner and IT—are guilty of ignoring each other's domains. In many cases IT has ignored the business focus and business needs and has concentrated on the latest toys or has focused too much effort on lower-level technologies. On the business side often there is too much of a tendency to very quickly brush off technology.

Service orientation is moving from point-to-point integration of systems and trading partners to more business-centric process and policy automation. Initially, especially with Web services, most implementations were simple proof of concept type of applications. This was primarily the experimentation phase. Companies started to experiment and to try to understand if this technology was just another fad or could truly deliver loosely coupled integration with their internal applications and with their trading partners. In this phase the technology was rather ad hoc. Relatively few Web services were deployed within enterprises or on the Web. Customers started using Web services development platforms to experiment and to understand this emerging technology.

Even in their earliest phases, organizations such as the World Wide Web Consortium and OASIS started to recognize the importance of additional standards to support issues such as reliability, security, and transactions across enterprise. So during this second phase, a number of key foundational Web services standards started to emerge. Large e-business companies such as Amazon, Google, and eBay started to provide programmatic Web services-based interfaces to their Web sites. This was a major trend, and suddenly with millions of Web services accessed on a daily basis, service orientation started to become mainstream. Equally important, in this second phase many large IT organizations started to use Web services as a viable technology to integrate back-office and mainframe applications. There are now serious efforts to establish business relationships and base them on Web services technologies.

In phase 2, the emphasis is on service composition and more robust standards for quality of service and management of services. Phase 2 also witnessed the emergence of BPM suites, which allow the automation of business rules and business processes involving human as well as system participants. ESBs are becoming the backbone of enterprise architectures and are providing the foundation for orchestrating services, as well as core enterprise integration features such as message transformations, protocol transformation, security, and reliability. This second phase witnessed the evolution and ratification of a number of core service standards for handling orchestration, such as Business Process Execution Language; security, such as WS-Security; transaction; and reliability. Also, registration of services and especially the UDDI standard became more robust.

In phase 3, connectivity solutions will evolve from foundational technologies of Web services (phase 1) to establishments of partner relationships (phase 2) to agile transformations, where business relationships can be discovered and deployed dynamically. In phase 3, software will be a service that becomes a formidable solution in end-to-end business processes involving internal enterprise applications, BPM systems, and ESBs. From the perspective of technology, the ubiquitous phase implies Web services will be everywhere. They will be part of every platform and will be used in all integration projects—the foundation of connectivity. From a demand perspective, customers will build and enact dynamic processes. The composition of Web services in intelligent processes—which have both the flows and business rules—is going to become essential in choosing and deploying Web services solutions. Phase 3 will also launch the next wave in software deployments and licensing, namely software as a service (SaaS). Service orientation will enable enterprises to search and use the service they need, often dynamically, without the overhead of costly and sometimes complex installation of enterprise software.

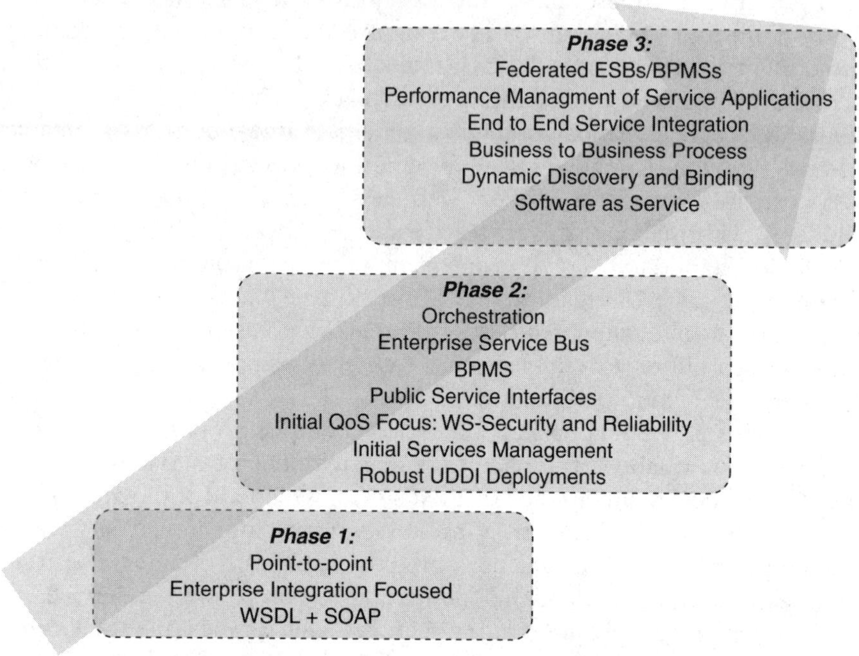

Phase 3:
Federated ESBs/BPMSs
Performance Managment of Service Applications
End to End Service Integration
Business to Business Process
Dynamic Discovery and Binding
Software as Service

Phase 2:
Orchestration
Enterprise Service Bus
BPMS
Public Service Interfaces
Initial QoS Focus: WS-Security and Reliability
Initial Services Management
Robust UDDI Deployments

Phase 1:
Point-to-point
Enterprise Integration Focused
WSDL + SOAP

Figure 1.16 The three phases of SOEs

1.5 Conclusion

The journey with service oriented enterprises has begun. At its very core, a SOE is the enterprise that builds on and realizes three functional layers: enterprise performance management, business process management, and a core underlying service oriented IT architecture. Service orientation is also a culture of services where not only systems but also human participants view themselves as servants. The servant principle emanates from inverse pyramids and creates a culture of service orientation involving trading partners, human participants within organizations, and services in the IT technology framework.

How will these phases be supported effectively in service oriented enterprises? Two pyramids capture the essence of service oriented enterprises (Figure 1.17). The first pyramid deals with the organization of three key technological components: enterprise performance management, business process management, and the underlying service oriented IT architecture for managing services, especially through technologies such as the enterprise service bus. The second pyramid is the service and empowerment pyramid, which encourages executives in service oriented enterprises to

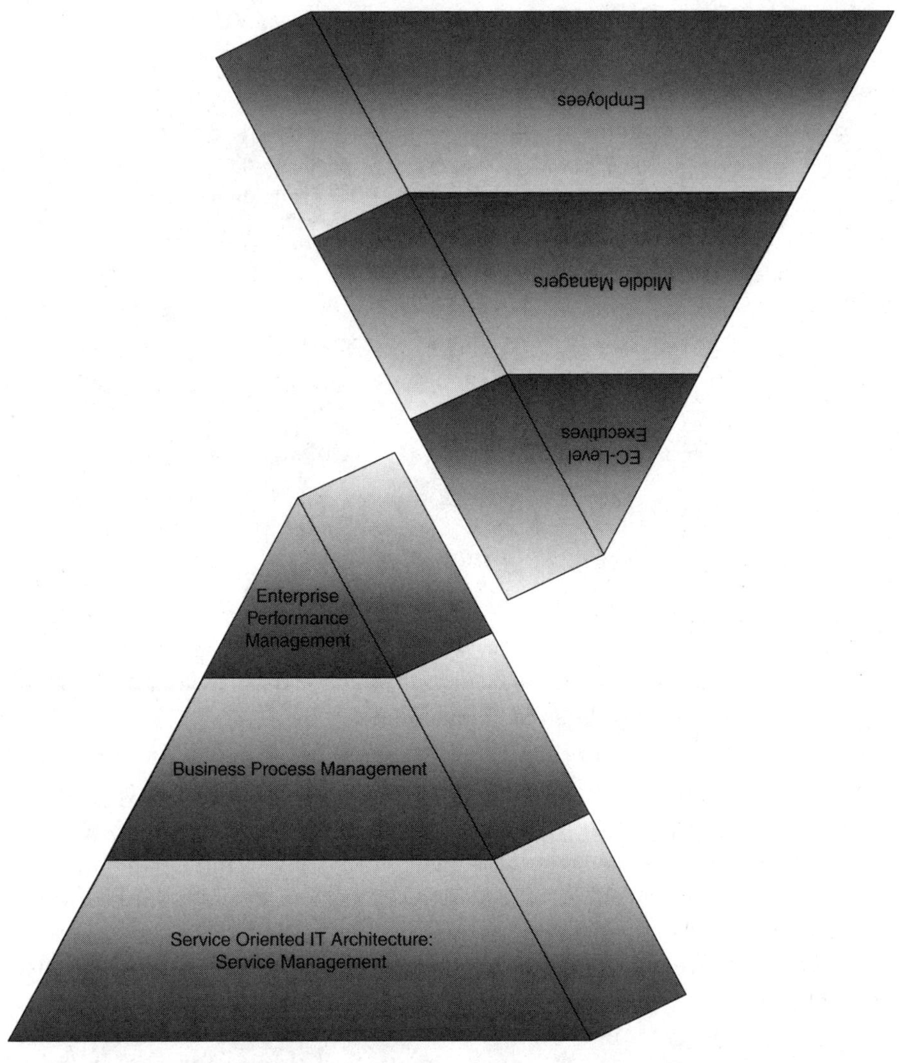

Figure 1.17 Servant technology and servant leadership pyramids

view themselves truly as facilitators, empowering their constituents to achieve the performance goals of the enterprise.

The two pyramids are about serving. The pyramid on the left hand side shows the more traditional view where enterprise objectives and goals guide the enterprise. Business process management systems and the lower-level service oriented IT infrastructures are facilitators that help an enterprise achieve its measurable business goals and objectives. But the pyramid

Figure 1.18 SOE serving different communities

on the right-hand side is equally important. After all, an enterprise is about people, and the customers, partners, and employees are the ones who will help an enterprise achieve its objectives. The role of the servant leader and the upside down effect of a leader serving the needs of those he or she manages are critical factors in the success of the service oriented enterprise. With technology as the facilitator and a strong trend toward servant leadership, a service oriented enterprise can succeed through serving the communities it is intended to serve: its customers, trading partners, shareholders, employees, the government, and the community at large (Figure 1.18).

Notes

1. Thomas L. Friedman, *The World Is Flat: A Brief History of the Twenty-First Century* (New York: Farrar, Straus, and Giroux, 2005).
2. And other industries as well, including biotechnology and computer hardware, as seen with the acquisition of IBM's laptop technology by China's Lenovo (see http://www.lenovo.com/us/en/). Lenovo is also interested in becoming a leader in high-end supercomputing, not just personal computers (PCs).

3. Setrag Khoshafian, "Web Services and Virtual Building Blocks: Virtual Enterprises," May 22, 2002, http://www.webservicesarchitect.com/content/articles/khoshafian01.asp.
4. After some investigations the FBI was urged to scrap the $170 million dollar project, which was intended to manage terrorism cases because of mismanagement. See statement of Robert S. Mueller, III, director, Federal Bureau of Investigation, before the United States Senate Committee on Appropriations Subcommittee on Commerce, Justice, State and the Judiciary, February 3, 2005, http://www.fbi.gov/congress/congress05/mueller020305.htm.
5. India had a revenue of about $17 billion from software outsourcing in 2005. See the ZDNet Research Blog on outsourcing titled "Outsourcing spending by Asia-Pacific companies to reach $16 bln in 2010," at http://blogs.zdnet.com/ITFacts/index.php?id=C0_29_1.
6. Dell computers used to have all its outsourcing functions in India. After dealing with a lot of complaints, Dell decided to move its technical support back to the United States, while keeping the home support in India.
7. James A. Champy, "X-treme Business Reengineering," *Optimize*, March 2002, http://www.optimizemag.com/article/showArticle.jhtml?printableArticle=true&articleId=17700684&queryText.
8. http://www.acm.org/classics/nov95/toc.html
9. Joseph Boyett and Jimmie Boyett, *Beyond Workplace 2000* (New York: Dutton, 1995).
10. James C. Hunter, *The Servant* (New York: Crown Business, 1998).
11. Tony Campolo, *Everything You've Heard Is Wrong* (Nashville, TN: W Publishing Group, 1992).
12. Richard Scrushy was the first CEO charged with violating the Sarbanes–Oxley Act. As reported in *USA Today,* he was acquitted. See http://www.usatoday.com/money/industries/health/2005-06-28-scrushy_x.htm?csp=34.
13. http://www.businessforum.com
14. KPIs combine several measurements or metrics to reflect performance of key performance criteria. KPIs can be leading or lagging. Leading is more dynamic and real-time. The processes that are executing can be continuously tracked, and the problem can be potentially fixed while in flight. The lagging indicators are after-the-fact measures.

Chapter 2

Service Oriented Methodologies

New technologies have enabled an increase in the pace at which businesses can form and reform value chains in order to create new products and services.

Thomas Koulopoulus and Nathaniel Palmer

2.1 Introduction

Business and IT: Methodologies are important for both business and information technology (IT). Even though there are tools for enterprise performance monitoring, business process management, and service oriented integration, phases are still needed to capture requirements and to design and implement specific target solutions. In other words, methodologies are needed. Methodologies involve roles, workflows with sequenced activities, and artifacts that are processed in each phase. Methodologies also involve the governance of the project as a whole.

Methodologies are necessary to help build new products and services and to continuously improve existing offerings. Methodologies help achieve productivity and maturity in building products and services. However, if one area in the service orientation suite were identified as the least mature, it is definitely this whole area of methodology for building and deploying services. This is interesting because a lot of the developments in service oriented technologies happened from the bottom up—where various infrastructure technologies, especially in Web services, provided pieces of the service oriented jigsaw puzzle without the comprehensive support of all the elements in the service stack.

For service oriented enterprises (SOEs), methodologies are necessary because the solutions will change. Internal and external challenges must be responded to, and solutions must be continuously improved. This chapter is helpful for both business and IT. On the business side, it helps provide an appreciation of the business roles and overall scope of SOE solutions. For IT, it provides an overview of the various concepts, notations, and approaches in service oriented analysis and design. Here the focus is primarily on the service oriented architecture (SOA) analysis and design methodologies. Chapter 5 elaborates more on business process management (BPM) methodologies. Until recently, methodologies have received little attention in service orientation. This is surprising because it is an important starting point for building successful service oriented applications. If the analysis and design is done incorrectly, there will be a price—sometimes quite high—to pay when building and deploying service oriented applications.

2.1.1 Methodologies

> Agile methodology has a lot of benefits and I believe that all organizations can gain from implementing some portion of it. However, to reap the true benefits of Agile, just like with SOA, you need to have good communication between business and IT.
>
> **D. L. Tyler, Jr.**

As discussed in Chapter 1, the architecture of service oriented enterprises involves three layers: enterprise performance management (EPM), business process management, and the underlying infrastructure of service oriented architecture (Figure 2.1). Corresponding to each of these layers are methodologies.

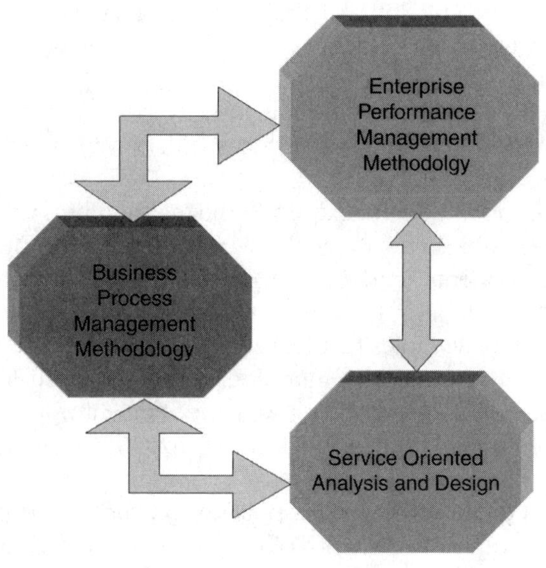

Figure 2.1 The three components of SOEs are interdependent

The methodology in the enterprise performance management layer is expanded and drilled down in the BPM methodology. Similarly, services and requirements identified in the BPM methodology are then analyzed and designed in the service oriented analysis and design (SOAD) phase. For instance, a balanced scorecard methodology will identify a number of internal processes for enhancements and optimizations. These processes are then designed and implemented using a BPM methodology. Similarly, within the BPM methodology are a number of services that need to be identified. The overall methodology spanning enterprise performance, business process, and service orientation is dynamic and iterative. Details of service definition, service registration, service deployment, and service QoS are done at the SOAD layer.

Service oriented enterprises deploy service oriented solutions. Building these solutions covers the entire spectrum of service oriented definition, analysis, and design—from higher-level business focus to the lower-level IT focus. This IT focus is primarily the service infrastructure with concerns focusing on integration performance, reliability, and security. In terms of the systems that are built, IT is also focused on maintainability, software life cycle, and overall productivity of the development team to meet business demands.

Business focus, on the other hand, typically starts top down with goals and objectives driven by business requirements. Businesses set goals—often measurable objectives—and then attempt to align the implementation of the various projects to meet these objectives and goals. It is not uncommon to find IT projects targeting business objectives that have incurred delays and cost overruns.

Business-focused methodologies are usually based on business process reengineering[1] (BPR) approaches that focus on approving organizations and business processes.

In a service oriented context, BPR means starting with higher-level strategic business objectives or goals, which identify the purposes of the proposed improvements, and then from this top-down determination of business objectives drilling down through a series of models into potential project plans and deliverables that realize these business objectives or goals. The overall focus of business methodologies is tangible business results. In contrast, the focus of IT methodologies is the efficient implementation and deployments of systems whose goal is to support and to implement the applications for business strategies.

A business is defined through its policies, practices, and processes. It is not surprising therefore to see a lot of emphasis on process redesign in the business-oriented BPR approach. So a major phase of the business-oriented approach is to focus on analyzing and simulating the current processes—sometimes called the *as-is* analysis phase. The goal here is to identify cost-saving opportunities as well as potential problems or disconnects. Put simply, this phase tries to identify such concerns about how effectively business currently is conducted. This could apply to the front office (e.g., call centers), the back office (e.g., fulfillment), human resources (e.g., employee performance management), or any other facet of the business. In fact, the analysis also shows the connections and dependencies between the strategies as well as the processes involving multiple functional areas within the enterprise.

Figure 2.2 illustrates the spectrum of methodology focus from a business and IT focus. The vertical axis represents the low- and high-level methodology focus for IT. This indicates if IT uses a continuously improving methodology. It is not uncommon to find lack of methodology both on IT and the business side. The overall usage and focus in deployed projects in IT has been coding. On the other hand, some methodologies have emerged that focus on the business community. The horizontal axis captures the level of deployment for a business-focused methodology. Here, BPM and especially BRE (business rules engine) methodologies put less emphasis on IT.

With service orientation, the entire spectrum from business objectives to lower-level service implementations needs to be covered. Service orientation changes the rules of the game. Businesses need to view themselves as service providers and service consumers.

The dynamic relationship between IT and business for service oriented applications means what is built attempts to provide robust as well as

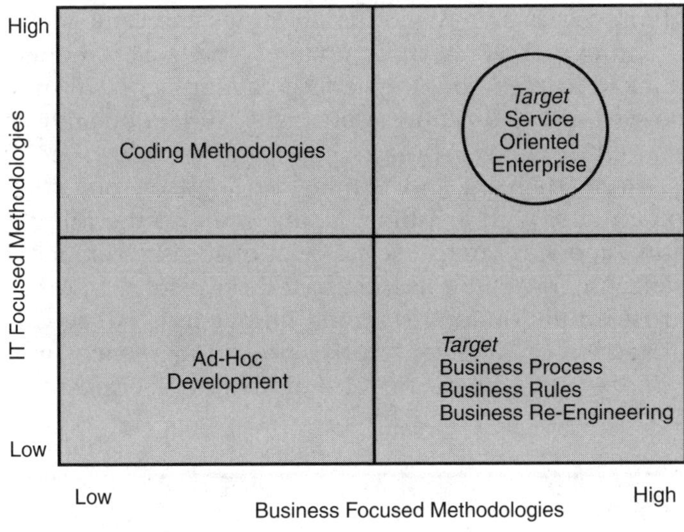

Figure 2.2 An SOE approach is focused on business and IT needs

extensible services to various communities. This sounds obvious, but it is a profound philosophical change that impacts every single aspect of the enterprise.

The target SOE methodology focus in the upper right-hand corner of Figure 2.2 implies that the SOE treats its integration, business process, information, and business rule entities as corporate assets. The methodology incorporates the ability to continuously improve, specialize, and change these assets. Bringing IT and businesses together in the lingua franca of business processes and rules will help them better communicate and build solutions by the SOE that targets its various communities.

Business and IT: The service provision is not just to the customers—although they should be the priority. The service focus should include also the employees, the shareholders, the trading partners, the suppliers, the government, and the community as a whole. The community could be global and diverse. For example, a service oriented enterprise that is globalizing with offices in foreign countries should try to adjust to the needs, culture, and the value systems of the foreign communities and not impose its own way of doing things and value system on others. Sometimes Western companies and governments have difficulties in foreign countries and create antagonism precisely because of lack of profound sensitivity and understanding of different cultures. In U.S. organizations, there is a lot of emphasis on short-term delivery and coming through on objectives. In Eastern cultures, such as China, Japan, and also the Middle East and Latin America, interpersonal relationships are much more important. Americans build trust based on results. In other cultures, trust is built on long-standing interactions. An agile multicultural service oriented enterprise providing services must be aware of the cultural nuances of its service requestors, and accordingly adjust its practices.

2.1.2 Why Should We Analyze and Design?

Computer science and software in general is an interesting discipline. There are intrinsic differences between computer science and other disciplines such as financial services, telecommunications, civil engineering, medicine, or manufacturing. One is creativity and innovation. Virtual universes and new paradigms can be practically created for any type of domain. Perhaps more important, this is a relatively new discipline, and hence some of the track records based on real-life experiences and accountability models have not been established. Furthermore, software is never finished. Any software needs to provide substantive improvements in its release history. The only type of software that does not change is legacy software, which sometimes is eventually retired. Software improvements are continuous. There is tremendous pressure to quickly create software and to put it out there, even though it may not be complete or may not have gone through quality assurance. This is problematic.

There is hope. Even industries such as automobile manufacturing soon learned the importance of rigorous methodologies and practices, especially those focusing on quality. The commitment to quality is starting to permeate other software disciplines, and maturity models are becoming more popular in software industries. However, by and large computer science has been more ad hoc and less disciplined than other disciplines.

So why should we analyze and design? Analysis captures the *what*: It provides a precise specification as to the purpose and scope of the software. Design then takes this analysis and converts it to a precise blueprint for implementation. Analysis and design help articulate the problem and then the solution. Different disciplines, such as object orientation, have their own approach to analysis and design. The next section will expand on analysis and design within the service oriented discipline.

Business and IT—the channels of service: This is an important dimension for services. Wired or wireless channels can be via different types of devices and browsers. The conventional browser on a laptop or a workstation is perhaps the most popular. But increasingly Internet access is through nonconventional browsing. For instance, technologies such as wireless handhelds are becoming quite popular, both for browsing as well as e-mail access. Now these devices focus on the end-user experience. Equally important are programmatic interfaces. Here the client or the requestor of the service is not a user but potentially another service. For example, Amazon.com can be browsed through a conventional Web browser or a Wireless Access Protocol (WAP) browser. However, Amazon.com also allows programmatic access through Web services. The added openness and flexibility offer tremendous benefits when linking various organizations together. The Amazon.com WSDL allows for items to be searched and checked for availability from within processes and internal applications deployed in the enterprise. The access is automatic and does not need human interaction through a browser.

2.1.3 Analysis and Design with a Twist of Service Orientation

> There are only two ways to live your life. One is as though nothing is a miracle. The other is as though everything is a miracle.
>
> **Albert Einstein**

In the analysis and design of service orientation, there are some fundamental differences when compared to more conventional application development. These could be described through three dimensions. When you either build or interact with a service, that service will have properties along each of these dimensions.

- *Leaf service or composition from other services:* New services can be built from existing services. For instance, a value-added service can be provided to customers while using existing services from other organizations: A bank can offer credit card services, a hotel can offer car rental services, an independent software vendor can provide consulting services. These are simple examples. In fact, services can potentially be composed from multiple vendors and new services offered as compositions of existing services. Services can consist of other services. So you can have leaf or building block services, and then these can be composed to build new services. A new service can be built through composition and then published. Other third parties can then take the service and build yet newer services. This is the composition value chain of services, and it is very important. This notion of treating software through composition of components has been around for quite some time. It is only now, with the popularity of services standards, that it is becoming a reality.

- *Exposing existing implementations or building new services:* When services are built, they could be built and consumed internally, or you might be interested in publishing interfaces of your existing enterprise information systems. The other dimension stems from the existence of many legacy applications. Whether in COBOL, FORTRAN, PL/1, CICS, or more recently C, C++, and Java, there are plenty of applications out there on mainframes and minicomputers where enormous investments have been made to capture complex business requirements. Instead of rewriting complex, sometimes undocumented, legacy from scratch, some of their functionality can be exposed through standard service interfaces. This is being realized both by the vendors of enterprise information systems as well as by third parties. It is a compelling approach that bridges legacy investments to modern service architectures.
- *Services for internal or external requestors:* Services can be used for either internal or external requestors. Typically enterprises have two firewalls: (1) an external firewall that allows external requestors to access Web content or services; and (2) an internal firewall that allows access to secure proprietary information or services. The external requestors can also get access to secure services or content via appropriate authentication and authorizations. For example, if information on customers as well as sales strategies is being published, the content and the service offered to search and navigate this content is for internal customers. On the other hand, e-commerce companies such as Amazon.com might offer services for external customers to browse their catalogs. The customers in the former case are the internal users or applications. The customers for the second scenario could be anyone who can access the service implementations externally.

Government is one of the great industry sectors that could and increasingly does benefit from service orientation, especially in standards-based service architectures as well as business process management. The Aberdeen Group stated, "Business process management enables government agencies to dismantle obsolete bureaucratic divisions by cutting the labor- and paper-intensive inefficiency from manual, back-end processes ... The BPM category may arguably provide the greatest return on investment compared to any other category available on the market today."[2]

Almost any sector of government, whether local, state, or federal, could benefit from service orientation. The government SOE initiatives are often focused on automating internal labor-intensive operations, such as processing tax forms or procurement. Increasingly, e-government Web sites are providing customer-facing Web sites both to search government sites and also to conduct online transactions.

One example where service orientation is used effectively in e-government is the WebDG platform. WebDG[3] is a project of Virginia Tech University in collaboration with Indiana Family Social Services Administration and the U.S. Department of Health and Human Services. The objective is to help the health-assistance seeker in Indiana obtain correct and timely information about available programs at the local, state, or federal level. A key premise and focus of the WebDG system is the notion of outsourcing to different government services and composing government services to provide even more value to the public. For example, a family looking for federal and state assistance with health needs during a pregnancy needs to visit several Web sites and offices for Medicaid and food assistance through Women, Infants, and Children (WIC). WebDG exports interfaces to different systems and databases through Web services and then composes them such that health-assistance requestors can search and obtain all the assistance to which they are entitled through a single interface. The platform can be used for such operations as processing benefits requests or transactions. A citizen's request for benefits or assistance could involve many agencies and services. Instead of going through multiple sites or locations chasing the different categories of benefits, citizens could use a single point of access and could have the service composition access various programs such as WIC, Medicaid, or Teen Outreach Pregnancy (TOP). This is done while protecting citizens' sensitive information and privacy, through a Privacy Profile Manger component. The figure provides a high-level illustration of the WebDG architecture.

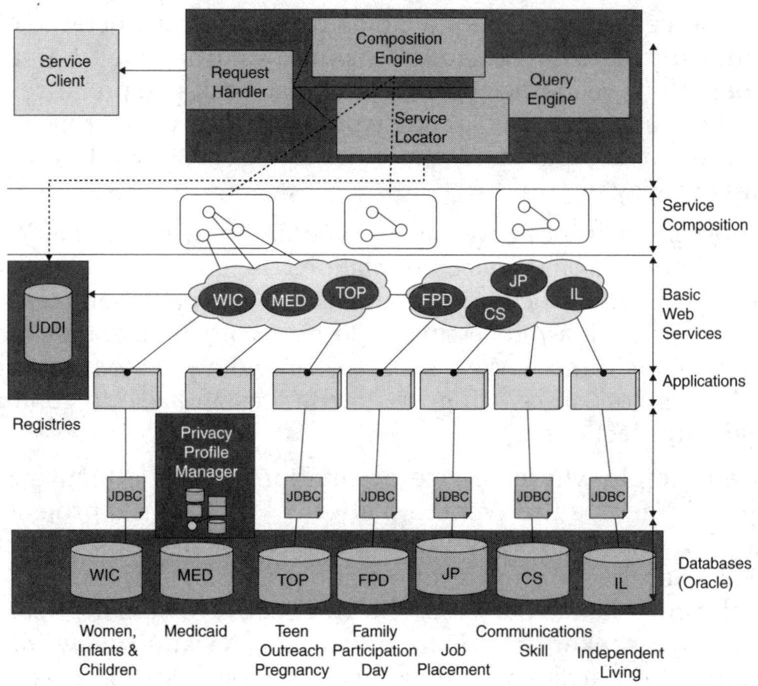

2.2 Service Development Life Cycle

> The waterfall model assumes that the only role for users is in specifying requirements, and that all requirements can be specified in advance. Unfortunately, requirements grow and change throughout the process and beyond, calling for considerable feedback and iterative consultation.
>
> **Russell Kay**

A key challenge when you're developing software-intensive systems is that you must cope with multiple developers organized

> into teams, possibly at different sites, working together on multiple iterations, releases, products, and platforms. In the absence of disciplined control, the development process rapidly degenerates into chaos.
>
> **Grady Booch**

Software that is used to increase productivity and the quality of life for individuals or corporation is never finished. The only type of software that eventually dies and finishes is legacy software, which is no longer maintained or used.

The traditional software development life cycle is the so-called waterfall model (Figure 2.3), which begins with requirements—what do the business owners or stakeholders want—and then proceeds through the major phases of analysis, design, implementation, and deployment. Sounds simple? Well, not quite. The problem with the traditional waterfall model is that usually the requirement, analysis, and design phases are too long. They end up being one-shot deals at the start of the project. Once coding starts, the developers typically prefer to change the code directly without careful analysis and design of the architecture. Though in the short term the quick coding changes appear to be beneficial, often they are detrimental to the overall maintainability of the code base. The changes to software are done in code, without rigorous analysis and design in continuous improvement development life cycles.

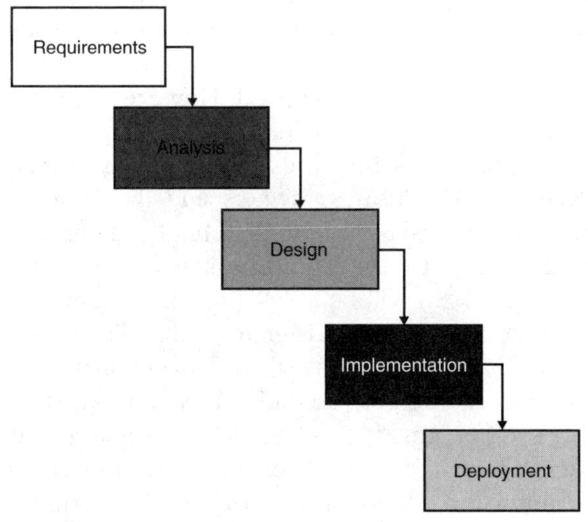

Figure 2.3 Traditional waterfall methodology for software development

Many elegant diagrams can be produced during these phases, which, though useful in the initial implementation, soon lose their relevance. Engineers will start to code and maintain their code without following any rigorous analysis and design phases. Even though this approach is still popular in many organizations, it is being replaced with more iterative and incremental approaches that involve continuous improvements.

Before getting into the details of analysis and design, here are some preliminary definitions of these terms, with the added elements of monitoring and interative continuous improvement.

- *Requirement:* The purpose of the requirement or define phase is to identify the business objectives. Two complementary objectives come into play here. One is to quickly show results and to provide the service automation that provides high value with high visibility. The other objective is to solve a pressing need. Sometimes the scope of the project is also determined. For instance, an organization might be required to provide service interfaces to its suppliers or customers, to link service requests to its internal processes, and to provide visibility of service request. There are situations where either in the context of a large project or in the abundance of candidate projects the choice must be made for the best return for the organization. In other words, the identification of the quick-win opportunity with the best return can be critical in this definition phase.
- *Analysis*: The purpose of analysis is to provide a precise representation and definition of exactly what is expected of the service. Usually business owners provide verbal or documented descriptions of their requirements. These requirements can then be translated into more precise representations through analysis. Usually a handful of analysis diagrams or notations can be used. However, the focus of analysis is not on the lower-level implementations but on making sure the business requirements are represented precisely. It is getting the right lingo between the business owners and the IT to implement the systems. So analysis is very important. It attempts to bridge and narrow the gap between IT and business owners. If the analysis is done correctly, both will be able to speak the same language and to communicate via analysis diagrams. Analysis in service oriented applications is similar to analysis in conventional software development. However, there is the added dimension of the interaction between service provider and service consumer. In traditional software development, typically the focus is on functionality. With service orientation, the trading or service oriented pr ovider partner—either internal or external—needs to be considered. In some situations the partner relationship could be pre-established—a current provider trusted and known to the consumer for specific

services. This is similar to procuring goods or services from certified or approved vendors. In other situations, the requirement could specify obtaining the best service that satifies the required functionality and quality of service immaterial of the service provider. Quality of service (QoS) analysis requirements are important from a technical and business perspective. Examples include reliability of the service: What percentage of the time will the service provider guarantee the service to be up and running? Another related QoS consideration is the overall performance of the service: What is the average response time that the service guarantees? Security of course is also a critical business requirement. Sometimes these services process sensitive customer information. The analysis phase is where business and IT come together to nail down the details of the requirements. It is essential for IT to talk the business talk and for business to appreciate what could potentially be realized through service automation. The analysis will cover not only the processes—how work should be processed and systems should interact—but also policies. These are the business rules. The rules-driven technology is critical. Here the analysis should also identify the business rules.

In fact, it is critical to provide the analysis of:

- Service building blocks: the interfaces or the provided services
- Flows that compose services (choreography or orchestration; the processes): the business analyst can specify the flowchart of core business processes
- Information models that are used to communicate between services: the attributes, relationships, and documents of the information processed by the services
- Organizational models: include the roles and the various groups involved
- Business rules involving constraints and decisioning logic; business rules also capture policies and control the process flows

- *Design:* The purpose of design is to provide a blueprint for implementation. The output of the analysis phase is the input for the design phase. Analysis focuses on the *what*; design focuses on the *how*. Think about your dream house. Suppose you set up a meeting with your architect and describe your dreams and requirements to the architect—that is requirement analysis. Now some notations could be used to make this semiformal. The architect then goes and comes up with a drawing of your dream house. Sometimes a small model is also provided. Then the architect goes into the blueprints and the details of the drawing or the model. Now things start getting very precise—sometimes painfully precise. For service orientation, design proceeds along two key detailed specifications:

- First, the focus is on identifying the services and their interfaces. These are the building blocks, the raw materials. In some cases existing legacy systems (e.g., CICS) can be exposed as services. In other cases new services need to be built from the ground up.
- Second, the focus is on building the business processes that orchestrate these services. These business processes will include the order in which the services are invoked when composing the services. These are the processes that get identified in the analysis phase.

- *Implementation:* There are two complementary approaches in implementing services—and hybrids of these two as well.
  - Harvesting services from existing systems: In almost any IT organization—especially in large enterprises—legacy applications typically exist. In many cases these applications are quite robust and fine tuned and do the job they are supposed to do. In other cases, the original developers have since left the organization, but the current IT staff does not have the budget or resources to replace these applications with extensible and maintainable alternatives. The programming languages or even the platforms used to support these legacy applications are older languages such as PL/1, COBOL, CICS, or C and C++. Another source of services is the relational databases containing departmental or enterprise data. These are typically Structure Query Language (SQL) databases; here again, certain techniques and tools can expose relational database management system (RDBMS) actions as services.
  - Building new services: In some cases the service needs to be newly implemented. This is the happy path for most developers. Here the requirement and the ensuing analysis and design are converted into implementation. There are many choices in how the use cases identified in the analysis phase are converted into code and deployed onto servers as services. Increasingly applications are being developed on top of business process management systems.

Business and IT—shortening life cycles: The requirement, analysis, and design phases were discussed as if they were completely independent or different. That is only one approach; increasingly, we are seeing the consolidation from requirements to implementation. This is important. The shorter the cycle times from design to implementation the better. There is always the danger of overanalyzing and overdesigning. Modern development platforms and tools allow increased productivity. These development tools are becoming browser based and are consolidating the life cycles from requirements to deployment and execution.

- *Monitoring:* Service oriented applications need to be monitored continuously. Both system management as well as business management are critical. System management involves monitoring, analyzing, and controlling the various software and hardware resources in the enterprise. Business management is monitoring, analyzing, and controlling the business processes and resources that participate in the processes. The monitoring of service applications spans higher-level business performance goals to low-level system-level implementations, the individual services. The monitoring can be categorized in one of three ways:
  - Primary use-case implementations that are providing the required functionality: These are the core functionalities supporting the use cases that were identified in the previous analysis phases. Here are examples of primary processes:
    - Procurement: Purchase goods and services with internal or external actors
    - Customer service: Process service request to support customer inquiries
    - Insurance applications: Process auto, personal, home, or business insurance application
  - Participants in different categories: The primary focus is on human participants, although partner and system participant performance could also be monitored. The focus is on how well these participants are processing the tasks assigned to them in the context of the use cases that are implemented and deployed.
  - Services and platforms: The entire area of services management and system monitoring is essential. A complex system implementation involves various types of containers such as component containers that host the service implementation, as well as system resources (e.g., memory, central processing unit [CPU] utilization, disk access, and network systems).
- *Iterative with continuous improvement:* Service oriented applications need to be developed in the context of iterative and continuous improvement methodologies (Figure 2.4). All modern methodologies such as Rational Unified Process,[4] Extreme Programming,[5] or

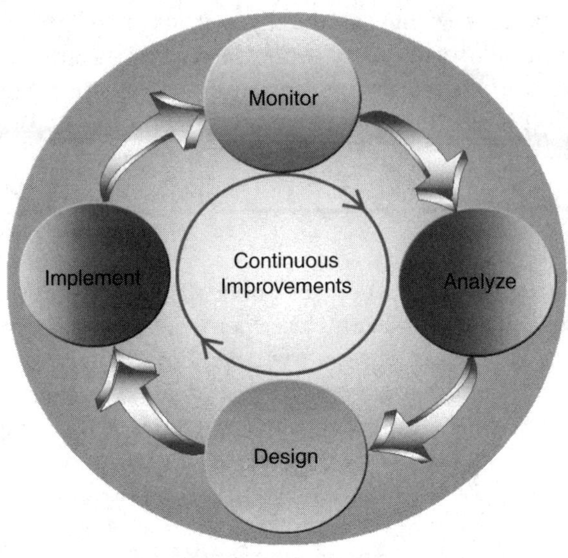

Figure 2.4 Basic continuous improvement iterative methodology

Scrum[6] are iterative and encourage continuous improvements. Usually iterations are understood in contrast to the more archaic waterfall approach discussed earlier. Depending on the specifics of the methodology, implementations are progressed through iteration phases. The solution can contain many use cases. In each iteration, focus on the analysis, design, and implementation of a number of the use cases. Consider a simple example. In attempting to automate the entire set of human resource functions, one choice is to break it up into major use-case packages: employee performance management, employee benefits, and employee time off. Then each of these will have multiple specific use cases. So iteration could proceed in major and minor implementation loops. The implementation of the use cases is not a one shot deal. Their performance should be monitored and implementations improved in subsequent iterations.

2.3 Enterprise Architectures

The previous section discussed the life cycle in building and deploying service oriented applications in service oriented enterprises. In fact, service orientation permeates all the levels of an enterprise architecture (EA), defined in one way as "a framework which is able to coordinate the many facets that make up the fundamental essence of an enterprise."[7]

Many categories of models get involved in enterprise architectures. In fact, some consider enterprise architectures as the milieu that brings business owners and IT together.[8] This is justifiable because it is the enterprise architecture and the descriptions as well as the models of the various components of an EA where you relate the business strategies and objectives to technology. Enterprise models are used to organize enterprise architectures along a number of key perspectives and abstractions. The most famous standard for enterprise architectures is the Zachman framework. This section provides an overview of the Zachman framework and relates it to service orientation. A word of caution: The Zachman framework is documentation and artifact intensive, with six columns and five rows and therefore potentially 30 categories of artifacts. So when trying to achieve quick wins and returns, Zachman is not necessarily the way to go. Figure 2.5 provides a high-level representation of the Zachman framework.

Figure 2.5 also illustrates how the three layers of SOEs (enterprise performance management, business process management, and IT SOA) relate to the Zachman framework. Basically, the higher level is closer to the business analysts. The lower layers are closer to the implementation perspectives. The middle layer is the bridge, which once again is the role of the ubiquitous business process management suites.

Within the same framework exist both business models and detailed system and technology models. Very briefly, the rows represent different

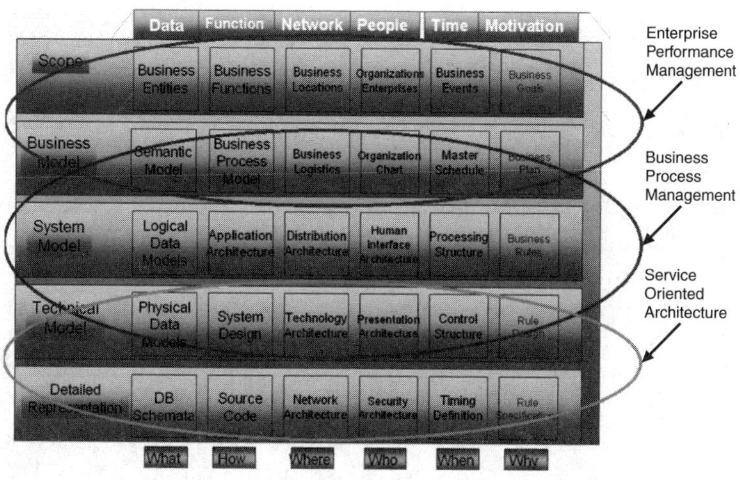

Figure 2.5 The Zachman framework (Source: http://www.zifa.com/)

perspectives: of a planner, a business owner, a designer, a builder, or a subcontractor. The columns represent different abstractions or focuses: data (what), function (how), network (where), people (who), time (when), and motivation (why). By and large, enterprise performance management and business process management focus on the first three rows of the Zachman framework. The service oriented architecture focuses on the lower-level rows of the framework.

Following are brief definitions of the various rows and what they represent, with special emphasis on service orientation.

- *Scope*: The scope artifacts and specifications focus on the highest business level covering the business goals.
  - The service oriented enterprise needs to view the entire enterprise as a collection of cooperating services offered to various parties, such as customers but also employees, trading partners, and financial institutions. Scope is the overall commitment to service definitions, service discovery, and service orchestration and choreography driving the service architecture.
  - Example: Motivation can improve customer retention by 10 percent or increase sales revenue by 25 percent. The business entities will include customers, products, and services. The business will deal with the sales, promotion, and marketing operations. Business locations will indicate the geographical locations of the enterprise.
- *Business model:* This layer gets into more detail from a business perspective and defines the objectives, structure, processes, and organization of the business. These are the business stockholders' views of the architecture.
  - For service oriented enterprises, the business models define the objectives and motivations of the business integration involving multiple back-end systems, departments, subsidiaries, and other organizations.
  - Example: Continuing with the increasing sales revenue example, here the overall process model is provided—the super process and their subprocesses involved in the marketing, sales, and production to support the revenue increase. This layer will also generate the business plan and will provide additional details on the delivery plan and schedule. This business modeling layer will identify the participants in the sales, marketing, and development organization involved in the project with tangible improvement milestones. It will also identify the services used in the various processes.
- *System model*: This layer goes into the more detailed logical models that form a system architect's perspective. Here the business process

and the business rules that drive these processes will be represented. The processes operate on data. The logical model of the entities is also captured in this layer.

- For service oriented enterprises, these models are used to describe and to define the services as well as the business rules and orchestration of the services. The information model and services also are specified for the message content that will be communicated across the service invocations and business rules operating on those services.
- Example: Each of the different areas for improving sales revenue (i.e., marketing, sales, and production) will go deeper into the flow logic and the business rules that drive them. For example, if development of a new product and its market penetration involves various outsourced third-party material or services, in this layer the flow logic of procuring the material or service will be identified as well as the overall choreography of message exchanges between the parties. The business rules also will be captured, such as service level agreements (SLAs) involving internal or external participants. If a particular component is late in delivery, the rules will proactively execute agents to mitigate the risks.

- *Technology model:* This layer focuses on the design details, providing a design architect's view. It is here where the detailed design involving the BPM platform, the underlying ESB, and the overall multi-tiered clustered architecture are provided.
  - For service oriented enterprises, the specifications here focus on the details of service orchestration and the business rules that drive the decisioning logic of service invocation as well as the various constraints associated with the service applications. Here the focus is on the service bindings and service invocation specifications. It is also necessary to decide how the service is going to be implemented—for example, component, pure Java code, exposing existing applications or legacy. In this layer the physical data models of the databases are provided, capturing the persistent information that will be communicated across the services. It is also necessary to specify the detailed design of the quality of service requirements for the individual service invocations as well as the aggregate application that composes the services.
  - Example: For each of the three main use-case models—marketing, sales, and production—it is necessary to provide the technology details of what are the back-end services or existing legacy applications that get invoked in supporting the process orchestrations of the use cases. For instance, sales operations might involve

back-end sales automation systems and invoke them via standard interfaces. When trading partners are involved, the detailed design and specification of the security, reliability, and performance service level agreements are needed.

- *Detailed representation:* This layer provides the implementer's view of the architecture. Moving from technology to detailed representation delves into the development and deployment platforms as well as the management tools that help with setting up the service oriented enterprise networks.
  - For a service orientation perspective, these are the most detailed artifacts used by the implementers of the service architecture. In terms of source code, there are two main categories:
    - For the BPM layer, the goal is to be able to directly represent the flow diagrams (for service orchestration) and business rules and to manage them as BPM layer resources.
    - For the service layer, the implementations have numerous sources including publishing BPM applications as services, publishing legacy as services, or writing code for new service implementations.
  - The networking, QoS, and implementation details are all handled in this detailed representation layer. For example, if the sales initiatives were built from scratch, the database schema will contain all the information needed to store the sales activities, such as all the geographically distributed sales accounts, the allocation of sales people quotas, and the overall process in identifying potential sales opportunities. The source code will be a combination of processes for automating the sales process and the business rules for guiding and controlling the sales activities. If the interfaces to various back-end systems such as finances and accounting are ready to be plugged in, there is little custom programming (in Java or C# or other) code that needs to be developed. Otherwise, the interface needs to be developed and the adapter built to the back-end accounting system. Another aspect that needs to be put in place is the communication infrastructure, including secure Web service, e-mail and Intranet access.

In terms of the columns of the Zachman framework, these could be described as follows:

- The motivation, or *Why* column—even though it is the right-most column of the Zachman framework—in a sense is the most important dimension because it sets the business strategies, the performance goals, and the objectives of the systems being developed. For service oriented enterprises, the motivation captures the objectives in building integrated service oriented products or services, specific key performance indicator goals, strategies for realizing agility, and continuous improvements.

- The *What* column focuses on entities (it used to be called *data*) and their relationships that are important for the application. For service oriented applications, the What column can be used to specify the persistent objects, the components used in the service applications, and the formats of the message objects exchanged between applications.
- The *How* column focuses on the policies, procedures, and practices used by the organization to solve problems. This is also called the *function* in earlier versions of the framework. In service oriented enterprises, these will be the processes that get executed in the BPM systems as well as the service orchestration flows that get executed in the ESBs.
- The *Where* column focuses on the geographical distribution of processes and activities in the service oriented enterprises, which are increasingly geographically distributed. Furthermore, SOEs involve various types of trading partners. The focus here is on how services will interoperate while supporting composite applications.
- The *Who* column focuses on all participants of the business solutions and processes. Service oriented enterprises involve organizational hierarchies within the enterprise as well as trading partners with various roles. The *who* models and uses the various individual participants, departments, groups, and roles within the organization and the value chain of delivered solutions.
- The *When* column focuses on the temporal dimension, especially on the various types of business events and their effects on the business solutions. Time-sensitive business events are critical in various service oriented enterprise solutions.

Zachman therefore provides a framework to organize, to layer, and to build service oriented enterprise solutions. Zachman is not a methodology. A methodology dictates what development phases and workflows are needed to go through in building an application. It is not necessary to apply the horizontal layers in Zachman strictly in a sequential fashion, which is akin to a waterfall model. That is not the intention. Zachman organizes the perspectives and context of deliverables. It is a framework. A methodology, by contrast, specifies the activities from inception to completion, with potentially continuous improvement iterations. It helps abstract the various types of deliverables. Zachman should be treated as a guideline. It helps in understanding and conceptualizing the overall EA. In service orientation, the trend is acceleration in development cycles and reduction in the number of mapping layers from the business to the underlying IT implementations. Central to this trend is the BPM layer, which is at the very heart of the SOE solution development methodologies—and is discussed in more detail in Chapter 5. The cells in the Zachman framework could provide guidelines in selecting the artifacts and activities that need to be enacted in the SOE implementation methodology.

2.4 Model-Driven Architecture

> Openness is the key to widely adopted, interoperable and portable implementation.
>
> **Richard Soley**

The previous section provided an overview of the Zachman framework. Zachman helps organize and conceptualize perspectives (i.e., scope, business model, system model, technology model, and detailed representation) and abstractions (i.e., why, who, what, how, where, and when). As stated already, Zachman is not a methodology: It is a framework for enterprise architectures. The model-driven architecture (MDA) takes a different approach, focusing on building systems with various levels of modeling abstractions. MDA is not a methodology but uses a rigorous modeling approach between perspectives. MDA uses metamodels—models that describe other models—to capture the concepts and layers of abstraction. Zachman can be related to MDA. For instance, the highest computation independent model could be mapped onto the business model in Zachman. The platform independent and specific models could respectively be mapped onto the Zachman system and technology layers.

The Object Management Group's[9] (OMG) model-driven architecture provides three levels of architecture and modeling abstractions: (1) a computation-independent model (CIM), which is oriented to model businesses; (2) a platform-independent model (PIM); and (3) a platform-specific model (PSM). (See Figure 2.6.) What is a *platform*? It depends. Typically a large and complex enterprise architecture has several layers, so a PIM from one perspective could be a PSM from another. A BPM system could be supported on a variety of platforms (e.g., WebSphere, WebLogic, .NET). Hence, the PSM models for the service oriented application are the application server infrastructures where applications are executed. However, for other domains such as component computing, the PIM could be the detailed design models of the components, whereas the PSM could be either a J2EE or .NET platform—corresponding to the code. In MDA architecture mappings

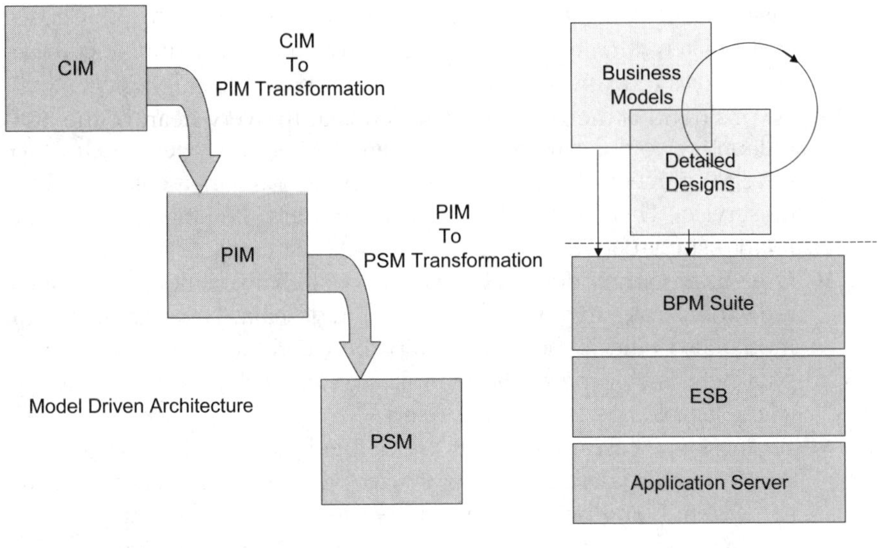

Figure 2.6 Model-driven architectures

will then be provided. Here again, every time mappings are used there is the danger of losing semantics. Once again, this could be problematic if the application is being continuously improved and iteratively built.

The overall premise is that there are business models that can be represented independently of underlying software models or implementations. Notations or modeling languages such as Business Process Modeling Notation (BPMN) or Unified Modeling Language (UML) can be used to represent certain aspects of CIM business models. CIM concentrates on the business use cases, the required business results, and the business processes to achieve them, independent of software or underlying implementation systems. In an iterative development methodology, the CIM will correspond to business modeling and requirements phases. The main idea behind the computational-independent models in SOEs is to capture the various stakeholders, trading partners, and enterprise departments and their relationships. CIMs also capture the processes and business rules that involve these various types of participants. The main idea behind CIM is not to worry about any underlying automation or computation model. CIM artifacts can be produced in modeling diagrams. CIM could be used to capture the business model as a requirement for underlying implementations.

Some of the artifacts produced in CIM or business modeling include the following:

- Vision chart or document: The vision document specifies the goals and objectives of the endeavor. For instance, the vision document could state a financial goal to increase sale volumes by 20 percent, could state quality goals such as to have less than 3.4 defects per million, or could state goals pertaining to the employees such as to have 80 percent of the employees certified on a particular product or service. This is also the place to express the dependencies or relationships between goals.
- Organizational model: The organizational chart or model describes the various roles involved in the solution domain. The organizational model also reflects the relationships between the various roles. The goal here is to capture the organization chart that pertains directly to the problem or solution at hand.
- Business use cases: Use cases are defined in more detail in Section 2.5.1. Here are described all the actors that will be interacting with the system being built as well as the use cases or major interactions that will be implemented via processes. Making a purchase, for instance, is a use case. The actors involved in the purchase are the buyer and the seller.
- Business processes: This delves further into the use cases providing process models, using for instance UML activity diagrams or BPMN. Here the business flow diagrams can be captured, as well as the business rules that further elaborate the use cases. For instance, the business interaction that needs to take place between the buyer and seller is a sequence of interactions in a specific order.
- Business information model: Any process or use case involves information exchanges. The business information model provides a high-level description of the data exchanged within and between use cases. For instance, the business information model of the purchase will include the fields of the purchase order and fields required to describe the items of the purchase.

The CIM models are then used by the PIM to provide the analysis of the business models. In PIM, the goal is to provide more details for the models while staying independent of underlying specific platforms. For instance, execution languages such as Business Process Execution Language (BPEL) can be used to capture execution of Web services orchestrations, independent of the underlying business process management system, at least in theory. The focus in PIM is on business analysis. PIM is more detailed than CIM. In fact, it takes CIM artifacts and models as input and produces specific analysis models. The focus in PIM is on the functional models: What are you trying to achieve for the system or solution being built or extended? Section 2.5 delves into more notational and descriptive details for analysis (PIM) and design (PSM).

The last layer, PSM, provides detailed specifications on implementation platforms, and this layer contains specific extensions and capabilities from various vendors. This layer incorporates not only the functional requirements but also nonfunctional architectural considerations and requirements. In fact, platforms such as the BPM system, ESB, enterprise portal server, application server, database management system, and security server are all involved in coming up with a PSM. PSM therefore extends and expands the PIM with detailed designs and also takes into consideration all the platform-specific requirements.

2.4.1 Metamodels

Common metamodels and standardized exchange formats between models facilitate sharing among tools, communities, and products as well as mapping between various platforms and layers. OMG has introduced a four-layered metamodel framework (Figure 2.7) and an exchange standard called XML Metadata Interchange (XMI) for interoperability between tools that support common metamodels. The model-driven architecture framework also attempts to standardize a metamodel for processes and organizational models. The MDA framework supports a four-layered metadata architecture:

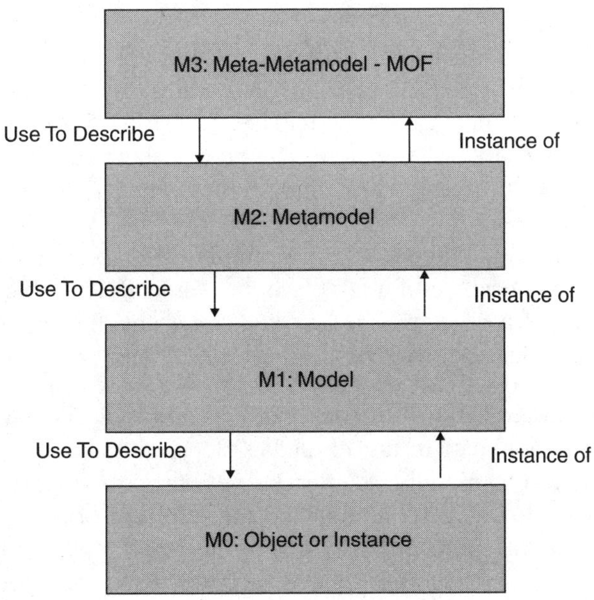

Figure 2.7 Metamodel layers

- M3: Meta-metamodel, the most abstract—and in some ways the most important—layer specifying the MetaObject Facility (MOF). MOF provides a way to define metamodels (M2). MOF uses UML.
- M2: Metamodels for specific domains or disciplines such as database management, business process management, or eXtensible Markup Language (XML). For example, relational database schemata are defined through tables. Products schema will contain a table for items, a table for product, a table for invoice, and so on. An organization's schema will contain a table for employees, a table for departments, a table for employees in the department and so on. The table metamodel in relational databases is defined at this level. The metamodel will specify that a table will have columns and rows. The columns will have names or labels and base types (e.g., integer, decimal, character string, date). Then this metamodel will be used to instantiate table models or schemata (M1). This book uses UML notation to describe metamodels. Similarly, the metamodel for processes will indicate that a process consists of activities, which can be basic or structured. Basic activities will have a participant—a human or a role or a system or a trading partner. Structured activities will consist of other activities. Decisioning, looping, and parallel split/join are examples of structured activities. So UML is used to define the metamodels for specific concepts or domains, and then models are created as compliant instances of these metamodels.
- M1: Models are instances of the metamodel in M2. For instance, there will be models for tables in a relational database. This is of course the schema of the database. Similarly, there will be models of processes in a BPM system. The processes will capture the process flows and business rules, and then instances of these (M0) are created.
- M0: Instances of models. For example, the table with all the rows will be an instance of a table schema. Similarly, an object will be an instance of a class, where the class represents the model. Likewise, a process instance will be the instance of a process model.

Metamodel standardization provides value in speaking the same language among various tools. For instance, OMG's Business Integration Task Force is working on a metamodel (M2) for business process definitions.

Metamodels also help us understand the different object types used in service oriented enterprise applications. In this book, metamodels (M2) are used to describe service descriptions, service directories, business processes, and information models. SOE metamodels provide a precise definition of the composition of the service oriented enterprise solution's building blocks. However, especially due to significant differentiations and extensions by various underlying platforms, it is still difficult to sustain interoperability simply by relying on the metamodel standards.

2.5 Service Oriented Analysis and Design

> SOAD must facilitate end-to-end modeling and have comprehensive tool support. If SOA is supposed to bring flexibility and agility to the business, the same should be expected from its supporting method, spanning from the business to the architecture and application design domains.
>
> **Olaf Zimmermann, Pal Krogdahl, and Clive Gee**

The previous sections provided an overview of a conceptualization framework—the Zachman framework—and MDA for SOEs. This and following sections delve deeper into phases and artifacts for building SOE solutions. Here the focus is on service oriented analysis and design (SOAD).

Before digging into the details of service oriented analysis, it should be noted that a very close relationship exists between SOAD and object-oriented analysis and object-oriented design[10] (OOA/OOD); the notation standard used for object analysis and design could also be used for service oriented analysis and design.

This book uses Unified Modeling Language notation to illustrate some of the analysis and design notation and concepts that can be used to build service oriented applications. UML has become universally accepted as the notation of choice for modeling complex enterprises and helps to visualize and specify service implementation as well as service dependencies. UML 2.0 was ratified in 2005 and provides a solid mechanism for building service oriented applications. Two main categories of tools are used to support UML.

1. Object-oriented analysis and design tools: UML tools support the design and analysis of advanced object-oriented applications using UML notation. These tools are typically IT oriented and not suitable for business users—even though parts of the UML notation are quite appropriate for business users. UML tools typically output source codes in target languages such as Java or C#. These tools also support XML and SQL.
2. Business modeling or process analysis tools: There are a handful of such tools that target business users. The business modeling and analysis tools can use UML notation for modeling information, organization, business processes, and business rules. The modeling and analysis tools also include the design and development

of other business-oriented artifacts such as strategies, cause-and-effect diagrams, organizational hierarchies, and, of course, business processes.

2.5.1 Use Case

Business and IT: Use cases are essential for IT and business. They constitute a common language for communication. These sections provide an introduction and overview.

Use cases provide a high level of description of service implementation. It shows the services provided or accessed—through oval shapes—and the service requestors who access them—through actor shapes (Figure 2.8).

The actors are typically humans. Actors can also be systems or trading partners. The classic example of an actor is an end user who is purchasing or checking the status of a purchase from an online retail store. Another example is an online banking customer conducting transactions online. Sometimes multiple actors are involved with the same use case.

Figure 2.9 illustrates several actors involved in the purchasing. The buyer's organization could be a user or a system. These external actors interact with the purchasing system to browse a catalog or to place an order. Another actor involved is the seller's organization. Also, financial services organizations like banks or credit card processing centers conduct the financial transaction. And the shipping organization delivers the goods. In this example there is a buyer actor—a person or a system—who browses a catalog. This browsing could be a simple search or a more

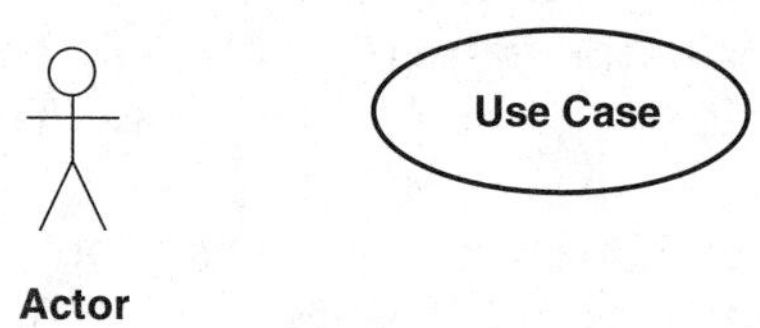

Figure 2.8 Shapes for actor and use case

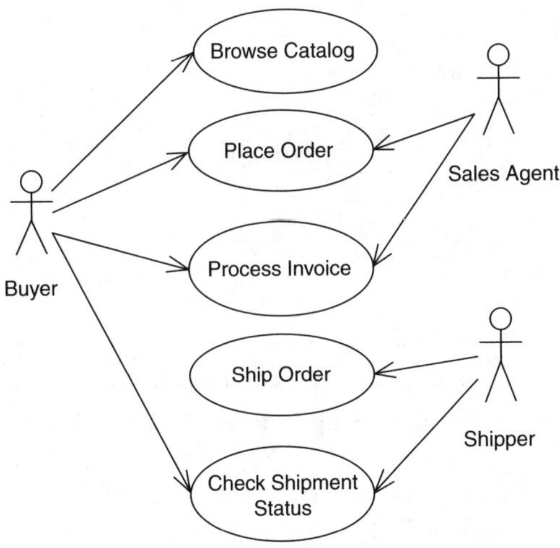

Figure 2.9 Use case model example

complex process involving decisioning that could most closely satisfy the buyer's request.

Use cases can have relationships with one another. Two popular relationships between use cases are specialization and extension.

- A use case can specialize another use case, which means the extending use case is specializing the target use case. This is similar to inheritance; for instance, a hardware purchase and software purchase can both extend a purchase, as illustrated in Figure 2.10.

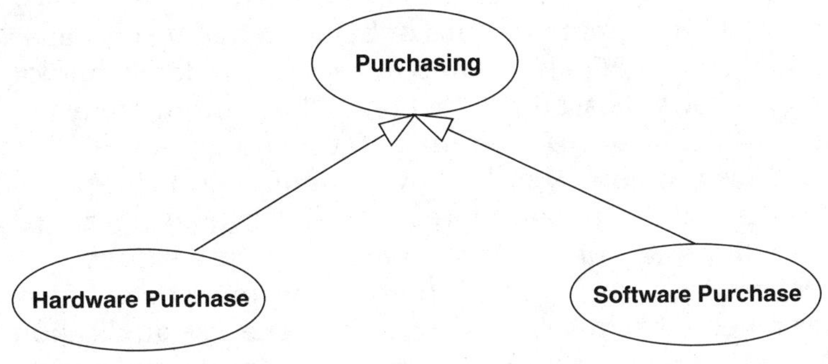

Figure 2.10 Specialization of use cases

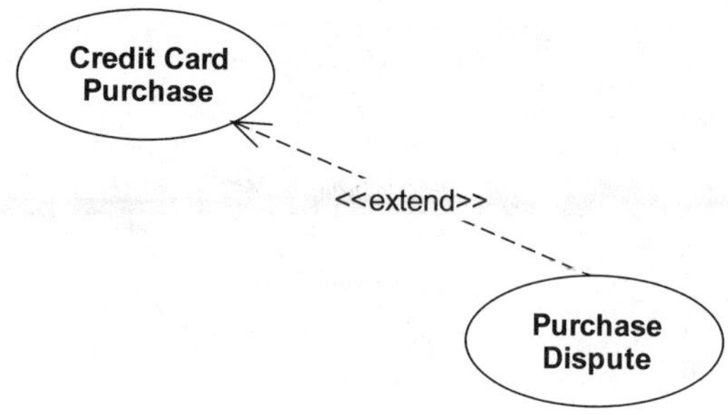

Figure 2.11 <<extend>> relationship between use cases

- A use case can extend another use case. This means the use case that is extending will be adding extensions to the behavior of the original use case without disrupting the behavior of the use case. Exception handling is typically handled through extensions (see Figure 2.11).

The following figure is an elaborate healthcare use-case model involving healthcare providers (e.g., hospitals, clinics) and payers. The use cases are implemented through process orchestrations and business rules as well as service (especially Web services)-based integration between providers and payers. This use-case model involves elaborate processes, business rules, and service interactions. Multiple interfaces and technologies in service oriented enterprises need to be considered while providing service oriented solutions. In particular one cannot always assume—even in the foreseeable future—that Web services-based access to remote systems or between trading partners will be available. Sometimes it is necessary to use older technologies or even browser-based interactions. The current state of the union in healthcare is ripe for process integration. Consider the following figure, which shows a multi-tier, multi-platform, multi-application, and multi-process milieu in a healthcare payer organization. Each of the boxes represents a use case.

There are many issues and problems with this heterogeneous environment that result in delays, bottlenecks, duplication of effort, and complex and error-prone processing of claims, to name just a few. Enter the service oriented BPM solution. Here the various internal as well as external applications are integrated through

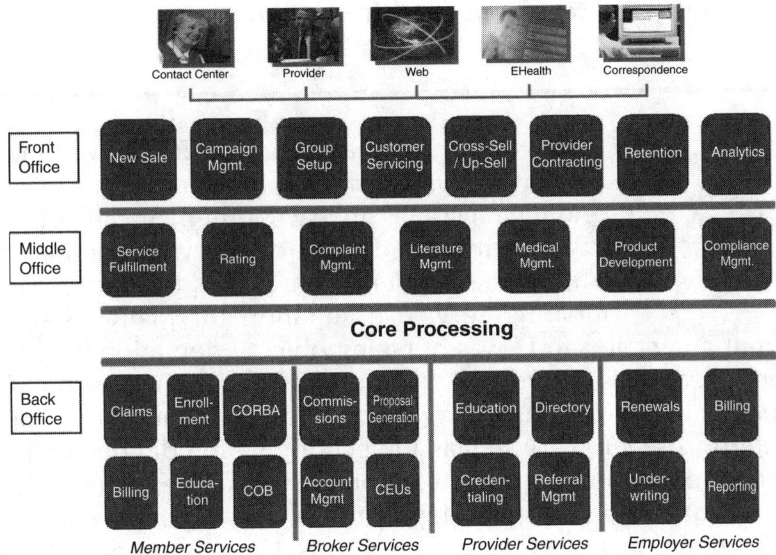

the robust BPM platform's service integration technologies using an underlying enterprise service bus. More importantly, business rules and process flow, spanning multiple applications, human participants, as well as trading partners are digitized and deployed across the extended enterprise as illustrated below.

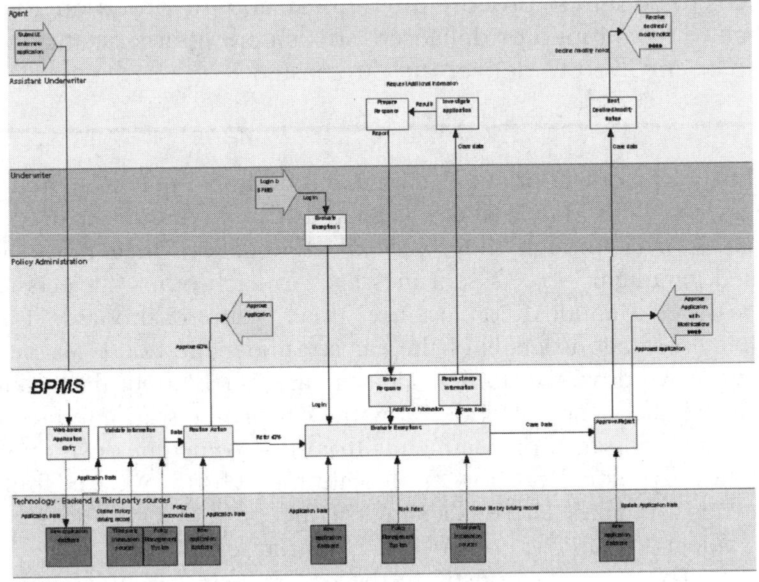

2.5.2 Service Messaging and Interactions

IT: *Messaging* has many connotations. Here messaging is discussed more in the context of services sending messages to each other. An analogy is drawn from a predecessor of service orientation, namely object orientation. Just as these days IT is pursuing service orientation for many reasons, about a decade ago IT was pursuing object orientation with the same zeal. It is interesting to note that the promises and the potential of integrating many objects or components in extended enterprises were very similar. Object orientation did deliver to a certain extent but is now ubiquitous. A lot can be learned from object-oriented concepts, deployments, and experiences when embarking on service oriented projects. Here the primary focus is on messaging.

IT: The following sections highlight a procurement example in which employees are trying to procure goods and services. Typically it is necessary to go through an approval process; in addition to the manager, finance will check if the request was budgeted. Once approval is granted, the trading partners—especially the provider or seller—get involved. The approved purchase order needs to be sent to procure the request, and the procured goods need to be shipped or delivered, so a shipping organization will also be involved to deliver the purchase.

The history of object-oriented computation shows that it started with languages such as Simula and Smalltalk. Today we hardly hear of these languages, even though they were the foundation. In a pure object-oriented paradigm, objects sent messages to each other. Objects represent real-world entities. For instance, think of the dashboard of a car. The implementation details of the car are under the hood. Most of the time when we drive we do not think or care much about the details, as long as we have a smooth ride. Now the car presents an interface to us and accepts messages or commands from us—sometimes even vocally. It satisfies a protocol on how to operate the vehicle. We can find it in the owner's manual. There is a similar concept in objects and services. Each object satisfied a protocol—an interface. These were called *methods*. The methods constitute the contract or the interface of the class. A class is a collection of objects with the same structure and behavior. The methods describe the behavior. The properties—also called attributes or instance variables—describe the structure of the class. These properties will contain values that will represent the state of objects.

Therefore, this whole notion of services sending messages to one another is not new. It had existed in object orientation for quite some time. In a more pure concurrent object paradigm, programs will look much different—more like a collection of collaborating independent and parallel objects.

Enter services. There are a number of techniques and mechanisms for demonstrating dynamic interactions between services.

- *Service invocation*: The simplest service interaction diagram that one could depict is the service invocation. These are service request/response messages that could be depicted through object interaction diagrams. The objects are actually the services that support interfaces. The interfaces are captured in the signatures[11] of the messages sent to the services (the invocation).
- *Communication and interaction between services:* A more elaborate diagram can be used to illustrate the interaction between services. With interaction diagrams—also called communication or object diagrams in UML—each service is depicted as an instance of the service in a particular context (Figure 2.12). The interactions between objects are numbered and labeled. So these diagrams illustrate the services as both service requestors and providers. The messages are numbered to indicate the order of the invocations.
- *Sequence of service invocations*: Sequence diagrams are another effective way of illustrating messaging communication between services. The sequence diagramming incorporates the temporal axis and illustrates how messages are sent between services along a time axis. Section 2.5.4 discusses sequence diagrams in more detail.
- *Service orchestration*: Orchestration of services provides a richer model for capturing the interaction between services. Standards such as BPEL allow you to capture the sequencing and decisioning of activities and various interaction models between services in executable processes. Chapter 5 expands on business process management. Process diagrams can model message interactions between service providers and requestors; sequential, conditional, and parallel service execution flows; data flows; looping; and several other constructs for a relatively complete execution language expressed in XML.

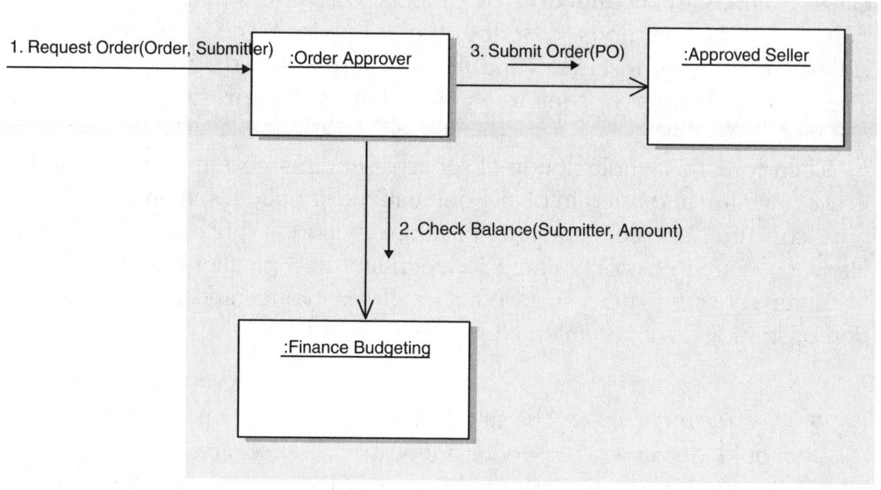

Figure 2.12 Object interaction notation in UML (could also be used for service interactions)

- *Service choreography:* Choreography takes a bigger picture and focuses on the sequence of message exchanges between service requestors and providers. The differences between choreography and orchestration might not be that apparent. Orchestration services are typically executed by a process execution engine. For instance, BPEL is a process execution language, so programs written in BPEL[12] will execute on an engine that supports BPEL. Choreography, on the other hand, can involve multiple engines. The message communication and exchanges of messages between service providers and requestors produce a protocol of exchanges. Behind those exchanges there could be several processes. For instance, a service provider can have an internal process that periodically interacts with requestors. Choreography deals with the sequencing of the exchanges between the two—or multiple—parties, not the internal execution of the entire process. It is the choreographed message dance of the service partners.

These five are the most important mechanisms of specifying message exchanges between services. The following sections will expand on some UML notations for capturing dynamic exchanges of services.

2.5.3 Activity Diagram

Services are often composed to create new services. The previous example illustrated a number of use cases and actors involved in purchasing. Now behind each of these use cases there will be business processes. A business process will consist of information models, or class models; organization models, which are the major players and their relationships; flow models, which are covered here; and business rules, or the policies guiding the processes.

Here the focus is on the activity diagram notation. There are many types of shapes (stencils in Visio) that could be used to represent the flow models in processes. The UML activity diagram is one of these. It is more popular with IT than business owners. The alternative notation used especially for composing business processes is the BPMN, which is covered in Chapter 5. The basic notations for activity diagrams are summarized in Table 2.1.

Figure 2.13 shows a procurement activity diagram. It starts with a request for a purchase, and the manager then makes a decision to approve or reject the request. If the request is approved, it is submitted to the supplier. At the same time the procurement department prepares to accept the shipment.

Table 2.1 Notations for Activity Diagrams

Start and End	and	Start and end of an activity flow diagram. Typically you have one start and one end symbol in a flow.
Activity		This is the most important building block of an activity flow. In service orientation activity will represent a service operation. Activities and other nodes are connected through *edges* (directed links or transitions).
Decision		Decisions are used to branch the next activity based on decision criteria : e.g. Yes / No or Approve / Reject. It does not have to be binary.
Split and Joins		Splits and Joins are indicated through a solid line. After the split there will be multiple activity threads which will execute in parallel. After the Join the parallel activity threads are synchronized.

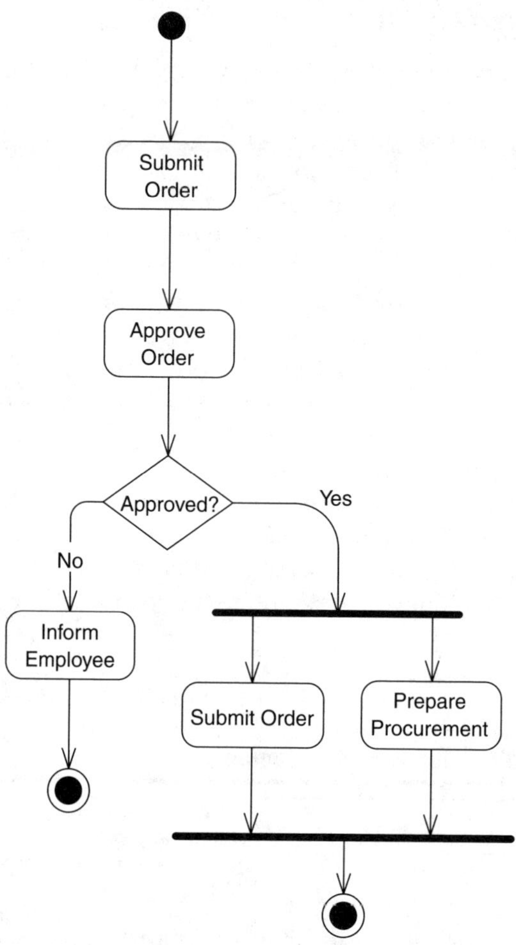

Figure 2.13 Example of an activity diagram

2.5.4 Sequence Diagrams

One of the more common diagrams used to model dynamic interaction of services is the sequence diagram. In sequence diagrams, each service is represented by a service object and a vertical line representing a sequence of time from top to bottom. This vertical line is called the lifeline of the service object. Methods or operations of service invocations are represented through arrows emanating from the service requestor to the service provider—with the name of the operation on the arrow. The service being invoked can return a result to the caller. Sequence diagrams can represent both synchronous and asynchronous interactions between services.

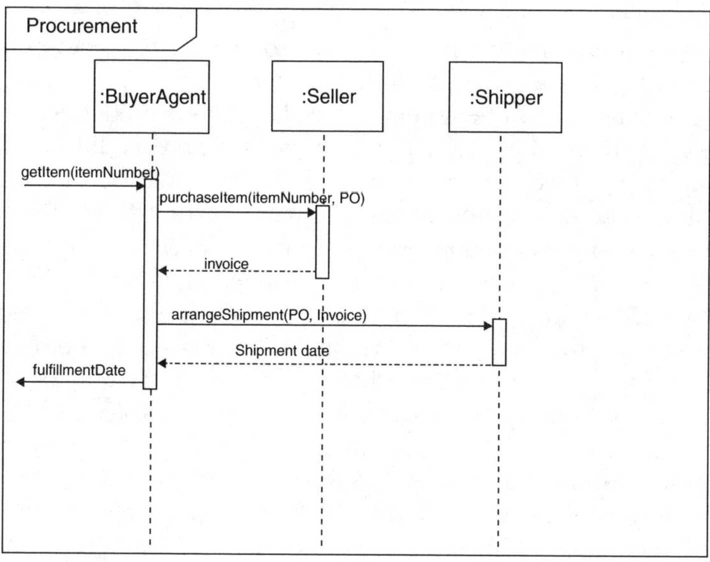

Figure 2.14 Example of sequence diagram

Figure 2.14 presents an example of a sequence diagram involving a buyer, seller, and shipper services.

2.5.5 State Transition Diagrams

Service state transition diagrams can be very effectively used in service oriented applications. There are two fundamental concepts in state transition diagrams.

1. *States*: Any service oriented application is dealing with states of objects. The service object being processed has a set of states, and based on specific events there will be transitions between states, such as purchase orders that have been submitted, shipments that are en route, or approval requests that have been closed. Each of these is an instance of service objects that go through a life cycle of state transitions. In fact, an object commences in a particular state and then goes through numerous states until it is resolved and completed. Some service objects have very short life cycles, and others have very long life cycles. The request for the balance of an account is an example of a very short life cycle object: There is basically a request for a service (e.g., obtaining the balance) and then its resolution (e.g., the balance is retrieved).

2. *Events*: What causes transitions between states of service objects? Events are quite common in service oriented architectures. Events occur at a particular point in time and cause transitions. Events can be business events or system events. Reaching a predefined revenue goal is an example of a business event. There could be external agents, such as humans or systems, which could be the source of the event. For instance, a business manager can decide to suspend a purchasing transaction. This is a business event and will transition the state of the purchase order to a suspended or pending resolution state. Other examples of business events include the receipt of a purchase order request, the resolution of a customer complaint, or the assignment of a task to a human participant. System-level events include exceptions in networking, security, reliability, CPU, memory, input-output (I/O), communication, and system performance-related events. For example, if the memory is too low, the system administrator can be alerted to remedy the performance bottleneck by adding another node to a cluster with additional memory resources.

In a state transition diagram the states are labeled and connected through transitions. The labels on the transitions are the events. Figure 2.15 illustrates the state transition for purchasing.

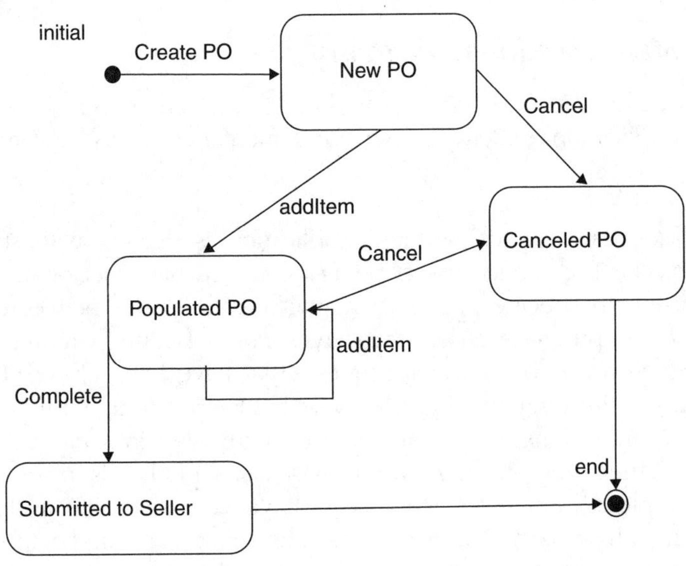

Figure 2.15 Example of state transition diagram

2.5.6 Component Diagrams

In UML notation and terminology, a component is a coarse-grained system that provides a service interface to other components or invokes applications. In pure object orientation, every object is an instance of a class. However, when more complex applications are built, they are typically organized in components.[13] A component provides implementation of interfaces. The component diagrams therefore depict the services and their interfaces, which denote the operations or methods that get invoked when the service is called. In UML, components can either provide or require interfaces. Think of these interfaces as the operations provided by the service. Required interfaces are operations that will be needed and used by the component. This creates service requirement dependency relationships between components.

A component combines and packages a number of classes—which are finer-grained elements in an overall implementation—and provides interfaces that can then be invoked by other components. For example, consider the implementation of a purchasing service. It can be represented as a component, which can have a number of interfaces such as CreateOrder; OrderStatus, or ChangeOrder. Figure 2.16 illustrates two components: Order and Customer. Order provides two interfaces—ChangeOrder and

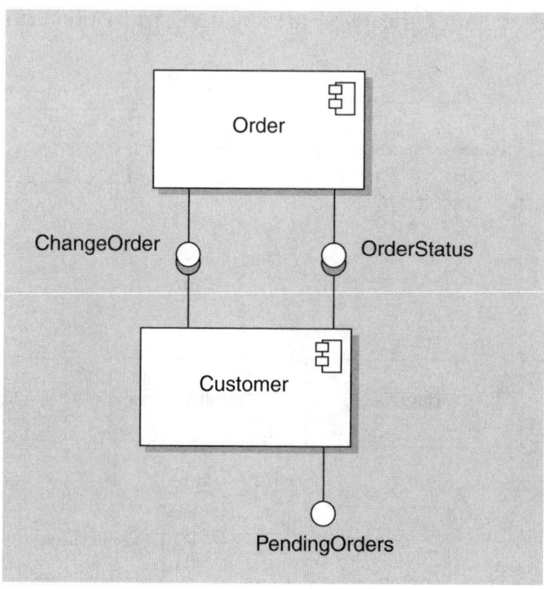

Figure 2.16 Example of component diagram

OrderStatus—used by the Customer component. The Customer component provides an interface: PendingOrders.

The interface of a component is very similar to interfaces of classes. In object orientation, there is a powerful concept called encapsulation. The abstraction or feature provided by encapsulation can apply both to classes and components alike. Dealing with the class or the component means only dealing with the interface—there is no need to worry about the implementation. In fact, the whole concept behind service orientation is to deal with the operations provided by the interface and not to worry, or to depend on, their implementation details such as the language or platform of the implementation, the operating system hosting the implementation, or other system or software components used in supporting the service. The WSDL described in Chapter 3 in more detail basically defines the operations of the service and where and how to invoke them—and nothing about their implementation. This is essentially encapsulation.

2.5.7 Class Diagram

Perhaps the most commonly used notation is the class diagram (Figure 2.17). Classes represent a collection of objects—often called *instances*—with the same structure and operations. Classes are factories that create objects. The focus here is on services. How do services relate to classes? The set of operations that a class supports constitutes the behavioral semantics of the class. That means instances of the class are created, and operations are called on

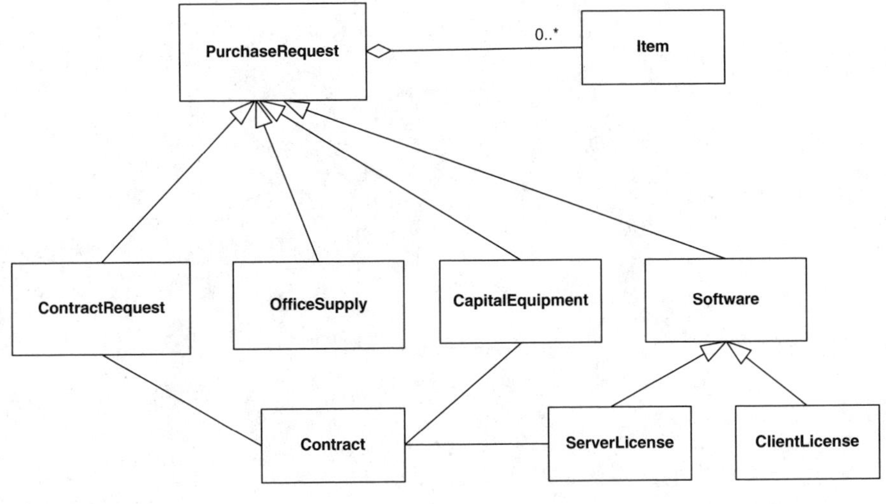

Figure 2.17 Example of class diagram

these instances.[14] A service invocation on a component might end up creating several objects, or instances of classes, and invoking operations or methods on these instances. Thus, the classes are the smaller-granule parts used to serve a request invoked through an interface.

Returning to services, each service will have a number of interfaces, which is another important term to define. Whatever is being implemented—*services* for the sake of this discussion—will typically have a programming interface. This means there will be a mechanism where a request can be sent to this service and a response will be received, sometimes called a synchronous invocation. The caller will wait until a response is given. This is like making a call to an organization and having an agent, such as a human operator, on the other side of the call respond to the caller's questions.

Remember a class represents a logical concept that has to be implemented through physical implementations. Typically this physical implementation is realized through a programming language such as Java or C#. Then the class implementations are packaged in components. The components are the physical units that get deployed. In most situations, service clients are calling the interfaces of deployed components. Several technologies are involved in going from a client interface all the way to the actual binary code that gets executed to respond to the request.

- Classes: These are the logical structures that contain the operations and attributes. They are the most important constructs in building new service oriented applications. Even when using legacy systems and wrapping or exposing them as services, it is helpful to model or wrap these through classes. The classes are the building blocks of the models. Each component will typically contain one or more classes. Both components and classes have interfaces. However, classes are used to create objects, which are instances of the class. So the class is like a factory that churns out instances when requested. Ultimately the implementation of a service will be done in an object-oriented language such as Java or C#. A service request will end up involving many classes, or actually instances.
- Interfaces: These group a set of operations whose combination provides a meaningful and complete purpose. An interface will have a name. Classes have attributes as well as methods. Interfaces only have operations. UML uses rectangles to represent interfaces but denotes the interface as such (e.g., by including <<interface>> in the rectangle). Classes can implement interfaces. Operations will have signatures. The signature of an operation indicates the name of the operation, the name or types of its input, as well as output parameters. UML uses two notations for interfaces: (a) circles, or "lollypops," the higher-level abstraction of the interface that mentions only the name of the interface; and (b) a stereotyped class,

which provides the details of the operations of the interface within the rectangle representing the class. Think of the interface as a contract. Interfaces specify what operations should be supported—without dealing with the details of the implementation.

- Attributes: These are used to contain the state of the instances of the class. Typically attributes are typed, and the type of the attribute is one of the supported base types, such as character strings, integers, decimals, or date.
- Relationships: There are a number of relationships between classes. A class might inherit structure and behavior from other more generalized classes. A class might use the interfaces of other classes. Classes are used to represent composite or complex objects and hence will have association and aggregation relationships with other classes.
  - Generalization: The UML notation of a generalization is a triangle. The subclasses inherit the attribute, associations, and the interfaces from their superclasses. Generalization could also be used with interfaces and components. Figure 2.17 provides a simple example of generalization. A client license is a specialized software purchase, which in turn is a specialization of a purchase request.
  - Associations: An association between two classes indicates that an instance of a class can be associated with one or more instances of another class. A classical example is orders and products. An order will have an association with many products: the products that are ordered. So there is an association between the order class and the product class. Associations have cardinalities: one to one, one to many, and many to many. For example, between products and orders is a many-to-many association: The same product is referenced in many orders (Figure 2.18).
  - Aggregation: Similar to association, an aggregation is also a relationship between classes. But unlike association, aggregations is effectively containment, or "parts-of" relationship. The children are part of the parent. A diamond is used on the parent's side to indicate aggregation. There can be one-to-one or one-to-many cardinalities between parent and child. For instance, a company can have several addresses; a car has four wheels. These are examples of aggregations with one-to-many cardinality. Aggregation captures "has-a" relationships.
  - Composition: This is a more restrictive type of aggregation. In aggregation, where the diamond shape is white, when the parent is deleted the child objects can continue to exist. With composition, the existence of the children depends upon the parent. When the parent is deleted, so are the children. Composition is indicated through a black diamond. For instance, consider

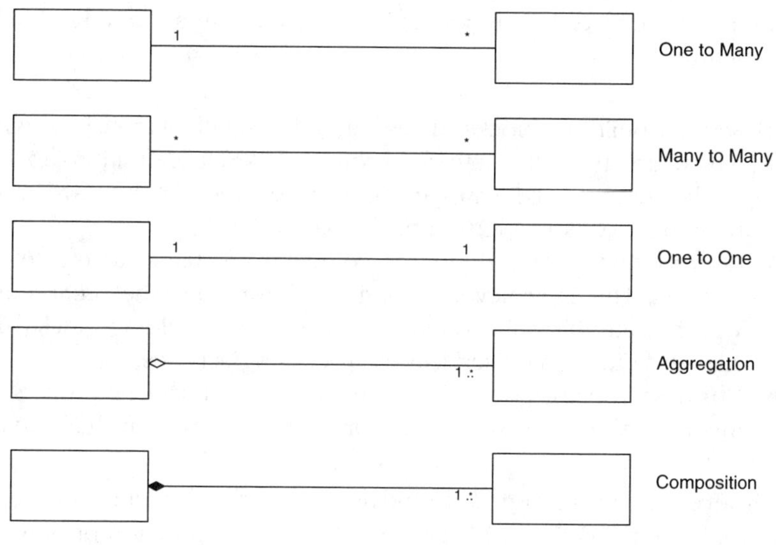

Figure 2.18 Association types and cardinalities

the relationship between the company and her business units. These business units cannot exist independently of the company; it is a composition relationship—also one to many and to illustrate service oriented concepts.

In this and subsequent chapters, UML notation is used to depict metamodels and relationships between service components.

2.6 SOA Methodology

So far the focus has been on notation for service oriented analysis and design. But how should these notations be used? In what order? And when is it more appropriate to use one notation versus another? These are very important questions, and to answer them an analysis–design–build methodology is needed that specifies step by step the processes in building successful service oriented applications.

Many projects have failed or at least have been delayed due to overdesign and overdocumentation. The opposite is also true. In fact, a lack of detailed design, especially in the earlier stages of the project, could be fatal. A dollar spent on design in the earlier stages could end up saving hundreds or thousands of dollars in later stages.

In building services it is important to look at a bottom-up, three-layered infrastructure.

- Service building blocks: These are the smallest-granule services, which are typically defined through a WSDL definition. Existing applications can be wrapped as services and can be used as the building blocks for SOA implementation.
- Composition services: Services could be combined to create new services. This is achieved through orchestration. The orchestration will indicate the call sequence of the service building blocks. This allows building new services from existing services.
- Business process: Going up the hierarchy, business process can involve either composite service orchestrations or individual services.

Several levels of abstraction and models are used in building service oriented applications. Figure 2.19 shows a UML[15] diagram that represents the services metamodel for processes: the relationships among services, their interfaces, and providers.

Each service will support a collection of operations. These operations will be grouped together to provide a logical function to the service requestors. A service provider will support a number of services, which are the logical groups of operations. Each operation will have an interface, which specifies the signature of the operation. Figure 2.19 also illustrates service orchestrations and business processes. Business processes provide yet a higher-level composition that can involve services, service orchestrations, as well as human participants and business rules. Chapter 5 discusses BPM suites in greater detail.

2.6.1 Service Discovery

An integral part of service methodology is the discovery of services. Discovery means finding the specific functionality of services (i.e., What are the functions or interfaces supported by the services?) and the location as well as invocation details (i.e., Where and how should the service be invoked?). These are of course defined by various elements within WSDL documents. However, one should be able to discover the existence of such a WSDL and its support via the implementation of the services. This is where directories come into the picture. These services could be internally deployed services within the organization or services that are published by trading partners. Initially, service orientation started with publishing services that were deployed internally in the organization. The services can be deployed to the ESB. Among other features, the ESB supports the discovery and overall life cycle of services: their deployment as well as deprecation. ESBs also support the quality of service:

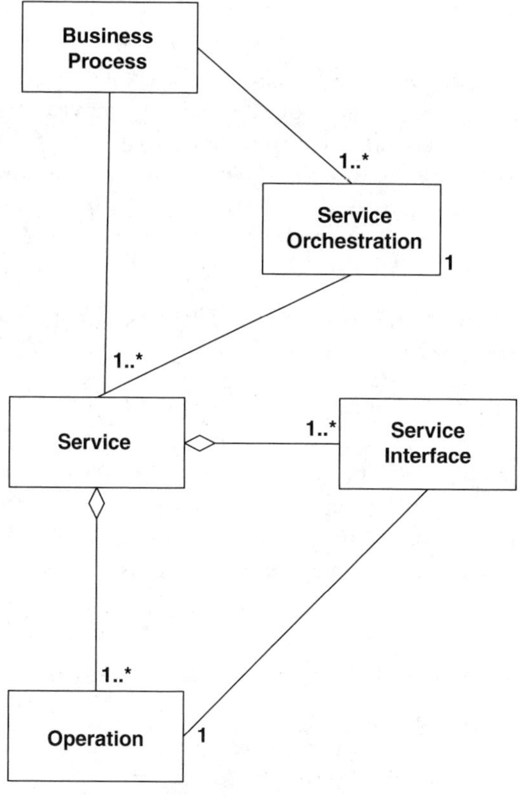

Figure 2.19 A metamodel for business processes using UML

security and reliability. The ESB is a container that manages the services deployed in its directory. More recently, we are starting to witness the emergence of services supported by trading partners. The discovery of these services is now primarily through partner or general communications: via direct communication, e-mail blasts, or Web sites. In other words, discovery does not necessary imply using a public Universal Description, Discovery, and Integration (UDDI) registry, although using a registry could be very helpful.

2.6.2 Iterative Methodology

Given the essential phases in developing service oriented applications, this section aggregates them in an iterative methodology. This methodology identifies a number of key worker roles. Depending on the particular organization, the roles could potentially have different titles. In many instances the same person will be holding multiple roles.

Service orientation by its very nature involves two parties: (1) the service consumer or requestor; and (2) the service publisher or provider. In fact, a third party is also involved: the service broker or registry. The service consumers need to find out about the existing services and be able to develop client service consumer applications that access the service.

This methodology is approached both from the perspective of the service consumer and service provider. Each will have its own sequence of steps and phases.

2.6.2.1 Continuous Improvement Methodology for Service Providers

Figure 2.20 illustrates the iterative continuous improvement methodology for service providers.

After implementing and deploying services, the provider monitors, identifies potential areas of improvements, implements the enhancements, and redeploys. For new services, the publisher analyzes service level agreements and requirements and then defines and implements the service. The following sections delve into the details of each of these phases. Note that in some cases, depending on the services being built, the publisher will skip over some steps in the iterative methodology. What is presented here is a general overview of

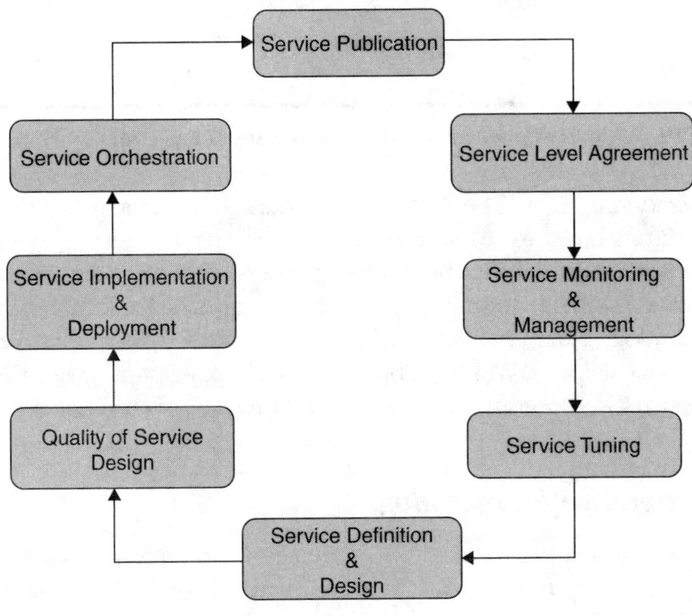

Figure 2.20 Continuous improvement iterative methodology for service providers

the steps that need to be implemented. Service enterprises need to adapt these phases to their particular organizations.

- Service definition and design: This is perhaps the most important step in the overall iterative methodology. Typically, there will be requirements feeding into this phase from internal customers, business stakeholders, or trading partners.[16]
  - In terms of service definitions, there are essentially two distinct paths.
    - New service, which needs to be defined and implemented from the ground up. The definition of the service results from the requirement and analysis of requests for the service. The service implementation can use other systems or services in the implementation of the service.
    - Exposing existing component, back-end applications, or enterprise information systems as services. This second alternative essentially exposes interfaces to existing components, back-end applications, or Enterprise Information Systems (EISs) as services.[17]
  - Hybrids can also exist, where a new service is defined through developing original code and invoking existing components or applications. In either case, the resulting artifact is one (or more) WSDL files that describes and defines the service.
  - Actors: Service designer and architect. This is an important role. The service designer will provide the model of the service and should be familiar both with WSDL and XML schemas, as these will be used to generate the service definition and description. Furthermore, service designers should be able to readily analyze interfaces and implementations of existing components as well as commercial off-the-shelf applications, such as enterprise resource planning systems.
  - Artifacts: (a) service component diagrams (in UML); and (b) WSDL and XML schema files.
- Quality of service design: This step takes the service level agreement requirements and the service definitions and comes up with a detailed implementation design that supports the required reliability, security, and performance requirements of the service. This book calls this QoS design since just implementing the WSDL and binding it to, say, a SOAP implementation is not enough. The QoS service design takes into consideration the best platform and technology for implementing and deploying the services. The designer needs to decide which type of application server to use, the language of implementation, and the components for reliability and security.

  - Actor: QoS designer and architect defines the details of the deployment architecture. This designer, who could be the same person or group as the service designer, will decide the details of the service bindings, where and how should the service be deployed, and other QoS services that need to be utilized or deployed for this service. Some of these include service failover support, continuous service monitoring and exceptions management, service security tokens and intermediaries, and service reliability.
  - Artifacts: (a) detailed deployment design documents (UML); (b) WSDL bindings; and (c) architecture diagrams.
- Service implementation and deployment: In this phase, the detailed designs and the WSDL bindings specified in the QoS design phase are implemented and deployed. The deployment typically involves pre-release staging and certification. Implementers also manage the configuration, versioning, and deprecation of deployed services. Other deployment activities include standards compliance testing (e.g., certification for Web service interoperability).
  - Actors: Implementer is the programmer responsible for developing and testing the implementation of the service. The service is typically implemented using an object-oriented language such as Java or C#. The QoS service designer would indicate to the implementer the implementation pattern to use for the service. The implementation also involves the reliability, security, and performance-related optimization to satisfy the required service agreements. Even though it is not explicitly represented here as a separate step, an important phase in the implementation is testing. So this implementation phase also creates test components and conducts certification testing before deploying the service implementations.
  - Artifacts: The implementation and deployment artifacts include (a) source code packages; (b) service packages; and (c) staging, certification, and deployment reports.
- Service orchestration: In some cases the service implementation involves composition and orchestration of services. This activity is quite different than implementing individual services, although there are some similarities. Ideally, orchestrating services should involve a minimum level of object-oriented programming. Instead, a graphical tool can be used to compose the services. The emerging standard here is BPEL.[18] Once composition of services is arranged, the orchestrated service can be published as a service. It is actually more complex than that. Orchestrating services and interacting with partners

will involve tighter coordination between service provider and requestor. In some cases the service requestor will need to provide asynchronous call-back service.

  - Actor: Service process designer. This is a higher-level role than service implementer, although as noted already the same resource might be playing different roles concurrently.
  - Artifacts: Some of the artifacts produced in this optional phase include (a) orchestration files (e.g., BPEL, WSDL) and deployments; (b) published orchestrated service interfaces (e.g., WSDL); and (c) service level and interaction specifications (e.g., BPEL, service documents).
- Service publication: Once services—including orchestrated ones—are defined, implemented, and deployed they need to be published. Publishing services includes several tasks.
  - WSDL file accessible to service consumers: If the service consumers are internal to the organization, the WSDL could be stored in a shared folder or repository. For external customers typically the WSDL is accessible through a Web address and hence is deployed to the Web server.
  - Service, business, and technical descriptions: Chapter 3 delves into the details of the different types of service information when discussing UDDI registries. The details and categories of the registration are not important. The goal is to have fully self-describing, meaningful, and useful categorization of services so that service consumers can easily locate and invoke the service.
  - Actors: Service publisher is a new type of role that contains elements of what is traditionally known as system integrator. This role is also important in the deployment phase. The publisher and the designers and implementers involved in deployments work closely together—and might be the same person or group.
  - Artifacts: The artifacts in this phase include (a) deployed WSDL (and potentially BPEL) files for service consumer access; and (b) UDDI registry entries to catalog, to categorize, and to support ease of service search and discovery.
- Service level agreement: SLAs include partners who are typically in service publisher and service consumer relationships with one another. There are several aspects of the SLA that can be represented in the agreement between the partners:
  - Reliability: This means the service needs to provide a specific and measurable reliability. For instance, availability of service 99 percent of the time is a concrete reliability measure. Another more

lower-level measure is guaranteeing one and only one time delivery of a message.

- Security: Authentication and authorization are the two concepts underlying security for services. Authentication addresses who is accessing the service. It deals with verifying the identity of the agent requesting a service, usually through a unique login and password mechanism. Authorization addresses the access privileges of an authenticated service requestor, agent, or user.
- Performance: The service agreement can specify both throughput as well as response-time service levels. A response-time service level indicates how fast a service request must respond, such as a response within two seconds. A throughput specification indicates the number of transactions or service requests per unit of time, such as 10,000 services per minute.
- Actors: It is difficult to characterize the actors involved in SLA. For purposes here they will be called service analysts. This is a higher-level role that gets involved in the requirement specification of the service and potentially negotiates with the trading partner on the SLA specifications. These SLA specifications are then fed to the service architects, designers, and implementers.

- Service monitoring and management: This is typically characterized as management or provisioning of the services. The management includes graphical monitoring of the service performance, analyzing service performance reports, and continuously tuning deployment systems to facilitate compliance to the service level agreements. Actors are service managers responsible for the SLAs who work closely with the service analysts to make sure there is continuous monitoring and improvements of SLA compliance.

2.6.2.2 Continuous Improvements for Service Consumers

The previous section provided an overview of the service producer's iterative methodology. In fact, there is a parallel continuous improvement methodology for service consumers. The methodologies have touch points—especially in designing service level agreements, which include not only service interface specifications but also QoS requirements (Figure 2.21).

Notice that here instead of service publishing there is service discovery. The SLA is similar and is a touch point where service provider and consumer come together to agree on the specifics of the SLA. The client also needs to implement the interaction and service access code and deploy it. There is similar QoS design and implementation on the client side as well.

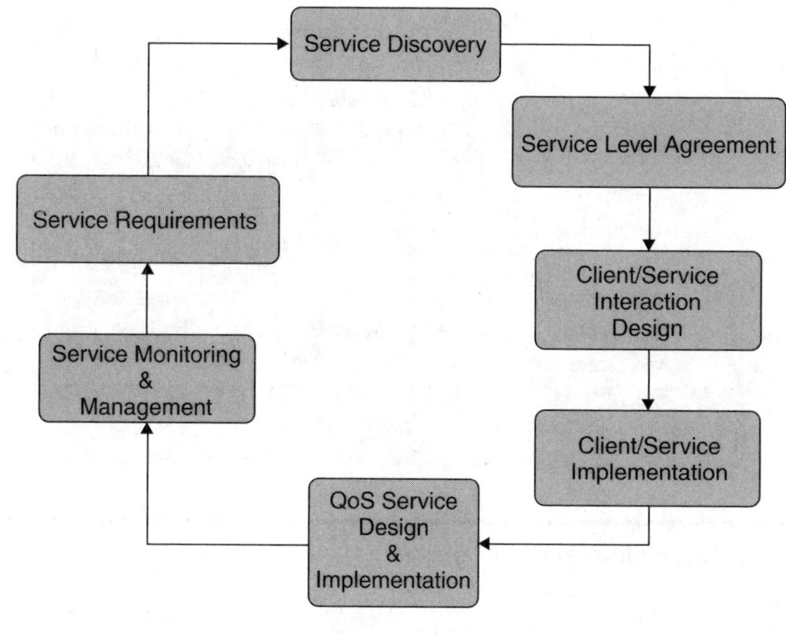

Figure 2.21 Continuous improvement iterative methodology for service requestors

2.7 Maturity Model for SOA

The original capability maturity model (CMM) was developed by the Software Engineering Institute (SEI)[19] and provides a robust discipline with practices and principles to help software development practices achieve maturity in their software development processes. A number of factors influence the maturity of the software development processes within enterprises, including the strategic plans of the enterprise, the enterprise's own organization and culture, and the technologies adopted within the enterprise IT architecture.

The five CMM levels are illustrated in Figure 2.22. The CMM has been applied to several software disciplines within the industry. It is not surprising that a number of software companies focusing on service oriented technologies came up with an initial proposal for SOA CMM.[20] Figure 2.23 illustrates the SOA CMM and how it relates to the original CMM maturity levels.

- Level 1—initial services: In this maturity level the enterprise is getting its feet wet with service orientation. This is the introductory level in service integration. The basic standards are WSDL and SOAP. The services are piloted and deployed over either Java or .NET platforms. The scope is research and development experimentation. Sponsorship is departmental.

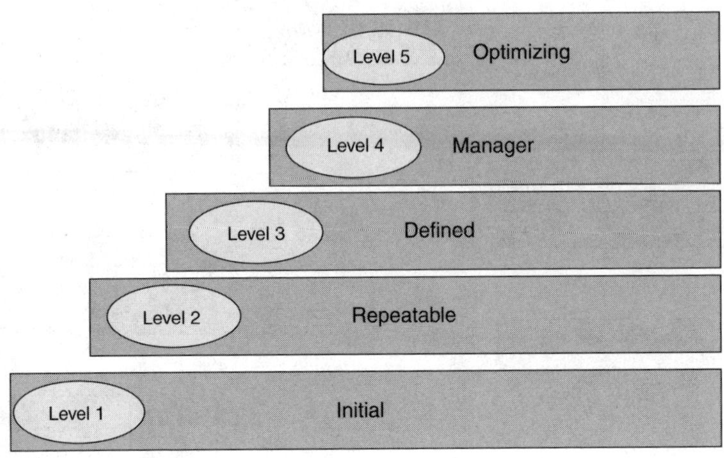

Figure 2.22 Traditional CMM levels

- Level 2—architected services: This maturity level demonstrates the beginnings of cost reductions for IT and moves from ad hoc experimentation to true integration using service technologies. Additional standards, especially for QoS, come into play. Examples include

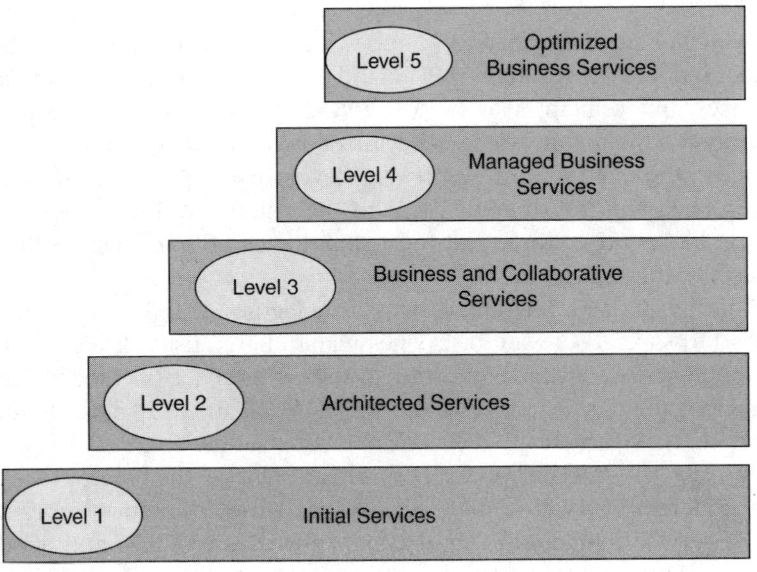

Figure 2.23 Proposed SOA maturity model levels

WS-Security and WS-ReliableMessaging. Chief information officer sponsorship is achieved.

- Level 3—business and collaboration services: This starts to touch on process orchestration and deploys composition of services involving trading partners. This maturity level starts supporting long duration transactions as well as event-driven processing. Standards such as WS-BPEL and WS-AtomicTransaction are significant in this maturity level.
- Level 4—measured business services: The main focus of this level is business performance metrics. Business activity monitoring is an essential technology that needs to be implemented at this level. Since business measures are involved, there may be other high-level sponsors, such as chief financial officers.
- Level 5—optimized business services: The main focus here is on business optimization end to end within the service oriented enterprise and the ability to automatically respond to change. This level attempts to achieve continuous improvements with chief executive officer sponsorship.

2.7.1 Maturity Model for Service Oriented Enterprises

The previous section summarized an envisioned maturity model that focuses on technology issues up to level 3 and then starts to delve into business value propositions in maturity in level 4 and 5. In fact, most maturity models—and as mentioned already, others have been proposed by IBM and BEA Systems, respectively[21]—have the bottom-up technology perspective. There is nothing wrong with having a technology and technical solution-focused approach. However, these tend to push the business-related value propositions to the higher levels of the maturity models. From its earlier days, SOA attempted to address the business needs and to claim it was addressing the business and IT gap. However, when the proposed solutions of SOA are carefully examined, it is clear that they tend to be technically focused and ignore core business perspectives and value propositions. A service oriented *enterprise* maturity model will approach it differently. The SOE maturity model is more holistic and focuses on bringing tangible return on investment (ROI) for the business as well as IT organizations (Figure 2.24).

Level 1: SOE foundation—initial setup of key performance indicators, end-to-end business processes and setup of SOA infrastructure. This means the SOE has embarked on getting its feet wet not only in the underlying Web services-based technologies but also the two additional layers: the enterprise performance layer, identifying a number of key performance indicators, and the business process

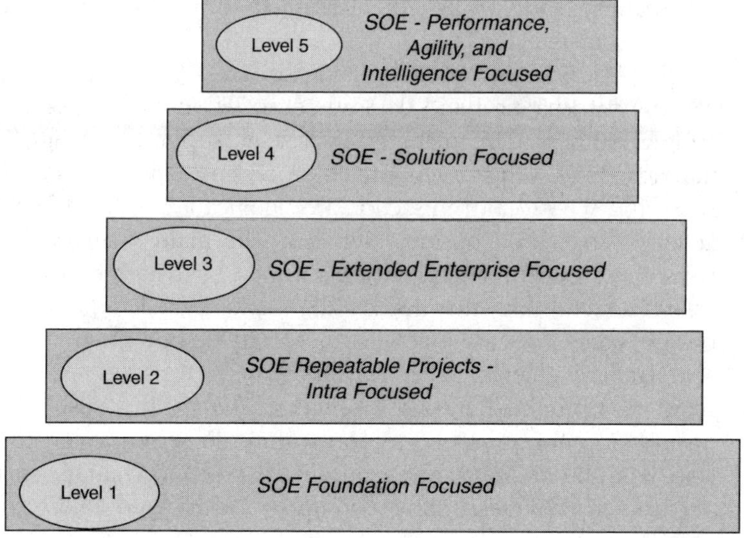

Figure 2.24 SOE maturity model levels

management layer, identifying initial processes that rely on the SOA/ESB layer to take care of high-quality, high-performance, and reliable integration using service technologies. This level has an initial setup of the three layers in an SOE.

Level 2: SOE repeatable projects—intra-focused: This level would have well-established SOA architecture, deployed ESBs, and implemented federation of ESBs. Level 2 has a good handle on identifying all the essential tasks for SOE projects involving tasks with roles and dependencies for (a) business users, especially stakeholders and business analysts; (b) process and rules architects for design and implementation of the policies, procedures, and end-to-end business processes; and (c) infrastructure SOA architects for design and implementation of service orchestrations and QoS service standards (e.g., WS-Security, WS-ReliableMessaging). Level 2 methodology can start with as-is processes and performance measures, can estimate the to-be gain, and can start showing tangible and repeatable ROIs for redesigned processes and service orchestrations. So here you have managed to have end-to-end ROI-driven optimization of processes, involving KPIs at the EPM level, business rules and processes at the BPM level, and underlying service composition at the ESB/SOA level. The focus though is still within the enterprise.

Level 3: SOE—extended enterprise-focused. Extended enterprise business-to-business composition and integration, with QoS standards support for the end-to-end business processes. The implementation of processes with underlying service integrations is more complex than process orchestrations. Here you have also to deal with process choreographies. There could be several processes executing internally within each business partner's organization. In this maturity level, partners are able to define and to deploy complex choreography of processes. Each might have its own internal process engines. The extended enterprise will be able to robustly execute the end-to-end superprocess-involved message exchanges choreographies in the context of internal processes. So in level 3 one has the ability to:

Effectively use registries: Search and discover not only services but actually potential business partners. When applicable, the role of business description and publicly available registries such as UDDI registries is increased. In fact, registration of businesses and their services is incorporated in the life cycle of SOE solution development.

Be able to negotiate and establish partner relationships: Trading partners are able to synchronize their internal processes and to coordinate with process choreographies specifying message exchanges. Some communities such as ebXML and RosettaNet attempt to provide standards for partners in horizontal and vertical domains that go beyond the core infrastructure Web services standards.

Efficiently align the QoS stacks: The businesses are able to establish service level agreements across their enterprises. The business partners are also able to align their security and reliability stacks so that end-to-end reliability and security are guaranteed.

Drill down from global and extended enterprise KPI or performance measures to automated processes: In level 2, the performance measures were driven primarily through internal processes. Here the monitoring and measurement span multiple enterprises. The stakeholders in an enterprise can compare and contrast the performance of trading partners. They are able to drill down from key extended enterprise performance measures and can analyze processes, internal operations, and external factors involved in the overall solution.

Level 4: SOE—solution focused: Up to level 3, the focus is on the maturity of the SOA infrastructure, BPM suite level, and the underlying infrastructure for intra- and inter-enterprise solutions. In level 4, the focus is on horizontal and vertical solutions that help the enterprise quickly build and deploy its customer solutions. A solution framework is essentially a foundation that can really accelerate the overall life cycle of projects deployed by the SOE. The solution framework comes with (a) predefined best-practice business process templates; (b) predefined best-practice information model definitions; (c) redefined best-practice business rules in different categories such as declarative expressions, declarative decision, event rules, and constraints; and (d) predefined service integration with either back-end or trading partner organizations. In level 4 maturity, engineering has developed best practices to reuse the existing predefined solutions and determine what areas need customization or extension. This is fundamentally a different and more mature approach to solution development. SOA and BPM systems are core horizontal layers. In this maturity level, not only best-practice architectures and solutions but also vertical as well as horizontal solutions that have predefined components can be leveraged for service integration and business process automation.

Level 5: SOE—performance, agility, and intelligence focused: This corresponds to the advanced features of SOE. Here there are optimizations, and the ability exists to quickly drill down from high-level KPIs to processes, participants, or services deployed in the underlying infrastructures. The system can also suggest optimizations and provide the ability to predictively improve KPI scores. Other key features of level 5:

Building service, process, and policy assets: In this maturity level, the ability exists to organize business processes, business rules, integration, and all other aspects of solutions so that depending on the constraints of a particular invocation the best process, participant, back-end service, or trading partner service is selected and executed. Process, rules, and integration facilities are treated as corporate assets, which can be easily reused and specialized. The system provides a separation of what is intended to be achieved in a particular solution versus how to achieve it—for example, which service to invoke, which trading partner to use, which process to activate, which human participant to assign tasks to.

Dynamic discovery: In this maturity level, there can be dynamic discoveries of services. Now you are able to semantically discover other services and sometimes even carry out automated negotiations, auctioning, and then accessing the service. The binding to service providers is dynamic. In this maturity level, designers focus on the type of services, quantifying them through the properties or meta-data of the services. The underlying system figures out what is the best service to invoke. The dynamic discovery and then subsequent binding goes hand in hand with the core registration, discover, and exchange of service request/responses that was illustrated in Section 1.3.3 and Figure 1.14.

The SOE maturity model is quite different from the SOA maturity model of the previous section. In some sense it is a superset of the SOA maturity model and other maturity models in technologies involved in the SOE stack (i.e., business processes, business rules, ESBs, performance management). It is a holistic approach that is critical for the success of the SOE engagement.

2.8 Summary

Service orientation is not just about technological layers. At its core, SOEs leverage three essential disciplines: enterprise performance management, business process management, and SOA IT architecture infrastructure, especially enterprise service buses. This chapter focused on development methodologies for service oriented architectures and the overall maturity models for service orientation.

The chapter contrasted traditional waterfall and iterative methodologies. It provided an overview of the Zachman framework, and it explained how service orientation relates to each of the rows in the framework.

Service oriented applications are built through service oriented analysis and design. The chapter covered the core UML notations that could be used in service oriented solution development. These include notation for use cases, activity diagrams (model processes), sequence diagrams (model service interactions), state transition diagrams (to model transition of service application states), component diagrams (to model composition of services in components), and class diagrams (to model information models that involve service properties). The chapter provided an overview of continuous improvement iterative methodologies for both service providers and consumers.

The last section focused on maturity models for service orientation. This section provided an overview of the SOE maturity model and elucidated the maturity levels in the context of the SOE layers and architecture. The capability of the development of SOE process matures from foundation- to intra-focused to extended enterprise to solution frameworks and finally to performance-, agility-, and intelligence-focused optimizations.

Notes

1. The concept of BPR is revisited in Chapter 5 when discussing business process management.
2. This quote was said by Darcy Fowkes of the Aberdeen Group in 2002. See March 25, 2002, Business Wire, http://calbears.findarticles.com/p/articles/mi_m0EIN/lis_2002_March_25/ai_84157557.
3. For an overview see "WebDG: One-Stop Shop for Social and Welfare Benefits," http://www.nvc.cs.vt.edu/~dgov/webdgtour/index.htm, Virginia Tech University, 2002.
4. IBM, "Rational Unified Process," http://www-306.ibm.com/software/awdtools/rup/.
5. Ronald Jeffries, 2006, "XProgramming.com: An Agile Software Development Resource," http://www.xprogramming.com/xpmag/whatisxp.htm.
6. Control Chaos, 2006, "Scrum: It's about Common Sense," http://www.controlchaos.com/.
7. From "Positioning the Enterprise Architecture," by Dennis A. Stevenson, http://users.iafrica.com/o/om/omisditd/denniss/text/eapositn.html.
8. Enterprise architectures so far—and for the foreseeable future—tend to tilt toward the IT and not the business owners. However, some entities and deliverables within enterprise architectures are very much relevant to business owners.
9. See Object Management Group, http://www.omg.org.
10. The history of object orientation is quite interesting. There are fundamental trends in object orientation, and we keep on rediscovering principles and techniques that have already been incorporated in previous generation products. Think of the promises and approach of CORBA. At one point we thought CORBA (or Microsoft's COM/DCOM and, more recently, .NET; or Sun's J2EE distributed architecture) would provide the infrastructure for implementing distributed objects throughout the enterprise. If you look under the surface all these distributed computing technologies attempted to (and continue to) achieve many of the claims of service orientation.
11. A signature consists of the name of the operation as well as the input and output messages using Web Services Description Language (WSDL) terminology.
12. That is, XML files that are valid instances of the BPEL schema.
13. Unfortunately, the term *component* often has different meanings—depending on who uses them and how. However, it does connote a large-grained object.
14. In fact, the operations and attributes of a class can pertain to either the instances or to the class itself. So in object-oriented jargon, there are class variables and class methods or operations as well as instance variables and instance methods or operations. In most cases, when speaking about the attributes and operations of a class, the implied meaning is the instance variables and methods. In some situations, references or discussions might be found on class variables and methods.
15. Section 2.5 goes deeper into some of the basics of UML.

16. This requirement phase has not been indicated, although it is perfectly legitimate to have a separate requirement step.
17. *Services* here means primarily concentrating on Web services, although a WSDL definition can specify other types of implementation bindings, not just SOAP.
18. This will be covered in more detail in Chapter 5.
19. Carnegie Mellon Software Engineering Institute, http://www. sei.cmu.edu/.
20. The companies were AmberPoint, BearingPoint, Sonic Software and Systinet. See Systinet, "SOA Leaders Introduce New SOA Maturity Model," September 20, 2005, http://www.systinet.com/pr/145.
21. See Ali Arsanjani and Kerrie Holley, "Increase Flexibility with the Service Integration Maturity Model," September 30, 2005, http://www. 128.ibm.com/developerworks/webservices/library/ws-soa-simm/; and David Groves, "Successfully Planning for SOA," November 9, 2005, http://dev2dev.bea.com/pub/a/2005/11/planning-for-soa.html.

Chapter 3

Service Definition, Discovery, and Deployment

The simplest and most basic definition that I can give you is that a Web service is an application that provides a Web API.

Ann Thomas Manes

3.1 Introduction

Business and IT: This chapter is primarily for IT. However, business users might find it useful to glance at it. It is common knowledge that service oriented architectures (SOAs) can use any standard technology, not just Web services, for registry, discovery and especially exchange of messages or invocations between service providers and consumers. That is true. However, Web services remain by far the most promising standards for robust inter- and intra-enterprise exchanges. Furthermore, the standards discussed here, especially Universal Description, Discovery, and Integration (UDDI) and Web Services Description Language (WSDL), can be used to publish and describe any type of business or service, respectively. As this chapter demonstrates, UDDI is used to publish information for Yellow Pages about businesses, not just technical specifications. A browser can be used to search and access information about business and the services that are supported by each—hence the relevance of UDDI to business users. WSDL gets more technical and provides additional details about the supported services. The third standard, SOAP, is the most technical and specifies the eXtensible Markup Language (XML) message structure for service provider and consumer exchanges.

Chapter 2 focused on the methodology to define and publish services. Through service oriented analysis and design the requirements are captured, and the services are subsequently implemented and deployed. The publishing and discovery are important phases in service application development. Typically the service provider and service consumer are loosely coupled, with standard message exchanges between service requestors and producers. The service requestors can actually discover the service providers and can bind to them or conduct business with them as they see fit.

There is nothing strange here. This is exactly what happens when someone searches for services through preferred search engines and then browses the Web sites that were discovered as a result of the search. Increasingly, the emergence of portals for specific types of services or verticals can be seen. Portals are Web sites that provide efficient access to services and information from a variety of sources organized in categories, such as travel, healthcare, and rentals. Yahoo! remains one of the more popular general purpose portals. Now both of these models of discovery are quite popular Web access mechanisms. Discoveries are made through (1) ad hoc searching using search engines such as Google, Excite, Yahoo!, MSN, AltaVista, HotBot to name a few; and (2) generalized or interest- and industry-specific portal site navigation, which could also provide some search capabilities.

Business and IT: It is interesting to notice how Yahoo!, Microsoft, and Google are competing ferociously to be the preferred landing page and portal for all users. Service orientation takes a different approach. It can let the individual user, enterprise, or application take control of the information that needs to be accessed for public and private sites. Interestingly, today millions of accesses are now conducted through Web services to these and other popular Web sites, such as Amazon and eBay. This trend will continue and in fact will accelerate.

Within the context of service oriented enterprises (SOEs) these more ad hoc approaches, which will remain very popular for the foreseeable future, are complemented with two additional techniques:

Service Registry: The portals for services provide a much more rigorous and well-categorized description of services. The categorization is similar to the familiar Yellow Pages for phone books. The White Pages contain detailed information about the services offered by organizations. Finally, registries introduce Green Pages to contain technical details for programmatic access of services.

Programmatic search and discovery: Registries also can themselves be accessed as services, through service client programs. Instead of a human agent browsing Web sites to discover services, the actual search and discovery could be conducted through client programs and search agents. Potentially programmatic agents could discover the best service and invoke it dynamically, either completely automated or with minimal human intervention.

Centralized registries are not the only mechanism for discovering services and binding (i.e., using them or calling) to the service dynamically. Customers or trading partners can access specific Web sites hosted by service providers to search and analyze the available services. This is definitely true of popular sites such as Google, eBay, or Amazon—all of which provide programmatic access to their Web sites through Web service invocations. However, the overall approach of searching standard registry and binding to services dynamically remains a very attractive option.

This chapter considers a hypothetical scenario of how this search discovery and binding can happen, using a reservation system. Suppose a customer requests the following: "Find me a sedan in the range of $65 to $75 a day and a hotel no more than $135 a day for June 19 to 21." Now, of course, there are a couple of conventional ways of doing this through either a travel sales agent or going to a number of dot-com sites to compare and shop. These options are always available. But now think of a completely automated option where a hypothetical intelligent software agent does the following:

1. Searches a public registry for auto rental and hotel reservation services
2. Locates the technical specification of these services
3. Dynamically generates the client interfaces
4. Invokes the services from qualified service providers
5. Attempts to locate the best deal for the customer—as specified within the required price ranges
6. Makes and holds the reservations
7. Returns to the customer an ordered list of possibilities from which to choose from

As mentioned above, this can be done today, but only with a lot of Web browsing—and it is rather inconvenient. Also steps 1 through 7 are not completely automated—but we are on our way. The availability of programmatic service based invocations is a key step in this direction. Chapters 4 and 5, respectively, delve deeper into the architectural plumbing needed to support these programmatic accesses to services as well as the higher-level business processes that orchestrate services.

3.2 Focusing on UDDI+WSDL+SOAP

> In 2000, we committed ourselves to the .Net strategy. That assumed XML and Web services would become mainstream. Looking back, one of the things that was a clear success was the bet on XML (eXtensible Markup Language) and Web services. People are just beginning to understand how profound they are as industry standards.
>
> **Bill Gates, 2003**

Business: You might find this section technical. Of the three standards, UDDI is the most relevant for businesses since it describes business entities and categories. Glance over it, or even go to one of the UDDI sites and search business entities and their services. The categorization could also be of some interest. The next standard, WSDL, allows service producers and consumers to communicate clearly and specifically the details of the service descriptions, which should be of less interest to readers. Finally, SOAP is the most technical and deals with the run-time structure of messages—skip over the SOAP section.

IT: These are the basic and core standards for Web services and service oriented architecture. If you are familiar with these standards you can skip over the rest of the chapter. The WSDL and SOAP are World Wide Web Consortium (W3C) standards (http://www.w3c.org). UDDI is an OASIS standard (http://www.oasis-open.org). There are always minor and major revisions of these standards, but Web Service Interoperability Organization (WS-I) profiles should always be reviewed. These profiles typically lag the most recent ratified standards. WS-I (http://www.ws-i.org) specifies the interoperability versions for UDDI, WSDL, and SOAP, as well as other standards. It describes the interoperability requirements in Basic Profiles. In August 2004, WS-I published its most recent profile, Basic Profile 1.1. In 2005, WS-I published several errata to Basic Profile. The versions of the three basic standards are WSDL 1.1, SOAP 1.1, and UDDI V2.

This chapter focuses primarily on the three core standards for registries (UDDI), service description (WSDL), and interchange (SOAP). Are these the only three mechanisms or standards for service orientation? Not at all. In fact these standards have been evolving, and a number of alternatives have been suggested and are pursued, especially for service descriptions. For instance, in addition to WSDL—which itself has several versions: 1.1, 2.0—you have other proposals on the table such as Norm's Service Description Language (NSDL),[1] SOAP Service Description Language (SSDL),[2] Web Resource Description Language (WRDL),[3] and Web Application Description Language (WADL),[4] to name a few. There are and continue to be others.

There are alternatives to SOAP as well. WSDL, for instance, can use Java Message Service (JMS)[5] binding instead of SOAP binding.[6] In addition, more recently the Representation State Transfer (REST) style of service invocation has become quite popular in research and development circles, even though the actual commercial viability and offerings supporting REST, are in short supply. REST provides a much simpler alternative to SOAP. With REST, service requestors communicate directly with service providers through a universal resource locator (URL) to the service provider. The request and response messages are encoded in XML directly. Basically the

SOAP processing component is deleted, and a direct invocation is used—it is simpler, faster, and appears to be more efficient.

However, at this junction and for the foreseeable future the primary focus in Web services standards will continue to be WSDL for service definition and SOAP for binding. One important aspect to consider here is the interoperability between Web services. WS-I has defined a number of interoperability profiles of Web services standards to support a baseline for interoperability among different Web services implementations. The main focus of WS-I standards has been on SOAP, WSDL, and UDDI. More specifically, the interoperability profile provides details and tests for interoperability using the following specific standards:[7]

1. SOAP 1.1, including material related to:
   a. Namespaces in XML
   b. XML 1.0 Second Edition
2. WSDL 1.1 including material related to:
   a. XML Schema 2001 Part 1: Structures
   b. XML Schema 2001 Part 2: Datatypes
3. UDDI 2.0, which includes support for UDDI 1.0 interfaces

This is important. Success in Web services deployments requires support not only of common standards but also their interoperability profiles. Service providers and consumers must exchange request/response messages using agreed on and mature standards for discovery, description, and deployment. This is critical. Today, WS-I has chosen these three standards (UDDI, WSDL, and SOAP) as the foundation of its interoperability profiles. Hence the focus here is on these three basic standards for service oriented enterprises.

3.3 Service Registries: UDDI

> An effective SOA implementation depends on an effective way to publish, discover, and consume business services.
>
> **Hurwitz and Associates**

Universal Description, Discovery, and Integration enables businesses and other organizations to describe and publish their service offerings in UDDI registries, and to discover other businesses and services through those registries.

UDDI registries implement the UDDI standard and are typically built on top of relational databases. A UDDI registry provides transactional access to search and update registry entries. As this chapter discusses, UDDI registries provide both Web-based and programmatic APIs to access and modify the registry content.

UDDI leverages standards such as XML, Hypertext Transfer Protocol (HTTP), and Domain Name System (DNS). The UDDI protocol is the building block that will enable businesses to quickly, easily, and dynamically find and transact business with one another using their preferred applications.

UDDI will enable organizations to publish information about their companies and services. These services and their technical details will be discovered by other potential trading partners. Once the service is chosen, the trading partners can exchange request/response messages and thus integrate with each other, potentially realizing extended enterprise solutions in Web services frameworks. It will also enable heterogeneous platforms and applications to discover and interoperate with existing applications.

Although UDDI is a core Web services standard, it has not gained the respect accorded WSDL and SOAP. Some view UDDI as not very useful in its current form, primarily because it is so open. UDDI operators do not monitor the entries in their UDDI registries. Entries include many companies that no longer exist,[8] and many other entries provide very basic information about an organization, which have contributed to the lack of mass endorsements of UDDI registries. Most public UDDI registries have shut down, as explained in Section 3.3.5.

UDDI includes technical specifications similar to other distributed object technologies. However, UDDI also introduces a much-needed business dimension to the concept and domain of registries. This business dimension includes categorization of the business and the services it provides.

Why is this categorization needed? The vision of Web services is to support dynamic discovery and binding of service requests to service providers. Service requestors can use UDDI's categorization of businesses to focus their searches on the specific service domains of their interests. UDDI registries also support information about the company and the contacts of the company via its registries. This enables e-business technical partners to discover and communicate with each other. Some business identifications also enable businesses to further investigate and evaluate their trading partners. In short, UDDI addresses the fundamental dimensions of service registries, including company information (White Pages), company and service categories (Yellow Pages), and technical service details (Green Pages). Subsequent sections expand on these three dimensions of UDDI registries.

3.3.1 Beyond Search Engines

Today one of the most important Web applications is the search engine. Were it not for search engines, the Web's usefulness would be very limited. Even with search engines, however, the process of finding information involves trial and error. Often a person searching for a specific company, site, article, or other content must deal with many misses before finding the desired information.

A number of technologies are addressing more intelligent searching on the Web. Some of these technologies include metadata support, the semantic Web (discussed in Chapter 7), and more specialized search engines.

UDDI is a better solution than Web search technologies—including advanced search techniques—when searching for businesses and services. UDDI enables companies to publish specific details about their companies, products, and services in a standard, structured way.

Finding businesses and services on the Web today requires the use of a search engine or knowing the URL of the business. Currently the Web has no standards as to how companies organize their Web pages. Typically they have an "About" company link, but every company does it differently. Also, the categorization of the products or services is ad hoc. Here again, each company has its own way of representing the categorization of its products.

UDDI improves on this chaos by providing a standard structure for companies to register information about themselves and their services. Under the UDDI standard, all registered companies will use the same elements for their contact information, standard business identification, standard categories of products, and standard mechanism to provide technical details about their services. Think of a UDDI registry as a powerful, well-organized discovery engine. UDDI benefits businesses of all sizes by creating a global, platform-independent, open architecture for describing, discovering and integrating businesses using the Internet.

3.3.2 Enabling External and Internal Integration

UDDI registries address and overcome the major hurdles to integration between and within organizations. In business-to-business integration, UDDI will enable trading partners to discover each other more easily and quickly because the categorization, contact information and other details about each business will be standardized. Furthermore, UDDI registries will store much more detailed information about business services than can be found on company Web sites.

UDDI will help to realize the vision of the virtual enterprise, involving many trading partners, by providing:

- Visibility of the partner organization, business category, and the services it offers
- Programmatic access to these services
- Process level integration between trading partners
- The possibility of dynamic discovery and binding
- New opportunities both for creating new relationships between existing partners and for discovering new partners around the globe

For internal integration, in addition to enabling trading partner relationships across the Internet, UDDI will facilitate integration within organizations.

In large organizations there are typically a plethora of applications, platforms, transport protocols, and middleware. As noted in Chapter 1, integrating these disparate components can be a formidable task. Of all the technologies available today in the arena of distributed object connectivity, Web services hold the most promise for achieving internal integration.

3.3.3 UDDI in the Web Services Stack

The previous sections described how UDDI goes beyond search engines to provide a structured representation of businesses, the categories of their services, and technical details about their services. Chapters 1 and 2 described several types of Web services technology stacks (e.g., Chapter 1 included a separate stack for registration). Figure 3.1 illustrates where UDDI fits within the overall stack of service oriented technologies, which includes registration and discovery.

Once a service has been described through WSDL, it must be published so that others can discover it. This is where UDDI comes into play. Service requestors will invoke these services either individually or within business processes. The communication infrastructure is typically via SOAP messages over HTTP protocol.

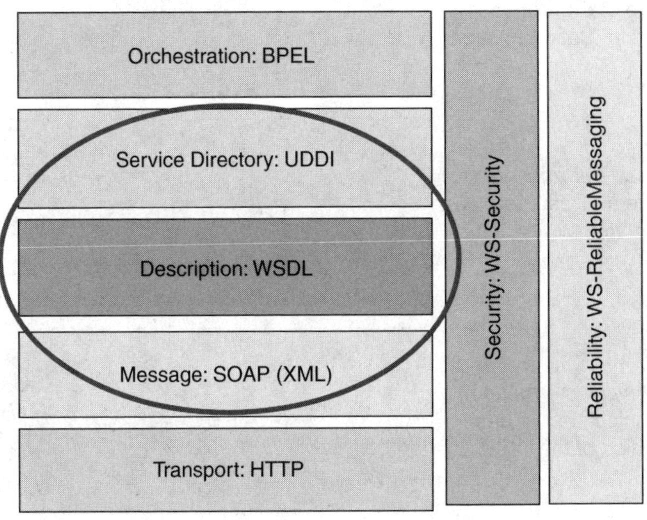

Figure 3.1 UDDI within the Web services stack

3.3.4 Organization of UDDI Registries

UDDI applies the familiar metaphor of telephone directories to Web services registries. As illustrated in Figure 3.2, the UDDI registry contains White Pages, Yellow Pages, and Green Pages entries.

- White Pages contain contact information about the publisher, such as the name and address of the business, phone and fax numbers, Web site URL, and description of the organization. In addition, the White Pages contain business identifiers, including Dun & Bradstreet's Data Universal Numbering System (DUNS) and Thomas Register.
- Yellow Pages organize the service providers and their services in various topics or categories, including categorization taxonomies such as the North American Industry Classification Industry (NAICS) industry codes, United Nations Standard Products and Services Codes (UNSPSC), and geographical taxonomies. These codes are useful in initial targeting of searches to specific industries within specific countries.

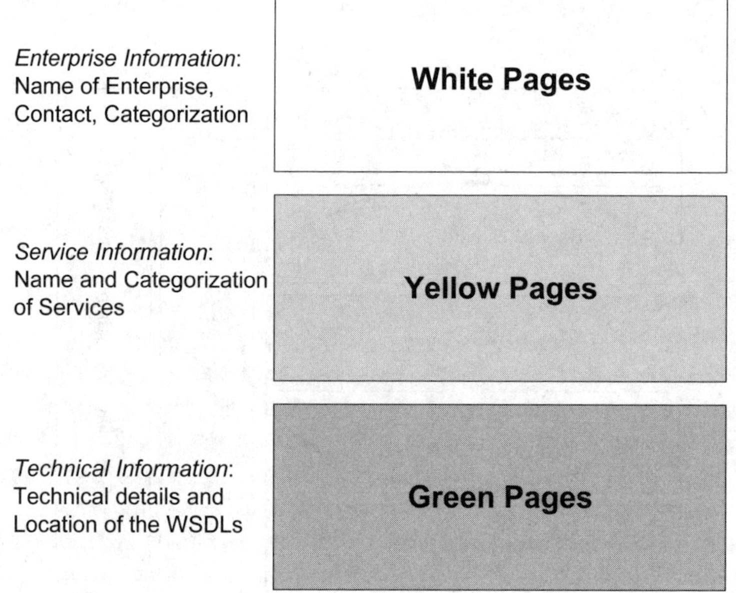

Figure 3.2 UDDI registries apply telephone directory metaphor

- Green Pages are more of a UDDI concept and are used to represent technical information pertaining to the services. These include where to locate the service and how to invoke the service operations, as well as the URL of the WSDL, which provides all the technical details necessary to invoke the service.

3.3.5 UDDI Business Registry Operators

UDDI registries have gone through several versions. Version 2 was ratified in May 2003 and version 3 in February of 2005. Initially a number of organizations such as IBM, Microsoft, SAP, and NTT provided support for public registries. This was important for proof of concept and validation of the notion of registries. The idea of a public registry was quite compelling: Using the White, Yellow, and Green Pages, businesses will publish information about their businesses and specifics of their services and be discovered. However, in January 2006 these public registries were discontinued. There are, and continue to be, several explanations for the shutdown, although these companies hosted the public UDDI registries for about five years. Perhaps the more compelling reason is that the public business registries did not take off as anticipated. Even the Web services-based interfaces to public Web sites are not growing as fast as anticipated. This also means the need for public registries is not as compelling as once anticipated. Furthermore, if a business is known and trusted, it could publish its WSDLs and allow other organizations to use their service interfaces, much the way Google[9] and Amazon[10] allow access to their services through SOAP messages.

In addition to the UDDI public business registry providers—which, as already noted, were shutdown in early 2006—other public registries allow Web service practitioners to experiment and have fun with service invocations. XMethods, [11] one such registry, provides a Web interface and is built on top of a private UDDI registry. Even though it provides a more basic interface, it is quite popular with Web services developers. XMethods lists services that can be invoked both for testing and production purposes. Some Web services listed on XMethods include checking for weather conditions and stock quotes and even entertaining services such as the joke of the day. Developers can easily publish and share their services with their peers.

XMethods is different from other public registries, which tend to capture the UDDI model through portal layouts—with

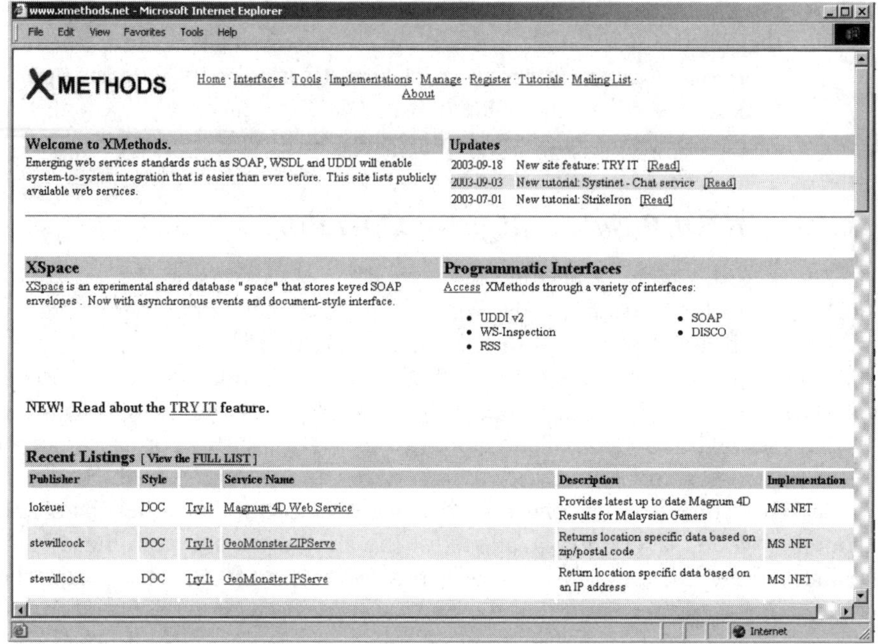

tabs and elements corresponding to UDDI concepts. XMethods provides a more direct listing of the registered services and their WSDL.

3.3.6 UDDI Elements

This section provides more detail about each of the elements of UDDI[12] that correspond to entries for White, Yellow, and Green Pages information. These elements, and their relationships to one another, are illustrated in Figure 3.3. As illustrated, each business entity contains a number of services, and each service contains business templates. The business templates reference the technical models and documents. These are discussed in more detail in the following sections.

3.3.6.1 Business Entity

The business entity represents the organization that is publishing its services. This element is required for any business; at the very least, the organization needs to indicate its name. The business entity also includes a business description, contact information, and a description of the services

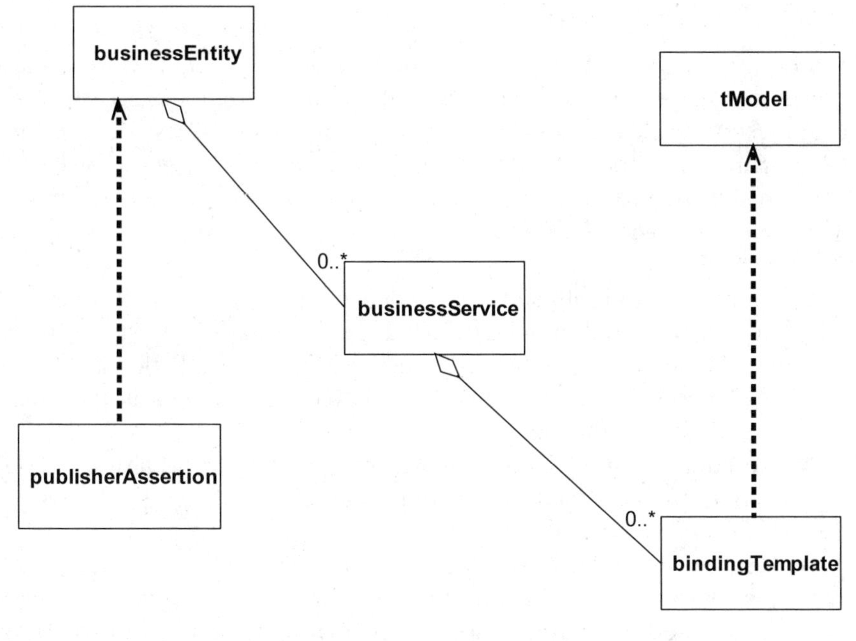

Figure 3.3 UDDI element types and their relationships

the organization is offering. It includes categories and identification of the business.

Some of the key attributes and elements of business entity are the name, discovery URL, identifier keys, and business categorization.

- Name (as indicated in <xsd:complexType name="businessEntity">): This is mandatory, and it contains the name of the business entity. Most UDDI registries support searching based on the name of the business entity.
- Discovery URL (as indicated in <xsd:element ref="uddi:discoveryURLs" minOccurs="0"/>): Each business entity can have one or more discovery URLs. Typically this will be the URL address of the business. There could be, however, additional URLs that provide information about the business or its services.
- Identifier keys (as indicated in <xsd:element ref="uddi:identifierBag" minOccurs="0"/>): A business entity will have business identifiers and business categorizations. Business identifiers used are Dun & Bradstreet DUNS Numbers and Thomas Register Supplier IDs.
- Business categorization: This includes NAICS, UNSPSC, and International Standards Organization (ISO) 3166.

3.3.6.2 Business Service

Each business entity will contain a number of business services. A business service will have a name, description, and categorizations. So by using business services, a business entity can organize its services. Each service will contain a number of binding templates which in turn will provide the details of the Web services under the business service. A business service includes the following features:

- Names (as indicated in <element ref="uddi:name" minOccurs="0" maxOccurs="unbounded"/>): It is good to have at least one name for the service. As indicated previously, a good practice is to have the same name as the name of the <service> element in the WSDL that describes the service.
- Descriptions (as indicated in <element ref="uddi:description" minOccurs="0" maxOccurs="unbounded"/>): Business services can have descriptions.
- Binding templates (as indicated in <element ref="uddi:bindingTemplates" minOccurs="0"/>): The business services are typically used to name and categorize a collection of binding templates. The latter provide the details of the service. The binding template provides information on the invocation method and location for the service. A business service can contain zero or more binding templates.
- Categorization of the service (as indicated in <element ref="uddi:categoryBag" minOccurs="0"/>): The categories include NAICS, UNSPSC, and the ISO 3166 geographical categorization.

3.3.6.3 Binding Templates

The binding template contains references to technical information about the services offered by the business. Specifically, these templates reference technical models (tModels) which in turn contain more detailed technical information about the services. The attributes and elements of the binding template are described as follows:

- Description (as indicated in <element ref="uddi:description" minOccurs="0" maxOccurs="unbounded"/>): There can be several description elements in the binding template.
- Choice (as indicated in <choice>): A binding template can have either an access point or a hostingRedirector.
  - accessPoint: This corresponds to the port element in the WSDL for the operation. For this choice the UDDI registry stores the URL type and the address to access the service.

    - hostingRedirector: This choice provides a pointer to another binding template. This element has an attribute that is the bindingKey (unique UUID key) of the binding template to which it points.
- tModelInstanceDetails (as indicated in <element ref="uddi:tModelInstanceDetails"/>): This points to the tModel through a UUID unique tModel key. This element contains zero or more occurrences of tModelInstanceInfo.
    - tModelKey: A required attribute of tModelInstanceInfo. This is very important, as it contains the unique key of the tModel containing the definition of the service, as discussed in the next section.
    - instanceDetails: This contains additional detailed information about the tModel.
- overviewDoc: This contains the URL for the service implementation document. For example, if a procurement service has a purchasingInterface.WSDL and an implementation document called purchasingAcmeCo.WSDL, the former will be referenced by the tModel, whereas the latter containing the implementation details will be referenced through a URL as the value of this overviewDoc element in tModelInstanceInfo.

3.3.7 Classification Schemes

The previous section demonstrated that three element types—businessEntity, businessService, and tModel—have category bags.[13] These category bags provide a mechanism for classifying the service offering using one or more of the available industry classification schemes.

Therefore, classification schemes can be used to categorize a number of elements in UDDI registries. These entries are business entities, business services and tModels. There are three main classification schemes: North American Industry Classification Scheme (NAICS), United Nation's Standard Products and Services Code (UNSPSC), and ISO 3166.

- NAICS[14] was created jointly by the United States, Canada, and Mexico. The classification scheme is a follow-up and revision of the Standard Industrial Classification (SIC) code scheme developed in the 1930s. NAICS provides a six-digit code, organized as shown in Table 3.1. Examples of two-digit industry sectors include 21 for Mining, 22 for Utilities, 51 for Information, and 61 for Education services.
- UNSPSC[15] was developed by the United Nations Development Programme in 1998. The UNSPSC is similar to NAICS in that it categorizes various industry sectors. The UNSPSC uses four pairs of

Table 3.1 NAICS Classification Scheme

XX	Industry Sector (20 broad sectors up from 10 SIC)
XXX	Industry Subsection
XXXX	Industry Group
XXXXX	Industry
XXXXXX	U.S., Canadian, or Mexican National specific

numbers, separated by hyphens, representing Segment, Family, Class, and Commodity to identify products and services. For example, the number for Office Equipment segment is 44; Office Supplies is 12; Ink and Refills is 19; and Pen Refills is 03. So the multi-part UNSPSC code for Pen Refills code is 44-12-19-03.

- ISO 3166 is a set of international standards that contains codes for all the countries in the world.[16] The ISO 3166 classification scheme facilitates browsing UDDI registries to find businesses, services, and tModels by country. This geographical classification scheme supports two-letter, three-letter, and three-digit codes to describe each country. Table 3.2 shows examples of ISO 3166 codes for several countries.

Table 3.2 Example of ISO 3166 Country Codes

Country	*Two-letter code*	*Three-letter code*	*Three-digit code*
Afghanistan	AF	AFG	004
Albania	AL	ALB	008
Algeria	DZ	DZA	012
American Samoa	AS	ASM	016
Andorra	AD	AND	020
Angola	AO	AGO	024
Anguilla	AI	AIA	660
Antarctica	AQ	ATA	010
Antigua and Barbuda	AG	ATG	028
Argentina	AR	ARG	032
Armenia	AM	ARM	051
Aruba	AW	ABW	533
Australia	AU	AUS	036

3.3.8 Business Identifiers

The previous section discussed the categorization schemes supported in UDDI registries. These are used in category bags for the service, binding template, and tModel elements. UDDI also supports identification schemes, which are used in identifier bags for business entities and tModels. UDDI registries must have a way of uniquely identifying every business listed in the registry. As noted earlier, these business identifiers are shown in the White Pages of the registry. This section discusses two commonly used schemes for identification (although many others that could be used in conjunction with UDDI registries): the DUNS and the Thomas Register schemes. Others include tax identifiers, and Global Location Numbers.[17]

- DUNS number: Perhaps the most popular business identifier is the Dun & Bradstreet Data Universal Numbering System number.[18] This is a standardized, nine-digit numbering sequence that is used to identify more than 70 billion businesses worldwide. Some government and private projects require that potential bidders have a DUNS number.
- Thomas Register ID: Another business identifier used by UDDI registries is the Thomas Register ID. DUNS provides identifiers for businesses all around the world. Thomas Register IDs are for Canadian and U.S. companies. There are approximately 173,000 companies and 152,000 brand names in the Thomas Register of American Manufacturers.[19] The Thomas Register organizes companies through a taxonomy of product catalogs. There are about 8,000 online catalogs in the Thomas Register.

3.3.9 Accessing UDDI Registries through SOAP Exchanges

The previous examples focused on UDDI registries accessed through Web browsers. UDDI registries also can be accessed through SOAP application program interface (API) exchanges, as illustrated in Figure 3.4.

Following are descriptions of the operations for finding businesses, services, and tModels in a UDDI registry:[20]

- find_binding: This element can find a binding—as in binding templates—within a service. It returns a bindingDetail element.
- find_business: This element can find businesses and return them in a businessList.
- find_relatedBusinesses: The business entity is a parameter to this call. It returns a list of business that are related to the given business entity.

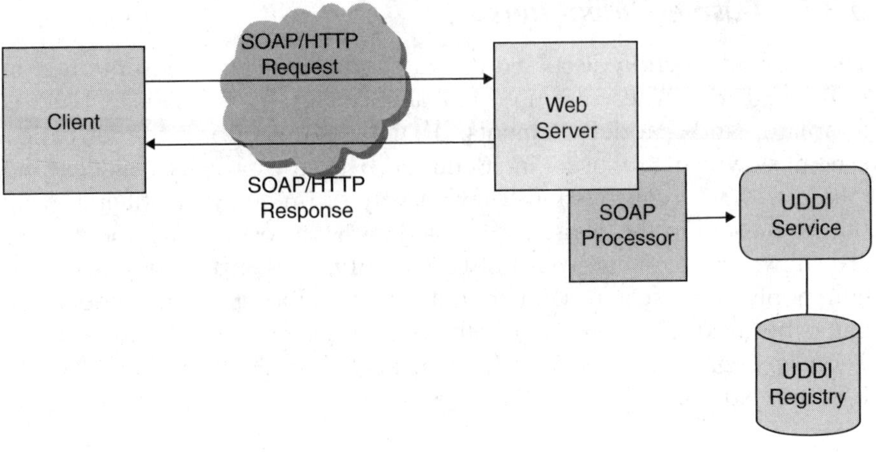

Figure 3.4 Accessing UDDI registry through SOAP

- find_service: This is used to find business services in a business entity. It returns a list of services.
- find_tModel: This is used to find and return technical models. It returns a list of technical models.

Once a business, service, or technical model is found in the registry, the user can then pass the key and obtain detailed information about binding templates, businesses, and services through the following API calls: get_bindingDetail, get_businessDetail, get_serviceDetail, get_tModelDetail.

There are operations for publishing, including the following calls for updating, saving, and adding UDDI elements: add_publisherAssertions, save_binding, save_business, save_service.

There are also operations for deleting UDDI entries, including the following: delete_binding, delete_business, delete_publisherAssertions, delete_service, delete_tModel, discard_authToken.

In addition to finding and getting details of UDDI entries, the specification also includes a publishing WSDL. The availability of the UDDI WSDLs means that many applications can access the UDDI registries programmatically. For instance, searches can be automated, and other interactive development tools can publish to UDDI registries from within their platforms. In short, UDDI WSDLs and their support via UDDI registries means that discovery and publishing of services are not restricted to browser interfaces but are available to any program that can invoke Web services. It also enables UDDI entries to be searched and updated dynamically.

3.4 Service Description: WSDL

IT: This section focuses on WSDL 1.2, although there is a more recent version, WSDL 2.0. The WSDL 1.1/1.2 versions have been around for a while, and many more definitions and tools can be found to support WSDL 1.2 than 2.0. WSDL 2.0 has introduced a number of significant enhancements. In the services interface or abstract service definition component, WSDL 2.0 introduces the notion of an interface, which combines a number of operations and the signature (messages) of these operations. So an interface contains a number of operations. Also interfaces can inherit from one another. WSDL 2.0 also makes explicit message exchange patterns (MEPs). For example MEPs can include In-Out, In-Only, Out-Only, as well as other combinations of sending and receiving messages. There are other extensions introduced in WSDL 2.0 that are described in: http://www.w3.org/TR/2004/WD-wsdl20-20040803/, http://www.w3.org/TR/2004/WD-wsdl20-extensions-20040803/, and http://www.w3.org/TR/2004/WD-wsdl20-bindings-20040803/.

Web Services Description Language is used to describe Web services. Clients and users of Web services will use the service descriptions in WSDL to create client proxies that access the service of the provider. The provider defines the operations (i.e., what is the service), the binding (i.e., how to access the service), and the endpoints (i.e., where to access the service) all in the WSDL document.

WSDL allows the messages and the operations for accessing services to be defined independently of the physical implementation and technical details, which is important. In the previous generation of service architectures and service interactions, such as CORBA or J2EE, there was not such a clear separation of the definition of the services from the physical implementations that WSDL achieves.

WSDL is important because it provides a self-describing, precise description of the location, binding, and operations of the Web services. More generally, WSDL schema provides the what, the how, and the where of Web services:

- What operations are supported by the Web service: similar to Interface Description Language (IDL) and interfaces in Java.

Table 3.3 Main Elements of WSDL

WSDL Elements (WSDL 1.1)	*Function*
Types	Define the input and out parameter types of operations; used in messages
Message	Specify the input and output parameters of operations. Messages have names and can have multiple parts.
PortType	A collection of operations
Operations	Use messages for their input and output parameters. Operations are Web services methods.
Binding	Specify how the operations of portTypes will be invoked
Port	A specific invocation endpoint, containing the address (the *where*) of the service
Service	A collection of endpoints

- How these operations are invoked: WSDL goes beyond mere specification of the interfaces and also specifies the serialized messages structures over the wire. Based on binding values specified in WSDL, the service requestor will send the request message in specific formats.
- Where: the location or port of the service.

WSDL is detailed and precise enough to allow the generation of client proxies from the WSDL file and to invoke the Web service's operations. As are all Web services standards, WSDL is in XML and hence is independent of any specific programming language or programmatic binding. WSDL only specifies the SOAP binding properties. As long as the call complies with the SOAP binding, the service will respond according to the operation's expected message response specifications. Table 3.3 illustrates the main elements of WSDL. The relationships among the various elements of WSDL are illustrated in Figure 3.5.

IT: WSDL 2.0 has cleaned up especially the separation between the abstract and binding parts of WSDL. WSDL 2.0 brings us much closer to a component-based service description. The specification has three parts: core specification, MEP, and bindings.

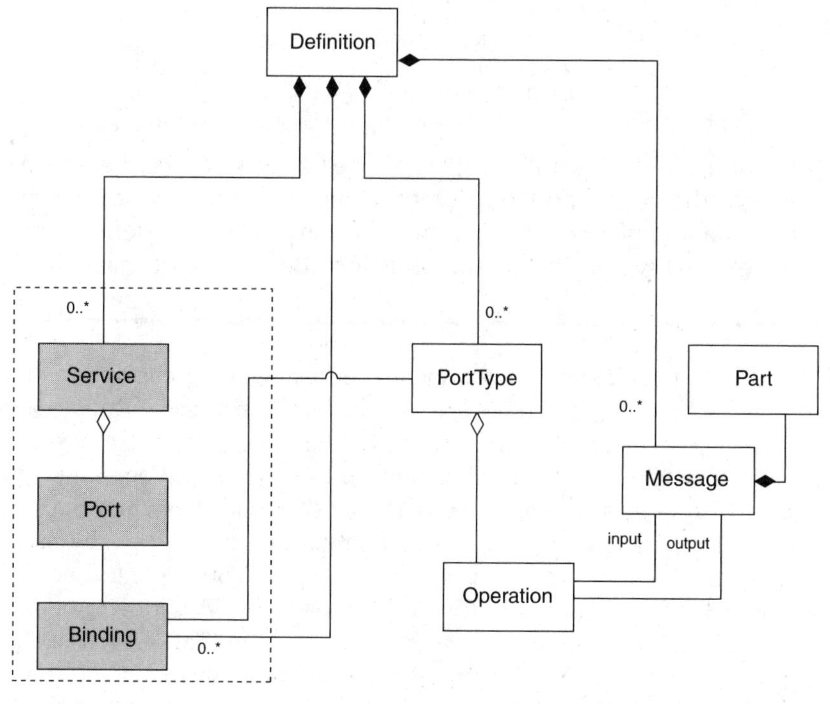

Figure 3.5 WSDL metamodel: relationships among WSDL elements

1. The core specification uses clearer constructs such as <type> and <interface> to define abstraction independent of protocol or the encoding, so <portType> does not exist anymore.

2. Interfaces can also inherit (object-oriented inheritance) from other interfaces. The interface that inherits extends the interface operations of its parent (through additional operations).

3. In interfaces <operations> are defined, which describe the signature as well as the MEP (e.g., In-Out).

4. The messages within operations are defined through types. It is cleaner and simpler than WSDL 1.1. These are not separate <part> and <message> elements. The types of the parameters of the operations are just specified within the operation element as follows (from the WSDL 2.0 Primer):[21]

```
<operation name="opCheckAvailability"
           pattern="http://www.w3.org/2005/05/wsdl/in-out"
           style="http://www.w3.org/2005/05/wsdl/style/uri"
           safe = "true">
```

```
        <input messageLabel="In"
               element="ghns:checkAvailability" />
        <output messageLabel="Out"
               element="ghns:checkAvailabilityResponse" />
  </operation>
```

The pattern indicates an in-out exchange pattern. Notice that there are only the input and output message and their types—both checkAvailability and checkAvailabilityResponse are defined as complex XSD types. The operation is included in an interface.

The WSDL specification is a bit unconventional when compared to other programming language definitions of operations or methods. Unlike other languages, WSDL first allows the user to define, or import, the types—that is, the types of input and output parameters of the operations. Then the user creates messages independent of operations, and these messages are then used in operations. In most programming languages, operations are defined with formal parameters referencing types. The separate message definition, which corresponds to formal parameter specification, is not used. The advantage of using messages as separate objects in WSDL is reusability.

Types, ports, messages, portTypes and operations within portTypes all provide the definition (i.e., what) of the various operations supported by the Web service. The operations contain operation names and input-output message parameters. Each message contains one or more parts, and each part has a part name and a type.

For the concrete elements—those that describe the how and where—services consist of ports. Bindings reference the operations in the abstract interface definitions and provide specifications such as SOAP binding, the style of the binding, and additional details pertaining to the serialized messages that get communicated over the wire.

The binding, or serialization and transformation of messages, does not have to be carried out only via SOAP over HTTP. It can be handled via SOAP over Simple Mail Transfer Protocol (SMTP) or even HTTP with GET methods. Furthermore, different ports of the service can use different bindings.

3.4.1 Client and Server Processes for WSDL

The overall usage and involvement of WSDL in Web services and its relationship to other Web services standards addressing registration, discovery, and request/response is illustrated in Figure 3.7. As the figure shows, the service provider can either publish the WSDL on a Web site, send the WSDL to its partners (e.g., via e-mail), or register the service with

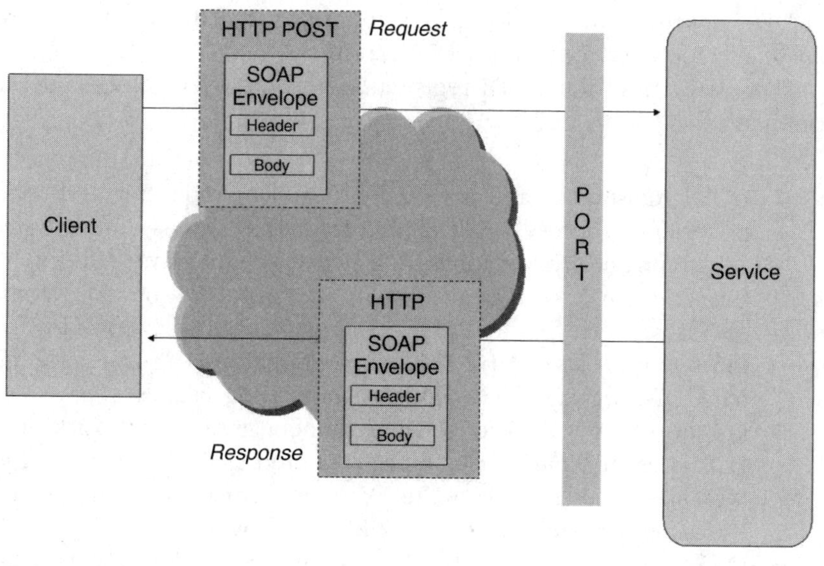

Figure 3.6 SOAP request and response over HTTP

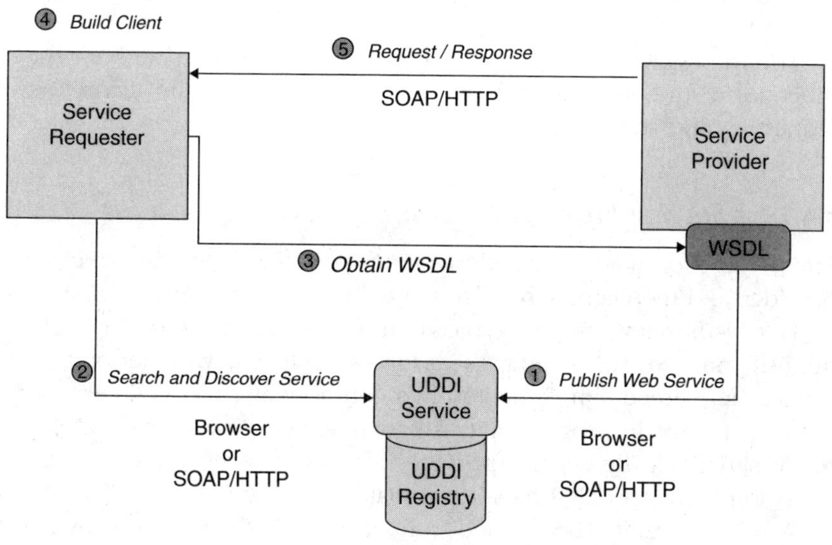

Figure 3.7 Relationship of WSDL to other Web services standards

a UDDI registry. If the service is registered at a UDDI site, the requestor can search for a service in the UDDI registry.

Three aspects of the UDDI registration and discovery process deserve comment:

- UDDI registration and search: The services requestor and service provider can access the UDDI registry in three ways—through SOAP, programmatically, or through a browser. The Java API for XML Registries (JAXR) can be used to register services. The requestor can also access the registry either programmatically (e.g., via JAXR) or through a browser. Most Web services platforms also provide internal UDDI registries, typically built on top of databases.
- Location of WSDL: The WSDL document itself is not stored in the UDDI registry; rather, it is typically stored at the service provider's Web site, accessible via a URL. Various elements and entries in the UDDI registry can contain the URL of the WSDL.
- Other mechanisms for communicating WSDL: Most discussions of WSDL and UDDI leave the impression that UDDI is needed to communicate the WSDL and that discovery always happens via a UDDI registry. This is not the case. Many companies know their trading partners and can directly access the WSDL. For instance, they could easily send the WSDL via e-mail or available authentication, or log-in accounts.

The following sections explore the processes involved in Web services description and invocation from the perspective of the client (service requestor) and server (service provider).

3.4.1.1 Service Provider Process

The process for generating and invoking the WSDL from the server/service provider and the client/service requestor is shown in Figure 3.8.

Here is how the process typically flows: A service provider decides to publish some services. The provider must determine whether or not these services are already implemented in a component, such as Enterprise Java Beans (EJB), or in programming language classes, such as C# or Java. In many situations the service provider already has the classes or components implemented; all it must do is make these available as Web services. So WSDLs can either be defined from scratch, or the service provider can generate the WSDL from existing classes or components.

Web services platforms typically support the component-to-WSDL generation module. A number of development tools[22] support editing of WSDL

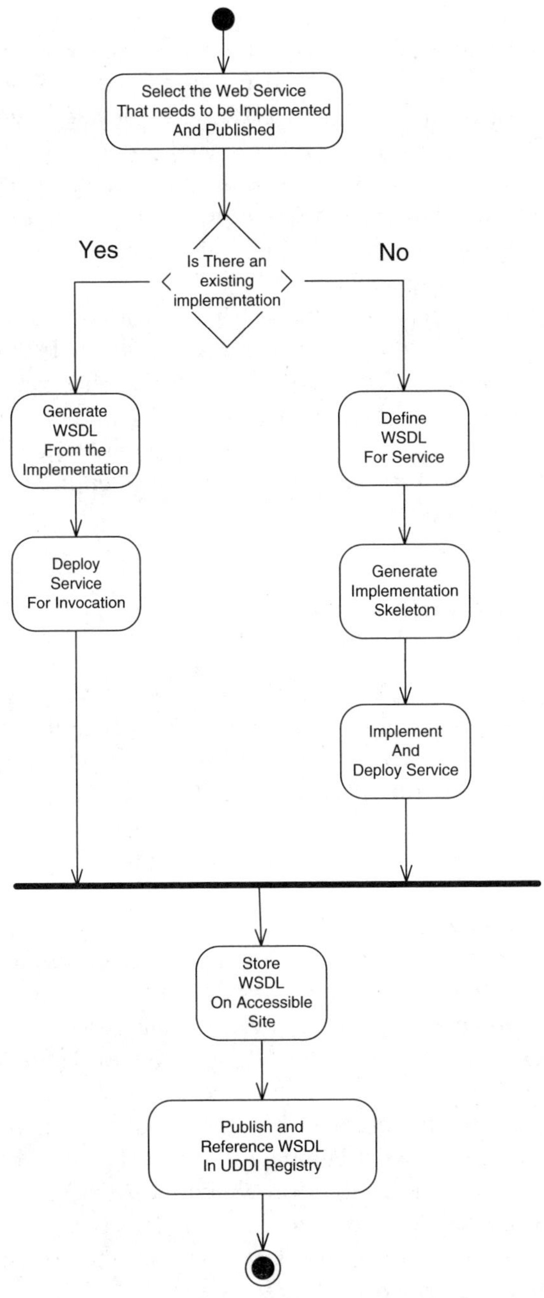

Figure 3.8 Invoking WSDL from the server/service provider and client/service requestor

documents and provide the automatic generation of WSDL from existing components. Using these tools, developers are able to design and edit the WSDL through easy-to-use graphical interfaces. These WSDL editors are becoming essential components in Web services development and deployment.

If the WSDL is new, the Web services development platform typically generates a skeleton for the service code in a target programming language or component. The service provider must then provide the detailed implementation and deploy the service.

After the service is deployed, the service provider must ensure that the WSDL is available. This could be accomplished through direct communication of the WSDL or via the URL of the WSDL that gets stored in the service provider's Web site. The service provider can then publish the Web service in one or more UDDI registries and can provide the URL of its WSDL to these registry entries. Typically this is done through the technical model, or tModel, of the service.

3.4.1.2 Service Requestor Process

The previous section discussed the service provider's process to generate and publish the WSDL. This section discusses the overall service requestor's process for searching, locating, and obtaining the WSDL and then invoking the service providers. The overall methodology of service discovery was touched on in Chapter 2. It needs to be reemphasized that invoking a service typically does involve some work on behalf of the service consumer. The client activity diagram (i.e., the process) is illustrated in Figure 3.9.

The service requestor first obtains the WSDL, which is done either through a URL from the technical model or description of the service in the UDDI registry or from a trading partner. Note that the Web services request/response is independent of the underlying operating system platforms, the application servers, or the implementation language of the service. This is crucial. As far as the service requestor is concerned, the communication is via the binding protocol specified in the WSDL; the requestor does not know what language the actual service is implemented in, or the type of application server on which the service is deployed. Both are hidden from the service requestor. The WSDL contract guarantees that once a request is sent to the appropriate port with the correct binding, the service provider will respond to the requests.

Once the service requestor gets the WSDL, in the vast majority of the cases a Web services development tool is used to generate a client proxy. The client proxy provides a programmatic API to the service. Thus service requestors can access the service using their preferred programming language

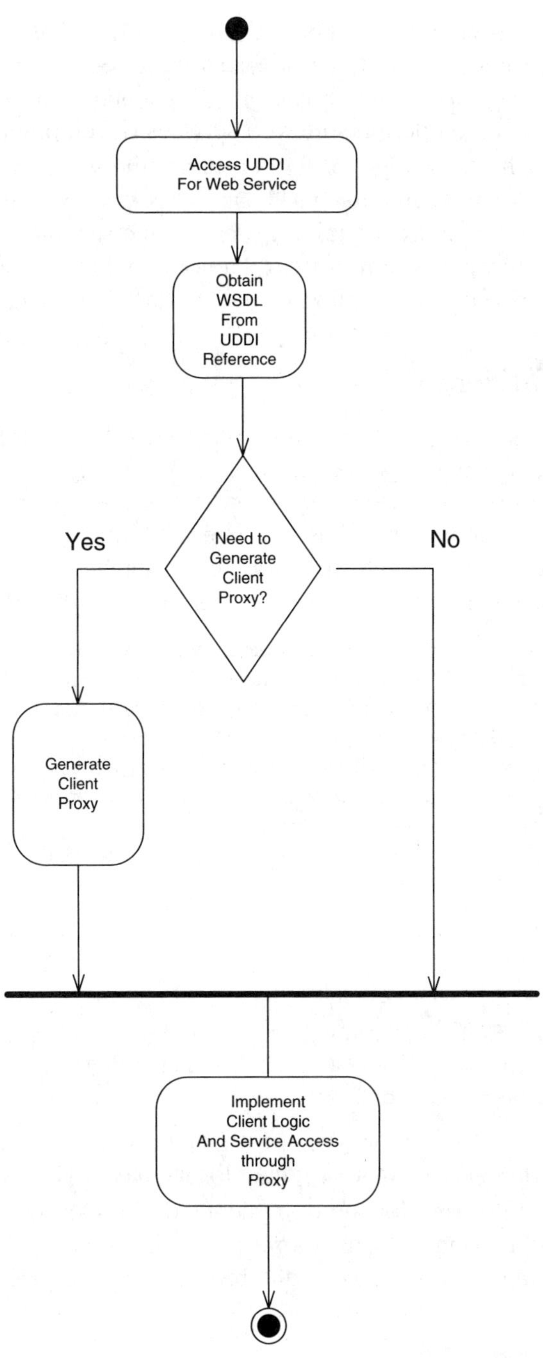

Figure 3.9 Service requestor process

(e.g., Java, C#, Visual Basic). There could even be a thin client tier that invokes the client proxy—using a servlet or Java Server Pages (JSP), for instance. The other option is to have a rich client that accesses the Web service via calls to the client proxy.

In rare cases, the client might prefer to generate the Web service call directly, without a client proxy programming API. Direct generation means, for instance, that the SOAP for the service request is generated and sent directly from a client program. This direct generation process is an option, but the process could be error prone. The client proxy option is much more convenient.

3.4.2 <definitions>

Now that the previous section discussed WSDL metamodel, this and the following sections go deeper into the specific elements of WSDL, beginning with the top-level root element of a WSDL, namely the <definitions> element.

The element <definitions> has a name attribute of type nmtoken, a targetnamespace of type uniform resource identifier (URI), and may also include additional namespace declarations, as shown in this simple example:

```
<definitions xmlns="http://schemas.xmlsoap.org/wsdl/"
xmlns:soap="http://schemas.xmlsoap.org/wsdl/soap/"
xmlns:http="http://schemas.xmlsoap.org/wsdl/http/"
xmlns:xs="http://www.w3.org/2001/XMLSchema"
xmlns:soapenc="http://schemas.xmlsoap.org/soap/encoding/"
xmlns:mime="http://schemas.xmlsoap.org/wsdl/mime/"
xmlns:y="http://new.webservice.namespace"
targetNamespace="http://new.webservice.namespace">
  <types>
   <xs:schema/>
  </types>
  <message name="messageName"/>
  <portType name="typeName"/>
  <binding name="bindingName" type="y:typeName"/>
  <service name="serviceName"/>
</definitions>
```

Using the <definitions> element, the WSDL namespace can be declared as the default namespace for the document. All the elements in the WSDL document will belong to this namespace unless they have another namespace definition and hence a different namespace prefix.

3.4.3 <import>

The <import> element references the URI or location of other XML Schema Definition (XSD) documents containing definitions. This allows the user to define a schemata separately and then use it within WSDL, such as in defining messages.

Following is an example of an import of customer.xsd:

```
<import
location="http://www.acme.com/schemas/
  customer.xsd"
namespace="http://www.acme.com/schemas"/>
```

3.4.4 <type>

Complex and other types can be defined within the <type> element. These types are then used in messages. WSDL uses the XML Schema type system, so XSD types can be defined within the <type> element. More specifically, the types element contains a <schema> element which in turn contains the type definitions.

Following is an example of a student type:

```
<xsd:schema>
  <xsd:complexType name="StudentType">
     <xsd:sequence>
        <xsd:element maxOccurs="1" minOccurs="0" name="ID"
          type="xsd:string"/>
        <xsd:element maxOccurs="1" minOccurs="0" name="Name"
          type="xsd:string"/>
     </xsd:sequence>
  </xsd:complexType>
</xsd:schema>
```

3.4.5 <message>

Messages consist of one or more parts, which reference the types. Messages are defined by a name and are used in the definition of an operation's input and output. The WSDL specification allows for defining messages independent from operations.

Following are examples of three messages: IDofStudent, Name, and Student:

```
<message name="IDofStudent">
  <part name="ID" type="xsd:string"/>
</message>
<message name="Name">
  <part name="name" type="xsd:string"/>
</message>
<message name="Student">
  <part name="student" type="xsd3:StudentType"/>
</message>
```

A <message> can contain zero or more <part> elements. The <parts> are the formal parameters and will be used for the input or return value of the Web service call.

3.4.6 <operation>

The <message> elements named and defined in a WSDL document are then used in operations. An operation can have a number of input messages and an output message. In WSDL a message represents a parameter of the operation. Operations are defined through the <operation> element. Therefore <message> elements are used within operations, which are then listed in port types.

There are four types of operations: request/response, solicit/response, one-way communication from the client, and notification.

Request/response. This is by far the most common type of operation. It includes an input message where the argument value will be provided by the service requestor, and an output message, where the argument value will be provided by the service provider. Following is a simple example of a request/response operation. In this example, the operation is requesting more detailed information about a student. The name of the student is an input parameter. The output is an XML message that contains the student information; in addition to name, it will include elements such as student ID and major:

```
<operation name="getStudentByName">
       <input message="tns:Name"/>
       <output message="tns:Student"/>
</operation>
```

Solicit/Response: In this operation, the request/response interaction order is reversed. The service requestor solicits a response and the service provides the response.

One-way communication from client: In situations where the client does not need a response, a one-way communication can be used with only an input message.

Notification: In this operation, the service endpoint simply sends a message to a client.

The <operation> element also has a parameterOrder, which specifies the order in which these parameters should appear in the messages. The parameters pertain to the input message. As noted earlier, messages have parts. The parameterOrder specifies the order in which these parts appear in the remote procedure call (RPC). For example, following is a simple message:

```
<wsdl:message name="getSchedulesByCourseRequest">
  <wsdl:part name="in0" type="xsd:int"/>
  <wsdl:part name="in1" type="xsd:int"/>
</wsdl:message>
```

Following is an operation that specifies the order in which the parameters should appear:

```
<wsdl:operation name="getSchedulesByCourse" parameterOrder="in0
  in1">
    <wsdl:input message="intf:getSchedulesByCourseRequest"
name="getSchedulesByCourseRequest"/>
    <wsdl:output message="intf:getSchedulesByCourseResponse"
name="getSchedulesByCourseResponse"/>
    </wsdl:operation>
```

As this example illustrates, the parameters appear in an order, separated by spaces.

3.4.7 <portType>

PortTypes capture the abstract interface definition of a Web service. They are similar to interface definitions in object-oriented systems. PortTypes contain the operation as child elements. As noted earlier, each operation can have input and output messages.

Following is an example of a portType:

```
<portType name="studentPortType">
  <operation name="getStudentByID">
    <input message="tns:IDofStudent"/>
    <output message="tns:Student"/>
  </operation>
  <operation name="getStudentByName">
    <input message="tns:Name"/>
    <output message="tns:Student"/>
  </operation>
</portType>
```

3.4.8 Binding

PortType definitions specify *abstractly* what the Web service operations are. WSDL, which is completely self-describing, also provides specifications of how and where to access the Web services. The services and port elements specify the where; the binding element specifies the how.

Bindings specify the details of the protocol for message exchanges and operations. These are the protocols for the portTypes and their operations and messages. The protocols can be either SOAP (SOAP over HTTP, SOAP over SMTP) or HTTP GET/POST.

3.4.9 SOAP binding

As indicated in the previous example, the binding specifies how messages must be invoked. The <soap:binding> element indicates that the binding is bound to the SOAP protocol format: envelope, header, and body.

The SOAP binding can specify a transport attribute and style. The most popular option for transport is HTTP. Style is discussed in the next section. Here is an example of binding:

```
<soap:binding transport='http://schemas.xmlsoap.org/soap/http'
style='document'/>
```

3.4.9.1 Styles

The binding example of the previous paragraph indicates the document style. This is one of two styles; the other is RPC. The document style indicates that the message contains an XML document and does not involve the signature wrapping of the invoked operation as it does in the RPC style. Document is the default style and is specified for the binding. As noted earlier, the binding contains the operations and additional constraints in the <soap:operation> elements, such as assuming a <soap:binding>. These operations can override the style specified in the binding element. Thus, the binding element might specify the document style, and one or more operations can override it with RPC style.

The RPC style is a remote procedure call with parameters, typically returning a value. The RPC style will include elements for the signature of the operation that gets sent over the wire. It includes the parameters as sub-elements of the operation element.

3.4.9.2 <soap:operation>

The <soap:operation> element is included in the <operation> element. SOAPAction appears in the HTTP part. It can be used by the server to identify the service—through its value or the URI. For the HTTP protocol binding of SOAP, a value must be specified. For other SOAP protocol bindings, it need not be specified.

The <soap:operation> also can specify the style for the particular operation, as follows:

```
<soap:operation soapAction="uri"? style="rpc|document"?>?
```

This will override the style of the soap message for the particular operation.

3.4.9.3 <soap:body>

The <soap:body> element specifies how to combine the different message parts that appear inside the body element of the SOAP message and is used with RPC as well as with document messages. As indicated, it contains:

```
<soap:body parts="nmtokens"? use="literal|encoded"
         encodingStyle="uri-list"? namespace="uri"?>
```

Recall that part elements in messages have types attributes. So some XSD types—complex types—could be used in messages. As noted earlier, these messages are the input and output parameters. When the use is encoded, it means the message parts are referencing abstract types, which are the types attributes for the parts elements defined for the message. These abstract types are made concrete through using the specific encoding style (e.g., SOAP for example).

Encoding is about serializing and sending the message over the wire. If the encoding is literal, the types that are mentioned in the WSDL actually represent concrete types and the instances, or specific SOAP messages will follow these types literally. These are easiest to understand, and many WSDL editors use literal as the default. The encoding type can have a list of URIs for the encodings used with the message (e.g., SOAP encoding).

3.4.9.4 SOAP Encoding

One of the more complex and confusing aspects of SOAP is the SOAP encoding scheme. An operation or message can be literal, or it can use an encoding scheme. Specifically, message types—types of the parts—defined in the WSDL could be either concrete (i.e., the literal option) or encoded, using SOAP encoding—the most popular scheme used to serialize operations.

There are actually four choices for concrete or encoded operations and messages (documents): (1) RPC/encoded, (2) RPC/literal, (3) Document/encoded (which is rarely used), and (4) Document/literal. RPC/literal and Document/literal are WS-I compliant. SOAP encoding uses XML Schema for the datatypes of the elements but has its own encoding rules. SOAP encoding supports simple values of simple types (e.g., long, int, short, float, double, short, date, time—all the primitive types of XML Schema). These primitive types are used for simple values. In complex structures, SOAP encoding uses array and struct for compound values.[23]

The rules for SOAP encoding can be summarized as follows:

- The values in the serialized message are element contents, not attributes. So the following, for instance, would not be correct: <grade value="A" />
- The simple values are character data.

- As noted already, compound values can be arrays or structs.
- Arrays can be multidimensional. As in programming languages, arrays are specified and accessed through ordinal positions. The type of array can be specified, as in the following example, which specifies an array of grades element:

```
<element name="arrayOfGrades">
<complexType base="SOAP-ENC:Array">
      <element name="grade" type="xsd:int" maxOccurs=
        "unbounded"/>
</complexType>
<xsd:anyAttribute namespace="##other" processContents=
 "strict"/>
</element>
```

  Here is an example of how arrayOfGrades could be used:

```
<arrayOfGrades SOAP-ENC:arrayType="xsd:int[2]">
     <grade>88</grade>
     <grade>90</grade>
</arrayOfGrades>
```

- For the struct, compound values are sequences of elements, with each element having a distinct element name.

```
<student xsi:type="s:studentType">
      <firstName xsi:type="xsd:string">John</firstName>
      <lastName xsi:type="xsd:string">Smith</lastName>
      <studentID xsi:type="xsd:integer">3245</studentID>
</hero>
```

SOAP encoding is particularly useful when you have cyclical references between objects.

3.5 SOAP

The SOAP protocol that is the focus of this section is the most important Web services core standard. The Simple Object Access Protocol supports distributed computing with XML by providing an effective mechanism for exchanging messages and accessing remote objects via XML. SOAP enables XML structures and typed messages to be exchanged between communicating client and server peers.

Figure 3.10 illustrates the central role of SOAP in the triangle of registering, discovering, and request/response interchanges. Even the discovery and registration of services is done through SOAP. The UDDI registry can

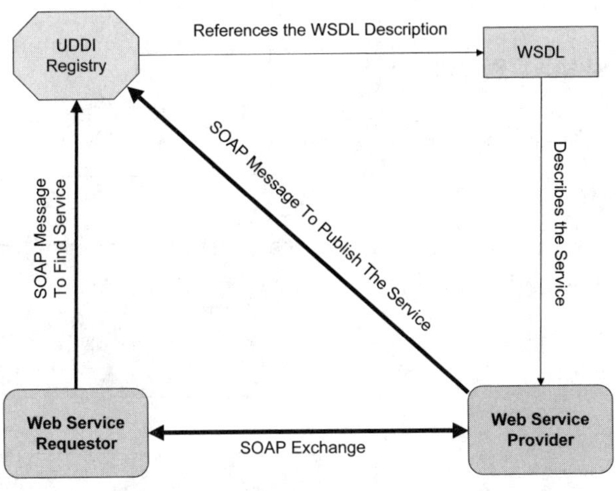

Figure 3.10 Role of SOAP in the publish, discover and request/response Web services triangle

have Web browser-based access, but its API is through XML messages in SOAP envelopes.

Assuming that HTTP is the transport, as illustrated in Figure 3.11, SOAP is the layer just above HTTP and other Internet transport protocols. SOAP messages are sent from requestor to provider for service requests. SOAP messages are also sent from provider to requestor for service responds. SOAP is therefore an XML message structure, and as we shall see it has its own XML schema.

Other than SOAP encoding, structure, and message typing, SOAP does not define a distributed object or application semantics. Distributed enterprise structures can be built on top of SOAP or using SOAP. Think of SOAP as an essential building block that allows heterogeneous systems pertaining to different object or component models to communicate with each other.

There is a great deal of flexibility—too much flexibility, some would argue—in using SOAP and building distributed computing models and remote procedure semantics with SOAP messaging. Flexibility is a double-edged sword. On the one hand, it provides distributed application developers with a lot of power. They can easily build their favorite extensions to SOAP and remain compliant with the core SOAP standard. On the other hand, this means different enterprises or organizations will invariably make their own extensions. The WS-I is attempting to bring some order to the potentially chaotic proliferation of incompatible extensions. In the meantime, the dangers of creating a tower of babble in the SOAP extension layer remains.

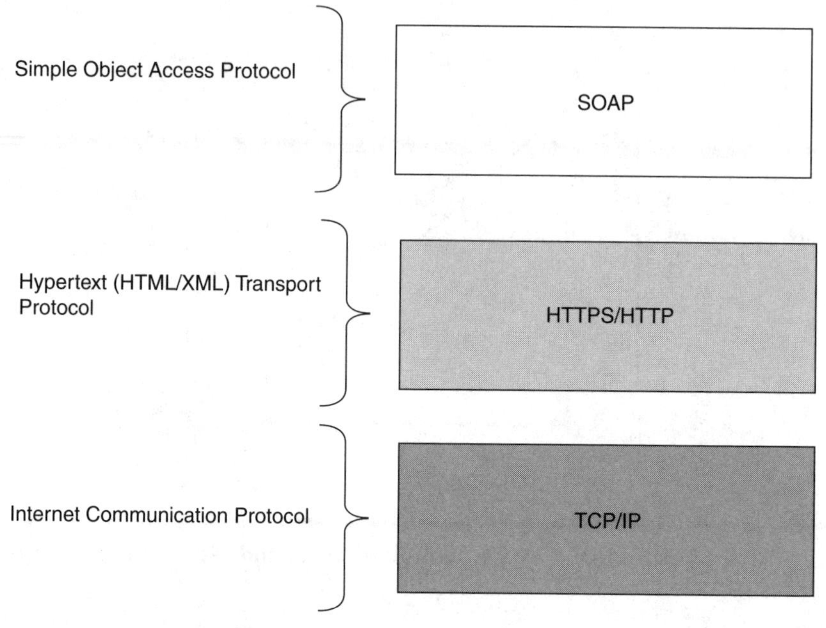

Figure 3.11 SOAP layer

There are several interesting examples on XMethods. One of the more popular examples is getting the 20-minute delayed stock quote values. For example, the following service[24] provides the quote for a symbol:

```
<message name="getQuoteResponse1">
  <part name="Result" type="xsd:float" />
    </message>
<message name="getQuoteRequest1">
  <part name="symbol" type="xsd:string" />
    </message>
<portType name="net.xmethods.services.stockquote.StockQuotePortType">
<operation name="getQuote" parameterOrder="symbol">
  <input message="tns:getQuoteRequest1" />
  <output message="tns:getQuoteResponse1" />
    </operation>
```

```
</portType>
```

The service could be called for a specific symbol such as "IBM" as in:

```
<soap:Envelope xmlns:mrns0="urn:xmethods-delayed-quotes"
xmlns:soap="http://schemas.xmlsoap.org/soap/envelope/"
xmlns:soapenc="http://schemas.xmlsoap.org/soap/encoding/"
xmlns:xs="http://www.w3.org/2001/XMLSchema"
xmlns:xsi="http://www.w3.org/2001/XMLSchema-instance">
  <soap:Body soap:encodingStyle="http://schemas.xmlsoap.org/
  soap/encoding/">
    <mrns0:getQuote>
      <symbol xsi:type="xs:string">IBM</symbol>
    </mrns0:getQuote>
  </soap:Body>
</soap:Envelope>
```

And the response:

```
<?xml version='1.0' encoding='UTF-8'?>
<soap:Envelope xmlns:soap='http://schemas.xmlsoap.org/soap/enve-
lope/' xmlns:xsi='http://www.w3.org/2001/XMLSchema-instance'
xmlns:xsd='http://www.w3.org/2001/XMLSchema' xmlns:soap-
enc='http://schemas.xmlsoap.org/soap/encoding/' soap:encoding-
Style='http://schemas.xmlsoap.org/soap/encoding/'>
<soap:Body>
<n:getQuoteResponse xmlns:n='urn:xmethods-delayed-quotes'>
 <Result xsi:type='xsd:float'>81.57</Result>
</n:getQuoteResponse>
</soap:Body>
</soap:Envelope>
```

Other services could be called subsequent to the resulting stock quote price. One example is

```
<?xml version="1.0" encoding="UTF-8"?>
<soap:Envelope xmlns:mrns0="urn:xmethods-CurrencyExchange"
xmlns:soap="http://schemas.xmlsoap.org/soap/envelope/"
xmlns:soapenc="http://schemas.xmlsoap.org/soap/encoding/"
xmlns:xs="http://www.w3.org/2001/XMLSchema"
xmlns:xsi="http://www.w3.org/2001/XMLSchema-instance">
  <soap:Body soap:encodingStyle="http://schemas.xmlsoap.org/soap/
  encoding/">
    <mrns0:getRate>
      <country1 xsi:type="xs:string">US</country1>
      <country2 xsi:type="xs:string">CHINA</country2>
    </mrns0:getRate>
  </soap:Body>
</soap:Envelope>
```

Which will return

```
<?xml version='1.0' encoding='UTF-8'?>
<soap:Envelope xmlns:soap='http://schemas.xmlsoap.org/soap/enve-
lope/' xmlns:xsi='http://www.w3.org/2001/XMLSchema-instance'
xmlns:xsd='http://www.w3.org/2001/XMLSchema' xmlns:soap-
enc='http://schemas.xmlsoap.org/soap/encoding/' soap:encoding-
Style='http://schemas.xmlsoap.org/soap/encoding/'>
  <soap:Body>
      <n:getRateResponse xmlns:n='urn:xmethods-CurrencyExchange'>
           <Result xsi:type='xsd:float'>8.0505</Result>
      </n:getRateResponse>
  </soap:Body>
</soap:Envelope>
```

These services can be composed and called in a sequence as illustrated in the figure—which is the essence of service orchestration discussed in Chapter 5.

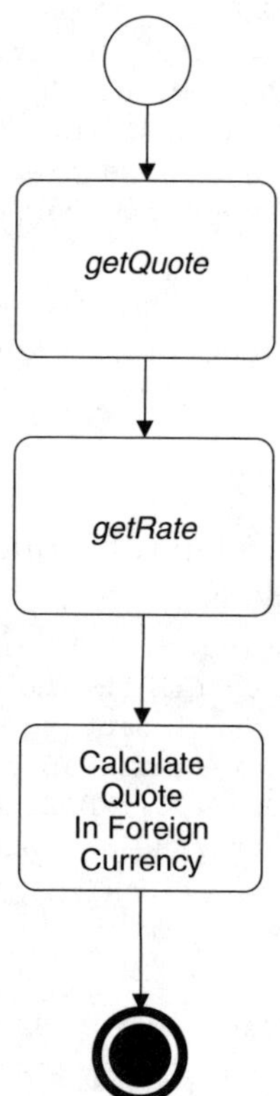

The last task is not really a service but a calculation of the quote in the foreign currency: 656.68 Yuans.

3.5.1 Overview of SOAP Elements and Message Structure

The overall structure of a SOAP message is rather simple. The message has an envelope, and this envelope contains an optional header and a mandatory body. The actual requests and responses of Web services invocations will be contained within the body element of the SOAP message. The SOAP message structure is shown in Figure 3.12.

As Figure 3.12 illustrates, SOAP consists of four XML elements. Two of these elements are mandatory; the other two are optional:

- **env:Envelope** As illustrated, the envelope is the root of all SOAP requests and responses. Every SOAP message must have an envelope and body. Among other attributes, it provides the SOAP namespace (e.g. http://www.w3.org/2003/05/soap-envelope/)[25] as well as other namespaces.
- **env:Header** This element is optional. It can contain additional information that can be understood by the requestor and service provider. Some examples include security or authentication elements, transactional information, and routing information.
- **env:Body** This is the other mandatory element, and it contains the main message. The body is used both for the request and the response. The body contains the main information in one or more SOAP blocks. An example would be a SOAP block for RPC.
- **env:Fault** When there is an error or a fault in the SOAP request, the body element can contain a fault element, which contains protocol-level errors.

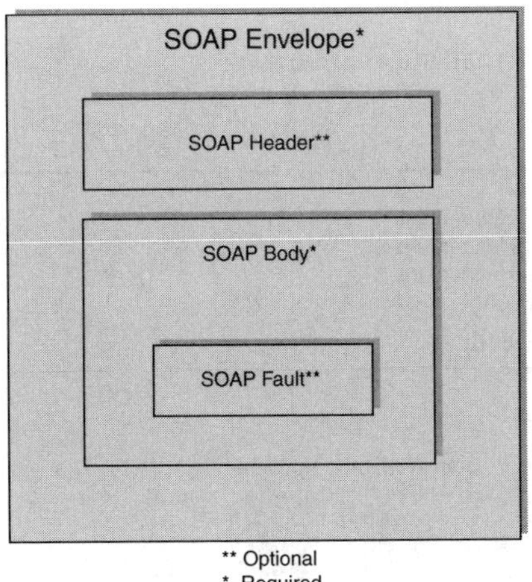

Figure 3.12 Structure of SOAP message

Each of these elements of SOAP messages is described in detail in Section 3.5.4. The current SOAP version is version 1.2, which became a recommendation in June of 2003.[26] In addition to SOAP 1.2, there is another version called "SOAP with Attachments."[27] As its name suggests, this version allows attachments such as faxes, images, and audio and video files to be attached to the SOAP message. Attachments allow nontext and nontagged documents to be included in the SOAP message as Multipurpose Internet Mail Extension (MIME) parts.

3.5.2 HTTP: The Leading SOAP Protocol

SOAP messages are in XML and can be validated with the SOAP schema specification. SOAP messages can be sent over any transport protocol, including JMS-compliant messaging middleware, file transfers, and e-mail attachments. However, by far the most popular SOAP transport protocol is the Hypertext Transfer Protocol.[28]

Increasingly, Internet architecture and protocols are providing the infrastructure for next-generation distributed object computing. Through its various technologies, the Internet is poised to support business-to-business transactions and electronic commerce. Web-based protocols—especially the HTTP protocol between browsers and Web servers—work remarkably well for static documents.

The structure of HTTP requests and responses is shown in Figure 3.13. The structure has three components: the HTTP start line and header lines, which are mandatory, and a body, which is optional.

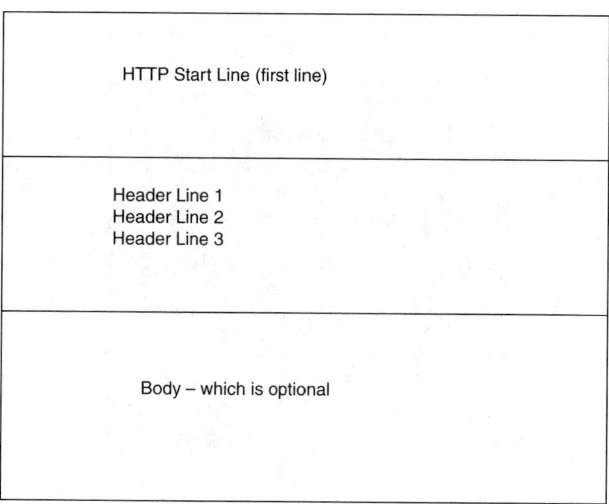

Figure 3.13 HTTP request, response structure

The HTTP Start line for requests includes the following information:

- The method (e.g., GET, POST, or HEAD)
- A path that designates the request URI. For example, if the file that needs to be retrieved from the host is /resumes, and the file is John.html, the path will be /resumes/John.html. This path is combined with the hostname for the request, to designate the eventual ultimate request.
- The protocol, which can be either HTTP/1.0 or HTTP/1.1

As an example in the following, GET is being used to retrieve UDDI version 3 features:

```
GET /pubs/uddi_v3_features.htm HTTP/1.0
Accept: image/gif, image/x-xbitmap, image/jpeg, image/pjpeg,
application/vnd.ms-excel, application/vnd.ms-powerpoint,
application/msword, */*
Referer: http://www.uddi.org/pubs/uddi_v3_features.htm
Accept-Language: en-us
Connection: Close
User-Agent: Mozilla/4.0 (compatible; MSIE 6.0; Windows NT 5.1;
Hotbar 4.1.8.0)
Host: uddi.org
```

The response to the request provides a response code and, if the request is valid, the requested HTML file. In most cases the desired response code is 200, which means OK (which means the response is valid). The GET request yields the following response (only part of the response is shown here).

```
[From Req: GET http://uddi.org/pubs/uddi_v3_features.htm HTTP/1.0]
HTTP/1.1 200 OK
Date: Tue, 22 Apr 2003 23:37:21 GMT
Server: Apache/2.0.40 (Unix) PHP/4.2.3
Last-Modified: Sat, 20 Jul 2002 03:19:14 GMT
ETag: "15b189-e2bc-89fd9080"
Accept-Ranges: bytes
Content-Length: 58044
Connection: close
Content-Type: text/html; charset=ISO-8859-1


[From Req: GET http://uddi.org/pubs/uddi_v3_features.htm HTTP/1.0]
<html>
```

```
<head>
<meta http-equiv=Content-Type content="text/html; charset=windows-
1252">
<meta name=Generator content="Microsoft FrontPage 5.0">
<title>UDDI Version 3 Features List</title>


<style> ….
```

The POST method can be used to send information or data to the server. This method is usually used in conjunction with forms in HTML pages. When the user completes a form, the data is sent to the server.

Following is an example of a POST request:

```
POST /search/search.aspx?frames=true&search=a911c860-f735-4ce5-
a70e-b83d51d52820 HTTP/1.0
Accept: image/gif, image/x-xbitmap, image/jpeg, image/pjpeg,
application/vnd.ms-excel, application/vnd.ms-powerpoint,
application/msword, */*
Referer:
http://uddi.microsoft.com/search/search.aspx?frames=true&search=
a911c860-f735-4ce5-a70e-b83d51d52820
Accept-Language: en-us
Content-Type: application/x-www-form-urlencoded
Connection: Close
User-Agent: Mozilla/4.0 (compatible; MSIE 6.0; Windows NT 5.1;
Hotbar 4.1.8.0)
Host: uddi.microsoft.com
Content-Length: 8489
Pragma: no-cache
Cookie:
MC1=HASH=7367&GUID=C2AE716F924945ED82727EB414FC209C&LV=20033&LCI
D=1033&V=3&LEVEL=3
```

Here is the response to the POST:

```
[From Req: POST
http://uddi.microsoft.com/search/search.aspx?frames=true&search=
a911c860-f735-4ce5-a70e-b83d51d52820 HTTP/1]
HTTP/1.1 200 OK
Connection: close
Date: Tue, 22 Apr 2003 23:07:58 GMT
Server: Microsoft-IIS/6.0
X-Powered-By: ASP.NET
X-AspNet-Version: 1.1.4322
Pragma: no-cache
Cache-Control: private
Expires: Tue, 22 Apr 2003 23:06:58 GMT
```

```
Content-Type: text/html; charset=utf-8
Content-Length: 15621
```

3.5.3 SOAP Architecture

Sections 3.5.1 and 3.5.2 provided an overview of SOAP message structure and HTTP,[29] the most popular transport protocol for SOAP. This section reviews the key components of the SOAP architecture.

In a SOAP message exchange, typically a client makes a request which goes over the wire via HTTP protocol. The request is fulfilled through an HTTP response.

How is the SOAP request generated? Typically programmers do not write SOAP messages. The client code is typically written in a host object-oriented language. A client proxy interface will be provided to the developer on the client side. The client code will invoke the remote service via this programming interface, as illustrated in Figure 3.14. The server side is also typically written in an object-oriented language. On the server side, the SOAP message is parsed and the appropriate server interface is invoked through an API.

This architecture provides tremendous flexibility in options of server and client programming languages. For instance, the client that calls the service can be written in Java. The server could just as well support C#, C++, or any other programming language. In fact, the service could be implemented as a component, such as an EJB component. Alternatively, the service could be invoked as a point-to-point message, through a messaging bus.

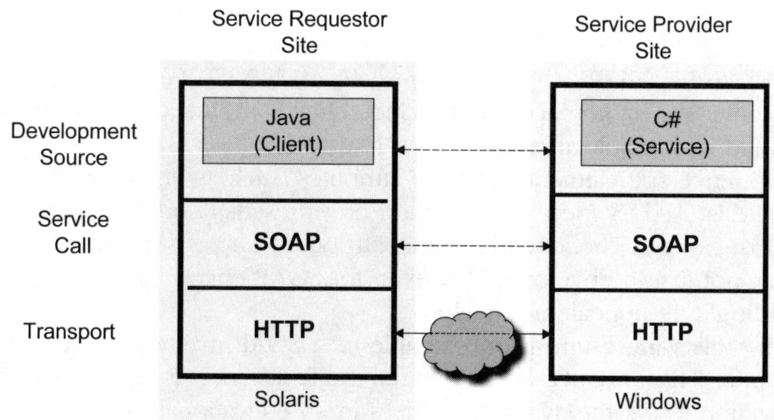

Figure 3.14 SOAP client request and SOAP response

3.5.4 SOAP Elements

This section provides a more detailed discussion of the essential SOAP elements: envelope, header, body, and faults.

3.5.4.1 SOAP Envelope

The Envelope is the root element of SOAP messages and is mandatory. The Envelope contains an optional Header element and a mandatory Body element. Following is the formal description of the Envelope, from the SOAP 1.2 standard:

- A [local name] of Envelope
- A [namespace name]
- Zero or more namespace qualified attribute information items among its [attributes] property
- One or two element information items in its [children] property in order as follows:
  - An optional Header element information item
  - A mandatory Body element information item

The term *element information item* comes from a different specification[30] called XML Information Set, which defines many types of information items and introduces terminology used in various XML standards.

The envelope namespace is http://www.w3.org/2001/12/soap-envelope. The xmlns namespace for envelope must include this namespace, as in this simple example:

```
<envns:Envelope
xmlns:envns="http://www.w3.org/2002/12/soap-envelope">
```

If the envelope namespace is not included in a SOAP message, the message is invalid and a fault message will be returned.

The Envelope element can have attributes, such as encodingStyle. This attribute is used to specify the method of representation of the data in the SOAP message. The encodingStyle attribute can appear in other elements, not just in envelope. However, for SOAP encoding, in most cases encodingStyle appears in envelope.

The following listing is an example of a SOAP message with the root envelope. This is a SOAP request for available courses in an e-learning application to get the available courses in an educational institution.

```
<?xml version="1.0" encoding="UTF-8"?>
<SOAP-ENV:Envelope
  xmlns:SOAP-ENV="http://schemas.xmlsoap.org/soap/envelope/"
```

```
  xmlns:SOAP-ENC="http://schemas.xmlsoap.org/soap/encoding/"
  xmlns:xsd="http://www.w3.org/2001/XMLSchema"
  xmlns:xsi="http://www.w3.org/2001/XMLSchema-instance"
  xmlns:ns0="capeconnect:eLearning:StudentServices">
  <SOAP-ENV:Body>
    <ns0:getAvailableCourses></ns0:getAvailableCourses>
  </SOAP-ENV:Body>
</SOAP-ENV:Envelope>
```

This will yield a SOAP response, which will have its own envelope:

```
<?xml version="1.0"?>
<env:Envelope
  xmlns:env="http://schemas.xmlsoap.org/soap/envelope/"
  xmlns:enc="http://schemas.xmlsoap.org/soap/encoding/"
  xmlns:xsd="http://www.w3.org/2001/XMLSchema"
  xmlns:xsi="http://www.w3.org/2001/XMLSchema-instance"
  xmlns:ns0="http://SONALI:8000/eLearning.xsd">
  <env:Body xmlns:methodns="capeconnect:eLearning:Student
  Services">
    <methodns:getAvailableCoursesResponse>
      <return xsi:type="ns0:ArrayOfCourse">
        <item xsi:type="ns0:Course">
          <courseId xsi:type="xsd:string">cs1</courseId>
            <courseName xsi:type="xsd:string">Web Based System</
            courseName>
            <courseDesc xsi:type="xsd:string">Understanding and
            implementaion of Web Services</courseDesc>
            <maxStudents xsi:type="xsd:int">25</maxStudents>
            <enrolledStudents xsi:type="xsd:int">1</enrolled
            Students>
            <daysOfWeek xsi:type="xsd:string">Tuesday,Thrusday</
            daysOfWeek>
            <courseTime xsi:type="xsd:string">8:00 to 10:00 am
            </courseTime>
          </item>
          <item xsi:type="ns0:Course">
            <courseId xsi:type="xsd:string">cs2</courseId>
            <courseName xsi:type="xsd:string">Distributed Systems
            </courseName>
            <courseDesc xsi:type="xsd:string">EJB, CORBA, RMI
            </courseDesc>
            <maxStudents xsi:type="xsd:int">25</maxStudents>
            <enrolledStudents xsi:type="xsd:int">0</enrolled
            Students>
```

```
        <daysOfWeek xsi:type="xsd:string">Monday, Wednesday
        </daysOfWeek>
        <courseTime xsi:type="xsd:string">10:00 to 12:00 am
        </courseTime>
      </item>
    ...
    </return>
  </methodns:getAvailableCoursesResponse>
 </env:Body>
</env:Envelope>
```

3.5.4.2 SOAP Header

SOAP messages can optionally have headers with multiple header blocks. The actual payload, such as the remote procedure call and the parameters, is contained in the body of the message. However, header blocks handle the transactional support, security, reliability, and other processing that is independent of the payload itself but supports the context and processing of messages.

The header includes the element name Header, followed by zero or more header block elements and zero or more attributes. Each header block must have a namespace qualified name. Each of these header block elements can have additional sub-elements and attributes.

The schema requirements for headers include:

- encodingStyle: Attribute that indicates the encoding rules used to serialize parts of a SOAP message; type is anyURI.
- role: Indicates the SOAP node intended for the given header block; type is also anyURI.
- mustUnderstand: Specifies whether the processing of the SOAP header is mandatory or optional; type is xs:boolean).
- relay: Another Boolean attribute that is used to indicate if the header block must be relayed, if it is not intended for processing by the current SOAP node.

Following is a simple example of a SOAP header:

```
<env:Header
      encodingStyle="http://www.myhost.com/encoding"
      role="http://www.w3.org/2002/12/soap-envelope/role/
      ultimateReceiver"
      mustUnderstand="true"
      relay="true" >
      ...
</env:Header>
```

3.5.4.3 SOAP Body

The body is a mandatory element that contains the message payload. The SOAP body can contain either the request or response: Service requestors indicate the remote message that is being invoked in the SOAP body, and service providers respond with the results, also in the SOAP body.

According to the SOAP standard, the body must include the following components:

- A [local name] of body
- A [namespace name] of "http://www.w3.org/2002/12/soap-envelope"
- Zero or more namespace qualified attribute information items in its [attributes] property
- Zero or more namespace qualified element information items in its [children] property

Following is the definition of Body, from the SOAP schema.

```
<xs:element name="Body" type="tns:Body"/>
  <xs:complexType name="Body">
    <xs:sequence>
      <xs:any namespace="##any" processContents="lax"
minOccurs="0" maxOccurs="unbounded"/>
    </xs:sequence>
    <xs:anyAttribute namespace="##any" processContents="lax"/>
  </xs:complexType>
```

All SOAP messages contain a body. Following is a simple example.

```
<SOAP-ENV:Envelope
     xmlns:SOAP-ENV="http://schemas.xmlsoap.org/soap/envelope/"
     SOAP-
     ENV:encodingStyle="http://schemas.xmlsoap.org/soap/encoding/">
     <SOAP-ENV:Body>
          <el:getGrades xmlns:el="eLearning">
              <el:studentName>John Smith</el:sudentName>
          </el:getGrades>
     </SOAP-ENV:Body>
</SOAP-ENV:Envelope>
```

3.5.4.4 SOAP Faults

When a SOAP request is processed and there is an error, the body element can contain a fault element that provides the code, description and other details of the fault. Web services will be deployed in distributed architectures. In distributed computing, the exception is the rule; there is always the potential for exceptions and faults. SOAP has introduced a fault element that can optionally be contained in the body element and can communicate error messages or exceptions from the service provider.

The Fault definition includes three key elements:

- FaultCode: This element contains a code that indicates an exception or error. The element is intended to be processed by the application that receives the fault.
- FaultString: This element contains the description of the fault.
- FaultActor: SOAP messages often involve intermediaries. This element can contain the SOAP intermediary or endpoint—the *actor*—that caused the fault.

Following is an example of a fault:

```
<soap:Envelope
xmlns:soap="http://schemas.xmlsoap.org/soap/envelope/"
soap:encodingStyle="http://schemas.xmlsoap.org/soap/ encoding/">
      <soap:Body>
            <soap:Fault>
                  <faultcode>soap:MustUnderstand</faultcode>
                  <faultstring>Mandatory Header
                  error.</faultstring>
                  <faultactor>http://www.eLearn.com/…</faultactor>
                  …
            </soap:Fault>
      </soap:Body>
</soap:Envelope>
```

3.6 Summary

Services are defined, registered, discovered, and invoked. This is the very basic life cycle of service oriented computing. Service orientation has emerged primarily through the popularity and robustness of Web services standards. The three core Web services standards are UDDI, WSDL, and SOAP. This chapter provided an overview of these three essential standards with examples.

The UDDI specification enables businesses and other organizations to describe and publish their service offerings in UDDI registries and to discover other businesses and services through those registries. This is not the only means for the partners to discover each other's services. In fact, if business partners can directly communicate their service descriptions once they become available, then UDDI registries can be used effectively within organizations to publish the services that become available—or deprecated for that matter—so that they can be searched and used throughout the enterprise.

UDDI registries implement the UDDI standard and are typically built on top of relational databases. A UDDI registry provides transactional access to search and update registry entries. UDDI leverages standards such as XML, HTTP and DNS. The UDDI protocol is the building block that will enable businesses to quickly, easily, and dynamically find and transact business with one another. UDDI registries could be accessed either through browsers or programmatically through an XML API, invoked through SOAP.

WSDL provides a self-describing, precise description of the location, binding, and operations of the Web services. More generally, the WSDL schema provides the what, the how, and the where of Web services:

- What operations are supported by the Web service, which is similar to IDL and interfaces in Java.
- How these operations are invoked. WSDL goes beyond mere specification of the interfaces and also specifies the serialized messages structures over the wire. Based on binding values specified in WSDL, the service requestor will send the request message in specific formats.
- Where, which is the location or port of the service.

Web service requestors and responds communicate via SOAP XML messages. The most popular transport is HTTP, although other transports such as SMTP or JMS could also be used. SOAP supports distributed computing with XML by providing an effective mechanism for exchanging messages and accessing remote objects via XML. The main elements of SOAP are the following:

- Envelope: Every SOAP message must have an envelope (and body). It provides the SOAP namespace as well as other namespaces.
- Header: This element is optional. It can contain additional information that can be understood by the requestor and service provider. Examples include security or authentication elements, transactional information, and routing information.
- Body: This element is used both for the request and the response. The body contains the main information (request or response) in one or more SOAP blocks.
- Fault: When there is an error or a fault in the SOAP request, the body element can contain a fault element. This element contains protocol-level errors.

Notes

1. http://norman.walsh.name/2005/03/12/nsdl
2. http://ssdl.org/
3. http://www.prescod.net/rest/wrdl/wrdl.html

4. http://weblogs.java.net/blog/mhadley/wadl.pdf
5. JMS is a messaging application programming interface (API) standard for the Java 2 Enterprise Edition platform. It lets applications use a standard API to create, send, and receive messages asynchronously over reliable messaging middleware.
6. SOAP can actually be over JMS; in addition there can be native JMS bindings.
7. http://www.ws-i.org/docs/charters/WSBasic_Profile_Charter1-6.pdf
8. Software companies that support UDDI sometimes create entries to do testing.
9. http://www.google.com/apis/
10. http://webservices.amazon.com/AWSECommerceService/AWSECommerce Service.wsdl
11. http://www.xmethods.com
12. Using UDDI Version 2.
13. Bags are collections or sets which also allow repeating elements.
14. The NAICS Web site is at http://www.naics.com/.
15. The UNSPSC Web site is at http://www.unspsc.org/.
16. More details about the ISO standardization body and documents can be found at http://www.iso.org/iso/en/prods-services/iso3166ma/.
17. http://www.ean-int.org/locations.html
18. The Web site for the DUNS number is http://www.dnb.com/US/duns_update/ index.html.
19. See http://www.thomasregister.com.
20. "Oasis UDDI Specifications TC," http://www.oasis-open.org/committees/ uddi-spec/tcspecs.shtml, publishes the various WSDLs to access UDDI descriptions (http://uddi.org/wsdl/inquire_v2.wsdl). You can also experiment with these calls through a graphical interface hosted by Microsoft at: http://www.microsoft.com/japan/msdn/columns/xml/12182000-test.htm.
21. http://www.w3.org/TR/2005/WD-wsdl20-primer-20050510/
22. Examples of products that support WSDL editing and processing include business process management (BPM) system vendors such as Pegasystems Inc. (http://www.pega.com), Web service platform vendors such as Cape Clear (http://www.capeclear.com), XML and WSDL editors (http://www.altova.com), and WSDL editor vendors (http://www.stylusstudio.com).
23. The namespace of the SOAP encoding is http://www.w3.org/2002/12/ soap-encoding. The most recent soap-encoding.xsd can be obtained from http://dev.w3.org/cvsweb/2002/ws/xp/spec/soap-encoding.xsd? sortby=file
24. http://services.xmethods.net/soap/urn:xmethods-delayed-quotes.wsdl
25. This is the main and most important namespace. If you go to http://www. w3.org/2003/05/soap-envelope/ you will find the SOAP schema. Another important namespace used in SOAP is the schema namespace that typically has the prefix xs and the value (http://www.w3.org/2001/XMLSchema).
26. The primer at http://www.w3.org/TR/2002/WD-soap12-part0-20020626/ provides a good overview of the SOAP 1.2 standard. Section 5, http://www.w3.org/TR/2002/WD-soap12-part0-20020626/#L4697, goes over the changes from Version 1.1 to Version 1.2. The SOAP 1.2 introduced several

improvements over SOAP 1.1. These span syntactical, SOAP HTTP-binding, RPC-related, and SOAP-encoding improvements.

27. See http://www.w3.org/TR/SOAP-attachments. There is also a SOAP with attachment working draft (as of September 2002) http://www.w3.org/TR/soap12-af/, which provides "an abstract SOAP 1.2 feature which can be used as the basis for defining SOAP bindings that support the transmission of messages with attachments."
28. Details can be found at http://www.w3.org/Protocols/rfc2616/rfc2616.html and a summary at http://www.w3.org/Protocols/rfc2616/rfc2616-sec10.html.
29. SOAP is an XML message or document, and like any other XML document, it can be transported as an e-mail attachment, an argument of a method call, or through a messaging transport protocol such as JMS. Even sockets or named pipes could be used to communicate SOAP messages.
30. http://www.w3.org/TR/xml-infoset/#infoitem

Chapter 4

Service Oriented Architectures

Service-oriented architectures are all about connections.

Douglas K. Barry

4.1 Introduction

In the software field we love acronyms, but sometimes they are not used consistently. Service oriented architecture (SOA) is one of those. This acronym is overloaded: It has different connotations and even meanings in various publications or discussions, and it is complex.

SOA adoption can achieve enterprise and cross-enterprise integration. SOA patterns attempt to address sharing of services within the enterprise and across enterprises. The architecture is complex. However, SOA can be achieved incrementally starting with elements of the SOA technology and then evolving incrementally to large, heterogeneous implementation. One healthy approach here is the notion of radiation, which begins with a small SOA project in one department, helps it to succeed, and then achieve buy-in from others. So radiation spreads with successful SOA deployments from one project to the other. Deploying the SOA approach in a departmental or project basis is a healthy approach.

SOA is not new. It is based on proven ideas from a number of sectors. The idea of having an interface as a contract between a provider and consumer has been around in both object-oriented as well as component-based computing. The notion of loosely coupling a client and service has also been around for quite some time. In fact, it is used every day when browsing Web sites on the Internet. SOA is a good architecture that has several salient features dealing with sharing of services, providing best practices in distributed service deployments, and quality of services features to support mission critical applications. Two key concepts are associated with service oriented architectures. One uses it synonymously with service orientation. The other emphasis is on the overall infrastructure that supports service orientation. This chapter elaborates on both of these complementary definitions, as both are important. But since the discussion concerns an emerging technology and a term with multiple definitions, it can get tricky.

Business and IT: A word of caution—many technologies and concepts are associated with service oriented architectures. A definition and a conceptual as well as standardization and technology stack for SOA will be provided. But if the plethora of technologies and terms seem somewhat confusing, do not worry. This and subsequent chapters delve deeper into the most important components of service orientation. Here the focus is on service oriented architectures.

In software, as in many other fields, architects specify what needs to be built. The programmers then realize the specifications of the architecture—at least in theory. At a high level the architects think and design service oriented; that is, they identify a number of collaborating services. Each service will have one or more callers, or service requestors. The callee, or service provider, will hide the details of the service implementations. The interaction between caller and callee is based on standards such as SOAP over Hyptertext Transfer Protocol (HTTP), but it is important to note that neither of these is necessary or sufficient to make an SOA—eXtensible Markup Language (XML) over HTTP could be used, as well as SOAP over Java Message Service (JMS) or Simple Mail Transfer Protocol (SMTP).

Think of it this way: The service oriented architecture specifies the overall multi-layered and multi-tier distributed infrastructure for supporting service oriented applications. Here is a more precise definition of architecture from the Institute of Electrical and Electronics Engineering

(IEEE): "The fundamental organization of a system embodied by its components, their relationships to each other and to the environment and the principles guiding its design and evolution." SOA therefore provides the organization of a system built from service components. It also specifies how these services can relate to one another. Here is another view of SOA: "Service oriented architectures define the overall structure that is used to support service oriented programming for service oriented applications in the service oriented enterprise." There is nothing like a recursive definition. These definitions are worked out step by step, or rather chapter by chapter, through the remainder of this book. This chapter starts with defining the SOA through service stacks (see Section 4.1.1) and then explains service oriented architecture with Web services (Section 4.2). This chapter also focuses on what is meant by service oriented programming (Section 4.3) and their run-time platforms in distributed infrastructures (Section 4.4). Section 4.5 is dedicated to the enterprise service bus (ESB), which is fast becoming the backbone of many service oriented enterprises. An entire chapter in this book is dedicated to defining these service terms, and their relationships are elucidated in this chapter as well as subsequent chapters.

4.1.1 Service Stacks

Stacks are commonly used to depict layers that depend and build on one another. Higher layers depend on lower layers. Higher layers are also typically closer to human interfaces or interactions. Two stack architecture illustrations for SOA are now provided. Figure 4.1 shows the service components in the stack.

Service oriented description, discovery, and deployment represent the very core foundation of service orientation. This topic was covered in Chapter 3. This foundation consists of service description, registration of these services by service providers, the discovery by service requestors, and then the subsequent interactions. Service oriented quality of service (QoS) deals with performance, reliability, and security of deployed services. Service oriented processes and rules provide the mechanism for composing services in orchestrations and association of business service rules with processes as well as service level interactions between service requestors and providers. Service oriented management addresses the overall maintenance, performance monitoring, measuring, and control of services—including management of service oriented processes and rules. Service oriented content and portals deal with aggregation of information via service oriented technologies as well as the human interface side of service orientation.

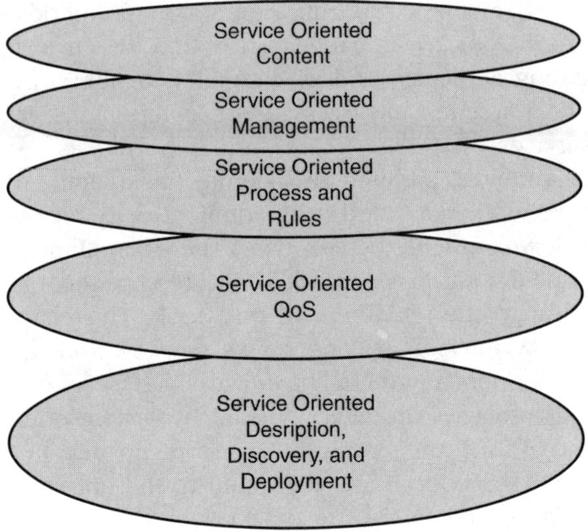

Figure 4.1 Service oriented architecture stack

Business: As the SOA stack illustrates, several layers need to work together to realize a comprehensive strategy. As stated many times, SOA is promising but complex. Each of the layers, though, provides essential functionality—spanning the whole spectrum from the user interface all the way down to the plumbing infrastructure.

IT: There are many different standards for each of the layers. The coming chapters will cover the most important standards; however, care should be taken because they are not all at the same level of maturity. Furthermore, the Web Service Interoperability Organization (WS-I) provides interoperability specifications, which is an excellent place to start (http://www.ws-i.org).

In service orientation, the layers of the service oriented architecture correspond to a service technology stack, which is illustrated in Figure 4.2. The service oriented architecture stack provides a number of service oriented standards corresponding to the service oriented layers. The focus here is on Web services (WS) standards, which are increasingly referred to in aggregate as WS-*.

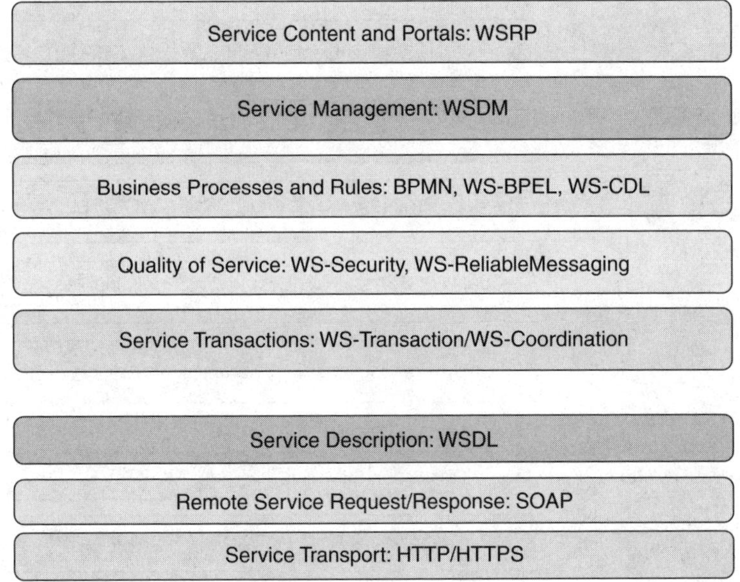

Figure 4.2 Service oriented standards stack

Business and IT: Service orientation is possible using technologies other than the Web service standards. For example, many folks simplify things dramatically by using a combination of HTTP (specifically the GET verb) and XML. This style of service orientation is often called Representational State Transfer (REST). Note that the advantages of this simplicity come with a cost: more custom development and documentation and less ability to leverage advanced development tool support for WS-*.

As Figure 4.2 illustrates, there are quite a number of WS-* standards and an impressive alphabet soup. These are not the only WS-* standards. There are many more such standards for service orientation with Web services. The layers of the standards stack correspond to the layers of service orientation as illustrated in Figure 4.3.

The stack on the left-hand side (the bubbles) represents elements of the service orientation suite. The stack on the right-hand side (the rounded

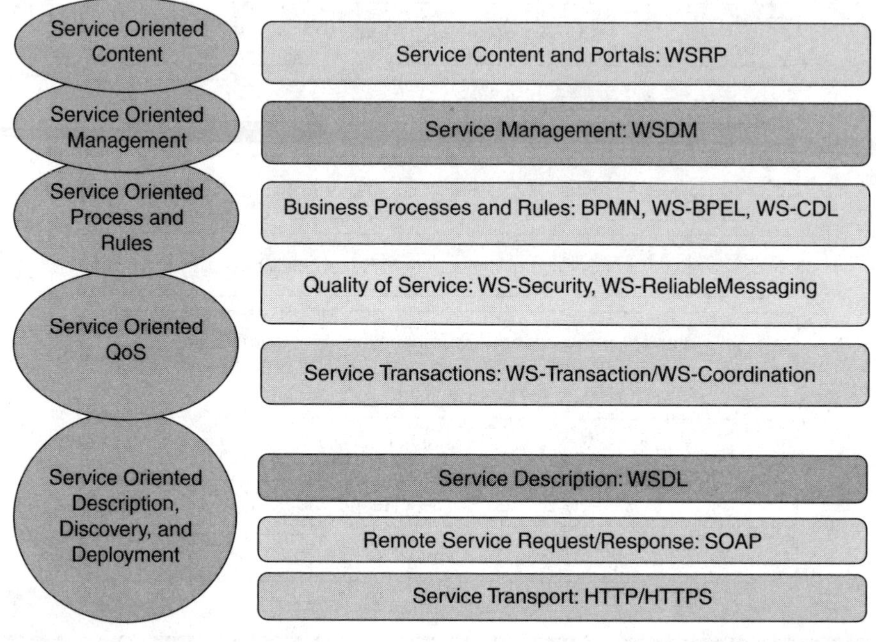

Figure 4.3 Correspondence between service oriented architecture and standard stacks

rectangles) represents the technology stack of Web services-driven service oriented architecture. The bubbles are functional components: They specify what needs to be accomplished. The rounded rectangles are specific core technology implementation layers: They specify how these functions are implemented, including standards used in the implementation. Both are important: one shows what needs to be done for a service oriented architecture, and the other shows how the service oriented functionality is implemented.

4.1.2 Service Architecture

> With SOA you can integrate your enterprise across departments, divisions, data sources, and applications. You can even reach out to your customer base to create virtual applications that span companies, countries and continents.
>
> **Alan Trefler**

The previous section gave an overview of the functional and technology stacks of service orientation. Let us now get a bit more concrete through an example:

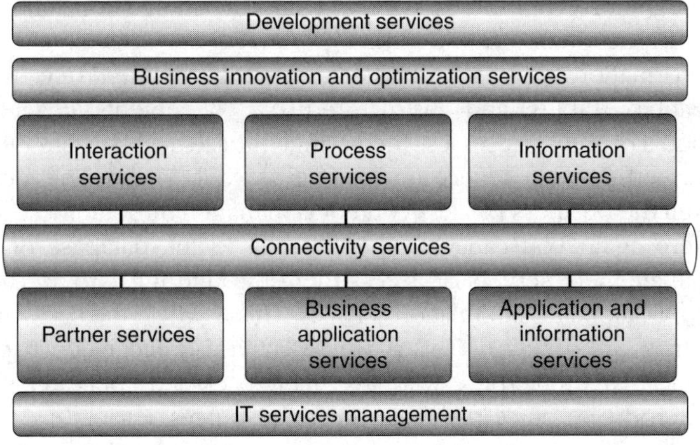

Figure 4.4 IBM's business integration architecture

How do these get implemented in an actual platform? To provide an overall perspective as to what a service oriented enterprise architecture might look like, Figure 4.4 provides an illustration from one large vendor known for its on-demand architectures and solutions for e-business: IBM provides an overall vision of a service oriented integration reference architecture.[1]

This rather complex-looking diagram illustrates several points. At the core of this service architecture is the enterprise service bus (ESB), which is covered later in the chapter. It shows that business integration platforms involve many components that could plug in to the ESB.

- Interaction services: These support the portal server and human interactions. Portals typically consist of portlets. According to Portals Community,[2] a portlet can be formally defined as "a 'building block' of a portal." It is a user interface for presenting data and functionality from multiple applications on a single Web page. Portlets encompass the presentation layer and the business logic. There is a tremendous synergy between user-facing Web services and portals. As noted earlier, Web services can provide the content of the portlets, so they thus become the user- or customer-facing representations of Web services, or services in general.
- Process services: This is the business process management (BPM) component. Many ESBs execute service orchestrations within the bus. The BPM also involves human participants as well as trading partners and other key components such as business rules. In fact, BPM also includes enterprise integration functionality. With the depicted architecture, the choice is given of performing direct

integration from the BPM or of using the integration infrastructure and functionality of the ESB.

- Information services: This reflects both the structured (e.g., relational database tables) and unstructured (e.g., documents, images, multimedia) content accesses. Increasingly, these accesses are being performed through service invocations as well. The business object as well the business process content is managed through these services. Here again you can go either directly to the database or content management servers or access them through the ESB.
- Application and information services: This is where the back-end applications are accessed. This is where enterprise integration happens. A typical large enterprise will have many back-end applications such as enterprise resource planning, human resources, legacy (e.g., COBOL) applications on mainframes, financial or accounting applications, and customer relationship management systems, to name a few. Increasingly, these applications are becoming accessible through standard interfaces, including Web services. However, in most cases integrating consistently and reliably with the enterprise applications is quite challenging. This used to be—and still is—the realm of enterprise application integration (EAI) servers and message oriented middleware (MOM). In fact, the ESB is the integrator of integration components, such as EAIs and MOMs. The key here is that an ESB provides standards-based integration versus the proprietary mechanisms of EAIs and MOMs.
- Partner services: This is where the business-to-business integration (B2B) happens. The security and service requirements of B2B are quite different than internal enterprise integration. Enterprises typically have external and internal firewalls. The integration here with the business partners could involve availability, reliability, performance, and security QoS requirements.

Increasingly operations in enterprise applications are being published as Web services. This support is provided either by the enterprise application vendor or by third-party adapter frameworks.

These applications' functionalities can then be composed into processes. For instance, a step in a process could deal with customer data; another step could read from a sales database; and a third step could update an accounting application. The key point here is that the entire transaction could involve operations provided by several different applications. The process can be published as a service.

Increasingly organizations are composing services in service oriented processes and publishing these processes as services.

In fact, processes can be used as sub-processes in even larger processes. The individual applications, or rather operations on applications, are the building blocks. Then these are composed into meaningful larger pieces and are used to build even larger constructs. It is cool, isn't it? Why haven't we tried or applied this approach earlier? Well, we have. A couple of technologies have tried to achieve this seamless and robust distributed computation, but they did not work, really. They were complex and convoluted. What sets apart service oriented architectures is the reliance on standards, especially XML and Internet standards. Note that Web services standards such as SOAP and Web Services Description Language (WSDL) are neither necessary nor sufficient for implementing an SOA. But they are becoming the most popular and ubiquitous mechanism for service orientation.

The previous paragraphs spoke about the building blocks and then the processes that compose them. So far the concentration has primarily been on applications within an organization. An increasing trend is now emerging among many large organizations to expose various functions typically supported through browser interfaces as Web services. For example, on Amazon people are used to browsing catalogs and searching for books and other items through their Web interfaces. Now catalogs can also be accessed and browsed programmatically through Web services. Products can also be purchased through Web service calls. There can be less human intervention or involvement in processes that span across organizational boundaries.

Increasingly organizations are integrating their internal and external processes in dynamic business to business interactions through services.

It is important to understand these three trends, even at a high level. So to recapture, applications are starting to expose their operations through Web services interfaces. The benefits are that it is much less expensive to interface with these applications than with custom-code or expensive proprietary software such as enterprise application integrators. The composition of internal back-office applications, as well as remote business partner applications, are emerging in service processes. The benefits are reduced human involvement, improved performance of process resolutions, reduced error rates, and opportunities for new partnerships and applications—all really cool stuff.

4.2 SOA and Web Services

The previous section provided an overview of service architectures. This book is about service orientation in general, but as will be demonstrated, increasingly Web services are becoming the pervasive means to realize service orientation. The compelling question is this: How do SOA and Web services relate to each other? Are they synonyms?

Chapter 3 hinted already to the fact that Web services are becoming the most prominent way to support service orientation. This section goes deeper into Web services and SOA.[3] Service oriented architectures could be built through many technologies. However, Web services are perhaps the best technology to implement service oriented architectures.[4]

There are two complementary perspectives reflecting the relationship between Web services and service oriented architectures.

1. One way to explain the relationship between SOA and Web services is through specialization. SOA is the general architectural framework that supports service oriented programming. Here are more acronyms (other alphabets in a different soup): CORBA (Common Object Request Broker Architecture), MOM (Message Oriented Middleware), .NET, J2EE (Java 2 Enterprise Edition). These technologies allow you to define a "service" with an interface. The interface of the service specifies how you can call the service: the protocol. The service will be deployed on a server and then invoked by consumers. Therefore, these frameworks are all a specialization of the SOA model. For instance, J2EE allows for components in a Java environment. MOM solutions support asynchronous service interactions. .NET supports exchanges between components potentially using different programming languages. The message here is that SOA can be realized through a plethora of technologies, including Web services (Figure 4.5).

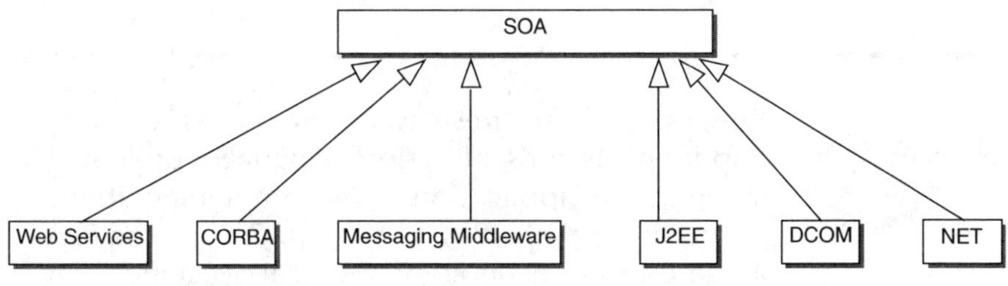

Figure 4.5 Various technologies as SOA, including web services

2. Another perspective is the increased level of independence achieved through Web services. As illustrated in Figure 4.6, the x-axis captures the operating system independence. For instance, J2EE application servers support almost any operating system. .NET on the other hand is supported only on Windows platforms. That is why J2EE is on the right and .NET on the left. The y-axis represents programming language independence. In this case .NET supports many languages, whereas J2EE is Java based. That is why .NET is higher up and J2EE is quite low in the programming language independence dimension.

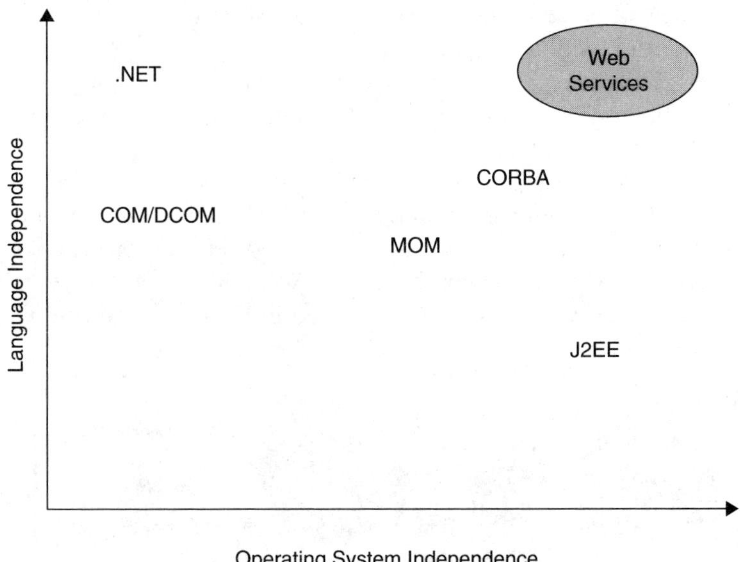

Figure 4.6 Web services are OS and programming language independent

Business and IT: These two dimensions are very important. Islands of various language, operating system, and application server implementations often will crop up. IBM, Microsoft, Oracle, and BEA agree on one technology: Web services and SOA through Web services. This means any effort or deployment with Web services standards will be supported by the major vendors. That is a safe bet.

4.2.1 Browser-Based and Browserless Access to Web Sites

Web service clients and providers communicate though SOAP exchanges. An important observation is repeated here: The clients as well as the actual services are written in host programming languages. A bit confusing, isn't it? The service requestor and service provider could be miles apart. The requestor could be running on a particular operating system platform (e.g., Solaris), using a particular programming language (e.g., Java), while invoking a service written in a different programming language (e.g., C#) running on a different operating system.

Analogy is an effective means to understanding an emerging concept or paradigm. This concept of heterogeneous systems, executing on different platforms and communicating to achieve a common goal, is not new. We use it every day. The Web has proven to be the most robust and ubiquitous framework for *information* exchange. Web services build on the success of the Web and allow operational, or browserless, exchanges between organizations.

When considering the Internet or the Web, immediately we think of browsers accessing various sites as illustrated in Figure 4.7. Web services, by

Figure 4.7 Conventional access to Web sites via browsers

contrast, are usually accessed programmatically without browsers—except in the case when a service is providing the implementation of a portlet. This is an important shift. This makes it possible for organizations to connect with each other seamlessly and streamline end-to-end straight through the process. One internal application in an organization can invoke another application as a service and can execute the integrated interaction as a complete whole: A financial application can programmatically check a stock quote from a financial institution; an organization can dynamically check the availability of courses from various e-learning organizations; a database query can check the temperature of a city as a function within a query expression. These are only a few examples illustrating the potential of Web services through programmatic access of Web sites. With Web services, organizations can access each other's services through browserless application exchanges while using the same Internet protocols (e.g., HTTP) for the exchange.

As illustrated in Figure 4.8, the interchange with Web services is through SOAP messages. HTTP is the most common transport protocol. Both request and response are in SOAP, which is an XML object access or method invocation protocol. As with other services, SOAP services can be invoked synchronously—where the service requestor has to wait and receive the result from the service provider. SOAP services can also be called asynchronously, which provides a lot of flexibility and performance advantages.

With Web services, programmatic interactions that span extended enterprises become more automated and intelligent. This means instead of requiring a human participant to carry out access, search, update (e.g., submitting forms), and browsing tasks every time, intelligent Web services application software can be used to implement the search, update, and browsing through a program—without human intervention. *Intelligent* here means the decision-making logic can also be implemented within the automated platform. This can reduce the need for human intervention and can streamline the integration between organizations. Browserless programmatic access through Web services can help realize loosely coupled integration between enterprises—an important step toward a virtual enterprise

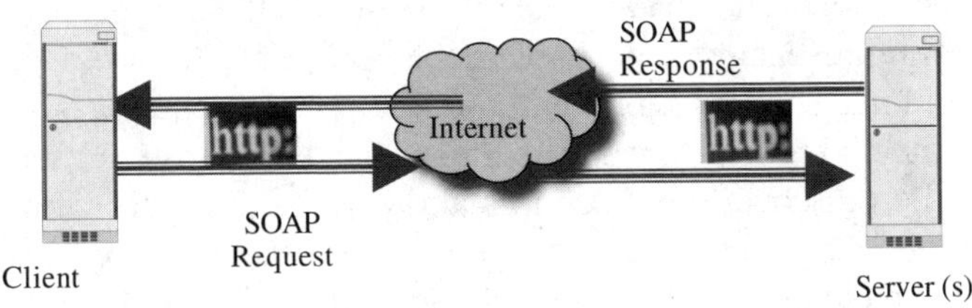

Figure 4.8 Browserless programmatic access

model: an enterprise that behaves and responds as an integrated organization, while in actuality consisting of an aggregation of independent participating organizations.

4.3 Service Oriented Programming

Section 4.1 provided an overview of different service oriented stacks. Service orientation introduces a new approach in thinking about solutions, connectivity, and interoperability, especially between applications and trading partners. Section 4.2 discussed SOA with Web services. Here the attention turns to service oriented programming. In the early and mid-1980s, the common phrase used to capture the emerging trends in object orientation was *Everything is an object*. Java and more recently C# are examples of object-oriented languages. The 1990s and early 2000s saw the emergence of constructs called *components,* which are coarser grained than objects. They typically provide particular functions that are self-contained and complete. Common Object Request Broker Architecture (CORBA)[5] and Enterprise Java Beans (EJBs)[6] are examples of component technologies.

In 2004 and beyond, the phrase capturing the emerging trend of service oriented architecture is *Everything is a service*. Each service is potentially a provider as well as a requestor of services. With service oriented architectures, enterprise resources are exposed and accessed as services. These resources include databases, documents, and applications. In an extended enterprise, SOA is used to access remote resource requests via service requests. Service oriented architectures are not limited to Web services-based solutions. But as this chapter shows, Web services provide the best infrastructure for implementing service oriented architectures.

The next wave of programming is service oriented programming. With service oriented programming, one thinks of the overall enterprise applications as a set of loosely coupled services. Services are implemented, published, and then discovered and invoked. As demonstrated in Chapter 2, services could be built from scratch, or adaptors to existing applications or components could be developed and made available as services. Service providers hide their internal representation and implementation details from service consumers. Furthermore, service publishers and the service requestors are loosely coupled.[7] Often a registry contains all the available or registered services. The clients can then discover these services and can interact with them—through invoking their public interfaces. Sometimes the services are composed into processes, which can in turn be published as services. Figure 4.9 illustrates the traditional service publication—service search and service interaction triangle with a twist. This figure takes into account the number of instances of public registries, service providers, and service requestors.

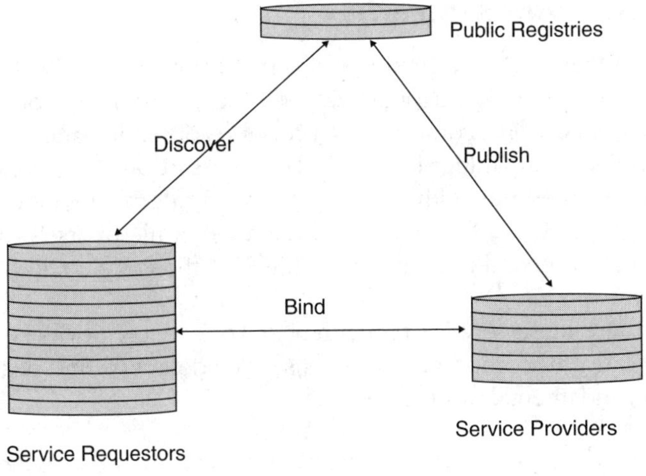

Figure 4.9 Relative weights (number of organizations) of registries, providers, and requestors

There are a handful of registry operators. As discussed in Chapter 3, most public UDDI registry operators were shut down. Every application category will have service providers (i.e., companies) that publish information about their services, which is similar to the Yellow Pages. There are a handful of Yellow Pages for any region, county, or city, and there are potentially thousands of businesses that publish their services—organized in categories. Then there are potentially hundreds of thousands or even millions of service requestors. This is not very different from the comparison between the number of Web site domains and the number of users who access these Web sites.

The concept of service oriented programming is not new. Services resemble objects—which hide their internal representations and only expose their interfaces. However, unlike objects, the state (i.e., values of instance variables in object-oriented systems) is not central. Instead the service can generate or consume messages corresponding to events. Component object computing also has a similar registration model and the invocation of the public interfaces through loosely coupled architectures. In CORBA, for instance, the interface invocation is brokered through a component object request/response brokering layer. The client and the service could be written in different programming languages and deployed on different operating systems. CORBA server objects could also be registered through CORBA's naming services. The server can provide a logical name to the service, and then clients can look up the object using that name to obtain an object reference.

4.3.1 What Are Services?

The easy answer is that everything is a service, with *everything* encompassing all the resources in an organization. These resources could be files, databases, applications, components, processes or participants in processes, business rules, or anything that could be accessed on a network. If it can be digitized or presented either as operations or information, it can become a service. This is kind of a stretch. For example, a file by itself cannot be a service; code is needed to manage the file. But the code could be exposed as a service.

So how are these services programmed? For service providers, Chapter 2 illustrated one of the important steps as service definition and design. There were two fundamental approaches.

- *Exposing existing components or applications or content as services*, through adapters. These adapters provide a layer that converts service calls to specific API calls to existing applications, components, or content. With this option the service designer selects classes, components, and interfaces that need to be exposed as services.
  - Determining what needs to be exposed and how is an essential ingredient in the overall success of service applications. The interface needs to provide a meaningful functionality to its clients. Yes, it is subjective, but there are techniques in identifying functionality that needs to be exposed as interfaces:
    - *Granularity:* Fine granules in interface definition are not recommended. For instance, if the service is encapsulating an object with state (e.g., a customer), it is completely unnecessary to expose each property of the object as an interface: setCustomerZipCode; getCustomerZipCode; and similar functions for each property. Instead, one interface can set or get a coarser-grained object such as address.
    - *Purpose:* Each interface should have a business or client purpose. Again, this is mostly subjective. But it goes to the very essence of exposing interfaces of components. Providing just Create, Read, Update, and Delete (CRUD) is not enough. It means the service consumer will have to implement the business functionality on top of these basic services. When a component is built, typically some functionalities pertain to its implementation, and some support the business purpose of the component. For example, interfaces for migrating the storage records of customers, when the underlying storage mechanism is a hierarchal storage repository, do not serve a business purpose. CRUD for customer properties or records

is also not very meaningful as a business purpose, whereas retrieving the transaction history of a customer within, say, the past three months, with a designation of the category of the customer, does serve a business purpose.

- *Building new services from scratch*: Here the service designer first decides what services are required by the organization. The service interface is first designed using service description standards. Then the service implementation is developed using one of the alternative technologies or languages such as Java or C#. This was discussed in the previous chapter. So it is possible to begin with a WSDL definition and then to generate target skeletons for target implementation alternatives. The actual service implementation is always in a target language. Once the service is deployed on a server that supports HTTP and SOAP, SOAP requests are translated to programming API calls to the service implementation.

Once the QoS of these services has been determined, the next steps are the implementation as well as publication of the services. Figure 4.10 is the service life cycle already seen in Chapter 2.

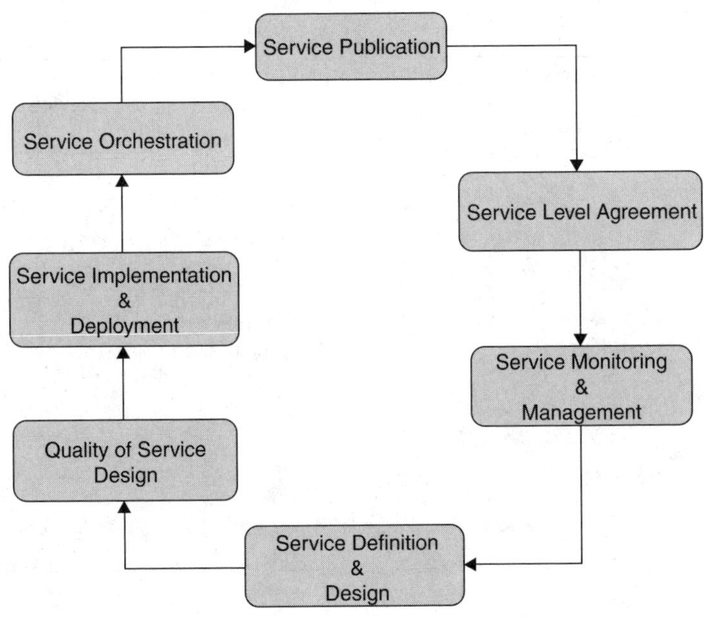

Figure 4.10 Service development life cycle

In this service life cycle is an implicit compositional hierarchy. Individual services are orchestrated and are composed into larger services, which in turn could be used in other orchestrated or composite services. A particular service oriented application or solution will use one or more of these composite services. The relationship between leaf services—indicated by service class—and composite services is illustrated in Figure 4.11. A composite service can have leaf services or other composite services. A service provider, for instance, can use other composite services as well as leaf services to build composite service oriented business applications (SOBA)

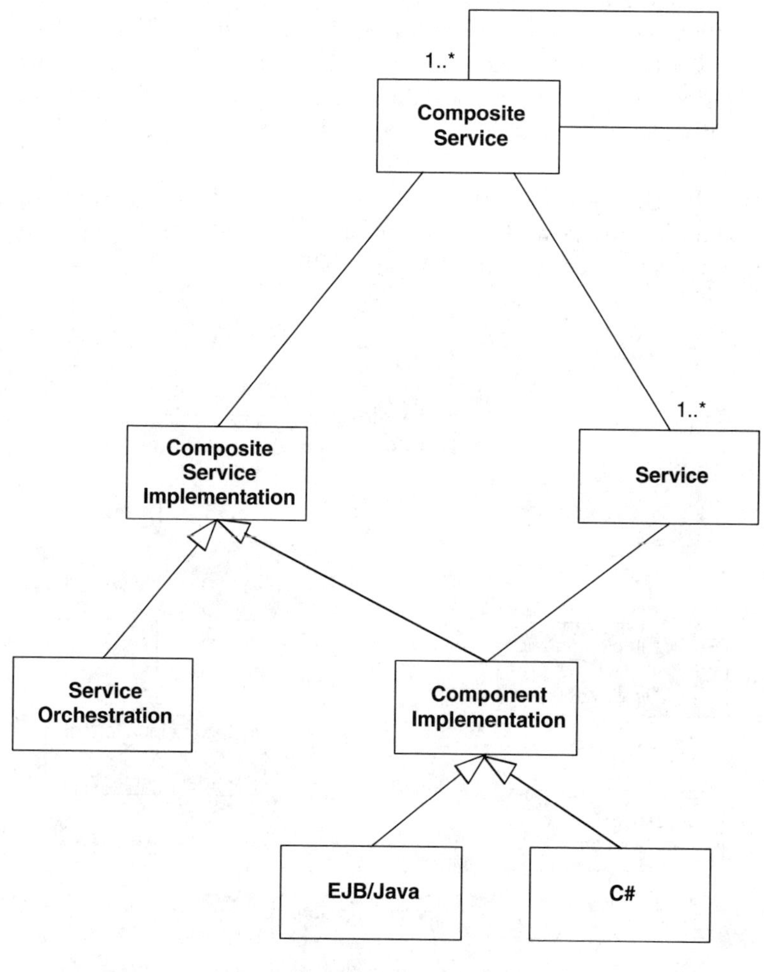

Figure 4.11 Relationships between leaf and composite services and their implementation

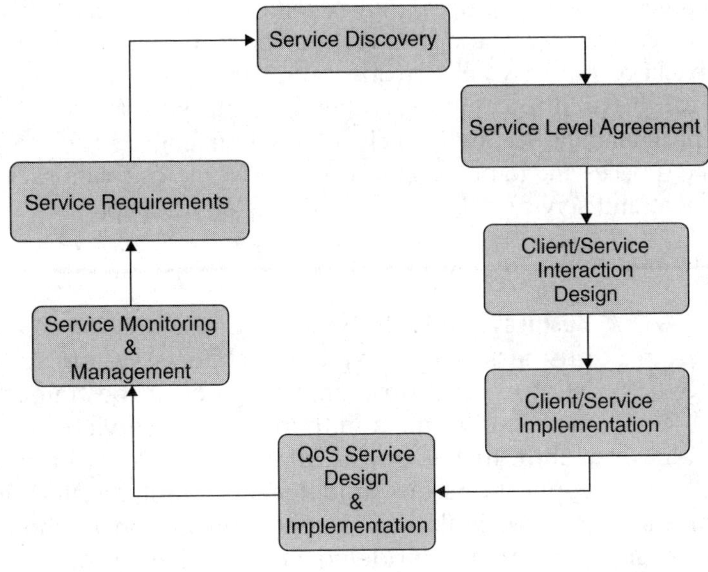

Figure 4.12 Service client development life cycle

and publish these as services. Figure 4.11 also illustrates the implementation options for leaf services and composite SOBAs.

This continuous improvement and development life cycle provides the service publisher's—also known as service provider—perspective. On the client side, many similar steps are depicted in Figure 4.12, a continuous life-cycle diagram.

These overall descriptions of service oriented programming from the client and server side are quite basic and do not cover complex issues such as reliability, security, and service level agreements or the composition of services.

Services that are implemented and published can be combined and composed in process flow charts. These processes can involve several services from the same or different organizations. In the SOA lingo, these are sometimes called partners. The classical example here is procurement. There are buyers, sellers, and shippers. Each provides a service: For instance, buyers generate orders, and sellers generate invoices and ship products relying on shippers. As can be seen even in this watered-down description, there is a specific order of the execution of these services, and there are specific roles for each service provider or requestor. In fact, a buyer can purchase several products, can combine them, and then can build and ship another product. Depending on the process, buyers can also become sellers.

Sometimes the entire process can become a service. This is definitely the trend. A travel agent, for instance, can provide one combined travel service package but may rely on many underlying services. This means services can be used to compose, to build, and to publish other services. Service programming therefore includes orchestrating services to create composite services and to publish those as more complex solutions. Process management and service orientation are discussed in Chapter 5.

Business and IT: To benefit from service orientation business analysts, system architects, system administrators, and programmers need to be trained to model, to think, and to implement services. This is a shift. Just as object orientation changed the way applications are modeled and implemented, in a similar way service orientation is also a revolution in the way program applications are modeled and administered. Do not underestimate this shift, and consider using a service orientation consultant to help make the transition.

With service oriented programming, all of the resources in an organization can be represented as services. These services can respond to synchronous and asynchronous requests. Services could also be composed into processes, and these processes could involve both humans for knowledge decisions and services—either internal or external applications. The composition of services in processes is the focus of business process management. Business process management components for SOEs are also discussed in detail in Chapter 5.

4.3.2 Service Requestors and Providers over Heterogeneous Platforms

Figure 4.13 illustrates a client program written in Java (i.e., a Java client) on a Solaris platform calling a C# service executing on a Windows platform. The Java developer does not know—or care about—the platform or the language of the service provider. The client communicates using standard SOAP and HTTP protocols, and that's it. Now that is the beauty of these independence dimensions of Web services and why they are best suited for service oriented architectures.

This is important, so the point should be reiterated.

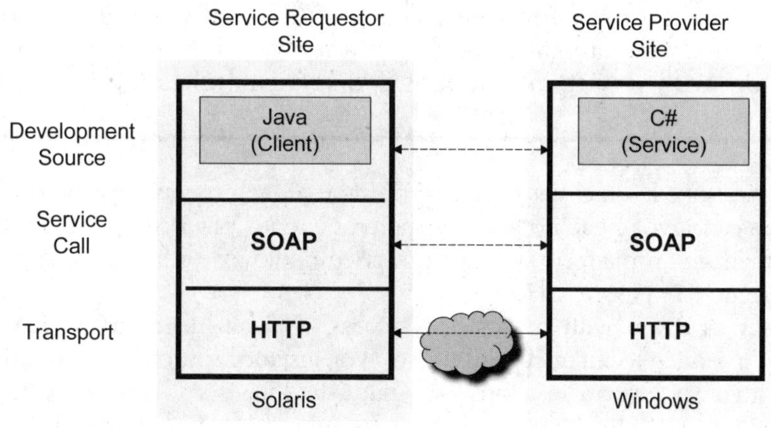

Figure 4.13 Client in Java invoking service in C#

1. Many technologies could be used in service oriented architectures.
2. From among these technologies, Web services are the most flexible when it comes to independence of operating systems, application servers, and programming languages for implementation.
3. Furthermore, because of this standards-based flexibility, disparate systems can be connected so they can communicate in service oriented interactions (i.e., request/response) with relative ease.

4.3.3 Call Sequence in a Web Service Invocation

Business: This section might seem too technical. That is okay; just appreciate the very many layers and technologies IT needs to deal with to satisfy a request from a browser or applications, initiated by a simple press of a button or by following a link. This might provide a perspective on the amount of traffic, conversions, and communications that take place between service requestors and service providers.

IT: This is of course only part of the picture. Things get really interesting when considering security, reliability, performance, transactional models, and, of course, business processes and rules. This book dedicates chapters to these specific topics, especially

Chapter 5 on BPM and rules. This and the next chapter should be a good place to start thinking of the overall enterprise architecture with service interactions and service orchestration.

So applications interact with external or internal Web services. Furthermore, services can invoke each other over heterogeneous platforms: Imagine that a client in a Sun platform invokes a service deployed on a .NET platform, as illustrated in Figure 4.13.

But wait: Even with browserless access, it is still necessary to have a human interface to interact with a user. For instance, purchasing an airline ticket involves a form in a browser that asks the user to fill in the flight information. But then once the request is submitted, the service requestor can query several airline Web services to find the best price. This is not what is happening today, but it is definitely the direction of the industry as a whole. So the move is made from a browser access to a browserless Web services access to other sites—eventually returning the result to the user probably using a browser. Think of procurement in an organization. The company can provide an application to allow its employees to carry out purchases internally using a purchase order application.

The scenario described here is an illustration of a direct point-to-point invocation. As will be demonstrated later on, there are other patterns. This is the simplest and clearest. Here the focus is on the chain of service invocations, from a user clicking a seemingly harmless "submit" button to the response, which could involve several sites and services. Figure 4.14 provides a simple illustration.

Now it gets a bit technical. All the terms and concepts are defined very briefly. If some are confusing that is okay: The main point is that moving from a browser access to the response involves several tiers. So in this scenario the following happens.

1. The user accesses a Web site from a browser and submits a form. This request goes to a Web container, which handles the sessions submitted to a Web site on the Internet or intranets. Therefore, Web containers handle the request from browsers and return Web pages to the user. The request and response use the HTTP protocol.
2. The Web containers manage Java server pages or servlets. These are programs that get a request and return either XML or HTML. The XML or HTML is generated dynamically based on the parameters of the request—in contrast to simple static HTML documents.
3. The servlet is a Java program that in turn calls a client proxy—also a Java program. As its name suggests, this proxy appears to the

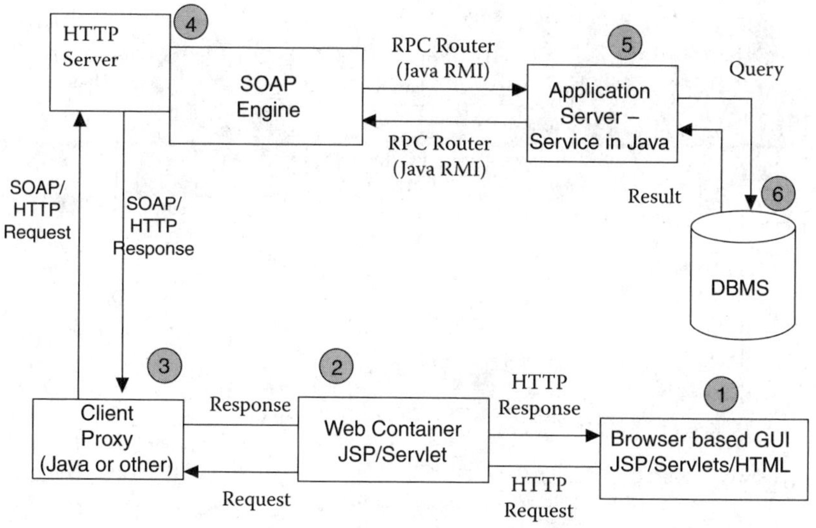

Figure 4.14 Multi-tier architecture involving a browser access

servlet as the actual service. The servlet calls it as it would call other Java programs and gets a response. The proxy actually translates the Java request call to a SOAP (i.e., XML) request and sends it over the wire also using the HTTP protocol.

4. The request is now submitted to another Web container or HTTP server. This time the Web container uses a SOAP engine, which is usually a servlet, and submits the SOAP request to this engine.
5. The SOAP engine therefore does the exact opposite of the client proxy: It takes the SOAP request and translates it into a Java request. It then calls the actual service in Java.
6. This service executes to create the response to the request, often relying on an underlying database management system (DBMS) to compose its response.

As can be seen, an innocent request from a browser can involve quite a few transformations. In fact, many of the boxes in Figure 4.14 could be handled or mapped onto different physical servers. Typically 1, 2, and 3 could be boxes on the client Web site. The interaction between 3 and 4 takes place over the Internet, and 4, 5, and 6 are on boxes on the server or service provider site. Figure 4.15 illustrates a potential mapping of the various rectangles to hardware boxes.

For instance, 1, 2, and 3 can all be on the service requestor site, with 4, 5, and 6 on the service provider site. The communication between 3 and

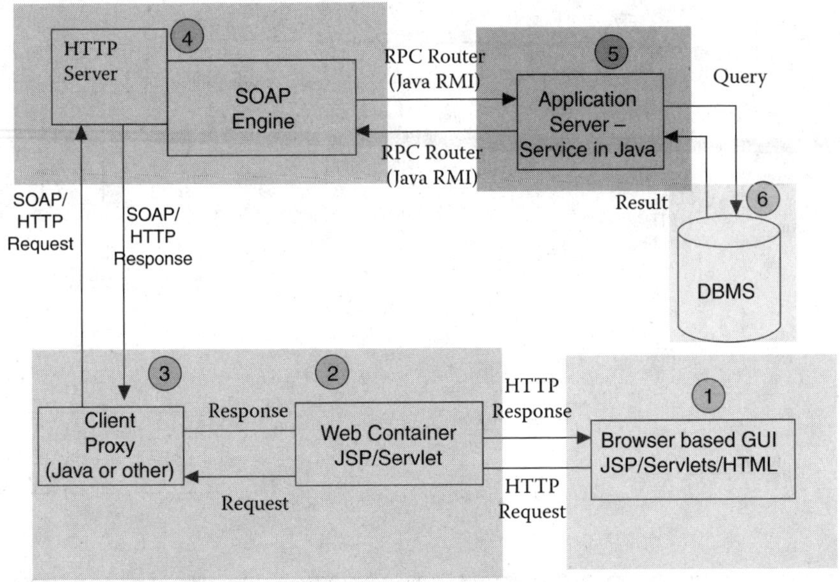

Figure 4.15 Hardware server in the SOA call sequence

4 can take place over the Internet, assuming the requestor and service provider are two different organizations. If this interaction is taking place within the enterprise, the interaction between 3 and 4 can happen behind the secure firewall of the enterprise internally in the intranet. Also, note that the mappings onto physical servers are just possible or potential scenarios. Several of these functions can execute on the same physical box. Why bother with all of these details? Well, because it makes a very big difference how services are configured. SOA applications will have various performance, reliability, availability, and security requirements. Chapter 6 will expand the SOA discussion with quality of service infrastructures and options for SOA deployments. What should be taken away from this chapter is a clear sense of the various elements of the multi-tier interaction that takes place from a simple push of a button by a user all the way to the database or back-end application accesses by the service providers. And it gets more interesting when the services are composed and combined in distributed architectures.

4.3.4 The SOAP Engine

The SOAP engine takes care of marshaling and unmarshaling the messages that get sent over the wire. What gets executed on the client and server side are actually binaries generated from compiled object-oriented languages such as Java or C#. The argument objects—corresponding to the parameters of the invoked operations—that are communicated from requestor and sent to the service provider need to be (1) serialized, which basically entails encoding of a complex object and all objects reachable from it transitively onto a byte stream; (2) converted to XML (i.e., SOAP Message); and (3) sent over a transport protocol—HTTP is the most popular, but there are others such as JMS and SMTP.

The SOAP engine supports client and server run-time components to enable programmatic client to server interactions while using XML to send and receive the message requests. Figure 4.16 illustrates how Axis[8] generates the WSDL and deployment descriptors for the service and the client proxy to invoke the service programmatically for the client. The Java client will use the generated client stubs to invoke the operations of the service. The Java operation and arguments are mapped onto XML (i.e., SOAP) and

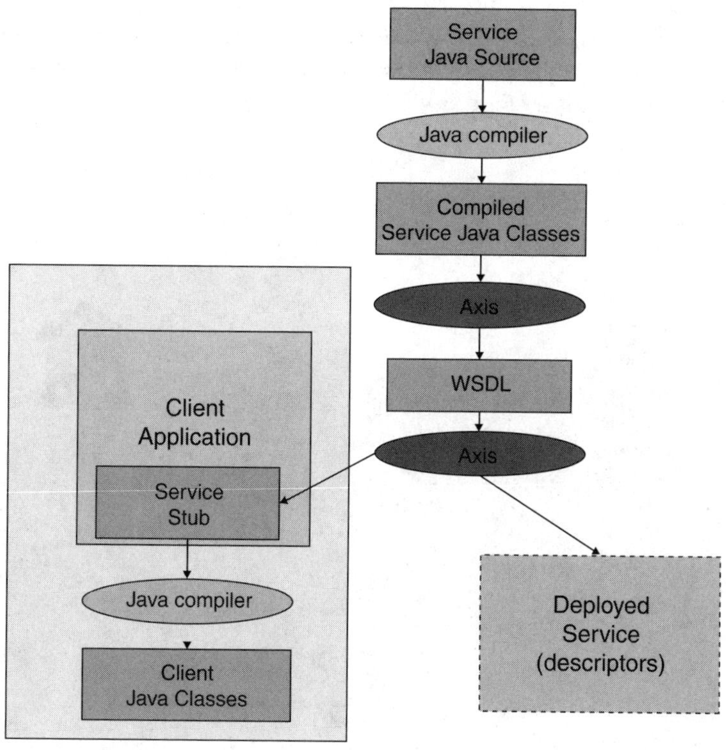

Figure 4.16 SOAP Engine (Axis) Tool generating WSDL, client proxy from service classes

sent over the wire, and then on the server side the corresponding operation is invoked and executed by the service implementation—also in Java in this case.

4.4 SOA in Distributed Architectures

The previous section illustrated what is involved when a client requests a service and a provider responds to this service. As can be seen, quite a bit happens from the initiator to the conclusion of the services. A number of the technologies and standards are used to guarantee the secure, reliable, and high-performance execution of service request/response exchanges. But this quintessential pattern is just the beginning. In a sense it is the building block of SOA applications. For example, say someone wants to purchase an appliance using services and then to ship it to his or her residential address. And say the transaction is approved only if the seller has the appliance in inventory, if the person's credit card has sufficient room for the purchase, and if the shipment can happen within the purchaser's prescribed dates. This is called a composition of three separate and distributed services, all cooperating in the context of a single appliance purchasing transaction (Figure 4.17).

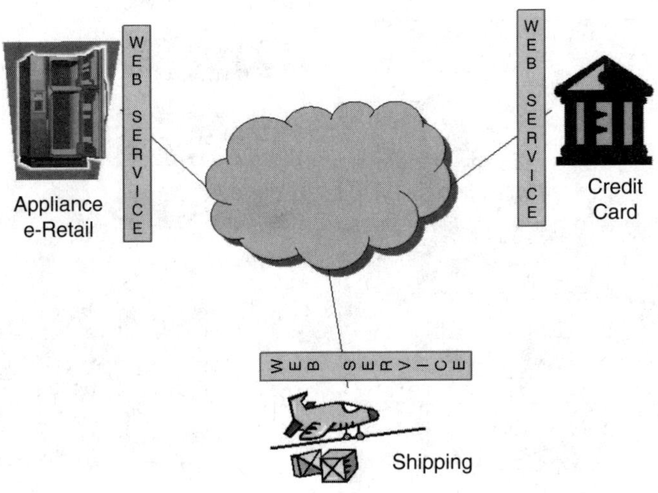

Figure 4.17 Appliance, credit card, and shipping services for a purchase

Business and IT: One of the most incredible advantages of SOA with Web services is the ability to create new partnerships, new products, and new possibilities from individual services that were created independently. Through standard interfaces and compositions, additional features can now be offered to internal and external stakeholders. Part of thinking and modeling service applications is the ability to come up with new and creative solutions through distributed service compositions.

The three services collaborating to achieve a single goal—purchasing an appliance—are a good example of distributed computing. At the heart of distributed computing, there is a healthy tension between the desirability of developing independent objects, components, and applications—called services—and the requirement to have them operate as an integrated whole. It would be desirable to have all the advantages of distribution, in terms of independence of the applications, as well as leveraging the investments that have been made in existing systems while also benefiting from integration.

Intel has introduced service oriented support through a number of initiatives. In addition to its core integrated communication and computing support, Intel supports and promotes a number of interesting service oriented architecture concepts. The Value Chain Operations Reference Model (VCOR) provides a common standardized language for value chain business applications. A value chain models a collection of interdependent businesses and processes that can be combined to provide value to the extended enterprise. VCOR focuses on the higher-level business processes and representations. The supporting infrastructure is supported by the underlying Federated Enterprise Reference Architecture (FERA), which supports VCOR and maps value chain business processes onto service oriented infrastructure. FERA has several components, one of which exposes enterprise data through open standards-based interfaces to facilitate connectivity and exchanges between federated systems. FERA actually uses Web services-based integration both for internal component integration as well as communication with external resources. For more details, see http://value-chain.org/.

So we decouple and distribute. Then, as soon a technology or a solution is developed for distributed and computationally independent technology, we search for solutions to reintegrate. Integration remains on the top-ten—if not the top-five—list of most important issues for Fortune 1000 companies. Today there is a proliferation of heterogeneous technologies that require integration (Section 4.5 on enterprise service buses elaborates more on integration).

- Multiple operating systems and platforms, including Solaris, Linux, and Windows
- Different distributed object computation solutions, such as CORBA, J2EE, and .NET
- Multiple applications within organizations, such as enterprise resource planning (ERP), human resources, and accounting applications
- A variety of databases and document repositories
- Different middleware and enterprise integration solutions

Often, IT managers attempt to discover the optimum form of integration through trial and error. Many of the integration solutions and middleware offered today have similar features. It is not easy for IT organizations to pick the right middleware for their increasingly complex and heterogeneous needs. It is not obvious exactly which solution best fits the need of a department or organization when delving deeper into the operating environment, specific requirements, and longer-term viability of a solution based on a particular platform. There are too many choices.

Service oriented architecture, especially through Web services, attempts to solve the dilemma by providing integration across a variety of heterogeneous systems.

Web services connect and integrate applications, distributed component objects, databases, and content repositories while each of these components

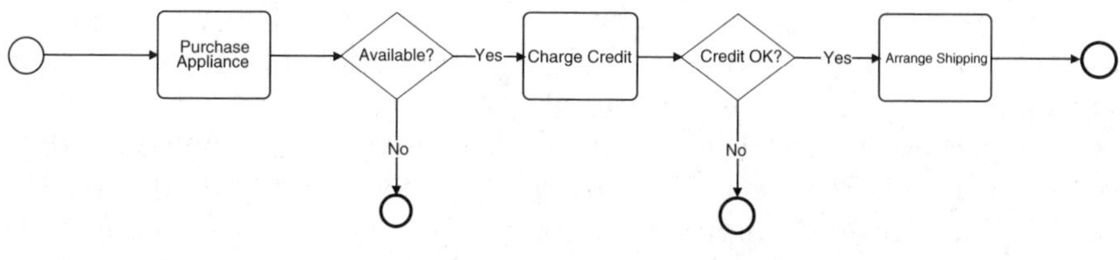

Figure 4.18 Business process for purchasing an appliance

maintains its independence and provides solutions that are best served by the specific platform or framework. Services become the common language that enables a variety of heterogeneous systems to communicate and share information. Web services thus represent the ideal distributed computing solution. In fact, various services are often combined and orchestrated together in processes. The three aforementioned service accesses (Figure 4.17) could happen in a process in the order shown in Figure 4.18.

Business process management, discussed in Chapter 5, is therefore essential to orchestrate the execution of the various services—and for two very important reasons:

1. Services that have been developed independently can be combined into a process to provide a useful value add service. In the previous example, the shipping, credit card company, and appliance vendor have developed their services independently from one another. Now a process can be created that combines and orchestrates them in a complete purchasing transaction.
2. Then the process can be published as a service, which in turn could be used in other processes. Think about it: The services that are the building blocks are distributed within the intranet or the Internet. Now processes are used to compose and to create a new service, which in turn could be made into a building block of a larger service.

This is very important, especially when companies try to connect to each other and to have visibility into their trading partner's processes. This means dealing with two fundamental types of processes: those that (1) access applications or services within an organization; and (2) access and interact with trading partners between organizations. The next chapter expands on BPM and shows how straight-through processing (STP) can be achieved from an originator process to a target process. STP begins connecting the processes of various trading partners in value chains, where each partner performs specific tasks in the chain to deliver specific goods or services to the end customer. Chapter 5 will help this become clearer, but just as a simple example think about building and shipping a customer computer with multiple parts and peripherals from different vendors. Each of the partners or players (e.g., memory chip vendor, central processing unit [CPU] vendor, chassis vendor, monitor vendor, printer vendor) is part of the overall supply chain. This chain also includes service and shipping companies as well as financial service organizations to complete the transaction. These transactions are carried out in distributed environments potentially involving many trading partners and applications.

4.4.1 Distributed Brokered Service Integration

The easiest way to build service oriented applications is through point-to-point integration. Figure 4.13 and 4.14 both illustrate point-to-point integration. This is the easiest and, not surprisingly, the most popular service integration. For example, many portals and popular sites—including Google, Amazon, and eBay—are providing Web services-based interface to their sites.

Here is a client code that can conduct Google searches within a client application:

```
GoogleSearch searchSOA = new GoogleSearch();
searchSOA.setKey("mykey");
searchSOA.setQueryString("Service Oriented Architecture");
GoogleSearchResult resultSOA = searchSOA.doSearch();
```

This is the simplest form of point-to-point service invocation, which could apply to both internal services as well as services invoked over the Web at remote sites. For example, with a key, which can be easily obtained from Google at http://www.google.com/apis/, the Google search can be executed anywhere on the Internet and will execute at the Google endpoint, http://api.google.com/search/beta2.

Point-to-point integration will remain quite popular because it is very simple to implement. However, in extended enterprise applications, quality of service is critical. The delivered messages need to be reliable, secure, and high performance. Transactional integrity, discussed in the next section, needs to be maintained. Here middleware or intermediary software lies between the consumer and producer. Service integration can occur internally within an organization or between trading partners. In fact, increasingly it will be a combination of both. Figure 4.19 illustrates the taxonomy of invocation tehnologies in extended enterprises.

At the very basic level, an intermediary lies between a service requestor client and a service provider. Many functions could be performed by an intermediary, especially for security, reliability, and overall monitoring of

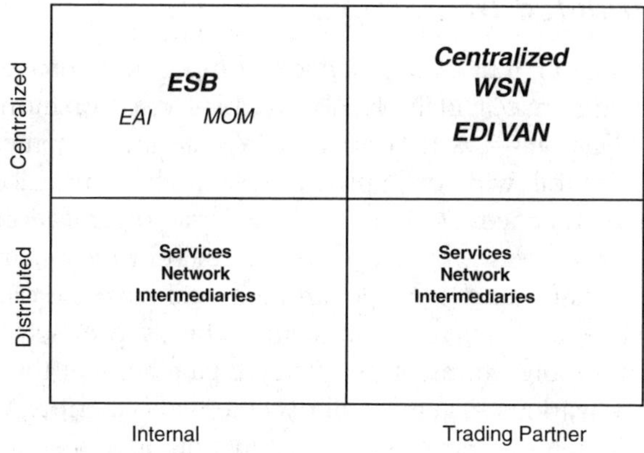

Figure 4.19 Taxonomy of service invocation technologies. VAN = Value Added Network, WSN = Web Services Network

the performance of the service interactions. Chapter 6, on quality of services, expands on this. Using SOAP as the protocol of message exchanges, an intermediary node is both a receiver and sender of a SOAP message. For example, SOAP intermediaries can process security and reliability portions of a SOAP header. The intermediary architecture works as follows. A SOAP message travels through a sequence of nodes on the way to its final destination, the service provider. Each of these nodes might do some processing of the message. Typically the nodes will use header blocks, discussed in Section 3.5, that are addressed to them (Figure 4.20).

Therefore, even though the request in the body of the SOAP message is targeted to the provider, sub-elements in the header of the SOAP message will be processed by the intermediaries. It is important to note that intermediaries can also process the message body (e.g., transformation). Needless to say, intermediaries are much more significant and important in trading partner exchanges than in intranet, but even within organizations security, reliability, and performance are essential requirements for robust SOA deployments.

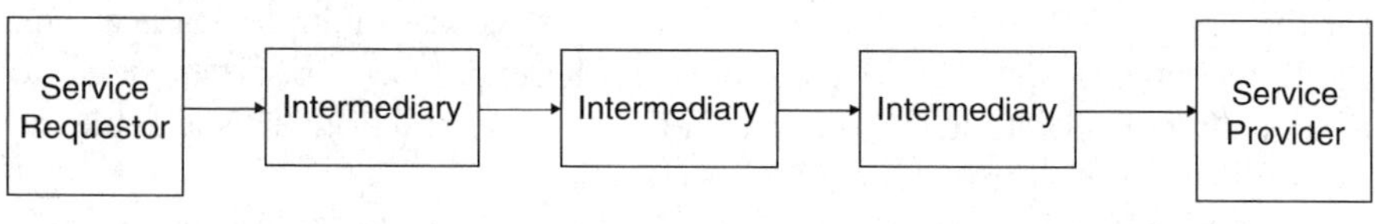

Figure 4.20 Intermediaries through which SOAP messages travel

4.4.2 Distributed Transactions

The previous section introduced service composition through processes. When integrating services in a distributed platform, sometimes additional constraints are needed—it is necessary to execute in the context of transactions. Consider the following example to explain why transactions are important in distributed services. Often within a large organization a customer address change has been provided to one branch of the organization, only to find out that other branches or departments still have the old address due to a failure while updating those systems. This is precisely the problem addressed by distributed transactions. They guarantee that the encapsulated logic, running on various systems, will execute without errors, or no updates are made. Distributed transactions are used in a number of systems, including distributed databases. The distributed transaction technology is also used in transaction servers for managing distributed objects.

Typical distributed transactions involve multiple sub-transactions cooperating to achieve the Atomicity, Consistency, Isolation, Durability (ACID) properties of the parent transaction:

- Atomicity: Transactions are either done or not done; they are never left partially executed.
- Consistency: Transactions leave the application or the database in a consistent state. There are always integrity constraints (e.g., referential integrity) associated with databases.
- Isolation: Transactions must behave as if they were executed in isolation.
- Durability: The effects of completed transactions are resilient against failures—that is, they persist through outages.

Whenever a service updates the states of objects involved in an application, these states must persist in databases, and the updates are done in the context of transactions satisfying the ACID properties. Examples include customers, purchase orders, invoices, employee information, and product status. Usually a back-end application and database store the persistent states of objects. These DBMSs support transaction management with ACID properties. However, in service oriented applications, several services could be collaborating in the context of the same transactions with ideally the same ACID properties for the composite service invocations. In other words, multiple applications, multiple databases, multiple messages, and multiple components need to potentially collaborate in the context of the same transaction. This is achieved through distributed transaction technologies.

Distributed transactions involve multiple services. As shown in the previous section, occasionally several services need to collaborate to respond to specific requests. For instance, there could be a travel arrangement Web service that involves a flight reservation, a hotel reservation, and a car rental. These three types of operations—reserving the flight, reserving a hotel room and renting the car—are executed in the context of the same transaction. As far as the customer is concerned, it is an all-or-nothing transaction. It is not terribly useful to have a hotel reservation for a particular date if no flight seats are available for that date.

Therefore, in many applications, it is required that several of these Web service requests execute in the context of a transaction. For example, if the information (e.g., address changes) about customers is distributed in two different applications or databases, these need to be updated consistently. In other words, either both address entries need to be changed or none. The two Web services need to be executed in the context of the same distributed transactions, each as a sub-transaction. Service applications do not involve just one request/response interchange; they involve several service interactions, or sub-transactions, which need to execute consistently. Transactions and coordination support are essential in the overall technology stack of Web services.

4.4.2.1 Two-Phase Commit Protocol

For a distributed transaction to commit, every sub-transaction, or participant, involved in the distributed transaction must commit. Each participant arrives at a commit or abort decision individually. Each participant has veto power over the distributed transaction. Once a participant decides either to commit or to abort, it cannot reverse its decision.

The decision to commit or abort a distributed transaction is carried out via the two-phase commit (2PC) protocol. Committing a distributed transaction involving several sub-transactions proceeds in two phases. The first phase involves preparing; the second involves committing to the transaction or aborting it.[9] Distributed transactions involve resource managers, which are the participants in the distributed transaction. For example, a Web service managing customer information is a resource manager. Distributed transactions also have a transaction manager, which is the coordinator of the distributed transaction. Some application programming interfaces are implemented by the resource managers and some by the transaction manager.

Figure 4.21 illustrates the 2PC algorithm through a sequence diagram. The example involves three sub-transactions. In this scenario, all three sub-transactions have voted to commit, so the distributed transaction will commit. In the scenario illustrated in Figure 4.22, one of the sub-transactions has indicated that it has to abort. Accordingly, the coordinator tells the other sub-transactions to abort.

The 2PC protocol is the most popular distributed transaction algorithm, and it is the foundation of all other distributed transaction strategies.

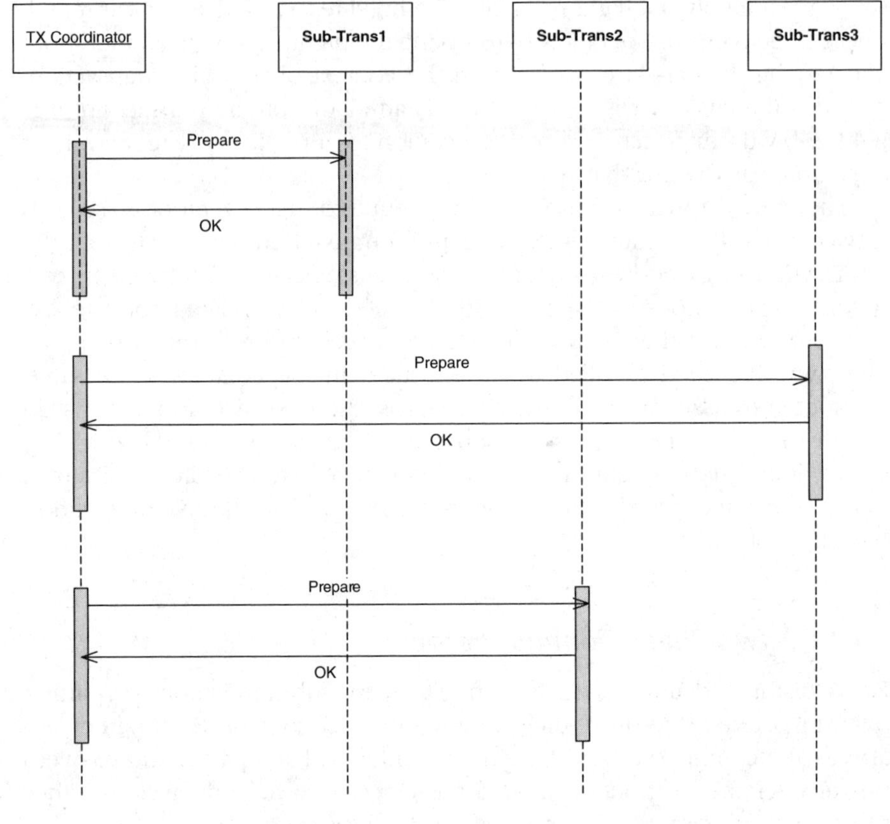

Figure 4.21 The prepare phase

With 2PC, coordinating resource managers can guarantee the ACID properties of transactions.

The next section discusses alternative standardization efforts to provide distributed transaction support in Web services applications. Here the Web services will be the resources. In addition to the strong isolation level provided by the 2PC algorithm, other algorithms will relax the strict isolation implied by 2PC, which is important. The 2PC protocol works best in situations where the transactions are short lived.

4.4.2.2 Distributed Transactions and Web Services

Web services are resources that can execute concurrently. The actual service can be supported within the intranet of the same organization. Alternatively,

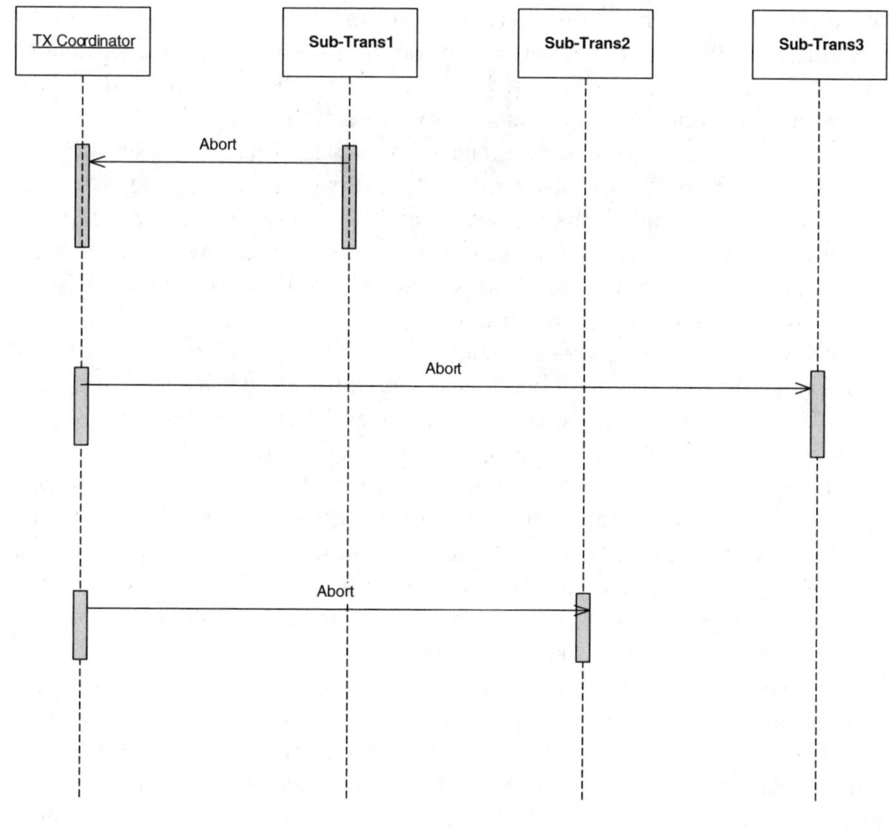

Figure 4.22 One sub-transaction aborts, so all abort

Web services can execute in a loosely coupled architecture involving many trading partners in extended enterprises.

Occasionally, several services need to collaborate to respond to specific requests. For instance, a particular Web service could process a customer line of credit application; another Web service could request credit bureau transcripts; and yet a third Web service could respond to the customer application. These three types of operations (application, transcript requests, and response to customer) are executed in the context of the same application.

Often it is required that several of these Web service requests execute in the context of a *transaction*. For example, assume the updates to customer information and records are performed through Web services. Also assume information about customers is distributed in two different databases. If there are common attributes or properties in the two databases, such as the customer address or customer credit score, these need to be updated consistently. In other words, either both address entries are changed or neither. The two Web services need to be executed in the context of the same distributed transactions—each as a sub-transaction.

Therefore, there are two interrelated aspects in combining Web services. The first is just the combination and order of invocation of the service operations. Earlier we called this orchestration. The second is making sure some of the Web services as an aggregate are invoked in the context of the same transactions. In other words, there will be transactional boundaries defined for some Web service invocations.

As Web services evolve—and they are evolving rapidly even as you read this book—transactions will become essential for more advanced and complex Web services applications involving several services. Web service applications do not involve just one request/response interchange.

Transactional support in Web services attempts to guarantee the appropriate levels of ACID properties for Web services distributed transactions. Distributed transactions sometimes involve short-duration transactions with few Web service invocations. The customer address update involving two Web services is a case in point. Here, ACID properties will be important.

However, in many other situations, distributed transactions involving many Web services in loosely coupled architectures are longer duration. For instance, processing a customer line of credit application could take several days and involve many Web services. Here strict serializability[10] or strict isolation with Web services is not realistic, desirable, or even possible. The distributed transaction 2PC protocol, which guarantees serializability, is also too restrictive.

Transactions that involve many loosely coupled Web services supported by different organizations need a less restrictive model. Nevertheless, it is important to have transactional boundaries involving several Web services. For instance, processing the line of credit can involve several Web services that can execute in the context of a transaction, without requiring serializability or all the ACID properties. In these cases some transactions could see the partial results of uncommitted transactions. The transaction boundaries are important for committing the transactions and also rolling back, or undoing, the completed subset of a transaction in case of failures.

Business process service integration allows service applications to combine several Web services in loosely coupled extended enterprises. Business process management technology orders the control flow and order of execution of the Web services that get involved. So there are two dimensions when dealing with multiple service invocations in the context of the same solution. One is the transactional consideration; the other is the service oriented process orchestration that controls the flow execution of Web services.

Table 4.1 Transaction Models and Service Oriented Processes

	Ad Hoc	*Service Oriented Processes*
ACID Properties	Programmatic invocation of few Web services in custom applications—with no particular flow order.	Internal application integration or tightly coupled business partner service combination. Typically enterprise application integration software implements distributed transactions with ACID properties.
Business-Oriented Transactions	Rare, since longer-duration business-oriented transactions will typically involve processes. Here also it will be done primarily through ad hoc programmatic invocations.	Long-duration transactions and sub-transactions involving loosely coupled services in business processes (i.e., orchestration or choreography). Typically involves trading partners.

Table 4.1 illustrates these two dimensions of service oriented processes and requirements for ACID properties.

So in the context of service oriented and Web services, new protocols and standards are emerging that relax the ACID property requirements and allow loosely coupled Web services to execute in long-duration business transactions. For example, in a business transaction there can be a parent coordinator and several child subtransactions as participants. The participants can inform the parent when they complete their sub-transaction. The parent can decide if the transaction should be committed or aborted. If the transaction is to commit, no action is needed by the parent or participants. If the transaction is to abort, the parent will tell the participants to compensate their subtransaciton. It will be up to the participant to decide how to realize the compensation. For example, if one of the participants changed the address of a customer and the transaction is aborted, the participant can compensate by setting the address to NULL. There are many variations of this weaker longer running transactional concept, but essentially they all relax the strict ACID properties of the 2PC protocol.

Business and IT: Two interrelated concepts are used to combine Web services. The first is the combination and order of invocation of the service operations in processes. Just because the Web services are invoked in a particular order does not automatically guarantee that they will be executed transactionally. The two concepts—service orchestration and transactional execution—are related but separate capabilities. The second is making sure some of the Web services as an aggregate are invoked in the context of the same transactions. In other words, transactional boundaries will be defined for some Web service invocations.

A number of WS standards address transactional coordination.[11]

- WS-Coordination: This is a WS-* that provides the specification interacting with the distributed transaction coordinator. As in the 2PC protocol, the role of the coordinator is essential. The coordinator is the transaction manager and is responsible for guaranteeing the appropriate distributed transaction semantics. As in all distributed transaction schemes, the coordinator sends messages to various participants in the distributed transaction, and participants respond with messages. Based on a particular protocol or transaction type, the coordinator implements a state transition protocol for the distributed transaction and guarantees the semantics of either business activity or atomic transactions.
- WS-AtomicTransaction: This standard uses the WS-Coordination standard and addresses distributed transactional support for Web services. The coordination control is achieved through a coordination context to coordinate service invocations that pertain to the same distributed transaction. The coordination context is included in the header of the SOAP message. The standard supports two types of 2PC protocols: durable and volatile. The volatile and durable variants are similar except that in case of the volatile 2PC, all the participants must respond to the transaction coordinator and vote that they will be committing before the coordinator starts a prepare phase with durable 2PC. Furthermore, the participants in a volatile 2PC are not guaranteed they will receive the final outcome (i.e., commit or abort) of the distributed transaction.

- WS-BusinessActivity: The third standard also uses WS-Coordination but is less restrictive than the 2PC atomic transaction protocol. It is a standard that addresses the long-duration business transactions. It provides support for compensations in case the transaction fails. Compensation provides less consistency than the rollback typically supported in ACID transactions. This standard supports two types of coordination for distributed transactions: Business Agreement With Participant Completion and Business Agreement With Coordinator Completion. The main difference is that with the former the participants decides the completion of the business activity and with the latter the coordinator decides when all the required business activity work is done by the participant.

4.5 Enterprise Service Bus

> The key to any ESB's effectiveness as an SOA foundation is its ability to noninvasively enable the enterprise's existing systems and application to participate as equal citizens in the SOA.
>
> **Eric Newcomer**

> An ESB provides the implementation backbone for an SOA. That is, it provides a loosely coupled, event-driven SOA with a highly distributed universe of named routing destinations across a multiprotocol message bus.
>
> **Dave Chappell**

Business: ESBs are the next phase in the evolution of enterprise integration technologies. They provide a powerful mechanism that allows an IT organization to mix and match various standard technologies for integration. They are the backbone of the enterprise. One big advantage of ESBs is that since they rely on standards for integration, it will be less of an issue to replace ESB solutions from different vendors—they are less vendor dependent, at least in theory.

IT: Be careful when choosing a particular ESB vendor. The larger companies and application server vendors are moving in this direction as well. However, smaller vendors can provide affordability, ease of use, and robustness. If the promise of standards-based integration holds, solutions might be prototyped and piloted based on an easy-to-use ESB platform first and then moving on to more high-performance and reliable solutions in subsequent deployments.

The previous sections showed two important and complementary elements of service composition: processes and transactions. Chapter 6 focuses on other critical features for service architectures, especially reliability and security. Why are these important? They are all key features and capabilities of the emerging SOA backbone: enterprise service buses. An ESB is a standards-based integration bus that supports synchronous and asynchronous exchanges between disparate applications. The ESB is intended to be the backbone of the enterprise architecture—the nervous system that connects all the applications, resources, and components.

Enterprise architectures will involve many applications that need to interoperate. It is also necessary to be able to compose existing applications and to publish the composition as a service. Many technologies attempt to realize this interoperability and application composition under the banners of integration or middleware. Some of these have already been mentioned: back-end applications (e.g., ERP systems), CORBA objects, EJB components, .NET components, MOM, EAI, and, of course, Web services. Many consider ESB as reincarnated and repackaged MOM and EAI. There is some truth to this because many EAI and MOM vendors are repackaging and repositioning their legacy integration or messaging technologies as the more modern enterprise service bus solution supporting SOA. There is nothing wrong with this approach. For instance when BPM became popular, workflow and EAI vendors started to position their products with the latest more popular industry denotation: BPMS, which is perfectly justifiable.

Business and IT: The word integration is rather nebulous. Each middleware has its twist and twirl on the semantics. For a long time EAI was supported by products that used proprietary technologies. So basically it was necessary to purchase an EAI product and then to develop adapters to the applications that worked with that particular EAI solution. Popular applications had their own adapters—prefabricated. The EAI hub became the clearinghouse that integrated all the applications, but it used proprietary messaging and application interface specifications. If one vendor's product was adopted for the EAI and adapters and solutions were developed with that vendor's tools, you were stuck. The application integration solution was tied to a proprietary vendor's platform. There will be differences in the definitions of ESBs for quite some time to come.

The various core functionalities and components that constitute an ESB are not new. The novelty is more on the standards adoption:

1. Web services XML-based core standards such as WSDL, Universal Description, Discovery, and Integration (UDDI), and SOAP
2. The QoS standards (covered in Chapter 6) such as WS-Security and WS-ReliableMessaging
3. Service orchestration standard, especially Web Services Business Process Execution Language (WS-BPEL) (discussed in Chapter 5)
4. Support for other incumbent standards such as JMS, SMTP, and CORBA

Most definitions of ESB will definitely support the first point, although some might not include a UDDI registry support. Also, increasingly Web services-based QoS as well as orchestration of services are being adopted by ESB solutions. Some ESB solutions consider process orchestration as a supported and pluggable process service, not a core component of the ESB.

The key point is that standards-based integration with reduced deployment and integration cost, relying primarily on Web services-based standards, is the salient capability of the enterprise service bus. One application could communicate (i.e., request) via a Web service call to an application that has a resource (application) adapter. The ESB can then conduct some transformations and can call the target application via a Java application interface call (e.g., using the Java connector architecture [JCA] standard). It will get the results and will create a SOAP response to the Web service call. It will also manage and store the message exchange and will make sure the exchange is carried out securely and reliably. So here are two applications: one communicating via the Web service SOAP request/response messaging standard and the other communicating via JCA protocol. ESB is the backbone plumbing that supports the transformation, the routing of messages, and round-trip exchanges between applications using standards.

This exchange can span beyond enterprise boundaries to extended enterprises. For instance, through an ESB, the request to a Web service server in SOAP can be submitted from an internal Web service client inside the firewall to an external Web service. Therefore, as the technology evolves, ESB technologies will also be used for B2B and business-to-consumer (B2C) integration. Extended enterprise ESBs—or federation of ESBs—provide openness and ease of plug-and-play support, aggregating all the standards-based technologies to deliver message exchanges securely and reliably.

This raises some important questions: What is the core reference architecture of an ESB, and what functionalities should be included in an ESB? These are important but difficult questions to answer.

This chapter has touched on some of the more obvious capabilities of ESBs: standards-based integration and application invocation brokering as well as transformations. How about other features such as orchestration and event processing? What should be considered core ESB functionality, and what should be considered optional add-on functionality? Does it really matter as long as the functionality is available to the ESB clients? There have been some attempts to standardize and to provide reference architecture definitions of ESBs. Sections 4.5.1 and 4.5.2 cover Java business integration (JBI) and the service component architecture (SCA), respectively. JBI provides a Java specification for ESBs.[12] SCA is a service programming method.

IT: The messaging communication between applications has two fundamental modes: synchronous and asynchronous. The synchronous communication or message exchange is a blocking send and receive mode of exchange. For instance, if someone makes a phone call to get some information on a product, in synchronous mode they are put on hold to wait usually with some elevator music in the background until they get their answer. In contrast, the asynchronous mode of communication is nonblocking. The request is made, and at some later time the answer is given. With this example, the request is left in some voice mailbox, and someone at a later time will call back to provide the answers. That is the gist of asynchronous communication. With a publish and subscribe model, service providers can publish on a topic, and service requestors can subscribe to the topic. The publishers and subscribers do not need to know about each other's protocols or requirements or even existence. The providers publish on various topics, and subscribers get the notifications. The whole interaction can happen using standards-based Web services.

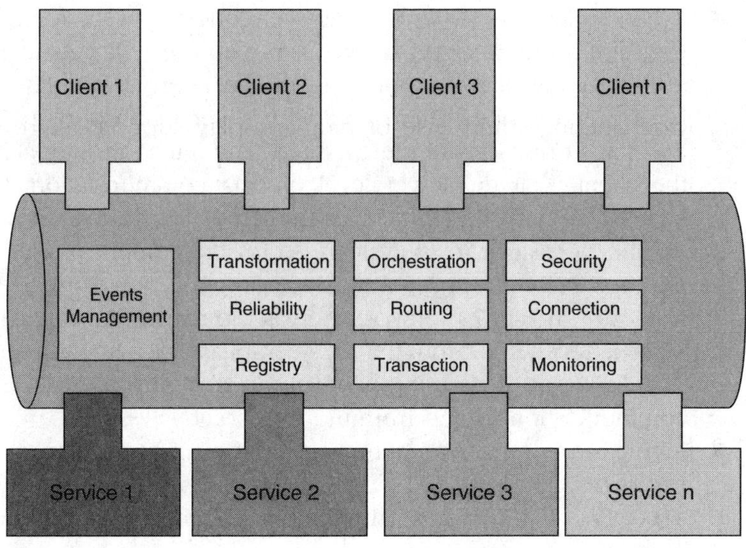

Figure 4.23 ESB Architecture

The focus here is on key features and functions of ESBs. A particular ESB software solution will provide its own level and approach in supporting these criteria. Some of these capabilities will be core capabilities, whereas others will be achieved through supporting pluggable components for the specific feature. For instance, some ESBs have built-in BPEL support for service orchestration. Others consider BPEL as part of the overall reference architecture of SOA but as an external component—and product—that could be plugged into the ESB. These distinctions were not made in Figure 4.23.

- Transport Protocol Brokering: With protocol translation, a service requestor submitting the request in one transport protocol (e.g., HTTP) can interact with a service provider with an interface in another protocol (e.g., JMS). The ESB handles the translation between the protocols. Note that the protocols supported by ESBs are all standards based. Some ESBs support nonstandard protocols (e.g., application specific). Nevertheless, as there is an abundance of standards, brokering capability is needed to translate and to map between the standard protocols. The service requestors and service providers can be decoupled from connection protocol dependencies, and it is necessary to rely on the ESB to perform the mapping between them.

- When a message is sent by a service requestor, at the requestor's end point, the transport mechanism with the ESB gets involved and communicates the message to the internal ESB layers for further processing. There could be several transport mapping and transformations of the message. The transport interfacing to the client is at the lower level of data communication. Other layers deal with the content of the data (e.g., to transform it to another format or to route it based on the content of the data). Figure 4.24 (a) illustrates a message or invocation from a service requestor in HTTP protocol whereas the requesting service provider is receiving through a JMS compliant messaging interface. The Transport Processing handles the mapping of the message communication to and from the end point.
- Figure 4.24 (b) shows a number of transport communication protocols. The key point here is that the underlying transport processing of the ESB allows for communication transport

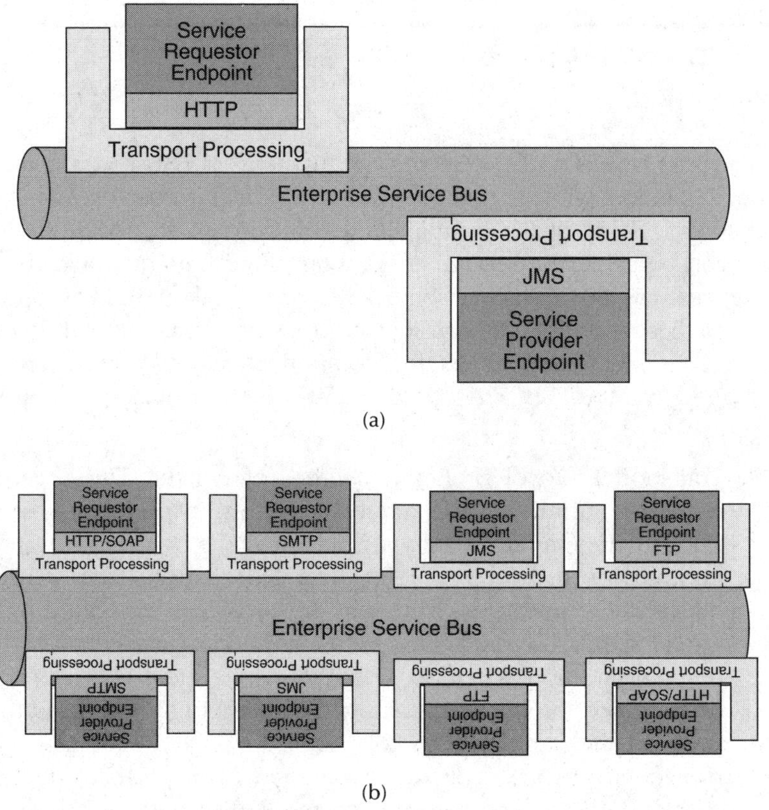

Figure 4.24 Mapping transport protocols

independence: A requestor can communicate with a provider via its own protocol without worrying about the provider's protocol. The transport processing mechanism within the ESB takes care of the mappings to and from the various standard protocols.

- Message transformation: Messages used by service providers and service requestors often have different formats for the same concepts or content. An address or customer information might have different representations or fields for customer name, customer status, or customer purchases. ESBs also provide mechanisms to convert or transform between messages. Thus participants in the integration can use their native message formats and let the ESB take care of the transformations. Here is an example of a message transformation. The content of the information is the same: customers and their purchase order, including items that were ordered. However, a source delivers it in one format and the target expects it in another format. Unlike transport mapping, Figure 4.25 shows transformational mapping between message formats.[14]
  - The messages being transformed could be in the same or different formats (e.g., XML, fixed-length ASCII, binary). The ability to execute such transformations requires that the developer provide

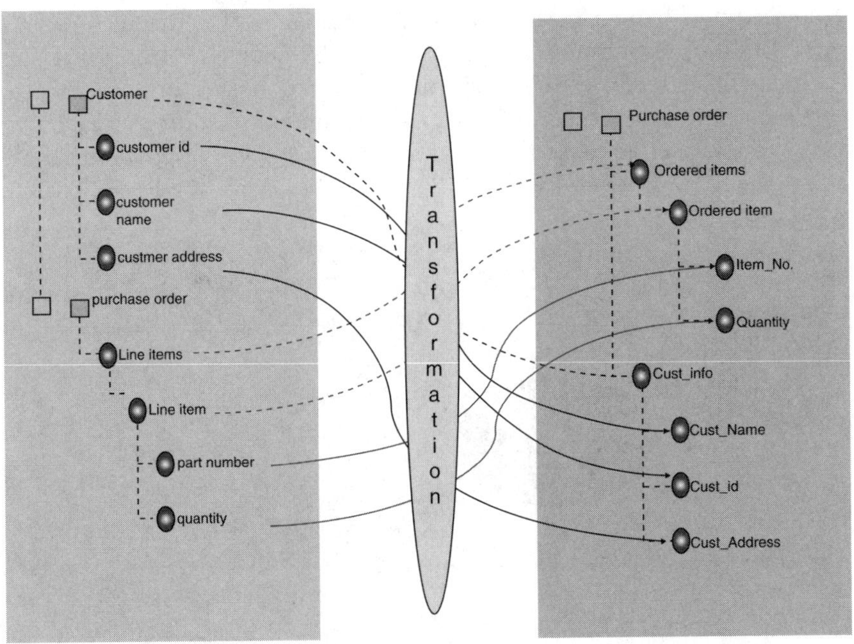

Figure 4.25 Message transformation

a mapping between message fields. Furthermore, whereas various ESBs may provide the ability to execute transformations among common formats, those involving proprietary formats may require the developer to provide the transformation implementation.

- Content-based routing rules: In many situations, the message delivery destination is content based. The ESB will have routing logic, which will inspect the content of the message and then will route it based on values of message fields. The decisioning logic can be represented as rules (e.g. if–then) that will decide which service to invoke or message to publish based on the content of the message itself. For instance, if the message contains information on insurance, depending on the field that indicates the type of the insurance requested (i.e, personal or vehicle), the message will be delivered to the appropriate service. Figure 4.26 illustrates a routing rule.
- Connections: Connecting to back-end systems in internal networks or trading partners through secure service networks are essential functions of an ESB. Typically there will be several back-end enterprise information systems (EIS) such as SAP or PeopleSoft. If such systems don't expose the required functionality via Web service interfaces, it is necessary to connect to these systems via resource adapters. The resource is the EIS interface. The adapter does the brokering to connect to the EIS, taking into consideration parameters such as security, reliability, and transaction support. An EIS can support a method-based (i.e., operation or procedure) service invocation or event-based interactions. Accordingly, the resource adapter will include a service invocation adapter, an event adapter, or both.

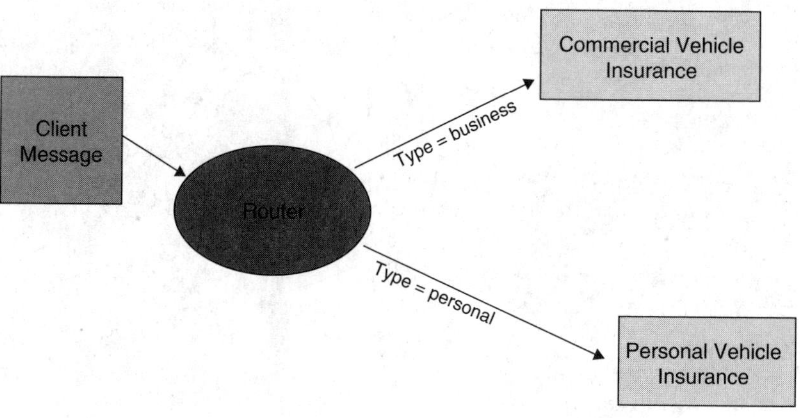

Figure 4.26 Content-based routing

In addition to the service and event options for adapters, ESBs support two modes of communications between service requestors and providers: synchronous and asynchronous. With synchronous integration, the caller invokes a service and blocks until it receives a response. This is exactly what happens in programming languages when one calls a method (i.e., operation or procedure) on an object within a program. It is also what happens with remote method or service invocations within distributed systems. In WSDL for instance, operations are defined, and these operations get invoked via SOAP messages. The invocation is typically synchronous: There will be a request, which is a SOAP message, and a response, which is also a SOAP message. The execution threads of all the components that get involved from the originator all the way to the service provider must block (i.e., wait for the service response). Most of the time this is fine. However, blocking the requestor and provider is more resource intensive, and there is the potential for several threads in the call path to get blocked until the call is served. ESBs also support *asynchronous* message calls. Here there are message producers and message listeners or consumers. The service client can submit a request message and the service implementation can provide the response at a later time. The service client will also pick up the response when it is ready. There is no blocking. There is more parallelism in the asynchronous connectivity.

- Security: There are several elements of security within ESBs: authentication, authorization, and encryption. Authentication information (e.g., username and password, a key) is used by a security server to authenticate the access to the service by a requestor or client. Authorization provides the mechanism to provide privileges to individual operations or objects accessed through the service. Another technique that is heavily used in service accesses is encryption. A number of security protocols use encryption and digital signatures. Chapter 6 covers security in greater detail.
- Reliability: This deals with the reliable delivery of messages from a source to a destination. When a client using a particular type of service invocation protocols invokes a service, potentially in a different protocol, the ESB needs to guarantee the secure and reliable communication of both the request and the response. Several fault tolerance technologies could be used by ESBs to guarantee reliable message or invocation exchanges. One of these is redundancy in the deployment of the ESB over distributed application servers. At its core, redundancy and replication is a common approach in handling recovery. Reliability will also be covered in more detail in Chapter 6.

- Orchestration: Either natively or through third-party services, ESBs support composition of Web services through orchestrations. The emerging industry standard in this area is BPEL, covered in Chapter 5. The orchestration represents the sequencing and interaction of services. The deployed BPEL process can be executed as a Web service either directly or through the ESB. Depending on the particular implementation strategy for the ESB, the orchestration can execute within the ESB, or the orchestration could execute at the higher BPM layer. There are no set rules. Some ESBs have embedded orchestration engines. Others invoke external BPM systems.
- Transaction: Transactional capabilities were covered in Section 4.4.2. Here again, the ESB will rely on transaction services from third parties, including the application server, which hosts the ESB. Transactions are particularly important within service orchestrations. Here several services could potentially be invoked in the context of the same transaction with either full ACID or less restrictive business activity transactional semantics.
- Registry: Registries were discussed in Chapter 3. This is an essential component of an ESB. The registry standard is UDDI—through which service providers could register their services, technical description of these services, and the location of the service definition, typically the WSDL. Even though UDDI is structured to handle business entities and service definitions for the extended enterprise, it is also used extensively[15] internally within enterprises, as an essential component of ESBs.

Finally, Figure 4.23 illustrates event management as an essential functionality of an ESB. In an event driven architecture (EDA), various applications (service requestors and service providers) transmit events to one another. The event publishers and consumers do not need to be aware of each other's existence. The underlying technology that is used to transmit the events could be, and often is, message based. Event exchanges are asynchronous. ESBs support both synchronous service invocations and asynchronous event transmissions in an EDA model. As with all the aforementioned features, the ESB could support these features either natively or through a third-party component (e.g., a BPM system or a business activity monitoring system). An event is an occurrence that includes a source, time stamp, and state information. In fact, many components of a computerized system deal with events. When you click on your mouse that is an event; when you press a key on a keyboard that is also an event. Then the operating system responds to these events. Events could be generated by programs, or devices, or just about anything else imaginable. A rather basic definition of an *event* is an occurrence that:[16]

- Happens at a specific time, such as 10:05:15 on July 30, 2005
- Has a code or description indicating unambiguously the type of the event
- Has the identification of the entity that caused the event to happen, such as unique ID of a process in a BPM system or a unique ID of a trading partner
- Event categorization data, such as priority or severity of the event
- Other event data, such as text messages pertaining to the event

This list is not exhaustive but gives an idea what is contained in an event. Since events are so generic, it is helpful to categorize them.

- Business events: This is the highest level or category of events that have direct relevance and semantics within business transactions. Examples include submission of a purchase order request to a trading partner, completion of the order, or the violation of a service level agreement established between a service provider and requestor. Typically, business events are generated by the BPM system.
- Application events: These get generated by various applications connected to the ESB. Examples here include ERP, customer relationship management (CRM), or human resources applications.
- System events: At the other end of the spectrum are the lower-system events that could occur at various levels of a multi-layered architecture. Here the events pertain to the system level occurrences and exceptions in the containers and hardware platforms that host the ESB and its components.

Events could be combined and correlated. For instance, if the service level agreement of a service request (e.g., shipping a product) has been violated (e.g., shipment is late by 24 hours), and the customer has voiced two complaints, then the combined occurrences of these events will elevate the issue and will raise a high priority exception. The raised exception can start another exception handling process.

Figure 4.27 illustrates events managed by the ESB, invoking the BPM system when necessary. It also illustrates a management layer that monitors the events.

4.5.1 Java Business Integration

According to the Sun Developer Network, "Java Business Integration (JBI) specification (JSR 208) defines the core of a service oriented integration bus and component architecture for SOA."[17] JBI corresponds to the JSR 208

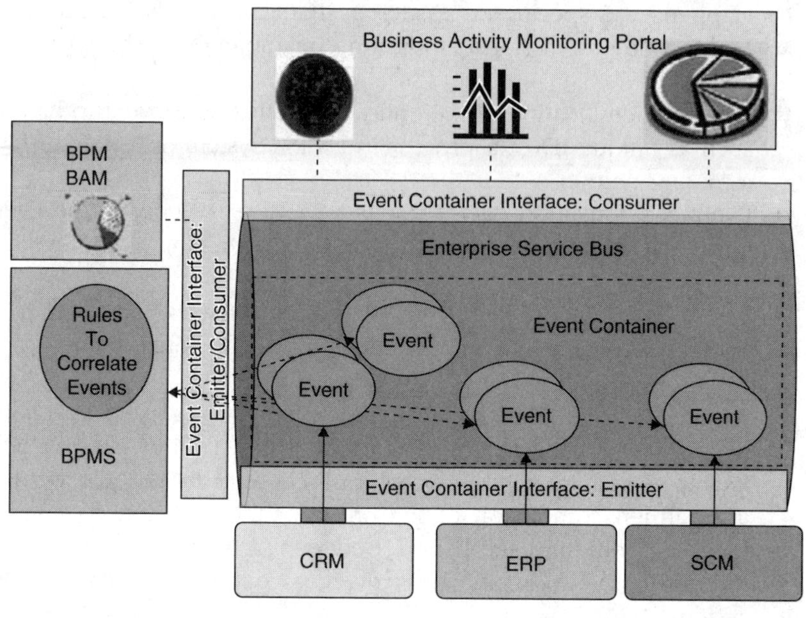

Figure 4.27 Event container within the ESB

specification in the family of the Java Community Process specifications.[18] Figure 4.28 illustrates the various components and capabilities of the JBI specification.

- Management: The management support of the JBI environment spans life-cycle and monitoring capabilities. This means the service engines and binding components can be installed, versioned, or deprecated through the management capabilities of the JBI environment. One of the emerging standards in J2EE service provisioning is Java Management eXtensions (JMX), which is discussed in Section 6.6.2. Complying to this standard means the graphical interfaces of external system management tools can be used to monitor and to manage the components (i.e., service engines and binding components) managed by the JBI compliant engine.
- Service engines: Service engines are service producers and consumers considered internal to the JBI environment. They provide business logic as well as other transformational, rule-based routing and orchestration (e.g., BPEL) services. Therefore, the JBI approach is to provide the framework for implementers to plug in JBI compliant services, which are then used by the overall JBI compliant engine to provide enterprise service bus functionalities.

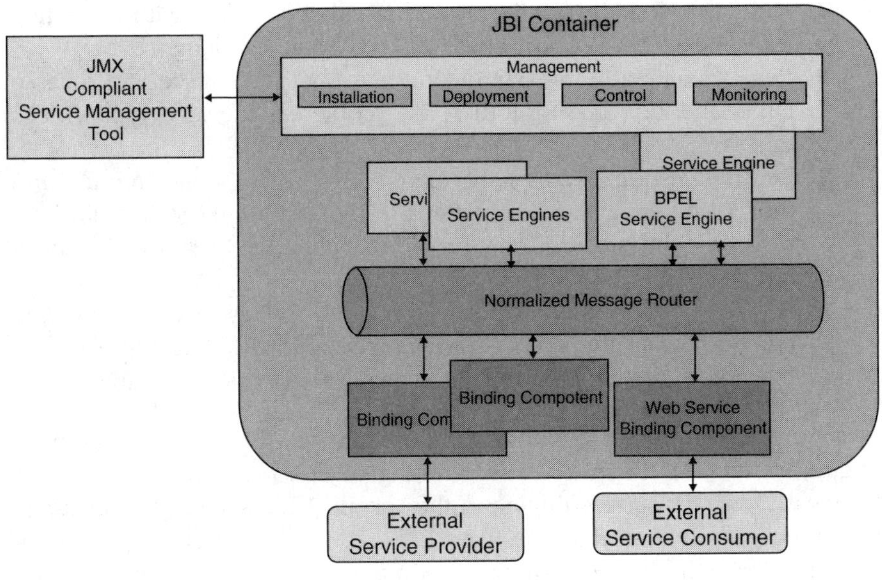

Figure 4.28 The JBI environment

- Binding components: The communication with external services, such as enterprise information services, is carried out through binding components. So these components take care of the all the mapping between JBI and the external service providers.[19] The invocation of external service providers as well as providing services to external clients is carried out via binding components. SOAP binding components are critical because, for instance, they can guarantee compliance to the Web services interoperability standard profiles.[20]
- Normalized message router: This is at the core of the JBI environment. JBI has a normalized canonical message format, the message exchange. The messages are defined in WSDL. A Delivery Channel API is used by both service engines and binding components to create message exchanges and to send and receive messages. The message exchanges represent in and out messages. The message is an XML document, complying to a WSDL and XML Schema Definition (XSD). In addition to the message, message exchanges contain metadata pertaining to the message such as security, reliability, or transactional context. Attachments are also supported.

JBI supports all the message exchange patterns as defined in the WSDL 2.0 standard,[21] which can be summarized as follows.

- One way: Here the service requestor makes a request without getting a response. This option does not have fault handling.
- Reliable one way: Similar to one way, but here there is a reliable fault handling response if there is a problem at the service provider's end.
- Request/response: This is the more conventional service request and then response invocation pattern. If there is a fault in handling the response, the provider may provide a failure response to the service requestor.
- Request with optional response: Similar to request/response, but the response from the service provider is optional. Here there is also the option for generating failure messages in case of a fault.

Figure 4.29 from the JBI standard[22] illustrates two JBI instances. A service engine in the first JBI instance is invoking a service implemented by the business logic of a service engine in the second JBI instance. The message exchange pattern is reliable one way (RobustIn). The service engines communicate through binding components. In this scenario, a fault is generated and is sent to the invoking service engine.

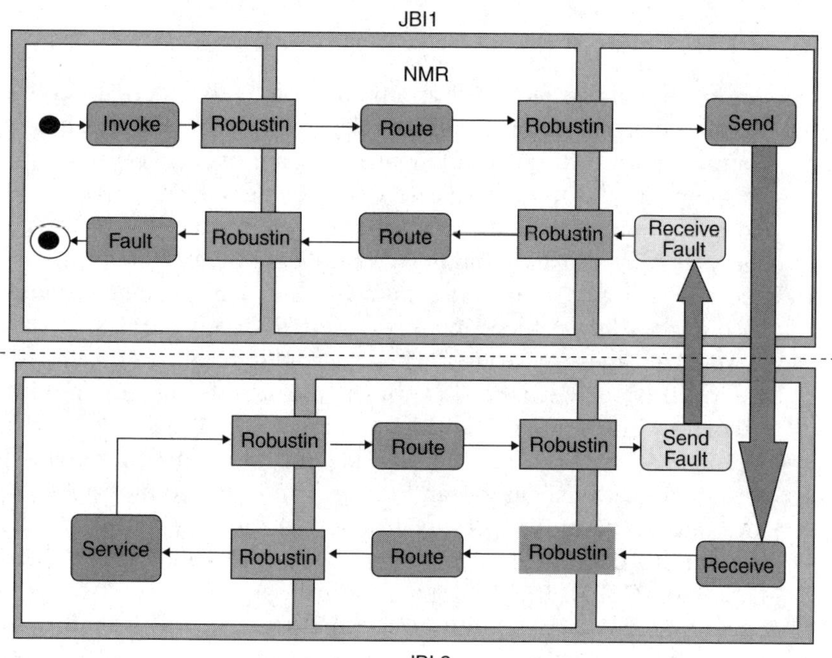

Figure 4.29 Two JBIs involved in service invocation from one SE to an external SE

4.5.2 Service Component Architecture

JBI provides a specification and APIs for implementing Java-based ESBs. The service component architecture is not, strictly speaking, an ESB standard or a collection of API for building ESBs but rather is a model for composing and assembling services from components. SCA contains a framework for composing and assembling systems from modules. JBI contains normalized message handling and specifications for service engines—containing business logic—and binding components, which provide connectivity and transport logic to support communication and integration with external services. Even though its focus is on service composition models, SCA can be, and is, supported by ESBs such as IBM's WebSphere ESB. It is a joint initiative by BEA Systems, IBM, IONA, Oracle, SAP AG, Siebel Systems, and Sybase. SCA describes declarative—versus programmatic—mechanisms for organizing and integrating heterogeneous components into service oriented applications. SCA allows for the capture of dependencies between service components executing within a system. SCA provides mechanisms for defining, deploying, and executing composite services, each of which may have multiple implementations. This is important. BPEL or process orchestration provides one core mechanism for composing services in the context of process flows. SCA provides another mechanism that allows programmers to compose and to deploy services whose aggregate provides a solution to a business problem. BPEL makes the call sequencing explicit. It is after all a process flow execution language. SCA on the other hand just specifies what the reference, or usage, is from one service to another without specifying the call sequence.

SCA building blocks consist of service components. Each service component has an interface and an implementation. The invocation of components, or dependencies, is defined by wiring the components together. The implementation can be in Java, C++, and, interestingly, BPEL. These are the current default implementation languages, but there can be others. The interface is specified using either a Java interface or WSDL.

The components are assembled into SCA modules. The objective here is to deploy the entire module to an SCA container that manages the modules and its components. Typically, these modules execute within the same server, or Java Virtual Machine. Modules correspond to projects and provide a way to capture the relationship and to references among components. Figure 4.30 illustrates an SCA module consisting of three components.

The I indicates an interface. The R indicates a reference. These references could be WSDL port types or Java APIs. The figure illustrates one Java implementation, another BPEL implementation, and a third component with a JCA implementation. The module can expose an EntryPoint to provide an interface to external clients. Modules define an ExternalService interface to invoke external components, so a module is a packaging construct.

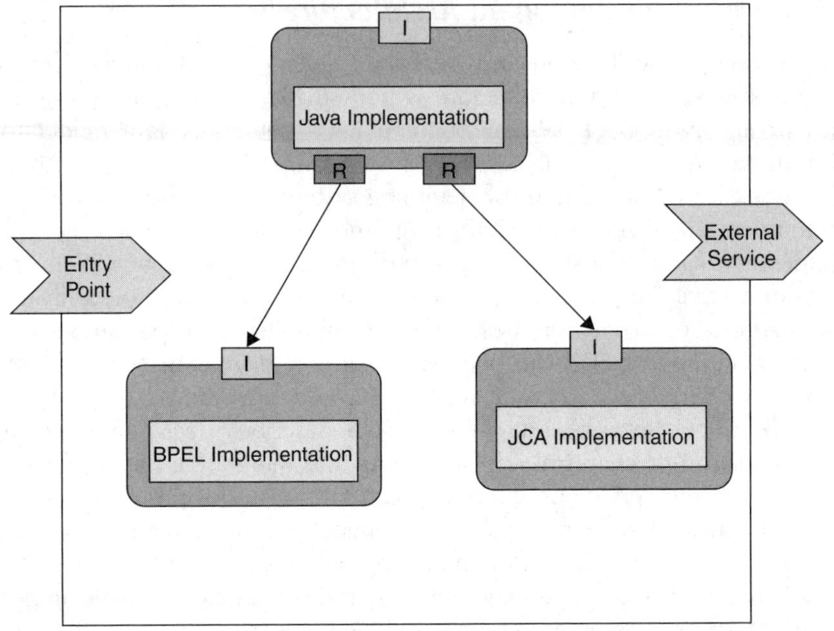

Figure 4.30 Service module in SCA

The services in a component are configured and are deployed together in a deployment package. The components provide configurations for the implementation. Configuration involves setting specific values for properties defined in the implementation. These properties could potentially capture various QoS values pertaining to security, reliability, and overall performance of the services. Other aspects of configuration involve the services and the references. So each service provides an interface and at least one implementation and references other services that it needs.

The components link the references and the services through wires. Wiring defines the source and target components and connects references and service interfaces within a module or between modules in a system. The reference corresponds to an interface supported by the service. The signature of the reference and service interface must match: The name of the operation as well as the order and types of the message parts must be the same. The service can have other interfaces, but it must minimally support the interfaces that are references, and with the right signatures.

The package (i.e., the module) is deployed in an SCA container. SCA calls configured modules that contain more general deployment configuration information moduleComponents, which are configured implementation instances of modules. Think of this as a second layer of containment. Just as there are components in modules with entry points and external services, moduleComponents that are configured implementations of modules also can be used. The wiring can be indicated between the various moduleComponents, and then the moduleComponents can be assembled in another containment concept called a system.

Like modules, systems can have entry points and external services for connecting to external services referenced in the modules. Logically related moduleComponents can optionally be packaged into an intermediate construct called a subsystem, which in turn can then be assembled into a system.

What we have here are two types of connectivity. Closely connected and fine-grained (smaller) components are assembled together within a module. Then these coarser grained modules are loosely connected together in coarser grained components within a system to create business solutions.

Figure 4.31 illustrates a high-level metamodel of the containment relationships among systems, subsystems, moduleComponents, modules, and components.

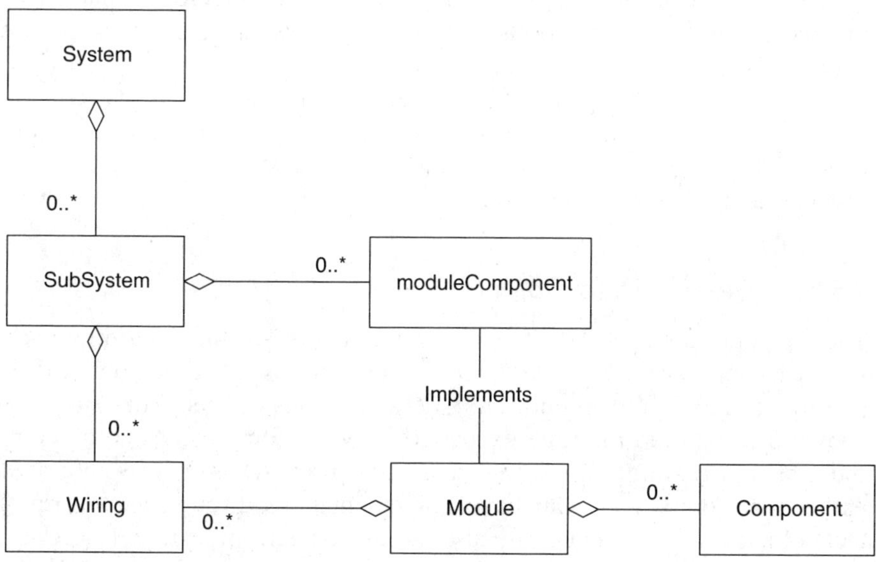

Figure 4.31 Systems and subsystems in SCA

4.5.2.1 SCDL

Components, modules, subsystems, and systems are defined in Service Component Definition Language (SCDL) files. These are similar to WSDL, except that they provide details on the interfaces, references, properties, and wiring. More importantly, SCDLs define the components of the modules and their relationships. Specifically, SCDLs contain deployment information specifying the following:

- The components of the module, including definition of the implementation as well as QoS (e.g., security, reliability) requirements of the component
- The interfaces of the components
- The references of components
- The wiring technology between components
- The entry points
- The external services

One of the main differences between SCDL and WSDL is that SCDL involves not only interfaces of service components but also the referential dependencies between components as well as the composition of subsystems and systems. Furthermore, SCDL also defines the quality of service requirements, including reliability and security, and messaging service agreements.

The SCA specification provides the XSD of SCDL. Figure 4.32 illustrates the schema tree for the module. As noted already, a module consists of components, external services, entry points, and wiring.[23]

There are several types of files for a SCA implementation that comply with the SCDL schemata corresponding to their respective elements. Examples of these deployment files include module.sca, sca.references, and <component_name>.component.

4.5.2.2 Service Data Objects

The communication of data between components is achieved through service data objects (SDOs). The SDO specification provides a common definition for the data communicated between components. This structure provides a common message exchange between components, so all communication over the wire within a module uses SDOs. It was indicated earlier that components can have implementations through a number of technologies. Components can also access data from external services. Service component architecture deployments will typically be across heterogeneous environments involving multiple data formats, languages, and platforms. SDO provides a unified definition of data that can be accessed and mapped onto the internal representation of the heterogeneous participants

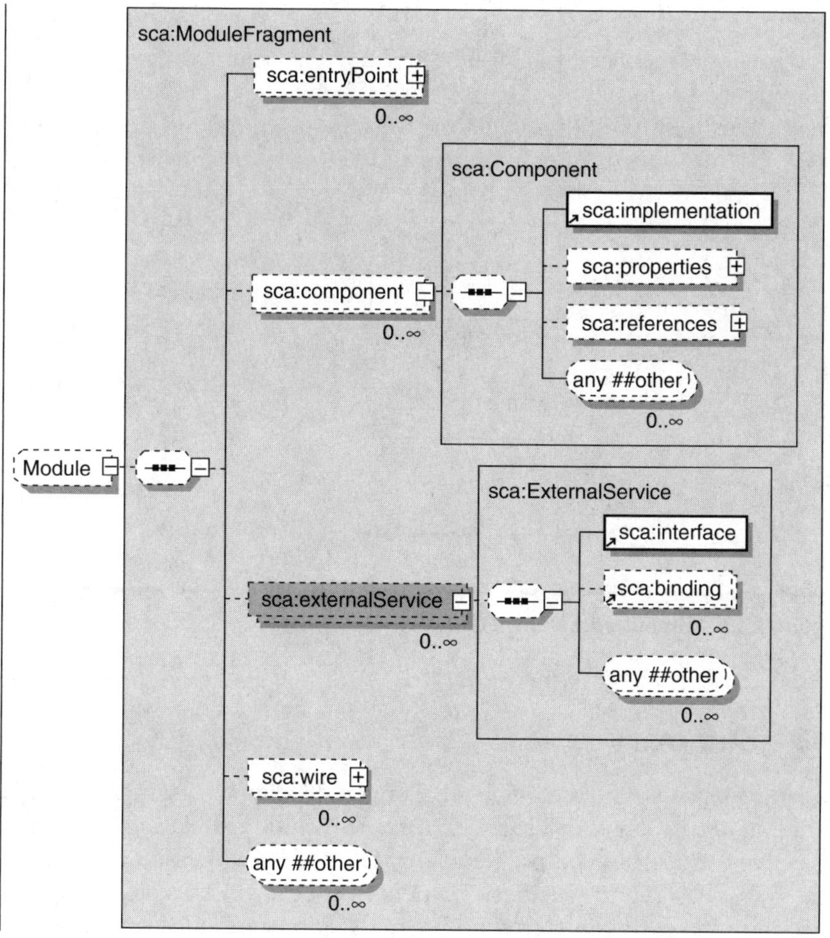

Figure 4.32 Module schema

in service oriented applications. There are other features and characteristics of SDO, but this common format is at the core of all of the other features and advantages of SDO.

The simplified metamodel of SDO is illustrated in Figure 4.33. Components will typically be communicating data graphs, which consist of data objects. These can be complex objects because data objects can contain other data objects. Data objects can also contain properties that are base types, such as character strings, integers, floating point numbers, and dates.

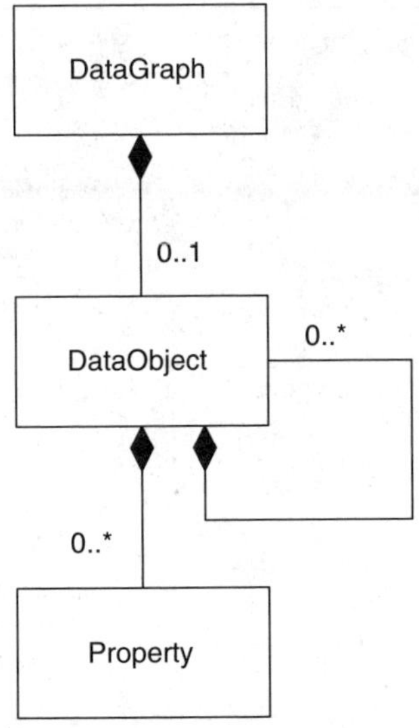

Figure 4.33 Simplified SDO metamodel

4.6 Summary

Organizations are facing huge challenges. Today terms such as *agility,* handling *change,* and dealing with *uncertainty* are circulating in enterprise objectives. These are real problems that need to be addressed continuously. The roles of IT and business owners—especially CEOs and CIOs—are becoming increasingly intertwined. Organizations are often given paradoxical challenges: Cut budgets while not only remaining competitive but also being innovative, producing new and successful products in Internet time. Furthermore, customers are demanding, not surprisingly, more customization. This business-oriented background is provided to make an important observation: One of the key solutions to addressing these problems is service oriented architectures. This chapter expanded on the key concepts of an SOA, especially one that uses Web services.

The technology stack of an SOA has many layers. For each of the layers the service oriented community is developing standards, especially for Web services. A service oriented architecture, in fact, operates in a distributed infrastructure. One can publish, discover, and then interoperate with services. When messages start being exchanged and remote services invoked, the realization surfaces that many components are involved, from a simple touch of a button to the ultimate response of the service call. And all these services operate in a distributed and heterogeneous environment—meaning many different types of systems and applications. SOAs are distributed by their very nature. Services can be composed through processes, and then transactional semantics can be imposed to guarantee consistency. The service oriented interactions often interoperate over the ESB, which acts as the core backbone for integration, providing standards-based integration capabilities together with support for synchronous and asynchronous messaging, message transformations, publish and subscribe interactions, and content-based routing rules.

This chapter provided an overview of SOA. The following chapters dive into the deep azure of service oriented components. The exuberance continues.

Notes

1. http://www-128.ibm.com/developerworks/websphere/techjournal/0508_simmons/0508_simmons.html
2. http://portalscommunity.com
3. In his book *Web Services and Service-Oriented Architectures*, Douglas Barry states, a "service-oriented architecture is essentially a collection of services. These services communicate with each other. The communication can involve either simple data passing or it could involve two or more services coordinating some activity." He goes on to note that the industry will define standard capabilities of CRM, enterprise resource planning (ERP), and other services. These will become standard services and could, in some ways, be seen as commodities. Barry, *Web Services and Service-Oriented Architectures* (San Francisco, CA: Morgan Kaufmann, 2003).
4. In many ways, SOA is synonymous with Web services. The distinction is blurry. But there are differences. Service orientation is a paradigm. Technologies other than Web services could be used for SOA, but Web services-based SOA will be the most pervasive.
5. CORBA is a distributed architecture specification that allows programs written in different programming languages to communicate with each other while maintaining the security and reliability of the overall distributed applications, which sounds similar to service orientation. As shown earlier, service oriented architectures are not limited to Web services. CORBA is a perfect example of an SOA. It is not more popular because it is complex and also relies on brokers—which basically take care of the plumbing and communication between the components—needing to be purchased from CORBA solution vendors. It is not that easy to set up, to maintain, and to migrate CORBA applications. Web services-based SOA, on the other hand, needs only Internet standards such as HTTP, which are pervasive within an organization and between trading partners. For more details on CORBA go to http://www.corba.org/.
6. Application servers such as WebSphere from IBM and WebLogic from BEA are J2EE application servers. A J2EE application consists of various EJBs as well as client- and server-side components. The J2EE architecture has server

and client environments. An EJB is a run-time server component that implements the business logic of the application. EJBs contain many classes and comply with the requirements and rules of the J2EE architecture.

7. The concept of *loose coupling* will be elaborated on in this and subsequent chapters throughout this book.
8. http://ws.apache.org/axis/
9. The essential and main source of the algorithm for 2PC is the *Distributed Transaction Processing: The XA Specification,* published by X/Open, http://www.opengroup.org/.
10. *Serializability* in the context of transactions means the order of execution of concurrent transactions is logically equivalent to a serial—one transaction after the other, where only one is executing at a given time—execution order of the transactions.
11. http://www-128.ibm.com/developerworks/library/specification/ws-tx/
12. There are other more vendor-specific standard architectures for service enterprise integration. For instance, IBM's service component architecture (SCA) implementation provides a unified application programming and integration model for language-independent solution assembly, application composition, and business integration.
13. As chapter 5 shows, a completely separate BPM system layer can serve either as a service requestor or service provider. As has been emphasized throughout this book, BPM systems are viewed as a complementary but separate and different layer than the underlying plumbing and infrastructure supported by the ESB. Both are important. Unfortunately, because of the business process claims of ESB and infrastructure vendors, there is a lot of confusion in the market. The BPEL standard can be used in BPM layer, but it is more appropriate at the ESB layer—orchestrating services.
14. Typically, ESB and EAI engines use XML-based standards for transformations. The most popular standards are eXtensible Stylesheet Language Transformation (XSLT) (http://www.w3.org/TR/xslt20/), XPath (http://www.w3.org/TR/xpath20/), and XQuery (http://www.w3.org/TR/xquery/).
15. Some would argue that it is also used almost exclusively, especially since IBM, Microsoft, and SAP have discontinued their support of the public UDDI Business Registries.
16. This definition follows some of the concepts in IBM's Common Event Infrastructure: ftp://www6.software.ibm.com/software/developer/library/ac-toolkitdg.pdf.
17. http://java.sun.com/integration/
18. http://www.jcp.org/en/jsr/detail?id=208
19. Both BCs and SEs can produce and consume services. There is very little difference, from an interface or component perspective, between BCs and SEs–JBI uses a Boolean to differentiate them. Functionally, they differ only in that BCs communicate with entities outside of (external to) the JBI container.
20. http://www.ws-i.org
21. http://www.w3.org/TR/2004/WD-wsdl20-patterns-20040326/
22. http://www.jcp.org/en/jsr/detail?id=208
23. For more details, see http://www.iona.com/devcenter/sca/.

Chapter 5

Business Process Management

Business and IT: This is one of the most important chapters of the book. Here we discuss how process management can align both business and information technology (IT). Increasingly, business process management (BPM) will become the common language for business and IT to communicate and to realize enterprise solutions quickly and robustly. Two words of caution are offered. First, as this chapter and other BPM literatures demonstrate, BPM has many moving parts. This will become clearer when looking at BPM reference architectures. Second, regarding the mismatches between high-level process definitions and low-level process implementations, the implication is that cohesive BPM system solutions that can easily execute models of processes and business rules created by business analysts are needed.

Definition of process: A set of one or more linked procedures or activities which collectively realize a business objective or policy goal, normally within the context of an organizational structure defining functional roles and relationships.

Workflow Management Coalition, www.wfmc.org

5.1 Overview

Every decade or so, a new technology trend arrives with the promise of finally resolving the conundrum of the extended enterprise connectivity. Two such trends have been gaining popularity since 2000. One is the emergence of Web services as perhaps the most significant Internet-based interoperability architecture. The other is the melding of a number of enterprise technologies, such as enterprise application integration (EAI), business rules, and workflow, under the umbrella of business process management.

This is a crucial chapter. Building on the service oriented analysis and design methodologies, Chapter 5 moves the threshold to further align business and IT. In fact, of all the building blocks included in service orientation, the one category that specifically addresses the execution gap between business objectives and business operations is business process management. This execution gap is the essence of the gap that exists between IT and businesses.

Why the gap? Well, partly because IT and business have different priorities. Business of course is focused first and foremost on revenue. The business objectives are also tightly associated with market share and branding of the products and services. Other high-level objectives include improvements in productivity, compliance governance, cost reduction, and innovation by a well-oiled enterprise with satisfied employees. In fact, businesses have several communities to keep at bay. The customers are of course the most important, but other communities include partners, suppliers, employees, shareholders, the government, and the community at large, which was demonstrated in Chapter 1. The culture of a business is often reflected in how the business views itself serving these respective communities.

IT, on the other hand, focuses on providing the necessary support and execution of systems that can help achieve the business objectives. Today large organizations rely on IT to manage its internal, partner-facing, and customer-facing operations. Given the complexity of the enterprise architectures, many worries or issues keep IT and especially chief information officers awake at night. IT organizations spend most of their time on maintenance, not innovation. Typically, there are IT backlogs and never enough resources to keep schedules on time. There are legacy systems and proprietary systems that are difficult to extend. These traditional IT issues from maintenance to increased backlogs and requirements for new applications are augmented with new challenges, especially globalization and compliance.

Business and IT: Business process management brings benefits to business users. It also brings benefits to IT. But perhaps more importantly, it bridges business and IT and helps them interact, think, work, innovate, and execute through business process flows and business rules. It becomes the common lingua franca of business and IT.

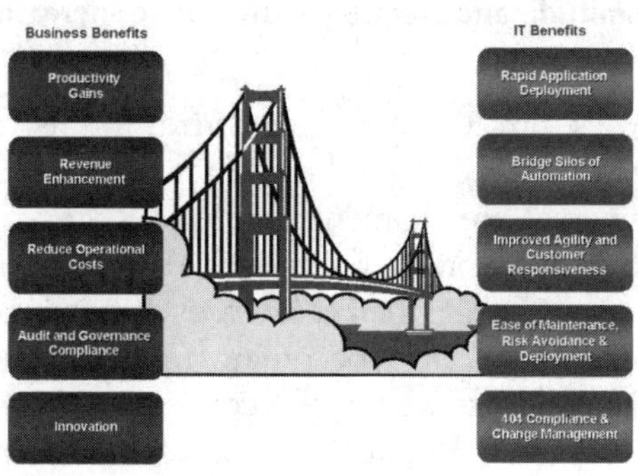

5.1.1 The Only Constant Is Change

Today, organizations are increasingly facing pressures to change and to respond to various types of challenges: internally, externally, and from the government and shareholders alike. Enterprises are increasingly global. Outsourcing of IT and processes is no longer an exception; it has become commonplace. This introduces challenges to the way IT and business respond to external marketing challenges, technological innovation, and increased partnerships with outsourcing organizations. In this milieu, change is the only constant. For instance, some organizations are shifting their outsourcing focus from front- to back-office applications. The phenomenon of software (e.g., call centers, sales force automation, human resources) is seen increasingly as a service. These trends often coexist and need to be integrated with existing legacy processes, software, corporate cultures, and employees. As organizations migrate to emerging enterprise solutions, the frequency as well as the magnitude of change is increasing. Market pressures, the need to integrate diverse departments, and global competition are driving management to constantly evolve the rules of the business—leading to massive increases in both the magnitude and the frequency of changes in business policies and procedures (Figure 5.1).

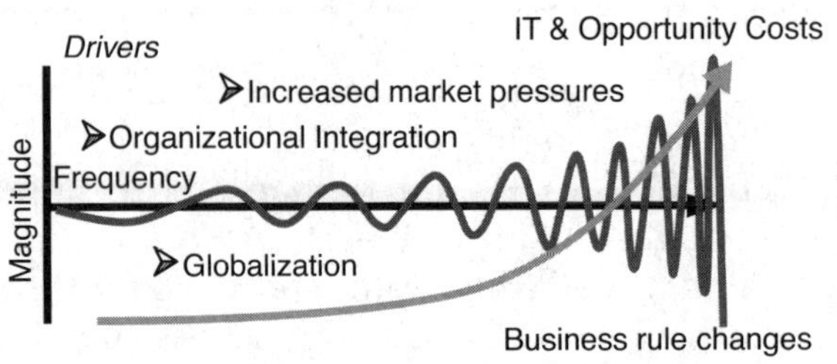

Figure 5.1 The magnitude and frequency of change increases

The industry analyst firm Gartner characterizes this as "chaos reigns." And it does. In this milieu of unprecedented pressures on businesses, the respective roles of IT and businesses are changing. Businesses are starting to learn how to utilize productive tools involving business rules and business process digitization. In fact, they are managing their businesses through continuous improvements and monitoring. IT is also becoming more business savvy through understanding the language as well as the concerns of business owners.

IT and business owners are partners that need to narrow the execution gaps from corporate objectives to operational implementations through IT technologies to realize the desired growth, productivity, and compliance. In fact, there is a difference in perspective between the priorities of IT and the priorities of business owners. In particular, many business objectives can be captured and implemented through digitized business rules and processes. What does it mean to digitize? It means the business objective is translated and mapped into a collection of process flows and business rules. These process flows and business rules are then executed by an underlying system that manages and monitors the automated processes. It is very similar to the execution of programs. As this chapter shows, modeling is necessary but not sufficient. It is not enough to draw flow charts indicating as is (i.e., current processes and rules) and to be (i.e., hopefully optimized processes and rules) solutions. You need to move further toward automatically executing those processes and rules. This is the very essence of business process management systems.

Business and IT: Activity-based costing (ABC) is one of the techniques often used to migrate from "as is" to "to be" process solutions. The main idea behind ABC is to identify all the activities carried out in the "as is" processes and to evaluate the cost of these activities and hence the aggregate processes where the activities are executed. Then "to be" processes can be modeled, which optimizes, automates, and eliminates some of the tasks of the as is processes. In other words, the return on investment (ROI) can be calculated and reflected, going from manual and ad hoc processes to modeled, optimized, and automated business process management solutions. The resulting process with all the digitized flows and business rules will be constantly monitored and continuously improved to sustain the advantages of the ABC models. BPM is not a one-shot solution. In fact, if a process does not involve change and does not require continuous improvement, it is not a good candidate for automation. This category of BPM solutions is used to manage continuously changing processes. As will be shown, the change can be due to changes in the process flow maps, changes in the properties or process data structures, changes in the system integration aspects of processes, and, perhaps more importantly, changes pertaining to business rules driving the processes.

5.1.2 BPM as a Platform (Software Product) Category

> The BPM value proposition evolution began with cost savings, moved to agility, and now has been raised to maximizing strategic performance metrics.
>
> **Bruce Silver**

This chapter focuses on BPM, especially in the context of service oriented architecture (SOA). Chapter 4 discussed several key concepts pertaining to service oriented architectures. It should be reemphasized that SOA is not a product category. Certainly some infrastructure technologies support SOA, such as enterprise service bus (ESB), which are being positioned as the next-generation EAI products. Other products that do support SOA include messaging middleware, Web servers with SOAP processors, application servers, and a plethora of productivity development tools for service oriented programming and service oriented application deployment. These are of course important categories. Going back to the definition of SOA introduced in Chapter 4, comprehensive service oriented architecture provides the overall organization of components that support the SOA and their relationships. Some consider all functions of enterprise software, including BPM, in different categories plugging in or supporting SOA. BPM concepts and standards attempt to address both business needs and underlying infrastructure

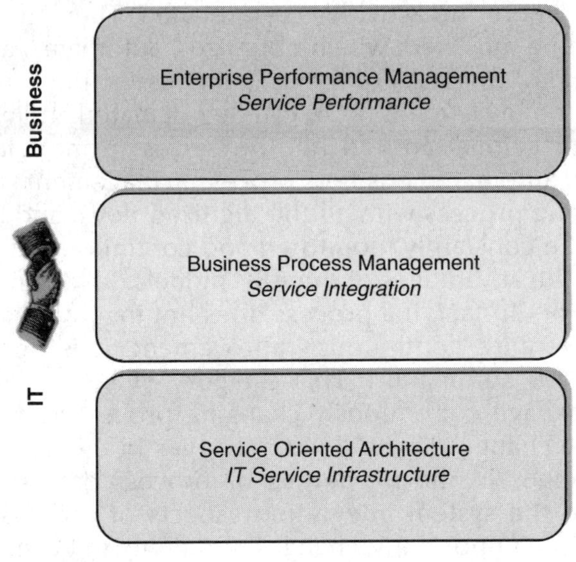

Figure 5.2 Business process management bringing IT and business together

integration constraints. As illustrated in Figure 5.2, BPM is bringing the two worlds—business and IT—together, and, depending on the perspective and priorities, BPM will be seen supporting one or the other. In fact, it supports both.

At the top layer of this service oriented enterprise (SOE) architecture are business intelligence and business performance management tools and products. The targets of enterprise performance management platforms, tools, and solutions are optimizing based on key performance indicators (KPIs) that could be lagging or leading performance indicators. Leading indicators is what the U.S. government uses to keep track of whether the country is moving toward economic growth or stagnation. Organizations can use leading indicators to adjust quickly and to introduce change. For instance, if there are indicators that certain supply chains will be diminished or certain markets will shrink, the enterprise can proactively introduce change to its processes or policies to quickly plan for and to adjust to the coming trends as reflected through the indicators. Lagging indicators are after the fact, which, unlike leading indicators, are a sure thing. For example, quality measures or analysis of the performance of processes in any front-, middle-, or back-office solution are examples of lagging indicators. In Six Sigma, for instance, defects are often measured per million opportunities. Through this quality improvement methodology, the Six Sigma practitioners can collect process performance data and can analyze them rigorously.

The measurement phase is followed by an improvement phase that introduces changes to the processes. The cycle is continuous with optimizations and deployments of the improvements. In either case, whether there are lagging or leading indicators of performance, change is inevitable: changes in process flows, changes in the business rules driving the processes, and changes in the information, organization, or integration aspects of the processes.

This is where BPM comes into the picture. Business process management is a platform and product category, and as of the writing of this book there are more than 100 products on the market that could be classified as BPM. So to reiterate the overall scope of service oriented enterprises, remember the position of the BPM in the overall three-layered architecture of SOEs. BPM brings IT and business together. It is the common lingua franca that enables business stakeholders to become potentially not only the source of improvement and requirements but also occasionally the owners of business processes and rules. BPM is about empowering both the IT and the business. Finally, through this layer the two communities can become partners, improving leading and lagging indicators through continuous improvement change cycles.

5.1.3 Three Types of Processes

> In today's information and knowledge based economy, process is the enterprise. Companies serve customers by executing business processes.
>
> **Sandeep Arora**

The previous section provided an overall motivational high-level perspective on BPM. This and subsequent sections go deeper into all the components of BPM platforms. Here the focus is on a taxonomy of processes spanning documentation, modeling, and execution. Within an organization exists three types of processes, which are illustrated in concentric circles in Figure 5.3.

1. Processes and policies: These are enterprise processes and policies, documented, automated, or ad hoc. Think about any type of work currently being processed. Checking your e-mail inbox is a good place to start. Of the very many e-mails only a small portion—some estimate less than 10 percent—pertain to well-documented or automated processes. Nevertheless, each work or task accomplished is part of a process, even though these processes are undocumented or ad hoc. A business is a collection of procedures and policies. Policy denotes guiding rules and principles that often have contractual bindings. Procedures designate how specific sequences of tasks or actions

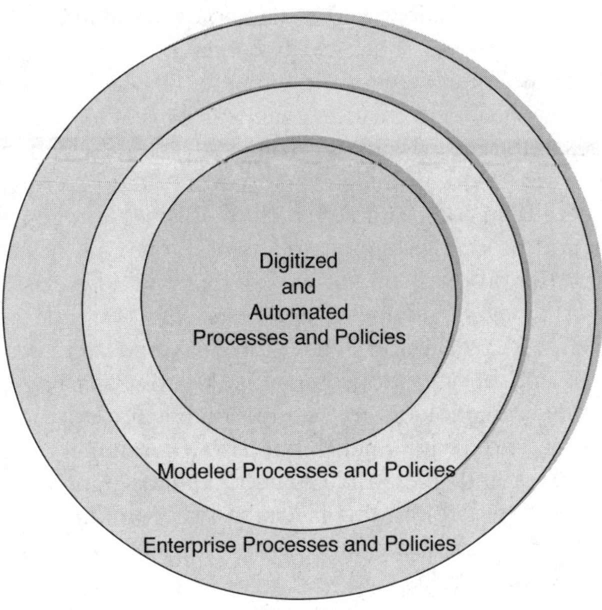

Figure 5.3 Three categories of processes

implement policies, and often the two are linked. Figure 5.3 is an inclusion diagram. The outermost circle includes everything. Every procedure and policy in the enterprise is included here. Typically—and especially in the absence of BPM—these procedures and policies are in (1) policy and procedure rule books, such as when companies publish their human resource policies and procedures, or policies and procedures for handling customer complaints and compliance policies; (2) applications or code—encoding the policy or procedure in enterprise information system application code, database integrity constraints, or raw programs in languages such as Cobol, Java, or C/C++/C#; and (3) people's heads, a third interesting locale of procedures and policies (e.g., "This is how things get done around here"). All these three major categories are used in many organizations. The fact that the policies and procedures are not factored out and managed as a separate asset has caused considerable confusion, complexity, and chaos.

2. Modeled processes and policies: The next inner circle includes all the modeled processes and policies. A diagramming tool such as Visio can be used to model the process diagrams. For instance, Sarbanes–Oxley compliance projects typically start with the documentation of all the processes, especially with the decisioning and

the roles involved in compliance. There are several types of models. The information model, for instance, deals with the business object classes involved in the procedure or policy. The organizational model captures the various groups, teams, roles, and individuals involved in implementing the procedures and policies. The process models are the most visible flows or flow-chart diagrams that depict the sequencing of the process activities.

3. Automated (executing or digitized) process and policies (business rules): The ideal is not only to model but also to deploy and actually to execute the processes. This means models are created and then instantiated. Instantiation implies users will see tasks appear in their work lists. The underlying BPM system monitors the assignments of tasks to users and can take proactive actions. For instance, if a user is supposed to finish a task within two days, and the task is late, the system could automatically reassign it to someone else and notify the user's manager. The process also includes back-end applications and trading partner services as participants, so human as well as system participants cooperate in completing the process. This third category, and in some sense the most important, is the digitized and automated processes and rules. Here the processes are executing. They are not just pretty pictures seen through graphical packages such as PowerPoint or Visio or printed to display on office walls. The processes and business rules are effecting change in the organizations through assigning tasks, monitoring currently executing processes, proactively informing interested parties if certain assignments are delayed, and observing the overall performance of processes.

Insurance: The following example illustrates a use case pertaining to a global insurance company. It is typical of other global and multinational companies. Before deploying a distributed BPM solution, most of the policies (i.e., business rules) and procedures (i.e., process flows) to operate the insurance programs were managed in silos, limiting the enterprise to effectively manage the existing programs and to develop new services worldwide. In addition, the current technology used to support the multinational business programs was dated, difficult to support, not accessible by all offices, and transactional in nature. This scenario is typical in many global and multinational organizations. When various branches are not connected through processes with service accesses, it becomes difficult to gather country-specific information required to develop multinational programs and to release accurate business processing instructions to the overseas underwriting offices. As a result, instructions to overseas issuing offices are released late and in many cases are incorrect, which in turn creates expensive rework and delays in the booking, billing, and collections of multinational premiums.

To continue to capitalize on its international markets, this insurance company deployed a service oriented BPM solution to automate and to evolve country-specific business rules quickly and to orchestrate the extensive process flows and multiple handoffs involved when creating international insurance programs. The service integration provided through business rules and process orchestrations provided the ease and flexibility to develop, to service, and to manage multinational programs throughout its extensive global network. The potential of service level integration and ability to provide various products and cross-sell or up-sell to the customer can span beyond a single organization and can span insurance value chains. BPM is a perfect fit for insurance, as most insurance activities are process intensive.

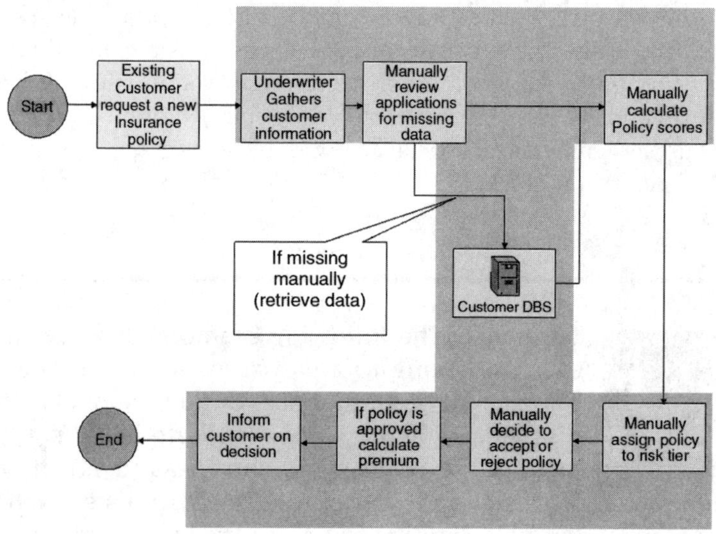

The figure illustrates an insurance process that can potentially involve many manual steps.

Gathering customer information, reviewing applications, searching customer data, calculating scores, assigning policy risk, deciding whether to reject or accept policy, calculating premiums, and communicating decisions are examples of labor-intensive tasks. This is a modeled process, but not an automated one. Automating this process will entail (1) integration via service invocation to gather customer information; (2) enacting rules to calculate policy score, to assess risk, and to execute business rules to accept or to reject policy and also calculate premium; (3) providing notification via service calls; and (4) streamlining the straight-through process.

The resulting process will minimize the human involvement, and for those steps still needing a human operator, the work processing will be less error prone.

The importance of handling change cannot be overemphasized. The policies and procedures within enterprise are in constant flux. On the one hand, it is important to model and to automate processes and business rules. On the other hand, the business or IT needs to be able to easily introduce change and to customize these processes, sometimes in real-time. The major focus of BPM, as this chapter and throughout this book demonstrates, is to facilitate the introduction of change to the processes in an organization to help innovate, to grow the business, or to deal with constraints such as compliance.

5.2 Evolution of Business Process Management Suites

> The third wave of BPM does much more than facilitate process design. It provides a direct path from vision to execution. It's not so much a matter of "rapid application development" as "remove application development" from the business cycle. BPM systems are remarkable in that they provide the capability for directly executing business process definitions and designs without traditional software development.
>
> **Howard Smith and Peter Fingar**

The automation of human activities, especially in the context of services deployed within organizations (internal services) and between trading partners (external services), is in some sense the last frontier in information technologies. The vast majority of process within organizations is either just documented or are ad hoc. The emergence of BPM targets more *digitization* of processes, a term originally coined by General Electric to denote modeling and automation.

Business process management is not entirely new. Figure 5.4 illustrates the evolution of BPM from its earlier days in workflow to now what have

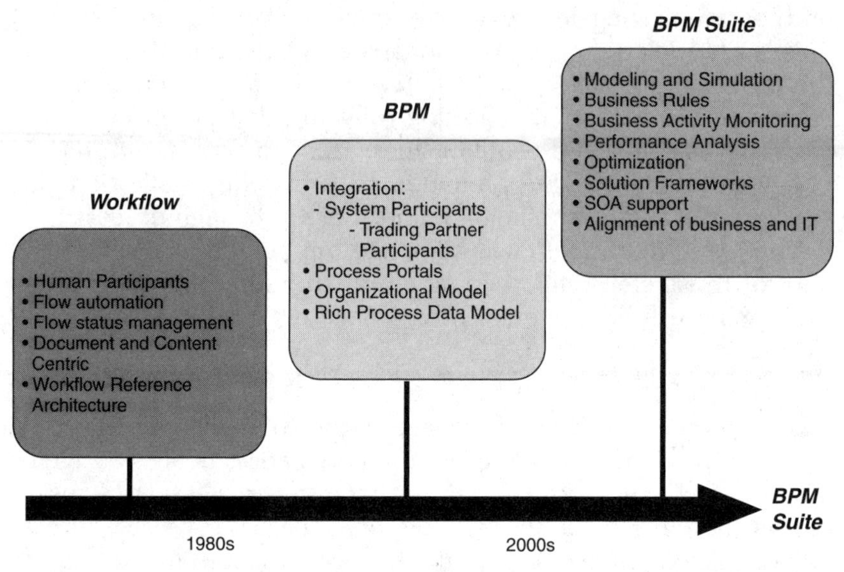

Figure 5.4 Evolution of BPM suites

become business process management suites. As Figure 5.4 shows, BPM suites have evolved from human-centric workflow to more comprehensive platforms. Workflow products, at least in the earlier stages of their evolution, were document, forms, and content centric. In fact, some of the earliest implementations of workflows focused on converting and processing paper-based documents through digitized media. Thus, scanners, specialized monitors for entering data from scanned documents, as well as back-end optical repositories were integral parts of workflow. Figure 5.5 illustrates a basic and typical workflow including a scanning station, indexing, and archiving. These workflows also involved activities to process, for instance, a loan application.

The main difference between the workflow systems up to the mid-1990s and the emergence of BPM systems of today is the involvement of system participants. Inclusion of system participants meant that in the same process flow some of the steps were performed by back-end applications such as enterprise resource planning (ERP) systems, human resources applications, or more generically database management systems (DBMSs). One of the earliest definitions of BPM included enterprise application integration as well as human-centric workflow and trading partner business-to-business (B2B) integration. EAI provides the solutions to connect and to interoperate disparate applications. These applications are typically back-office

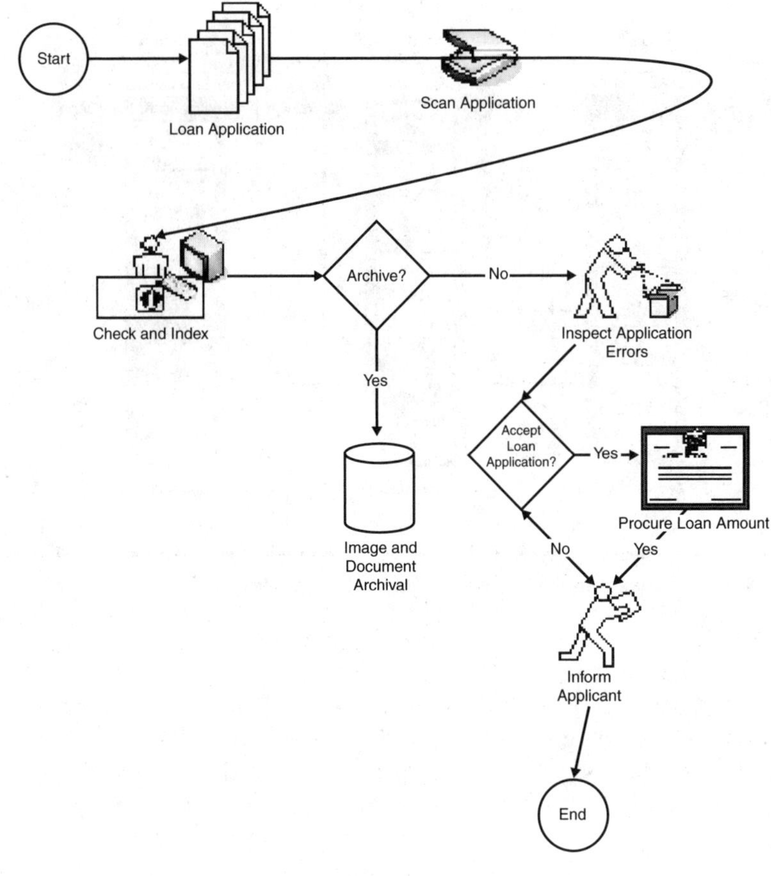

Figure 5.5 A document imaging workflow

applications such as human resource, accounting, customer relationship, sales automation, or general ledger. In this scope, the emphasis is on interoperability and integration between these functionally different applications. As the previous chapter showed, ESBs are starting to provide robust, more affordable standard-based—versus proprietary—enterprise integration. EAI is evolving into the ESB, which is becoming the essential plumbing backbone that integrates applications, systems, and partners.

B2B integration, on the other hand, involves business integration through supply or value chains. Processes in B2B integration involve different trading partner services. Typically B2B integration has specific message and information exchange choreographies between trading partners. The exchanges not only define the structure of the various messages that get exchanged but also the business rules of these exchanges, timing constraints, security

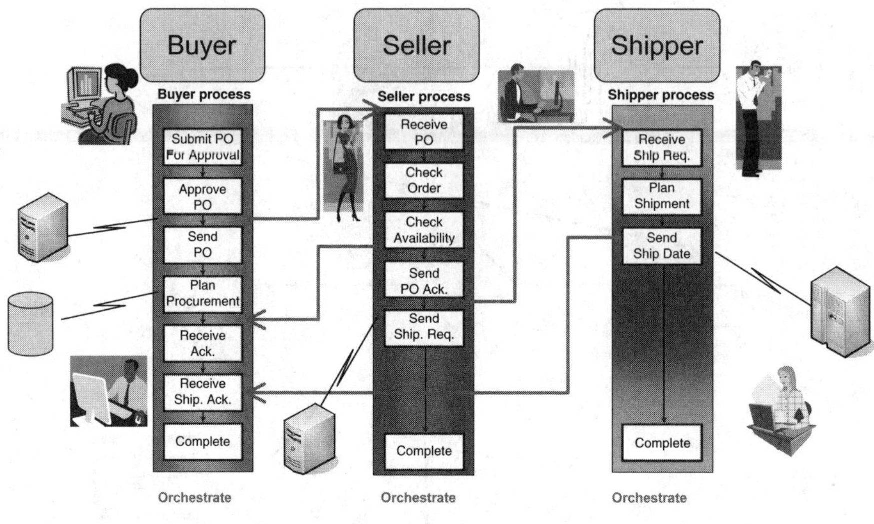

Figure 5.6 Business processes between trading partners

requirements, and process flow logic. So in the late 1990s and early 2000s, definitions began emerging such as BPM = Workflow + EAI + B2Bi.

Figure 5.6 illustrates a classical example involving an internal process for procurement (the buyer), another process for sellers, and yet a third process for shippers. Each of the trading partners will be executing its own internal processes. Procurement, for instance, could involve approvals at multiple layers. These business processes are the orchestration of the activities within each partner.

The following figure shows another example of a superflow for managing risk in purchasing securities. The process includes back-end applications such as customer relationship management (CRM), human workflow, and trading partners. The process also includes business rules for decision making and exception management. The process starts with selecting accounts, which also involves accessing a back-end CRM system. It then proceeds to a fully automated risk benchmark evaluation, which involves business rules. The next step is getting account positions including both equity and currency positions from back-end systems. The computation of the risk uses a secure hosted service and

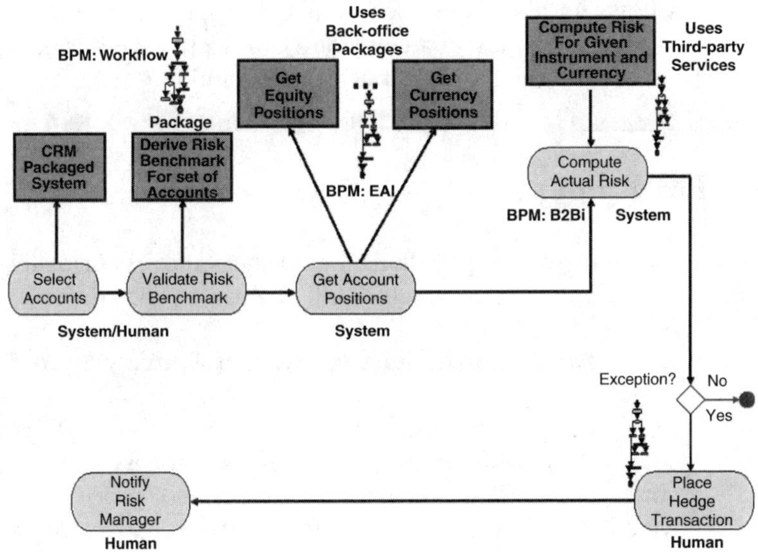

involves a B2B interaction. Finally, the process proceeds with human participants placing a hedge transaction and notifying a risk manager.

There is another significant evolution toward business process management: the evolution of business rules management (BRM) technologies. In fact, initially business rules engines were deployed in isolation, solving often niche and complex business rules problems. As time passed and complexity, especially in developing and deploying business applications, started to increase, it soon became evident that rules should not be executing in isolation. As BPM technologies evolved, the realization emerged that process flows and rules are two faces of the same coin. Any organization is an aggregation of policies and procedures. Procedural flows indicate how things should be done, and policies indicate the guidelines that dictate and drive these procedures. The procedures and policies are specified and executed in the same context. In drawing closer and closer to executing what is specified in processes and policies, it becomes evident that artificial boundaries in systems concentrating on process automation (i.e., procedures) versus business rules (i.e., policies) automation is counterproductive and often introduces additional complexities, especially in mapping or integrating disparate systems. The conclusion is that the evolution of BPM suites has demonstrated a single cohesive system that can digitize both procedural flows and declarative rules is the ideal solution. An optimized BPM system needs to be able to treat process flows and business rules as first-class citizens within a single system. Only with this cohesive architecture can declarative business rules drive the processes. Figure 5.4 illustrates this evolution.

5.3 BPM Primer

> There are so many interpretations for Business Process Management that twenty people might well provide twenty different answers.
>
> **Sandra Lusk, Staci Paley, and Andrew Spanyi**

As the coming sections demonstrate, there are several alternative approaches and models when it comes to business process management. Here a very basic and preliminary overview of business process management is provided. Even though differences can be found in theoretical foundations, models, and BPM products, most provide support for the core concepts presently discussed. This is not an exhaustive list but provides an idea of the core building-block concepts in business process management.

5.3.1 Business Process Modeling and Analysis

> The first point that helps us understand process in BPM is the fact that the processes of key importance to BPM are defined by their business attributes and functions, not their workflow expression (workflow includes the steps, routes, activities and rules of the process).
>
> **Terry Schurter**

Business: There is some confusion in the BPM market when it comes to tools, especially differentiating business process analysis and BPM systems. Some tools characterized as BPA focus primarily on modeling. The deliverables of BPA tools are models. Business analysts can use these tools to perform such tasks as to draw information models, to model and simulate processes, and to model organizations. The focus in BPA is on graphical models and their relationships. The focus of business process management systems (and suites) is on execution.

In BPM systems modeling also occurs: All the modeling concepts discussed here—information modeling, organizational modeling, process modeling, business rule modeling, and modeling integration—are also supported in BPM system tools. A fundamental difference is that BPM systems are also ready to execute. It is not necessary to go through a separate, and sometimes difficult, mapping phase between the models and what gets executed. This is especially critical for handling change. The continuous life cycle of BPM applications needs to very quickly move from models to execution.

To start with a BPM solution, a number of models need to be created. In fact, BPM application development is really a different paradigm and model of computing. This is essential. BPM deals with typically graphical models for a number of artifacts that are essential to the BPM solution. Programming in BPM is different. It consists of flows, business rules, process data models, and integration driven through direct manipulation of the corresponding models graphically. Developers think of processes, the business rules, and the information they manipulate as the building blocks (i.e., components or objects) of their application or applications. This is very different from traditional IT-intensive development methodologies used so far. In fact, it would be ideal to have business users and IT come together and collaborate in a rich browser-based development environment—sharing common development tools as much as possible. It is this collaborative environment that will help align IT and businesses[1] in closing the execution gap.

Chapter 2, specifically Section 2.5.7, introduced the notion of class. Classes represent a collection of objects with similar structure and behavior. Think of how a class is modeled in conventional IT development. Each class will have attributes, or properties, and operations. Classes have different types of relationships with other classes: generalization, association, aggregation, and composition. These models are also needed in BPM. But now it is necessary to view the classes much more holistically and to think about and to model flows, business rules, interfaces, and integration, all within the same model. Figure 5.7 illustrates the migration from conventional classes to process classes to build BPM applications. There are attributes and operations as usual, but now there are also process flows, business rules, integration, and the human interface constructs as essential elements in process class.

In business processes analysis and modeling, a number of tools and notations exist for modeling the processes. These tools provide various modeling constructs to design business process applications at a higher level and then to deploy them to a process engine.

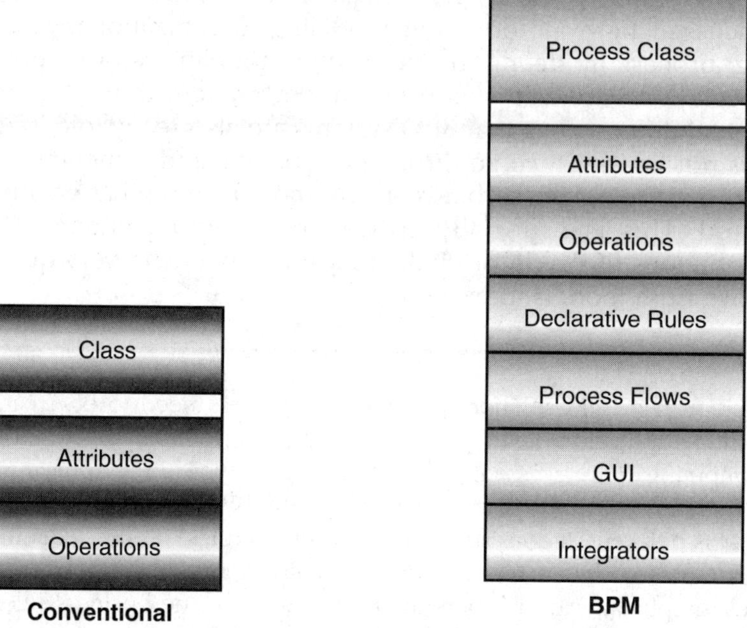

Figure 5.7 Conventional and BPM classes

Here are some of the modeling constructs in BPM suites:

- Strategy diagrams: BPM suites often have high-level graphical representations for corporate goals and strategies—for cause-and-effect analysis or strategic goal setting or as a general framework. Examples here include the balanced scorecard and fishbone illustrations.
- Process diagrams: This is perhaps the most important component for BPM. The process diagrams typically include swim lanes, tasks, or activities; defined roles; and the overall flow of the process. Processes can have subprocesses, and it is possible to specify simulation parameters and to simulate the process.
- Business policies and decision rules: The processes provide the procedural flow models of work, involving human participants, systems, and trading partners. It is also necessary to model the business policies and decision rules. Rules such as risk-level determinations, service level agreements, and approval levels are examples of business policies and decision rules. These can be associated with processes and can pertain to the application or even the enterprise as a whole.

- Class or information modeling: This allows the modeler to provide the analysis of the business classes. Typically Unified Modeling Language (UML) notation is used to represent the class hierarchies. Depending on the specific capabilities of the modeling tool, the classes can be used in processes, for process properties or messages.
- Interaction and integration models: A number of interaction models are used to represent use-case diagrams, sequence diagrams, or object-interaction diagrams. These depict external actors using the system or internal objects interacting with one another.
- Organizational model: The organizational model is used to represent the various organizational units and their relationships. Usually this is illustrated as a hierarchy. An organization can have divisions and units, and involve various roles or individuals.

There are dependencies and associations between these models. For instance, a process model will use the organization model—that is, the participants in the flows, which are typically in the swim lanes—the class or information model, and also the business policies. The strategy model will use both the processes and policies (Figure 5.8).

The key thing to remember is that all these models are defined in the context of process classes. So a process class such as procurement will contain the following:

- Information model properties for the procurement, such as type and amount of purchase, requestor, and items of purchase.
- The process model of the procurement: the flows that involve approval cycles and notification of the procured items.

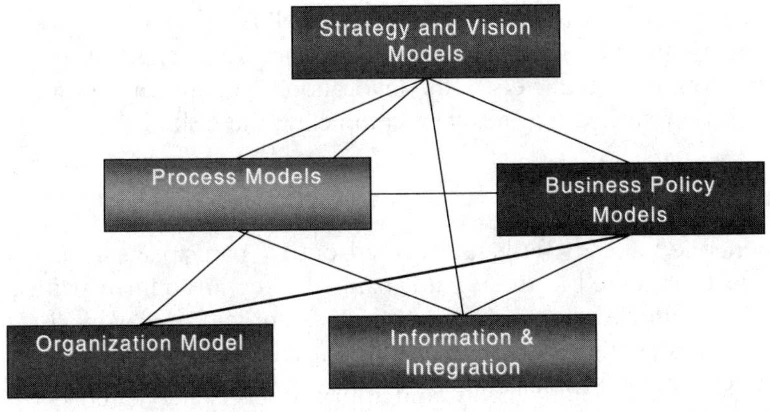

Figure 5.8 The different categories of models and their relationships

- The integration model: all the messaging and services involved in communicating either with back-end human resources, accounting systems, and interactions with the sellers or with providers.
- The various business policies and rules for procurement: the business rules that guide the number of approvals based on amount, expressions that calculate the taxes based on where the items are purchased, and the service level agreements associated with approval delays and the procurement cycle.

The key thing to remember is that all these and other elements such as the user interface are defined in the context of process classes. Comprehensive process classes provide common object semantics that increase overall system performance and the ability to streamline application changes.

5.3.2 The Ubiquitous Activity (Task)

This section starts with the notion of an activity,[2] which represents a step in a process where a particular work needs to be carried out. If a human participant is doing the activity, typically a form is presented to the user to complete the activity. If a system[3] or trading partner is completing the activity, the work is processed in a similar way; however the system carries out the request/response messages: There will be a request message from the process and a respond message from the system to the process. Then when the system assigns the task to the user, a form is presented (i.e., the request), the user carries out the task (i.e., the response), and then the work is complete.[4]

Put in the context of service orientation, an activity represents a service invocation. In a service call, a request is submitted to a service provider, which then responds to the request. The response completes the activity. The call will correspond to one of the operations supported by the Web service.

Now at a particular task, the participant will be manipulating forms and documents. In case of systems, the forms and documents will be sent as part of the input parameters to the invocation. Output forms or documents will also be returned as a result of completing the task.

5.3.3 Participants

As mentioned already, tasks are carried out by participants. The work of the activity is routed to these participants. If they are human participants, the routing implies the work will appear as an item in a work list. If the participant is another system, then this will entail a procedural invocation to the responding system. In case of human participants, the task could be assigned to a group or a role. The assignment to participants can also be more intelligent (e.g., based on skill sets, availability). Figure 5.9 illustrates a hierarchy of participant types using UML notation.

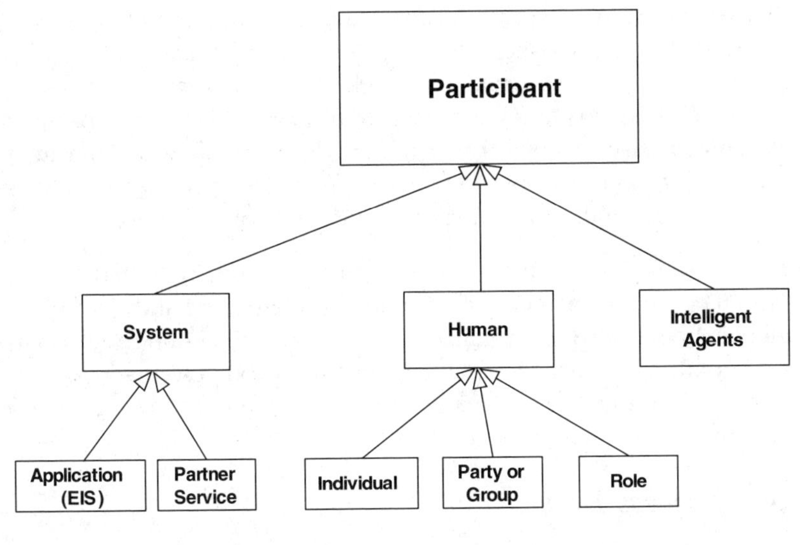

Figure 5.9 Categorization of business process participants

The EAI and B2B integration manage automated system involvement and are discussed in Sections 5.3.7 and 5.3.8, respectively. With workflow systems, most of the participants as well as the emphasis of the process are on human participants. Examples include back-office processes such as human resources (e.g., time off, new hire), processes for procurement and finances, processes for building and deploying products or servers, and front-office processes such as customer service and order processing. Typically these are long-duration processes.

The human workflow support in business process management is one of the most important features, because "we are what we do." Much of an individual or a group's identity comes from what and how work is conducted to earn a living. Through workflow, the sequence of activities carried out while performing work are orchestrated and, more importantly, automated. This automation means that an underlying process engine knows what activity or task to assign to which user. The engine also keeps track of the audit trail of all the instances of the process. So the idea is to define the sequence of the activities and then to assign them to workers. This assignment is completed via several models.

- Assign to an individual operator or worker: This is the most obvious and straightforward option. A task is assigned to a particular worker, such as John or Mary or Tim. In designing the workflow, the process designer assigns the task or activity to a particular individual user, resulting in work being routed to their individual work queue.

- Assign to a group, queue, or workbasket: Another option is to assign work to a workbasket or group. Here the individual user might either pick up or be assigned the work from a community workbasket, which contains tasks assigned to an entire group or department.
- Assign based on roles or skills: A third option is to indicate what type of work is to be done and to let the system intelligently assign the work to the most qualified and available employee.

These are some of the types of assignments used in human workflow systems. The human participant support goes hand in hand with the organizational model used to organize the enterprise, including the usual suspects: departments such as finance, human resources, marketing, sales, support, and product development. Within each one of these departments are organizational divisions and units.

5.3.4 Process Data

As indicated in the previous section, at each activity the participant manipulates data: These could be process-specific data, structured data from relational DBMSs, or unstructured multi-media data such as documents, audio, or video. The process data, as all other elements of BPM application, are defined in the context of process classes.

The richness of the process data is illustrated in Figure 5.10. Process data represents the information model in business process solutions. The process data includes properties such as when the process instance was created and by whom, the purpose, and properties specific to the application. For

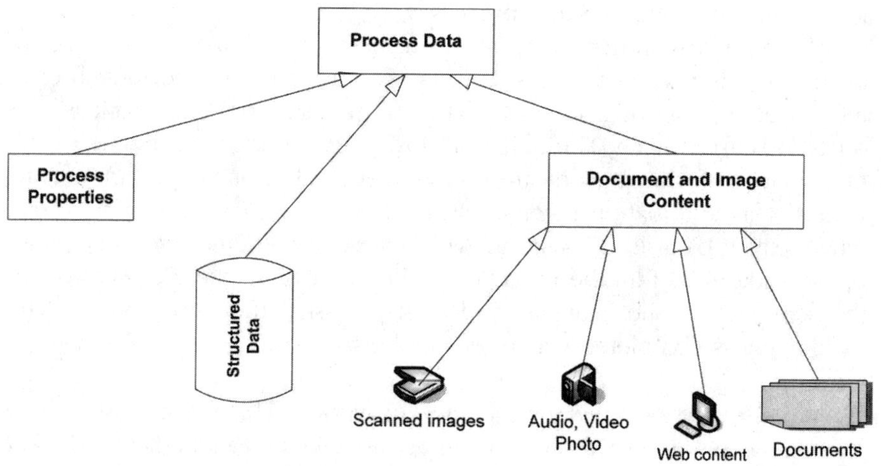

Figure 5.10 Categories of process data

instance, for a procurement application this will include such things as the purchase order, the purchase amount, and the items being purchased. Process data also includes structured data that are typically mapped onto relational databases, as well as unstructured data such as documents and images. An example of the former includes a database that stores information about customers or suppliers. An example of the latter includes digital images of products, contract documents, and user guides.

At a particular task or activity, a participant will be manipulating the process data. The manipulation means accessing the data and in some cases updating it. This data will appear in the forms displayed to the user. Examples include forms for customer support, purchase order requisition, and risk analysis assessment, to name a few. The user will fill in the data that will then be used in the process, especially for decisioning.

5.3.5 Business Rules

> Business rules are abstractions of the policies and practices of a business organization.
>
> **Wikipedia**

Business process management tries to capture and to digitize policies and procedures. The procedures typically correspond to the procedural flow diagram of activities. This takes the form of a two-dimensional diagram with the participants in one dimension and activities depicted in the other. In conjunction with these, it is necessary to analyze, to design, and to implement the business rules. To date, not many notations or standards can be used for business rules analysis or design.[5] However, business rules are essential for capturing the policies, constraints, and compliance rules within the overall end-to-end application.

A key concept in the definition of business rules is the word *declarative*. When business rules are labeled as declarative, it means a rule can be authored without worrying when, how, or in what order it is executed. For instance, the business rule can determine when a contract should be considered risky. A legal or contract coordinator can make the decision based on conditions such as the track record of contractor, the amount of contract involved, and the status of paper work. This rule then is used in processes, when flows are used to implement contract requests.

Rules are critical in business processes. If flows are just modeled and automated, only part of the end-to-end automation of procedures and policies in the service enterprise has been dealt with. Without business rules driving the processes, there will be weak links. The ultimate rules and decision-making criteria are still either in rule books or in the minds of the decision makers or in legacy code. The business rules actually provide an additional dimension to advanced business process applications. So, for instance, in most BPM systems that do not digitize the business rules, the workflow typically indicates a human participant making a decision prior to the decision split (e.g., approve or do not approve; accept or reject). The decision does not have to be binary; it can involve several options in the decision branch. For example, a mortgage company can decide if a customer mortgage application is low risk, medium risk, or high risk and in each branch can process the application accordingly.

Each of these examples involves a decision being made. The question is, Who made the decision? With a rule-enabled BPM system, many decisions are made through rules. This implies there will be less human intervention and fewer opportunities for errors. Rules provide the intelligent reasoning and dimension behind each decision. With declarative thinking, the focus is on declaring the intention, not the execution sequence of the rule. In most businesses, rules or policies are enacted through various documents. Company memos are sent either to announce new policies or to change existing policies. Examples of declarative business rules include stating that from now on all customer complaint correspondences need to be forwarded to a complaint task force or stating that starting October 1, 2005, any type of purchase exceeding $5,000 requires two levels of approval.

In fact, business rules are quite common. Other examples of business rules include (1) rules to calculate taxes, which can take into consideration the country or state in which an item is purchased; (2) rules to decide the level of risk for a customer—accessing the current status of the customer and his or her past history and then deciding accordingly whether the customer is a high, medium, or manageable risk; and (3) rules for service level agreements (SLAs), which determine what actions to take when a service level agreement is violated, such as escalating and assigning the task to the manager.

Business rules can be associated with a process or shared across processes. For example, Figure 5.11 illustrates a rule associated with the diamond shape in two processes. Note that the same rule, calculating the risk level, is used in both processes. The business rule determines the level of risk.

Many types of rules can be used in conjunction with processes. Some of these declarative rules could apply to the process as a whole. For instance, there can be a declarative rule action for implementing service level agreements and associated with the entire process. Others could be associated with specific activities. The decision as to who should be assigned a task at a particular step could be determined through a business rule. Also within the topology of the process there will be decision points. As mentioned already, this is typically represented through a diamond shape, behind which are decision maps or decision trees that get evaluated; the result of this evaluation will then help select one or more of the branches emanating from the diamond shape. Rules can be triggered when the values of certain process properties are modified. Rules are also cascaded, meaning the result of one rule could be fed to another rule.

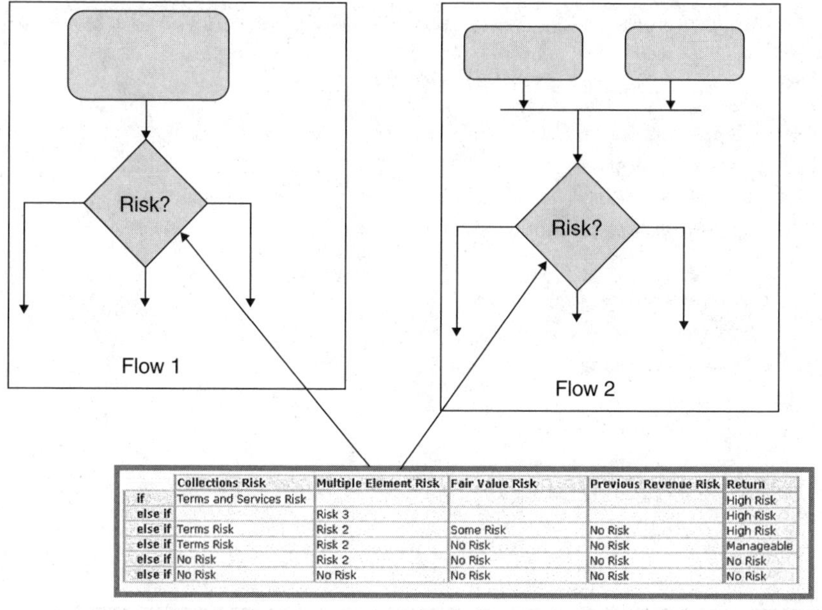

	Collections Risk	Multiple Element Risk	Fair Value Risk	Previous Revenue Risk	Return
if	Terms and Services Risk				High Risk
else if		Risk 3			High Risk
else if	Terms Risk	Risk 2	Some Risk	No Risk	High Risk
else if	Terms Risk	Risk 2	No Risk	No Risk	Manageable
else if	No Risk	Risk 2	No Risk	No Risk	No Risk
else if	No Risk	No Risk	No Risk	No Risk	No Risk

Figure 5.11 Same risk rule used by two processes

The following illustrates the classification of the declarative rules used in processes.

- Decision rules: Common examples of decision rules include decision trees and decision tables. A decision tree is a rule that may contain a tree of if–then productions. Decision tables, on the other hand, have a series of decisions represented in rows, with a return value. These are typically used in various decision steps within a process. Decision rules can also invoke other rules.
  - Examples: (a) Figure 5.12 illustrates a decision tree for offering discounts on an invoice depending on the type of customer; and (b) Figure 5.13 illustrates a decision table to evaluate if a customer is in good standing.
- Declarative expressions: These can establish inferential dependencies between properties that are part of the process data. For example, the total amount of a purchase depends on: (1) items; (2) quantities; (3) total amount before tax, calculated as an expression involving item and quantity (Price * Quantity); (4) tax amount, which depends on country and state and the total amount before tax (tax percentages could also use rules); and (5) discount. The discount expression depends on the total amount and the type of

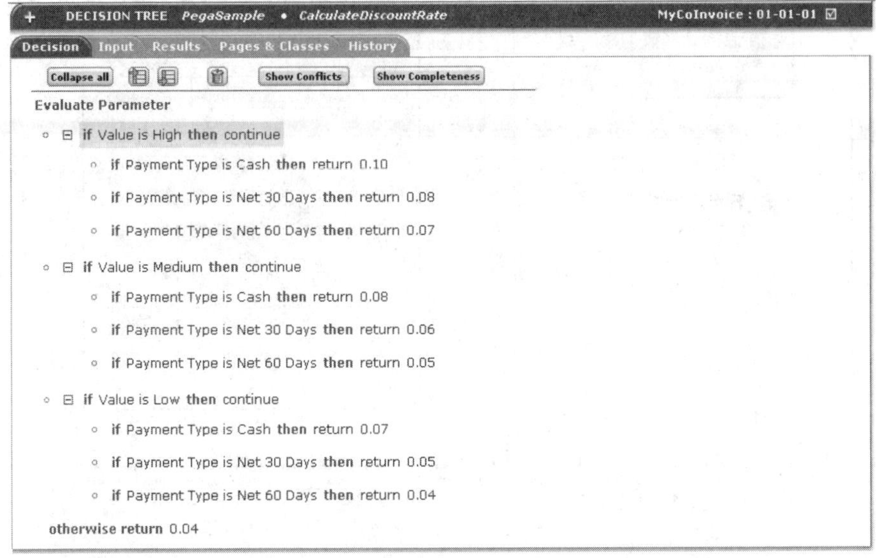

Figure 5.12 A decision tree

customer—again evaluated through another rule. The expressions are defined recursively, and there are dependencies between properties.

- Event rules: An event is any type of occurrence. An event rule examines, correlates, and executes actions based on the event occurrences. Events are defined in greater detail in the next section. Several types of rules deal explicitly with events:

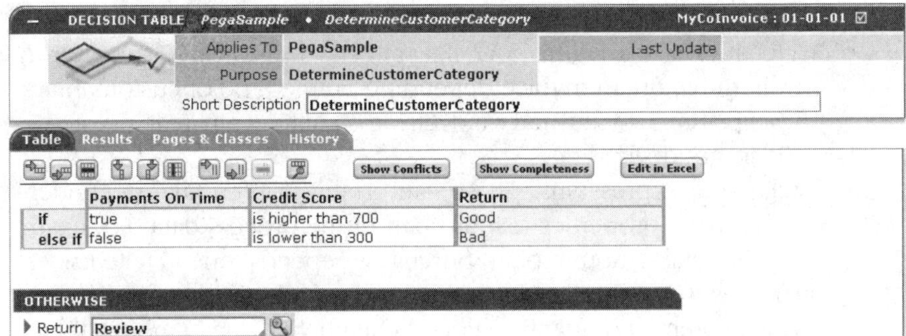

Figure 5.13 A decision table

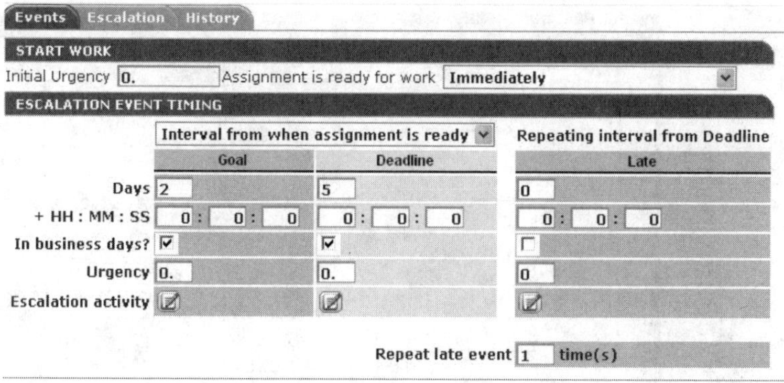

Figure 5.14 A service level agreement

- Service level agreements: These rules deal with temporal events. An SLA rule can specify goals and deadlines and then can invoke methods or services on the occurrence of the temporal event. For example, a particular human participant needs to complete a task within a prescribed amount of time—that is, an SLA. Figure 5.14 is an example of an SLA involving goals and deadlines.
- Change of state: The process instance's change of state, including status of the process as well as values of process data, is another important category of event that could cause methods or service to execute on the occurrence of the change. Another example of change of state include completion of a task or assignment of a task to a specific participant.
- Event correlation: Event rules enable a BPM system to correlate events and to take actions based on the outcome of a correlation. For instance, if an external CRM system publishes an event when a customer changes addresses and a sales fulfillment system publishes an event when a purchase order is submitted, the underlying system could correlate these two business events to make sure the items are sent to the correct address.

5.3.5.1 Business Rules Driving Business Processes

Business processes are driven by business rules.

Microsoft[6]

The relationship between rules and process elements could be illustrated through a three-dimensional cube (Figure 5.15). One of the edges of the

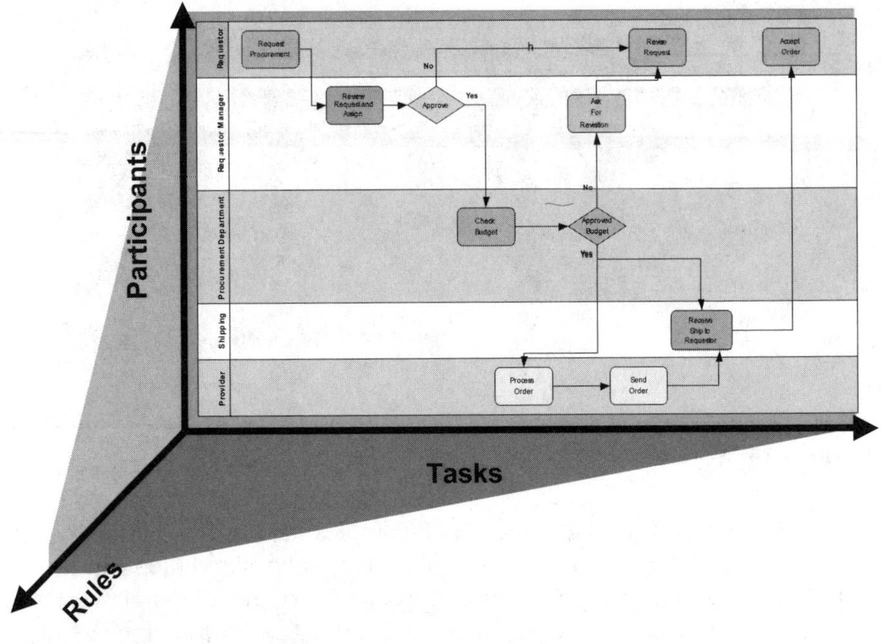

Figure 5.15 Business rules drive business processes

cube represents participants such as humans, back-end applications, and trading partners; the other edge represents activities or tasks; and the third edge represents declarative rules, such as those associated with a node (i.e., a participant assigned a task) in a flow. In other words, the declarative business rules drive the processes.

There are in fact two patterns in using rules for BPM. Figure 5.15 captures one of them. The rules driving processes could be decision, expression, constraint, or event rules. The other pattern involves selecting the most appropriate decision logic, GUI, integration, or process and it is illustrated in Figure 5.16. Different types of business rules (e.g., policies, best practices) can be used to select the appropriate constraint, user interface, decision rule, or flow. For example, depending on the type of customer, a rule might approve a certain credit amount for the customer. The approval will be a decisioning diamond shape within the process. After coming to that decision point, depending on the process instance data (e.g., the customer), the decision will be made as to whether credit should be granted. Similarly, depending on the geographical location of the user, the selection will be made as to whether the user interface needs to be displayed in a localized language. For instance, if the user is in Montreal, the interface will be

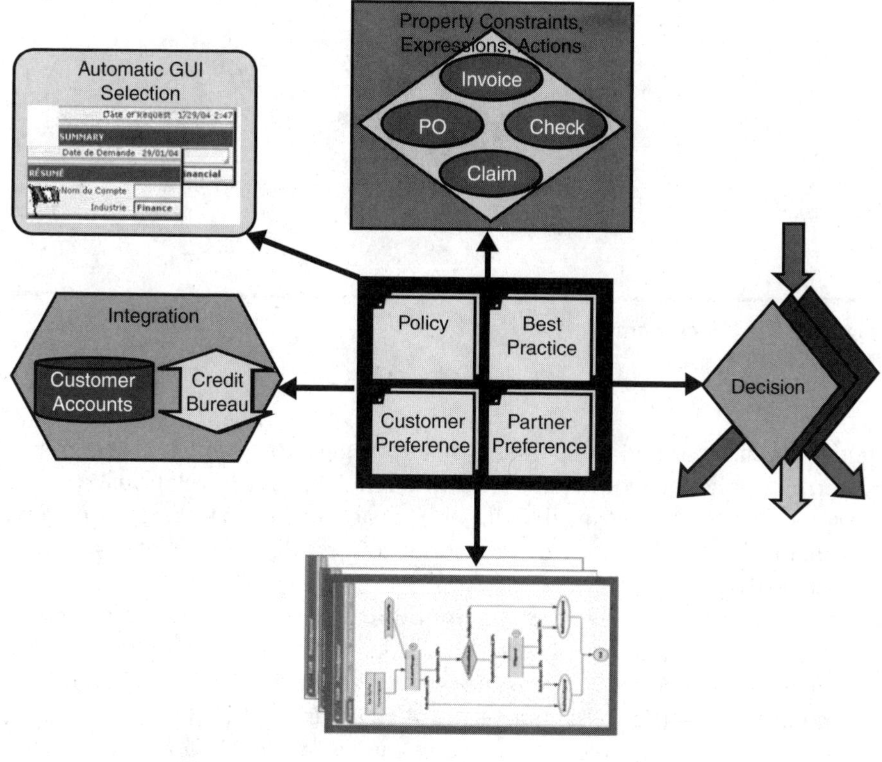

Figure 5.16 Policies, preferences, and practices can help select process elements

displayed in French, whereas users in Toronto will see the interface to the same application in English.

Figure 5.16 also illustrates a property constraints, expressions, and actions box. Using property expressions and dependency rules, the system will automatically calculate the process property values. For example, an expression might evaluate the amount of a payment as (Total-Amount*DiscountRate + Tax). Tax could be an expression that takes into consideration state as well as federal tax and the type of the merchandise as well as its TotalAmount.

Selection can also drive integration choices. The underlying BPM system will use rules pertaining to integration to decide when to invoke services and which services to invoke. For example, a request requires information about a new credit application—the business rules will be applied to the existing information and may decide to start by not issuing an expensive external credit bureau report until examining internal accounts. The underlying system managing the rules understands that to

Figure 5.17 Decisioning

get account information it must first interrogate the customer records to determine which accounts are appropriate to the whole relationship. The system directs the retrieval from the customer records and then goes automatically to the relevant accounts to get all appropriate in-house credit history.

As an example of selecting the appropriate rule in a credit card dispute application, the decision should be made as to whether to write off a payment or not (Figure 5.17). Hence, there is a decisioning rule behind the diamond shape—the third dimension of rules driving the process.

In case (selection criteria) the credit card is World Master Card and the customer type is VIP, the write-off rule is:

IF
  Dispute Amount is less than $51; AND
  Transaction is not disputed as a fraudulent transaction; AND
  The customer has disputed less than 2 transactions this year;
THEN
  Fully credit the customer without even initiating the dispute, i.e., write-off the transaction.

5.3.6 Process Definitions

> I saw an angel in the block of marble and I just chiseled 'til I set him free.
>
> **Michelangelo**

The previous section provided an overview of the different types of elements involved in defining and orchestrating processes. Here is a review.

- Activities or tasks: These are the building blocks. Activities are automated actions that indicate what needs to be done at a particular step in the process. A task is an assignment that involves a participant to contribute in resolving the work.
- Participants: These are the doers of the work at each task step. Participant assignments indicate who needs to do the work or to carry out the task (e.g., human, partner, system).
- Process data or the information model: These are the objects processed at each activity by a participant. These indicate which objects are read or processed at the activities.
- Business rules: These are the driving nervous system of the process. These indicate how the process is assembled and why (i.e., the logic driving the process).

A basic definition will use these elements to define the flow of the process. To do so, some flow constructs and patterns are essential for process definitions. Following is a description of a few of the very basic intraprocess flow patterns. Also presented are a number of interprocess patterns, especially subprocess invocation and interactions between processes.

- Sequence: The sequence pattern is perhaps the most basic. The tasks are sequenced so that a subsequent task cannot start until its predecessor has completed. For example, when going on a trip in a car, the following sequence of tasks is conducted. Task 1: Get in the car; Task 2: Turn on the ignition; Task 3: Go on your way. For a process example, consider fulfillment of a purchase. Task 1: Receive the ordered merchandise; Task 2: Deliver to the recipient; Task 3: Acknowledge receipt (Figure 5.18).
- Parallel split and join: In the parallel split, two activity threads are executed in parallel. Typically, the parallel split is followed with a join or a rendezvous. For example, suppose in a product development process the desire is to execute two subprocesses in parallel, where one of the subprocesses does the market analysis of the product and the other subprocess does the engineering requirement

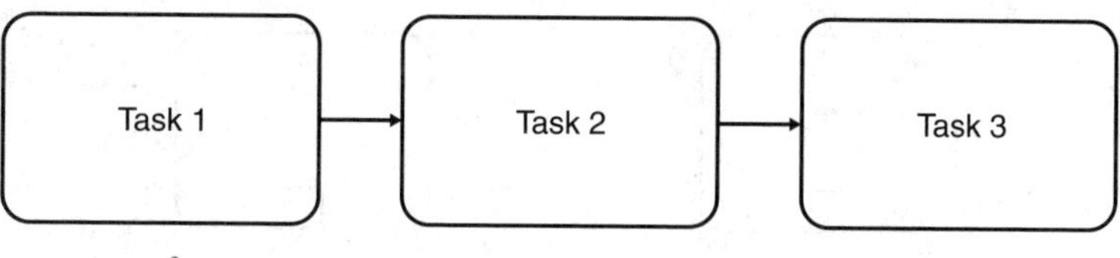

Figure 5.18 Task sequencing

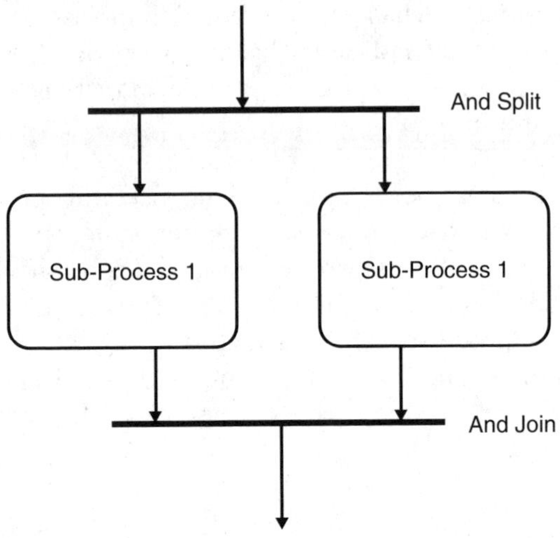

Figure 5.19 Parallel split and join

analysis. After the two subprocesses have completed, then the potential of the product can be assessed and a decision made as to whether to proceed with it (Figure 5.19).

- Decision split: This is also called an exclusive or inclusive disjunction (XOR, OR, respectively). Typically, in BPM flow diagrams the diamond shape is used to indicate the decision split. In XOR exactly one of the alternatives is selected. In OR one or more alternatives can be selected (Figure 5.20).

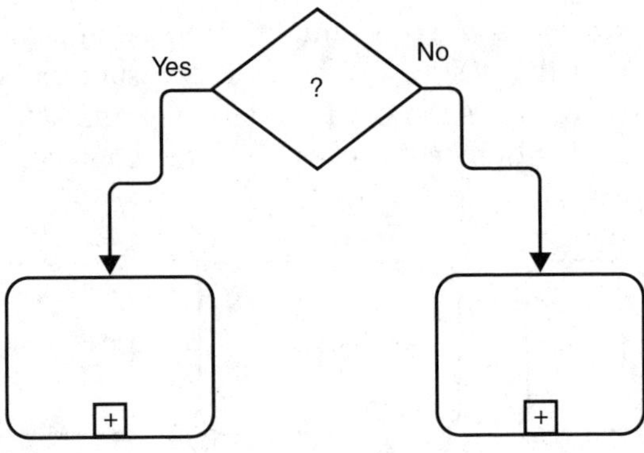

Figure 5.20 Decision split

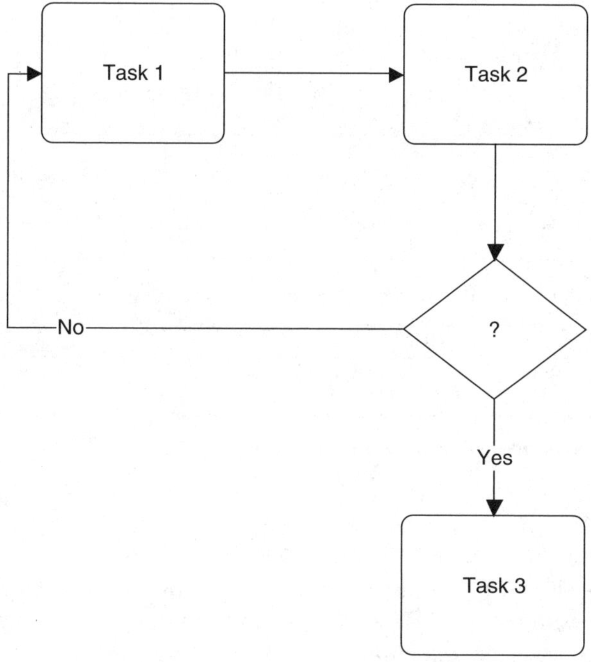

Figure 5.21 Loop

- Looping: In many workflow applications after proceeding with a decision, it is necessary to return to a predecessor step. This is achieved through a looping pattern. Looping is quite common in processes—in most cases a decision branch goes back in a loop to repeat one or more steps (Figure 5.21).

The aforementioned patterns are not the only patterns for processes. Currently, more than 20 process patterns have been identified, and the count is growing. However, these four are the most common intraprocess patterns.

As mentioned already, there are also interprocess patterns.

- Synchronous subprocess: The simplest pattern for a subprocess is the synchronous subprocess invocation. In this pattern, a super process (the parent process) invokes a subprocess executed either in the same or a different process engine. The semantics is that the calling process will wait until the subprocess execution is completed (Figure 5.22).
- Chained subprocess: Another pattern used quite often in business process applications is the chained, or spin-off, subprocess invocation,

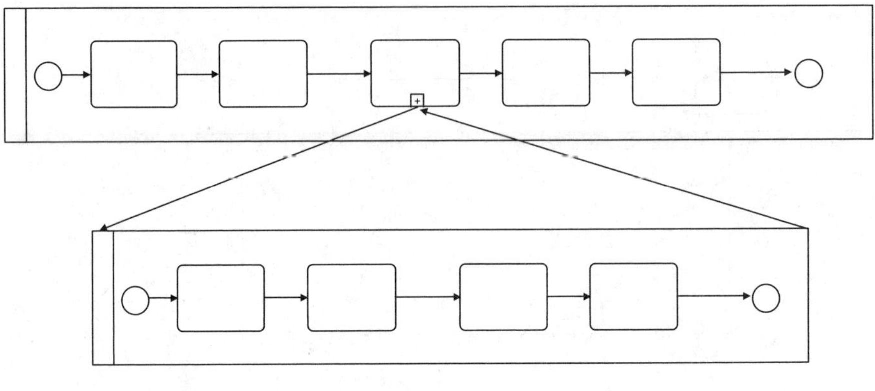

Figure 5.22 Synchronous sub-flow invocation

in which the parent process does not wait for the process to complete—it just starts the process and continues (Figure 5.23).

- Process interaction: The third pattern of interprocess communication is the message exchanges between processes. This is particularly relevant when multiple processes from different departments and organizations are involved. The interaction provides rendezvous points between the processes. Figure 5.24 illustrates a buyer and seller. Each has its own process, but they can also rendezvous and exchange messages to coordinate the buying and selling tasks.

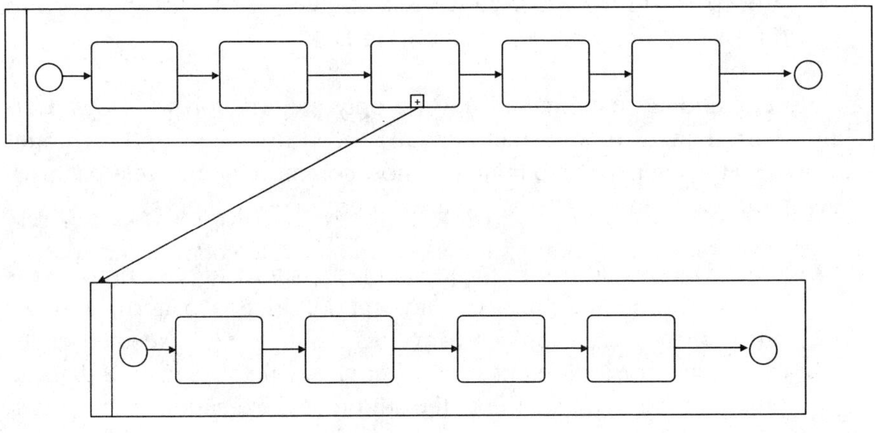

Figure 5.23 Chained sub-flow invocation

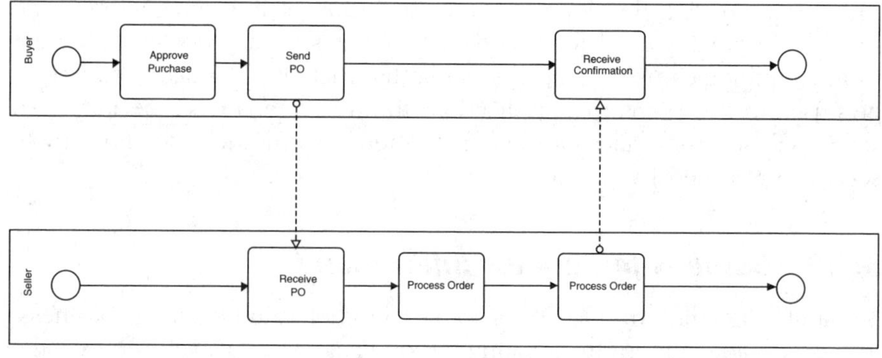

Figure 5.24 Process interaction

5.3.7 Enterprise Integration

BPM includes the active participation of enterprise systems. These systems could be databases, ERP applications, legacy applications, document management systems, or any enterprise application required to complete the work. System participation was the forte of earlier EAI products. The participation of these internal systems, updating them transitionally, and providing an overall flow-based integration continue to be an important requirement in many BPM solutions.

Traditional EAIs were typically implemented as a hub-and-spoke architecture with message transformation or mapping features. How does application integration manifest itself? It is achieved through invoking back-end systems or applications in process activities, either synchronously or asynchronously. These activities can be as simple as making an application programming call through an application programming interface (API) on the activity, publishing a message, or transforming messages. Since applications have different data types, the activities can involve transformations of the data or messages exchanged between the activities. The connotation of EAI is that they mostly consist of flowcharts or maps for invoking applications or sending and receiving messages in specific orders. Often several of these applications need to be involved in system transactions.

Earlier EAI systems tended to be proprietary: The message formats, APIs, and the overall enterprise integration functionalities in reliability, transformation technologies, and security all tended to be proprietary for specific EAI platforms and solutions. Starting in 2003, standards-based enterprise integration technologies began to emerge. The ESB, as discussed in Chapter 4, is providing functionalities similar to the EAI systems of almost a decade ago, but it uses standard and especially Web services-based technologies.

Another interesting development is the inclusion of B2B integration in the ESB. Technologies used for accessing intranet sites are not that different from technologies used to access public Internet sites. Similarly, technologies used to access internal applications through standard—especially Web services-based—interfaces are not that different from ones used for remote services published by trading partners.

5.3.8 Business-to-Business Integration

A popular integration practice for trading partner value chains is business-to-business integration. In revisiting the original vision of Web services, the main focus was on B2B integration. This is why from their earliest conceptions, Web services and service oriented architectures focused on discovery, hence the famous triangle of publish, discover, exchange.

BPM includes trading partners as participants. Here the process is no longer an internal one; it involves trading partners in streamlined flows. The most important technological development in this area is the emergence of Web services-based service oriented architectures. In short, these SOAs allow trading partners programmatic, or browserless, access to Web sites or portals via the Internet within the context of processes that often link internal activities with external trading partner requests. B2B vendors started to offer such extended enterprise connectivity, but now this is becoming a hallmark of all BPM products.

Supply and value chain management are typical examples of B2B integration. B2B is important since it provides the connectivity and aggregation of organizations in extended enterprises. In a value chain there are several companies in a chain of interactions, where each company takes in what is produced from its predecessor, adds value, and forwards it to the subsequent organization—toward the completion of the end product. The value chain progresses from raw material production to component production to the completion of a product (such as a television in consumer electronics) and ultimately to selling the goods to an end customer. This is an oversimplified illustration of what happens between organizations, where often the Internet and increasingly Web services are used to exchange messages to implement the processes spanning the value chain.

5.3.9 Orchestration and Choreography

Two terms often associated with business processing involving Web services are *orchestration* and *choreography*. It is important to pay close attention when these terms are used because sometimes they are used interchangeably. The distinction between these terms is often blurry. The concepts, though, behind the two terms are important. Orchestration deals with the ordering of Web service execution in process flows. The orchestrated Web services are typically executed by a process engine that invokes and controls the services. These ordered services can include trading partners, and some of the Web services can be executing in the context of a transaction. Orchestration of Web services implies the orchestrated process is actually executed by an underlying process engine. On the other hand, choreography represents abstract processes—in the sense that it is not necessary to have an actual process engine executing the choreography—which illustrate the order of message exchanges between applications or more often between trading partners. Therefore, multiple parties are involved, and these parties exchange messages of specific types and invoke prescribed operations. So orchestration means a process engine executes the process while interacting with or involving internal and external participants. Business process management systems support this model. Choreography, on the other hand, captures distributed processing involving multiple engines and participants without centralized control (i.e., the process engine). In fact, multiple process engines could get involved to realize choreographies.

A typical example of choreography is the procurement of goods and services. The choreography is the exchange of messages that occur between the buyer and seller (as illustrated in Figure 5.6). The overall process flow can involve the following.

- Submit purchase request: with purchase order number from buyer to seller. This is the first message that needs to be sent from the buyer to the seller. The message can indicate a purchase order number and also the list of items to be procured. The seller can accept the purchase request and can reply with an expected purchase delivery date.
- Request shipping: For the same procurement transaction, the seller can submit a shipment request from a shipping company to send the procured items to the buyer. This can also be submitted via a Web service operation and an input message that indicates details of the items, pick-up date, and destination address. This exchange is between the seller, the buyer, and the shipping company.
- Submit invoice: The seller sends the shipping notification message and the invoice to the buyer.

In between these three major steps could be additional steps for handling payments, delays in shipments, and changes to the requests if items are not available. The overall process can also include various types of service level agreements between the partners. These are captured in the decision logic of the process. This process can be represented as a choreography, where each party tracks the message exchanges and what it needs to do—following the agreed on partner message exchange sequence. For instance, after the buyer sends the purchase order request, an invoice is expected at some point[7] from the seller. Thus the choreography is an overall process that involves the buyer, seller, and shipper parties. Each of these parties will be executing their own internal process orchestrations while participating in the overall choreography of message exchanges and interactions.

5.3.10 Process Instances

The process definitions discussed in the previous section are like templates: There are process definitions to hire a new employee, to purchase new equipment, to deliver a service, to deal with customer complaints, to build or to release products or service offerings, and so on. Now for each of these process definitions there will be many process instances, or instantiations, of these processes. For example, hiring an executive assistant, a quality assurance manager, and a call center agent will use the same process definition. However, there will be three separate instances of the process: one for each new hire. That is the main idea of process instances.

A process instance is associated with an instance of a process class. The object is an instance of a process class, and process instances exist in manipulating this object in its various steps. The relationships among process definitions, process instances, process classes, and instances of these classes are illustrated in Figure 5.25.

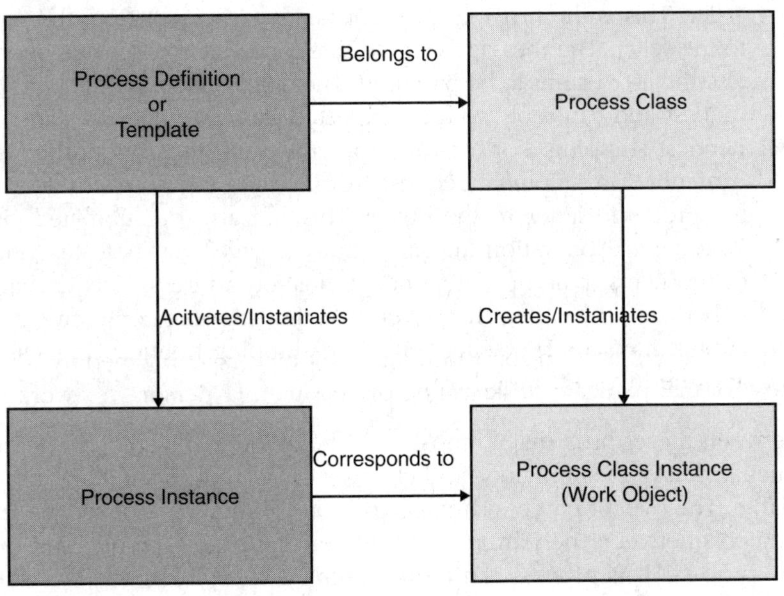

Figure 5.25 Process instances and process classes

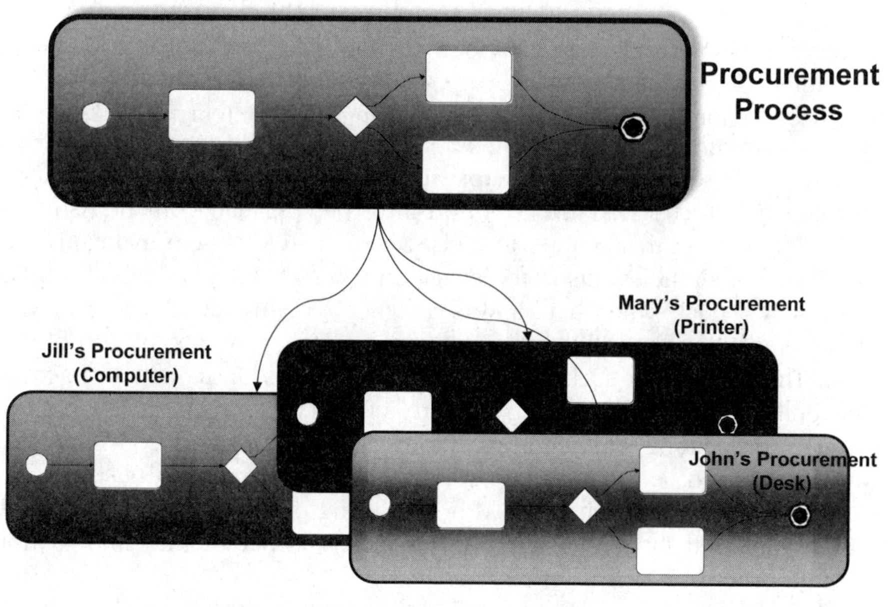

Figure 5.26 Process definition and process instances

Creation of process instances—that is, instances of process classes and processes manipulating these objects—is sometimes called activation of the process. A process instance can be created by either a human participant or a service call. For instance, a Web service call that wants to place an order can start a process instance. As mentioned previously, processes have process data. Each process instance will have its own copy of process data. For example, if the application is to process new hires, each instance will have process data pertaining to the specific new hire, such as the hire's name, department, date hired, resume, skill set, references, special accommodations, equipment, and office. As the process instances execute, work items will be created and placed in participant's work lists. For instance, assembling a workstation for a new hire will be a task assigned to IT. The request for that particular task will be placed in an IT personnel's work list.

Figure 5.26 illustrates the relationship between process definitions and process instances. Associated with a process map or definition will be many process instances, which provide the ability to run reports on processes.

5.3.11 Monitoring Performance of Processes

Information is power, and access to timely and accurate information about business operations gives executives and managers the edge they need to compete effectively and operate more efficiently.

Colin J. White

Business is about the bottom line and performance. Business is also about timely responses to events that happen in business operations. Performance management focuses on the "M" of business process management. As mentioned already in this chapter and elsewhere, a BPM system maintains the audit trail of all the events in the enacted processes. For example, the BPM system will track when a task was assigned to a user and when it was completed, as well as all the relevant process data in the completion of the task. This is done for each process, for all its process instances, and across the entire enterprise involving human, system (e.g., back-office applications), and trading partner applications. Two interrelated concepts and approaches can be found in monitoring the performance of a business: (1) data warehousing, which is based on analyzing primarily historic data; and (2) business activity monitoring (BAM), which is used to monitor and control current processes in real-time.

The historic analysis of the data is an approach associated with business intelligence that can be gained from a data warehouse. The sources of data within the data warehouse are many. In particular, the data warehouse could be populated through the process data generated from a business process management system. The historic data in a data warehouse can be analyzed through cubes, which have dimensions and measures. A dimension is an organized hierarchy of categories, known as levels, describing data in data warehouses. For example, in a BPM application, time is typically used as a dimension, with year, month, day, and hour as levels. Dimension members are the discrete values or choices at a level, which may be numeric or text. A measure is a numeric quantity, representing the numeric columns of the tables containing the cube data. Examples of generic BPM cubes include the following:

- Workload: This measures the number of process instances created and completed over time. Figure 5.27 provides an example of a workload throughput comparing process instances that have been completed and those that have been created per day for March.
- Human participant performance: The actual performance of human participants can also be analyzed. Dimensions here include the actual user, the process type, and the time. Measures include elapsed completion times and number of tasks completed. Figure 5.28 shows an example of a cube comparing the performance of three users.

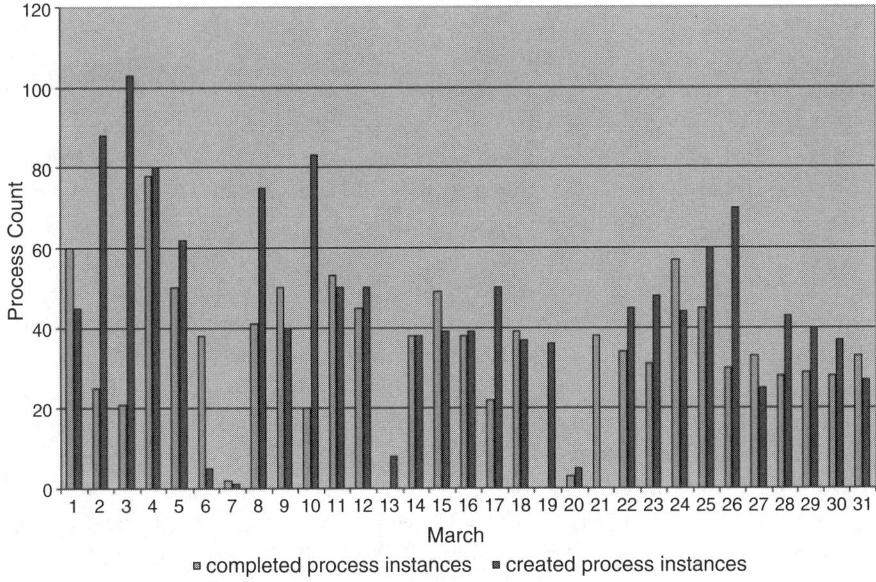

Figure 5.27 Work throughput

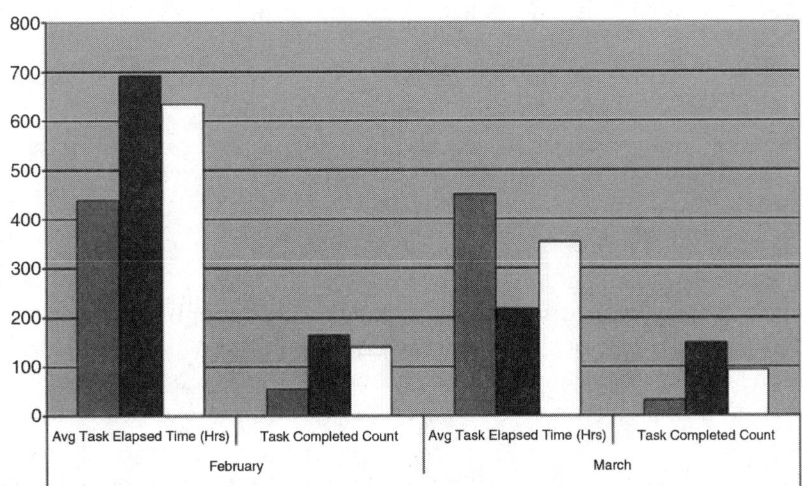

Figure 5.28 Performance of participants

Data warehousing is for analyzing historic data. There can actually be several sources of the historic data, and the source data can be transformed onto the schemata of the data warehouse to populate the tables. Analysis then can be used to slice and dice and to view the data measurements along its dimensions. Typically data warehouse tables are about a day old, although the database can be refreshed more frequently. The goal in data warehouse historic data analysis is for decisioning: to discover trends. For overall performance monitoring it is also necessary to monitor real-time process data. As noted above, business activity monitoring is used for real-time monitoring and control. It indicates the software that monitors, correlates, and allows users to respond to operational events in an organization. BAM can be used with any type of enterprise software or system that generates events. BAM monitors and correlates the context and information of these events and notifies decision makers in real-time. This combination of real-time monitoring of events and the ability to associate related events and then to interact with decision makers is a key feature of BAM software.

Even though BAM can be used in conjunction with or separately from BPM systems, more recently and especially in the context of BPM suites, BAM has been offered as a built-in component of BPM. The monitored and correlated events are generated from business process applications. Business rules can be used to correlate the events. BAM extends management's ability to examine business processes, assignments, works in progress, and data generated and executed by BPM and related software. Through business activity monitoring the following can be realized:

- Real-time monitoring the performance of processes and identifying areas for process improvement
- Monitoring process, work, and assignment performance for quality, effectiveness, and efficiency
- Managing capital and human resources
- Continuous process improvement activities

Business activity monitoring is typically achieved through a business manager dashboard. The business stakeholder can drill down and analyze the real-time data provided through the dashboard. Figure 5.29 illustrates examples of graphical reports that could be viewed from a business manager's dashboard.

Group managers and business analysts can monitor and analyze processes, work, and assignments based on criteria such as (1) timeliness, or the amount of time an assignment or work item has been in progress in a process instance; (2) work or process instance status, or the estimated amount of time needed to complete work and the actual

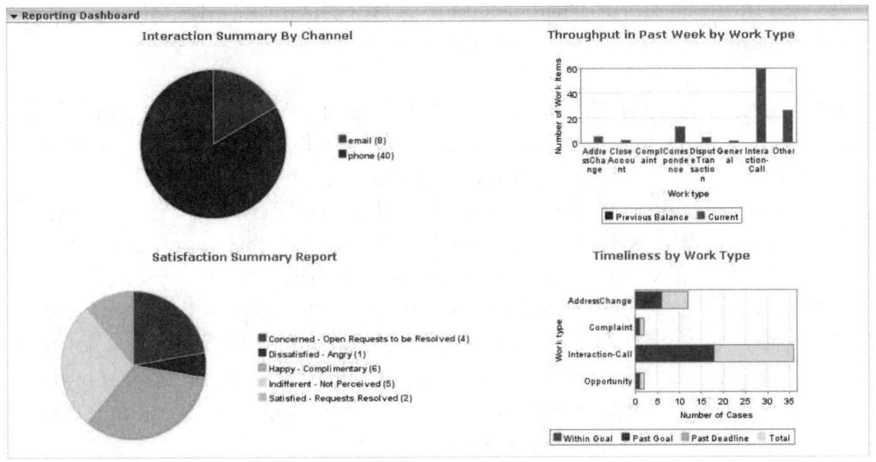

Figure 5.29 Example of a process status dashboard

amount of time applied toward completion; (3) throughput, or the number of items open during a given time period and the number of items open in the previous time period; (4) customer satisfaction and resolution quality, or timeliness and SLA performance of completed process work; and (5) root cause analysis, or a review of the underlying reasons of the performance characteristics of process instances, through summary or detailed reports. In a BAM portal, any of the graphics can be drilled down and managers can control and influence the execution of process instances. For instance, if a particular participant's performance is not on par with the manager's expectations, he or she could reassign the task to someone else.

5.3.12 Process Portals

Portals are becoming increasingly important and commonplace. The portlet is the human-facing interface of services. The term *portal* is somewhat overused. A clearer definition is emerging, but currently many horizontal and vertical frameworks, solutions, and applications claim to provide portals to their users. BPM systems are a case in point. The user interacts with the portal typically through a browser. The content and the subsequent user actions through the browser are submitted to the portal server through the Web server.

Portal framework functions include personalization, integration, content management, security, and community.

- Personalization: This is one of the most important functions of the portal framework. It allows users to decide which portlets and links to include in their personal portals. Personalization addresses various preferences, such as color tabs and positions of portlets. It includes the selection of specific portlets for the user, such as stock quotes, newsfeed sources, and other feeds.
- Integration: This includes the ability to easily define and access portlet content from a variety of information and application sources. Integration can span enterprise applications, content integration, and technology integration (e.g., file servers, messaging servers, distributed objects, Web services).
- Content management: Portal frameworks typically provide the ability to organize, to navigate, and to search for information from a variety of structured and unstructured information resources.
- Security: The portal accesses applications and information from a variety of resources. The administration of security is crucial for the single sign-on and overall authorization and authentication of portal and portlet users. Security features include support of Lightweight Directory Access Protocol (LDAP) services, distributed administration of security, access control, and role-based security.
- Community: Community groups and the corresponding portals and portlets are a foundational feature of portal frameworks. Employees, customers, and partners are examples of large community groups. Community support implies collaborative and groupware capabilities. Examples include shared calendars, shared spaces, and live online meetings.

5.3.12.1 Portlets

Portlets are the components in a portal framework. They provide the content and definition of the components within the portal Web page. Information and application sources provide the content for these portlets so that customers interacting with an institution can have the option of using the portlets supported by the organization. A portlet can have four modes: view, edit, help, and design. In view mode, portlets depict their functionality and content. For example, if the portlet is displaying weather information, the view will show the temperature in degrees Fahrenheit and perhaps will depict graphically the weather condition (e.g., clouds, rain, snow). This could consist of simple content—text or multimedia—or it could be more interactive and sophisticated, involving multiple screens. In edit mode, users can edit the portlet data. For example, if it is an address update portlet, a new address can be entered to submit for updating. The help mode provides explanations of how to use the portlet. The design mode is usually reserved for portlet developers or administrators. In this mode, developers and administrators can change the look and feel of the portlet. Portlets are the user- or customer-facing representations of Web services.

5.3.12.2 Portals and Business Process Management

Two fundamental alternatives involve BPM and portals.

1. Business process management systems typically come with a number of customizable BPM-focused portals. Typically the portals will expose BPM capabilities based on the authorization and role of the user.
2. It is also possible to have various functions and features of BPM as portlets within an enterprise portal.

This means BPM functionality can be accessed via portals provided by the BPM system vendor. Figure 5.30 illustrates a portal of a user in a BPM

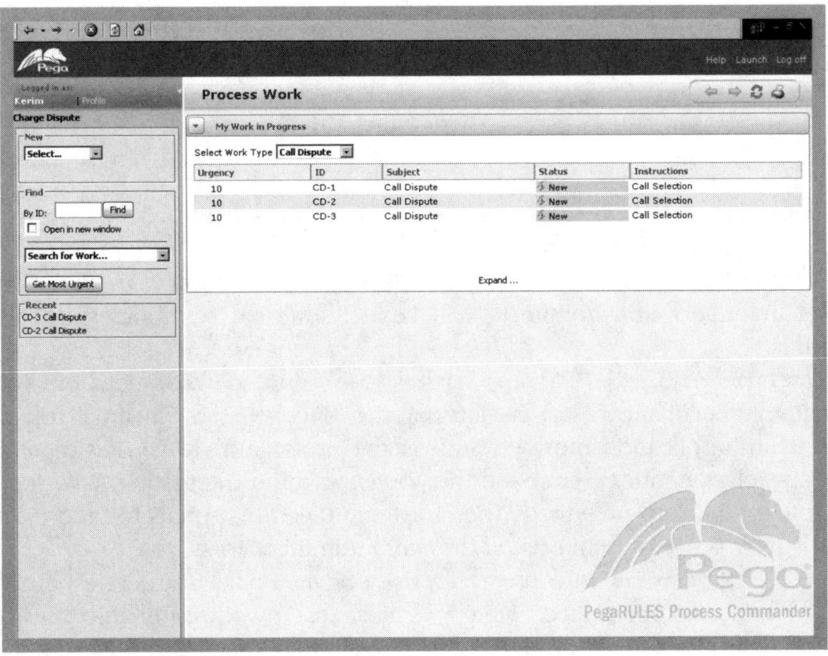

Figure 5.30 Example of a user portal

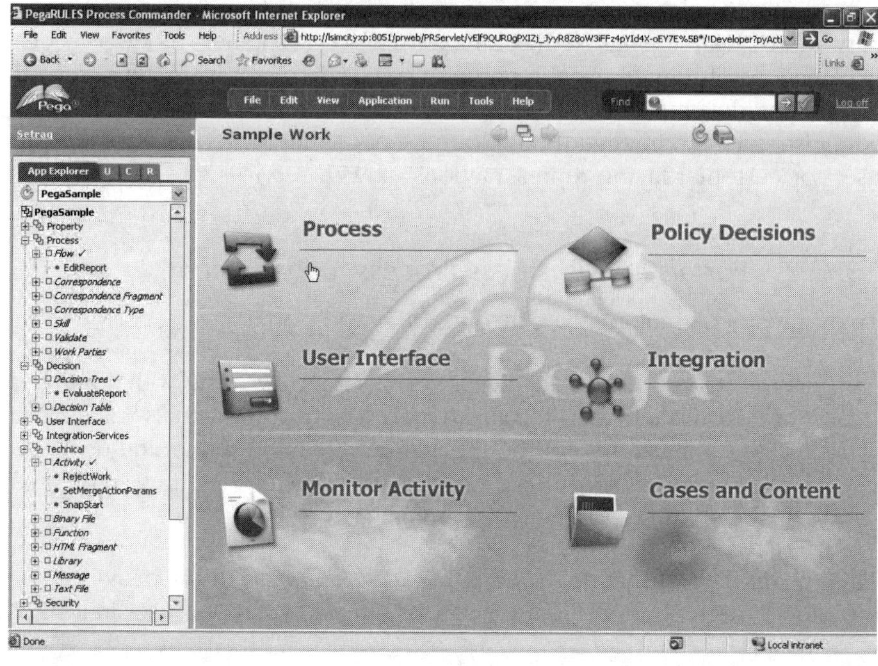

Figure 5.31 Example of a BPM system developer and process architect portal

system. The portal shows a number of work items in the user's work list. The user has the opportunity to customize the portal organization, as mentioned earlier. This is an example of a basic portal for end-users. BPM managers and architects will have additional capabilities in their portals.

In browser-based BPM approaches, the entire development environment can be in the portal, as illustrated in Figure 5.31. On the left-hand side is an application browser, and on the right-hand are various types of process class entities (process flows, decision rules, integration, user interface, etc.) that can be edited. Therefore, there can be portals for end users, managers, process architects, and system administrators.

BPM solutions can also use enterprise portals. Portlets can correspond to BPM functions. For instance, Figure 5.32 illustrates a work list in an enterprise portal. This is achieved through compliance to the emerging portlet standard JSR-168.

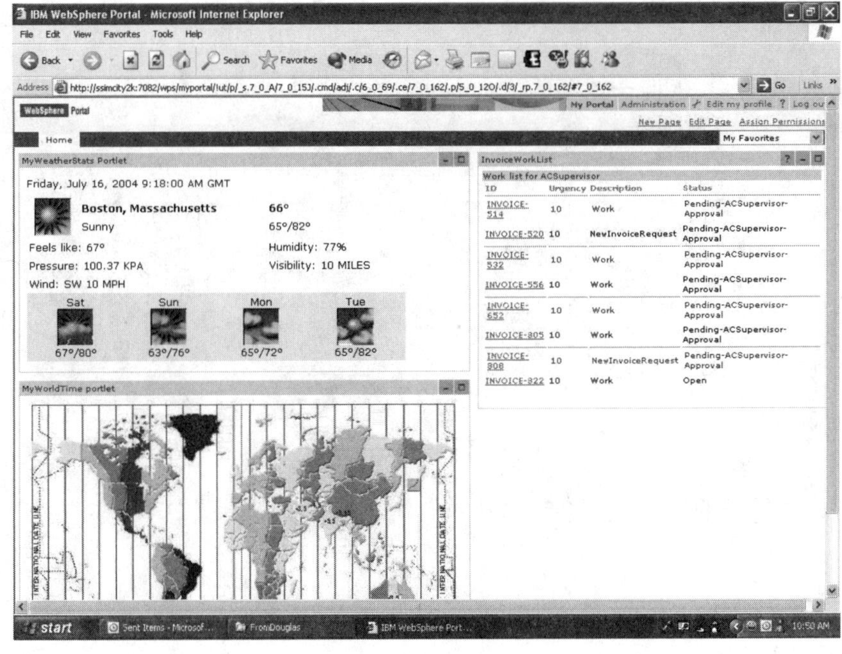

Figure 5.32 Example of BPM system work list in an enterprise portal

5.4 BPM Reference Architectures

> Customers want a system that is change-aware, that will help them "decide and do," and one that forms the core of their operational nerve center.
>
> **Jay Sherry**

Business process management typically includes a designer environment to design the processes; a BPM engine that executes the processes, adapters, and integration framework to leverage back-end systems (i.e., EAI); and B2B integration to collaborate with trading partners. Processes can involve human participants, roles, back-end applications, and trading partners. Figure 5.33 illustrates the overall architecture of a modern BPM. The top layer is the design environment for building BPM applications involving all the model types illustrated in Figure 5.8 (process flows, business rules, organization, integration). Figure 5.30 illustrates a BPM designer's portal. Once a BPM solution is built, it is deployed to

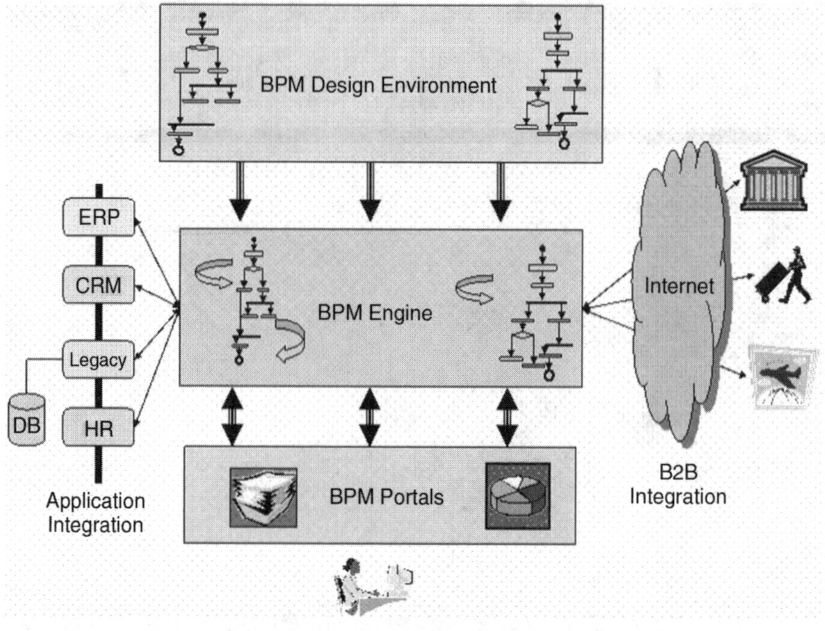

Figure 5.33 High-level BPM architecture: design, engine, and portals

the BPM server engine. This is the middle layer and the run-time execution environment that processes the flows, business rules, and integration involving EIS and B2B services. The figure also illustrates the portal layer for different communities, especially users and managers. The following sections provide an overview of two leading BPM reference architectures.

5.4.1 The WfMC Reference Architecture

The Workflow Management Coalition (WfMC) introduced a workflow reference architecture in the mid-1990s.[8] The goal was to identify the key components of a workflow system as well as various APIs to standardize the exchange of workflow information with other applications. In terms of the overall architecture of workflow systems, the WfMC provides the reference architecture and standards for each of the five interfaces they have identified (Figure 5.34).

- *Interface 1:* This specifies a common interface between the design and definition of processes and the underlying process engine.

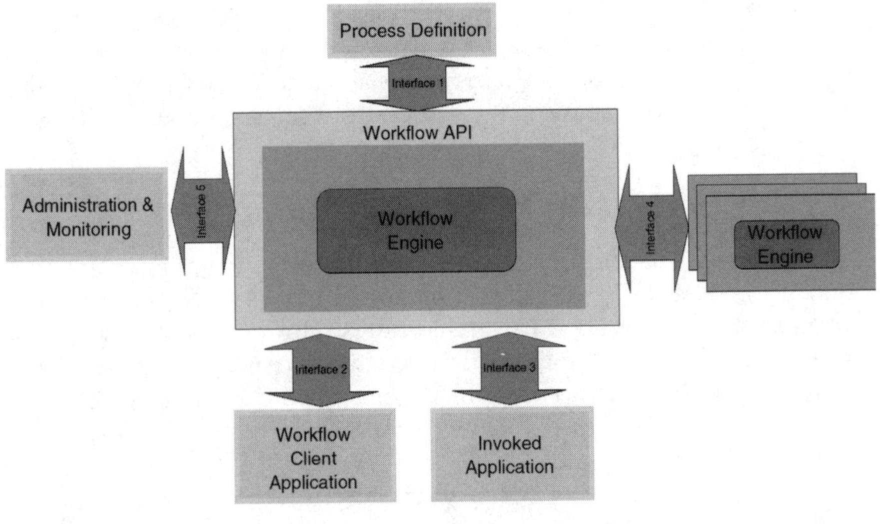

Figure 5.34 The WfMC reference architecture

Typically, the same BPM or process vendor provides a graphical process or workflow map editing tool. Once the process is designed, it is deployed to the process engine. This is similar to designing a Web Services Description Language (WSDL), providing the implementation, and then deploying it to a Web service server.

- *Interface 2:* This provides the workflow client application interface; it is the API of the workflow engine, which allows the development of rich or thin client applications to handle work lists, to process instance activations operations, to process control and status, and more.
- *Interface 3:* Sometimes the workflow engine calls other applications to complete or to perform activities or tasks. This interface facilitates cooperation between invoked applications and workflow engine invocations. For interfaces 2 and 3, workflow engines provide extensive workflow APIs to enable interoperability with clients and other applications invoking the workflow engine programmatically over distributed networks.
- *Interface 4:* This interface addresses interoperability between workflow engines. Typically, in a large organization there could be several workflow engine deployments. In these distributed and heterogeneous architectures, it is desirable to have cooperating workflow engines through common interfaces.
- *Interface 5:* This specification is for administering, monitoring, and auditing interfaces. This is an important functionality for workflow and

BPM engines. Often the monitored data is presented in graphical charts to be analyzed by business owners. Monitoring the process instances and historical process data is essential for taking real-time corrective actions or for improving the subsequent versions of the processes.

5.4.2 Doculabs' BPM Reference Architecture

The Workflow Management Coalition's architecture was an important contribution for BPM. Even though it dates to the mid-1990s, it still resonates with most practitioners of BPM architectures. However, in the 2000s we saw the emergence of more modern multi-component service oriented architectures for business process management. One of these is Doculabs' BPM Reference Architecture[9] (Figure 5.35).

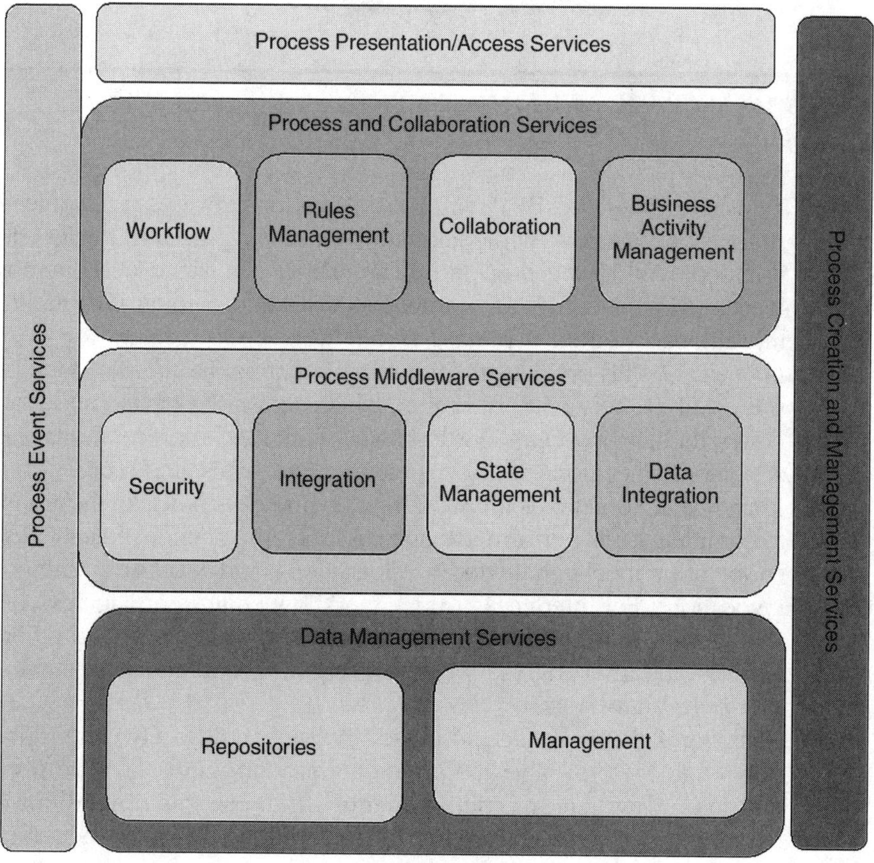

Figure 5.35 Doculabs' BPM reference architecture

There are many moving parts in a business process management system.

- Process presentation/access services: This layer deals with the portals to carry out work processes (e.g., work lists, queues) as well as BPM portals and process design.
- Process and collaboration services: This layer is the core process engine that includes automatic workflows that include human participants. An important component here is the business rules management. As indicated previously, business rules drive processes. This layer also includes collaborative components to process work as well as business activity monitoring functions.
- Process event services: There are several sources of events, some of which are generated and consumed by the processes or business rules and others that occur externally to the system but that need to be processed by the event architecture components.
- Process middleware service: This layer deals with the security and integration functions of the BPM system. This is the layer that either directly accesses back-end systems or trading partner services or, alternatively, interacts with the ESB through standard interfaces (e.g., SOAP). The layer can also conduct message transformations and mapping onto the properties of the processes.
- Data management services: The process data is managed by this layer. This includes all the data pertaining to the process instances (i.e., the values of properties), as well as contextual data such as data warehouse or enterprise content management data. This is the data that includes all the audit trailing of the process life cycles.
- Process creation and management services: The services in this layer are used to create and to manage processes. In this layer, the processes are designed and optimized for execution. Designers can use standard shapes, such as Business Process Modeling Notation (BPMN).

5.5 BPM Methodologies

> To ensure success, it is vitally important that the organization develop a repeatable BPM delivery methodology. At its heart, a methodology is a series of steps that, if followed, will dramatically improve the chances of a successful outcome. Think of a methodology as a recipe for success.
>
> **Derek Miers**

So far this chapter has covered the main concepts and features of business process management. It is easy to see that BPM has many moving parts:

It is like a soup with almost everything except the kitchen sink thrown in. The main question is this: How can successful BPM applications be built? Chapter 2 discussed the iterative methodology for building services—both the server and client side of development. This section focuses on BPM development methodologies. As Chapter 7 will illustrate, the enterprise performance management methodologies in conjunction with the BPM methodology, the service development, and access methodologies provide a comprehensive roadmap for success projects in service oriented enterprises.

Business and IT: Traditional software architecture frameworks (e.g., Zachman) and methodologies (e.g., Unified Software Development Process) do cover some elements of process management but are not well suited for the emerging BPM approach. BPM methodology should include declarative rules. There are a number of boutique methodologies both for business rules as well as BPM. Business rules have methodologies such as Proteus from Business Rules Solutions (http://www.brsolutions.com/) and the Rule Maturity Model from Knowledge Partners Inc. (http://www.kpiusa. com/). BPM methodologies include the 8 Omega from Business Process Management Group (www.bpmg.org) and SmartBuild from Pegasystems Inc. (www.pega.com).

To understand the significance of business processes for service oriented enterprises, a basic question must be asked: What is a business? A business is a collection of processes, policies, and procedures. Think about it—in any enterprise there are processes that need to be followed to get things done. A business process can be defined as a network, sequence, or organization of activities. Activities represent by and large what is done in a task. The term *network* here means that these activities are somewhat ordered. Merriam-Webster defines it as "a series of actions or operations conducing to an end." For instance, an employee first submits a purchase order; then this order is approved; then a purchase order is generated and submitted to a preapproved vendor. Purchasing is an example of a procurement process. There are processes and policies everywhere: finance, marketing, sales, and, of course, the processes used to develop and to implement services or products. Each of these areas has activities and business rules that drive them. BPM systems allow you to capture, to model, to automate, and to continuously improve the solutions.

Before starting any BPM system driven project, two issues need to be considered:

1. The business case: A BPM system solution starts with a business case that corresponds to the scope and motivation of the whole project or solution. Several factors make up the business case. Higher-level motivations include the following:
   Innovation: This is the ability to create and to quickly introduce new products and services.
   Growth: Related to innovation is the focus on growing the revenue as well as the market share of the business's products and services.
   Productivity: A service oriented enterprise attempts to increase not only the productivity of its employees but also its customers, trading partners, and other serviced communities.
   Compliance: A substantial percentage of IT and business resources are spent dealing with compliance issues.

   Careful analysis and quantitative and qualitative ROI is critical in this initial business case phase. Several factors come into play in determining the business case for the business process management projects. Some of these are illustrated in Figure 5.36.

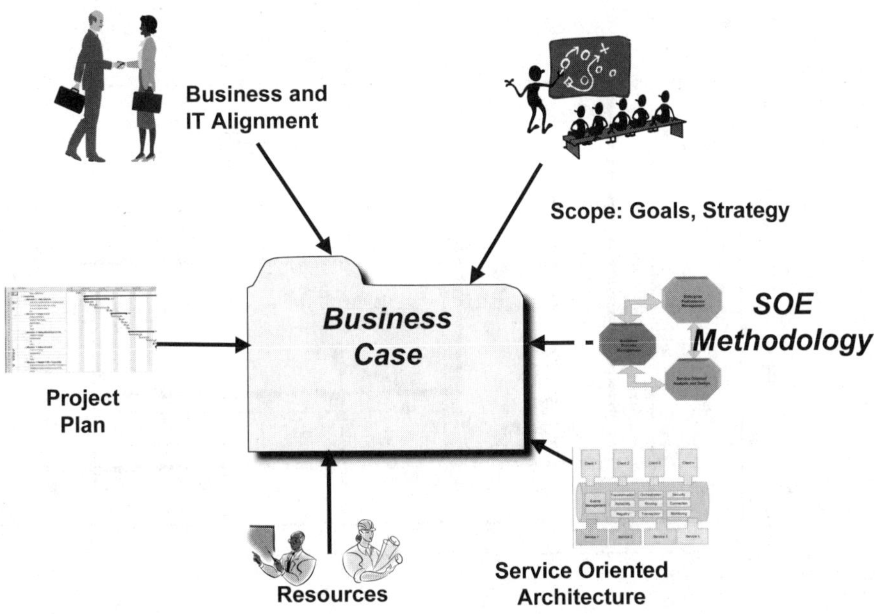

Figure 5.36 Business case for BPM system project

2. Best choice opportunity: The second issue could be less obvious. Once a business case is made, typically many use cases could potentially be digitized and automated. The BPM project leadership needs to decide where to start and which candidate use cases need to be deployed first. This is critical for the overall success of service oriented enterprise projects. Unfortunately, sometimes IT projects get a bad rap of long-running projects that cost much more than the initial estimates. Business and IT need to identify and agree on which use case to automate first. This is an extremely important success factor during the initial phases of the BPM system project. One approach that can be used here is to choose a quantitative strategy in balancing effort with business value. The effort is the IT implementation dimension (Figure 5.37).

The essential ingredients in business process management include (1) modeling, which also often includes simulation; (2) detailed design; (3) execution; (4) activity monitoring; and (5) performance analysis. These phases in building BPM applications are iterative: You go from modeling, to design, to execution, to monitoring and analysis. You then identify areas of improvement and go back to modeling changes and iterate over the other phases. As a result of monitoring typically changes or improvements emerge, hence a return to modeling and simulation, and the cycle iterates.

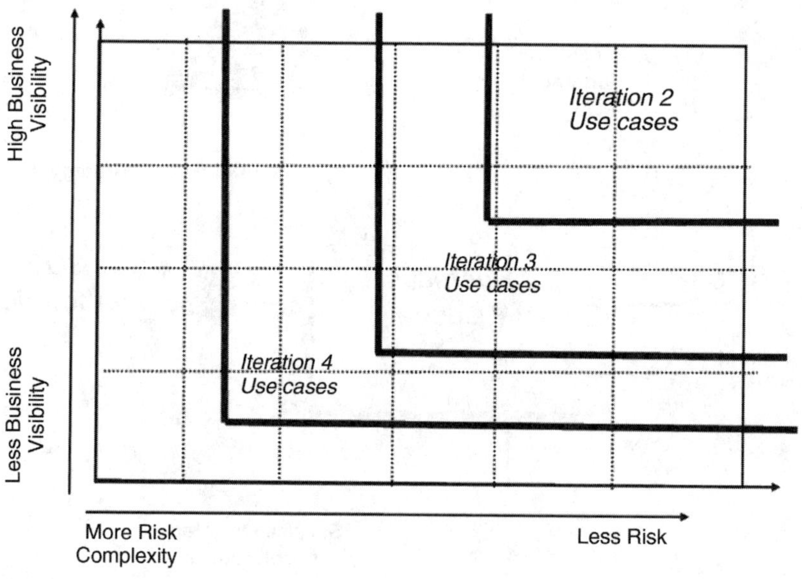

Figure 5.37 Selecting use cases with less risk and high business visibility first

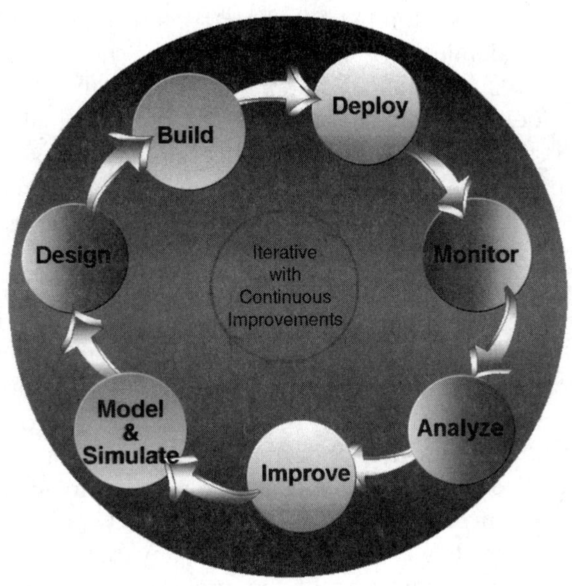

Figure 5.38 Iterative and continuous improvement methodology

It is a continuous life cycle. In fact, during monitoring business owners could analyze the performance of processes and request improvements. Modeling generates an information model, process model, and rules model. Chapter 3 discussed the definition of information models—through class diagrams—and process models—through state transitions and activity diagrams. Figure 5.38 illustrates the full life cycle of the continuous improvement of a business process. This is important as it shows how with BPM, applications are not only modeled but also are automated.

- Modeling and simulation: Methodology typically starts with modeling. Business users should be able to easily design processes and author the rules associated with decision steps, service level agreements, or constraints within these processes. Modeling involves capturing the "as is" processes and then suggesting the "to be" processes with clear articulation of the benefits (i.e., return on investments) justifying the BPM system solutions.
  - The architects can provide additional detailed design. The diagrams that businesses come up with should be either executable or very close to being so. The rules that the business manager authors should also be executable. Thus, this new approach brings IT and business together to rapidly deploy BPM applications and to continuously improve with incremental and iterative

changes. It is often helpful to model and simulate as-is processes and to identify potential opportunities. The as-is process simulation will illustrate requirements for additional resources and will identify scheduling bottlenecks and cost analysis. A simulation scenario can include statistical distribution and patterns for work arrivals as well as durations of tasks. In fact, the analyst can use both statistical distributions and historic data on operators, systems, or trading partners to analyze simulation results. Simulation can assist in identifying bottlenecks before deployments. Simulation run results can then be compared to results of historic data to elucidate potential improvements in the performance of operators, processes, or applications as a whole. Simulation will also involve the business rules and will identify potential automation opportunities. The simulation will provide tangible cost analysis as well as comparative analysis with historic performance. The improved processes and applications can then be immediately piloted to analyze any potential issues in the overall implementation of the process application. Real-world experiential feedback is essential to the success of the project. The pilot then can immediately be rolled forward to deployment.

- Participants: Two participants primarily get involved:
  - Business Stakeholder: The business stakeholder typically has the high-level goals, objectives, and requirements. The stakeholder funds the BPM project.
  - Business Analyst: The business analyst works closely with the business stakeholder and produces a precise business model of the requirement. This model includes information, participants, workflow or process, as well as business rules models. Business analysts also simulate some of the modeled processes and compare as-is and what-if use-case scenarios. The resulting output will be a number of artifacts that are then detailed by the process architect and designer.

- Design: In the design phase, the requirements produced will be detailed for implementation. The design phase includes design specification of the information models, the process models, the business rules, design of what needs to be integrated with or published as a service, and of course the design of the user interfaces. The deliverables are detailed design specifications. The initial requirements and use-case models from the modeling and simulation phases will contain the foundation of the design artifacts. Here analysis deliverables are used to provide a more detailed blueprint design toward implementation. So the fundamental difference between design and analysis is that the design phase moves quite close to implementation.

- Process architect: The process architect takes the drafts of the process definitions, the models, and even the business rules specified by the business analysts to create more precise design specifications. In fact, the process architect's detailed designs could potentially be the actual deployed processes. In other words, in more modern BPM systems, the gap between design and implementation is disappearing.
- SOA architect: The SOA architect is responsible for the detailed design of the underlying SOA IT architecture, including the design of the microflows and all the integration, communication, and QoS-specific functions that are needed in the ESB. The SOA architect needs to work closely with the process architect in identifying the best technical and viable approaches for invoking service orchestration microflow for integration, transactional contexts, QoS parameters, and invocation of external B2B services. The end-to-end application process will typically involve several subflows, some of which will be executed in the SOA or ESB layer, whereas others will be executed in the BPM system.

- Build: What is being built? The process flows and the accompanying business rules. There are three essential requirements here. Typically, most of the detailed design implemented by the process architect will be ready for deployment and execution. Occasionally process engineers will provide more detailed integration support when needed. For instance, in some cases additional integration logic code needs to be developed for integrating with systems that do not have out-of-the-box adapters. Another aspect of execution is the system security, reliability, scalability, and overall performance monitoring of the BPM application. This typically will involve system administrator-level effort for the overall deployment. Other efforts include interoperability with existing tools, application server platform, or infrastructure plumbing. Two participants primarily get involved:
  - Development engineers: They will be responsible for the implementations of the parts of the application that involve lower-level coding (e.g., Java, C#). The purpose of the required code will vary (e.g., integration, procedural logic). This is overall a more conventional procedural programming role. A BPM application needs to undergo rigorous quality assurance and then subsequently be deployed. Typically quality assurance and deployment engineers work closely with the administrators to go from staging servers to deployment servers.
  - Administrators: These include database, SOA, and system administrators. The administrators deal with the overall quality of service of the deployed application as well as key enterprise deployment issues such as performance, security, and reliability.

- Deploy: This is where the application goes into production. It is not uncommon to deploy a business process management in phases. Deployment is typically preceded by user acceptance testing to make sure the BPM system indeed meets the expectations and requirements of the stakeholders and its user community. For instance, an initial deployment could limit the number of users who will start using the automated and digitized business rules and business processes. As the application gains success in production, perhaps through some enhancements and extensions, the solution is deployed within larger and larger communities. In deployment, a key element to look for is early success and acceptance of the projects. BPM system applications in most cases will change what the user community of the solution is used to. To succeed in acceptance, tangible benefits in the early stages of a deployment is critical. Deployment will definitely involve various participants from the IT deportment. Database and system administrators as well as other information system personnel involved in configuring hardware and software resources will all be involved in successful deployment of BPM system applications.
- Monitor and analyze: This is the "M" of business process management. As soon as applications are deployed, they can be monitored. This could be as simple as tracking where one is within an in-flight process. It could also be running real-time reports on the performance of operators and applications, service level agreements, or specific task categories. The analysis of BAM could be done by managers on the technical and business side. Organizations need a platform that enables them to easily measure the effectiveness of their processes and to analyze them through online analytical measures. Business measures could be viewed and analyzed through a pool of real-time or historical analytical reports.[10] The participants for the monitoring and analysis are primarily the business stakeholder and the business analyst. The business stakeholder should be able to monitor and measure the KPIs of his business. Then if certain bottlenecks are identified, the business analyst can conduct a number of what-if analysis scenarios and can suggest improvements, going back to the model and simulate phase.
- Improve: Business process management is about continuous improvements. This means the monitoring and control identify potential opportunities for improvements. For instance, in revising a process flow, opportunities can be discovered to introduce additional automations through using business rules or external services. The flow could achieve a purpose such as processing a customer claim, a purchase order, or a credit card dispute or improving the quality in a production context, but now an improved version of the flow can get created for the same purpose.

Business process management systems are used to define, to execute, and to manage processes. Just as database management systems manage the data of the enterprise, BPM systems are used to manage the processes of the enterprise. Individual steps or activities in processes correspond to service invocations. The process flows as well as other entities (see Figure 5.7) involved in BPM solutions are continuously improved. Services are essential building blocks in BPM. As service oriented architectures become more popular and as organizations start to expose more of their systems and offerings through service interfaces, the services can be combined in processes that specify the flow of execution of the component services. In fact, the combined aggregate process can be then published as a service. BPM systems, therefore, provide the platform to build and to deploy compositions of services.

5.5.1 EPM, BPM Systems, and SOA/ESB

Figure 5.39 illustrates the interdependencies and the larger continuous loop of improvement involving the higher-layer enterprise performance management, the business performance management system layer discussed in this chapter, and the lower-level SOA/ESB infrastructure plumbing layers.

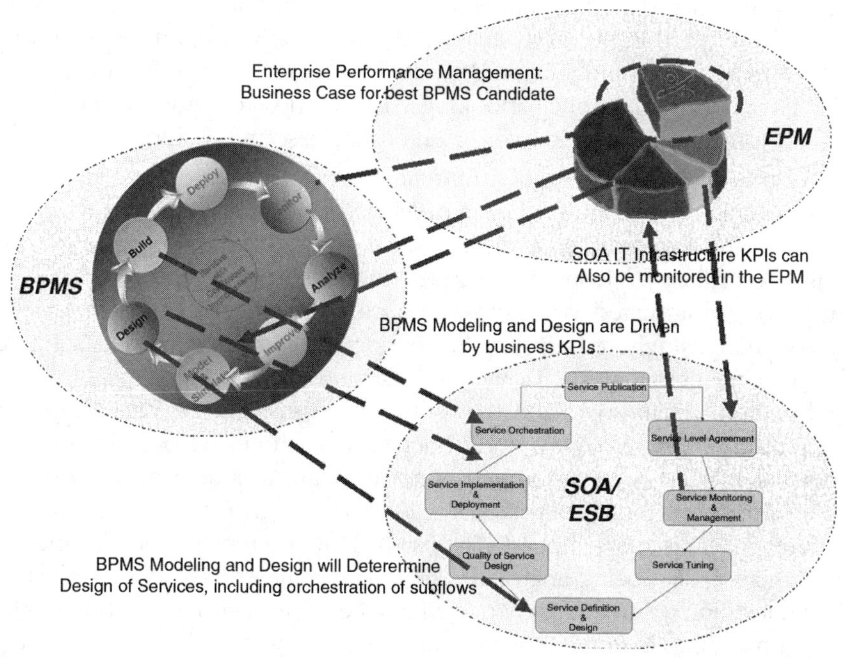

Figure 5.39 Continuous improvements with EPM, BPM system, and SOA/ESB

From a top-down, especially business-oriented perspective, it starts with what you are trying to achieve and your KPIs. One of the recurring problems in most organizations is that the higher level you are in the organization hierarchy, the less connected you are to the enterprise data needed to make critical decisions. Often decisions are made with the wrong or insufficient information.

However, it is not practical for higher-ups to be inundated with data. The enterprise performance management—especially business intelligence—system can aggregate the information for the various levels of the organization and can provide the most relevant and critical information to each party.

- Strategic performance: For instance, C-level executives such as chief executive officers and chief financial officers might be interested in strategic performance indicators that cross various departmental boundaries. For instance, they might be interested in sales bookings across all product and service lines and departments. Similarly, they might be interested in the number of customer complaints across products, procurement expenses, or liabilities across the enterprise.
- Tactical or departmental performance: The departmental or functional units will focus on the performance of their respective constituents. Here management at the vice president or director level is interested in the performance of its respective departments or areas of responsibilities. Concrete measures are still needed in terms of expenses, revenues, bookings, inventories, or any aspect of customer, human resource, or enterprise resource planning data.

It is possible to go even further into detailed operational data for the back-, middle-, and front-office applications. The more challenging aspect is the ability to drill down from values in the higher levels of the organization to underlying automated or digitized policies (i.e., business rules) or processes. Increasingly, enterprises are endorsing scorecards and dashboards for performance analysis. However, it is still difficult to make either short- or long-term changes to the executing processes and policies within the organization. Drilling down and understanding the exact policies and processes that need to be improved is not enough. It is also necessary to be able to improve them continuously, as illustrated in Figure 5.40.

The x-axis is the temporal dimension: How current is your business or performance data being analyzed? The y-axis is the efficiency of introducing continuous improvement or change within the organization. Even though identification of historic trends is important, it is desirable to have executives at all levels to introduce change continuously. This can be achieved through BPM.

A key concept in continuous improvement is this whole notion of treating the modeled and digitized processes as assets. What does this mean?

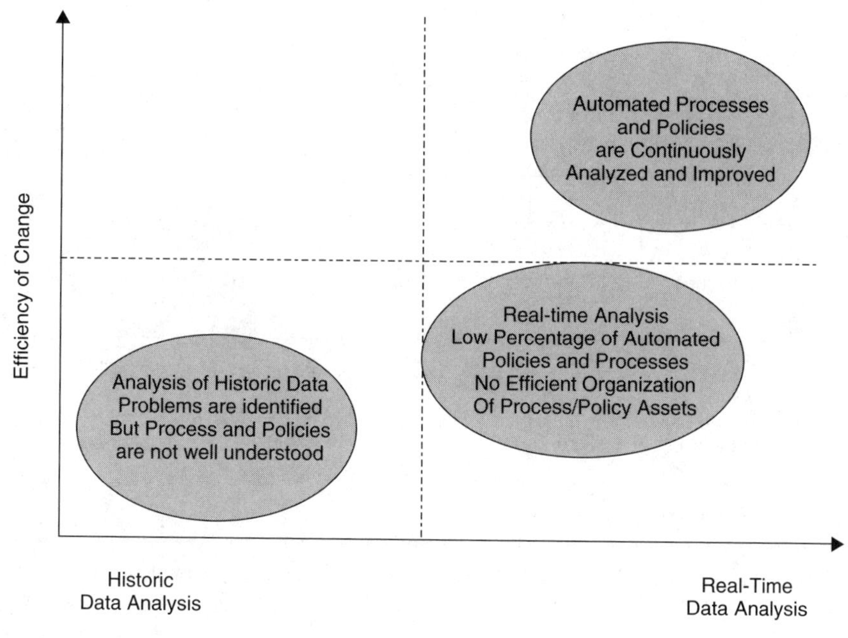

Figure 5.40 Data analysis versus efficiency of change

Think of what DBMSs gave us in the past 30 years. They allowed for a separation of the management of structured data from the applications. The databases are used for enterprise resource planning, sales force automation, human resources, supply chain management, customer relationship, inventory management, and product management. And one of the most important trends for DBMSs is data warehousing and business intelligence. Business intelligence attempts to extract business relevant information from data sources. More specifically, the data is mined and knowledge is extracted: trends that could help one predict the market or make improvements in core business processes and policies. There are multiple sources of the data from the DBMS. They are typically extracted, transformed, and then organized in the data warehouse. The source of the data includes BPM and enterprise data from other applications. So DBMSs treat data as assets. BPM systems allow you to organize your operational artifacts (processes, business rules, information models, service integrators) and treat these as assets. Increasingly these applications are becoming BPM system applications—often built as specializations of solution frameworks. The challenge is to take performance indicators, to analyze trends, and to immediately drill down to the processes or policies that need to be changed or improved.

Figure 5.41 illustrates a process with several subprocesses. Some of these subprocesses have microflows executing in the ESB level. The gray shaded

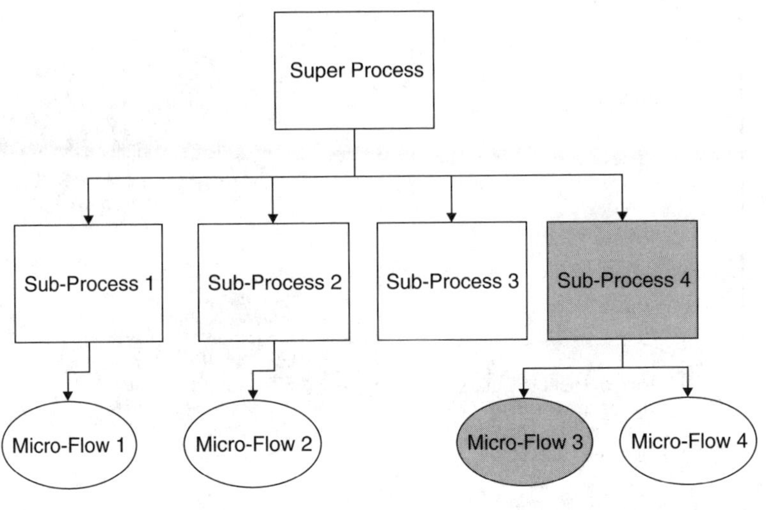

Figure 5.41 Process hierarchy with BPM and microflow subprocesses

boxes indicate changes that need to be made for the process and its subprocesses. Here subprocess 4 and microflow 3 need to be modified. The process involves business rules (constraints, decisions, SLA, expressions) as well. The parent process and the subprocesses are executed in the BPM system. The microflows are executed in the WS-BPEL engine or the ESB.

What is a microflow?

- Microflows do not involve human participants directly: you might send an e-mail or a message to the human participant, but human workflow with human participant model and capabilities are not supported in microflows.
- Microflows are of relatively short duration with few steps: no set rule but probably 5 to 10 steps.
- Microflows can be transactional, which means the service participants in the flow can be involved in the same transaction. Typically, distributed transaction technology is used to guarantee two-phase commit (2PC) transactional semantics.

Therefore, the essential life cycle starts with KPIs evaluated primarily through executing process data. Ideally managers are able then to drill down and to identify potential improvements in processes, human participants, and system participants and business rules. The improved processes can have several subprocesses, some of which will end up executing as microflows within enterprise service buses.

5.6 Business Process Standards

> The nice thing about standards is that there are so many to choose from.
>
> **Andrew S. Tanenbaum**

Business and IT: This section gives a good overview of the most important standards in business process management. But there is a bigger question: Are standards necessary in BPM? The problem is that the raison d'etre of standardization has thus far not been clearly articulated. For instance, if standards are used to export from a BPA tool and to import it in a BPM system execution environment, there is a problem. The underlying conceptual models—the metamodels—of the two environments will be quite different. Even though organizations such as Object Management Group (www.omg.org) are attempting to have common metamodels, it will take quite a while for these metamodels to be ratified and deployed extensively in BPM products. So a least common denominator needs to be assumed. That approach will severely hamper the round tripping and the continuous improvement cycle. Furthermore, the standards—and all the ones discussed here—in BPM do not thus far incorporate business rules, organizations, and information as well as integration models. Most process standards focus on the flow and are not holistic. This means, for instance, that rules that actually drive the processes are not incorporated in a cohesive fashion when it comes to BPM standardization. There are other challenges. There is thus far—and for the foreseeable future—no clear and accepted approach in exporting a modeling diagram (e.g., via BPMN or UML) to an executable eXtensible Markup Language (XML) document. XML Process Definition Language (XPDL) is attempting to do this. BPMN, on the other hand, has defined a BPEL binding. Part of the conundrum is that the various standards are sponsored by different consortia and organizations. Web Services Choreography Description Language (WS-CDL) is sponsored by the World Wide Web Consortia (W3C); BPMN and UML are sponsored by OMG; XPDL is sponsored by the Workflow Management Coalition (WfMC); and BPEL is sponsored by the Organization for the Advancement of Structured Information Standards (OASIS).

These issues need to be taken into consideration in building a BPM application with a BPM tool.

There is an abundance of BPM standards. At least four standardization bodies have standards pertaining to BPM, including OMG, Organization for the Advancement of Structured Information Standards (OASIS, www. oasis-open.org), Workflow Management Coalition, (WfMC, www.wfmc.org/), and World Wide Web Consortium (W3C, www.w3C.org). In fact, not too long ago there were at least five organizations working on different BPM standards. There has been some consolidation among the standard bodies. For instance, the BPMI consortium (www.bpmi.org) merged with OMG. In addition to these standardization bodies, some organizations also publish standards focusing on business exchanges between trading partners. Examples include ebXML (www.ebxml.org/, also part of OASIS) and RosettaNet (www.rosettanet.org).

So what do these different standards cover? Several dimensions could be used to taxonomize BPM standards. The motivation, perspective, focus, and bias of BPM standards are quite different. Figure 5.42 illustrates three essential layers in process standardization.

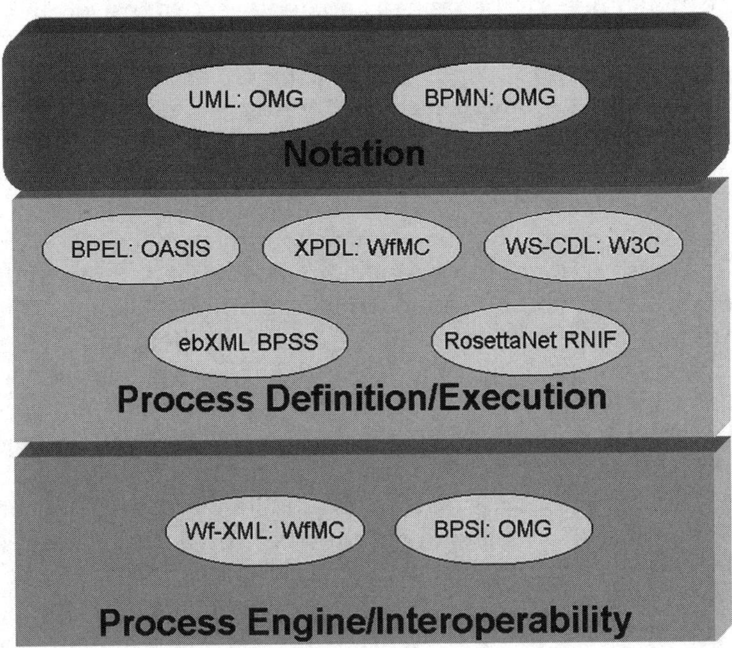

Figure 5.42 BPM standards

- Process notation: Through notation come the shapes and their semantics in designing processes. So process notation standards are graphical and result in process diagrams using the standard notation. This book primarily uses the BPMN notation for depicting the various process patterns in Section 5.3.6. BPMN, sponsored by OMG (and previously by BPMI.org) is the most popular notation in this category, although UML's activity diagram is also used extensively to model processes.
- Process definition and execution: These are typically XML standards that define the process that gets executed by the underlying process engine. Typically, process definition starts by creating a visual model of the process using a standard (e.g., BPMN) or proprietary notation. Then an XML-based process definition is generated from the notation. The two main contenders here are WS-BPEL and XPDL.[11]
- Process engine and interoperability: Once processes are designed and deployed on a BPM system, users or service requests can create instances of these processes. These process engine and interoperability standards focus on the run-time interaction of process engines. Typical engine interfaces include interfaces to create process instances as well as interfaces to receive events, to check on process instance states, and to change the states. The two standards indicated in Figure 5.42 are the Wf-XML standard from WfMC and the Business Process Service Interfaces (BPSI) from OMG.

The following sections describe the three most popular BPM standards in more detail: BPMN, WS-BPEL, and XPDL. The Choreography Description Language (WS-CDL) that supports standardization for process choreographies is also covered.

5.6.1 BPMN

The BPMN notation is becoming quite popular. It provides a standardized graphical notation for modeling business processes. There are notations to represent the following:

- Events: Figure 5.43 shows some of the events that could be used in BPMN processes and their categories. As indicated there are start, intermediate, and end events. Internal or external occurrences could cause events to be triggered. The BPMN flow can indicate what happens when an event is triggered through associating the event with an activity. For instance, if an error condition happened and it is necessary to compensate, a compensation event and an association are used emanating from the compensation event to the activity or

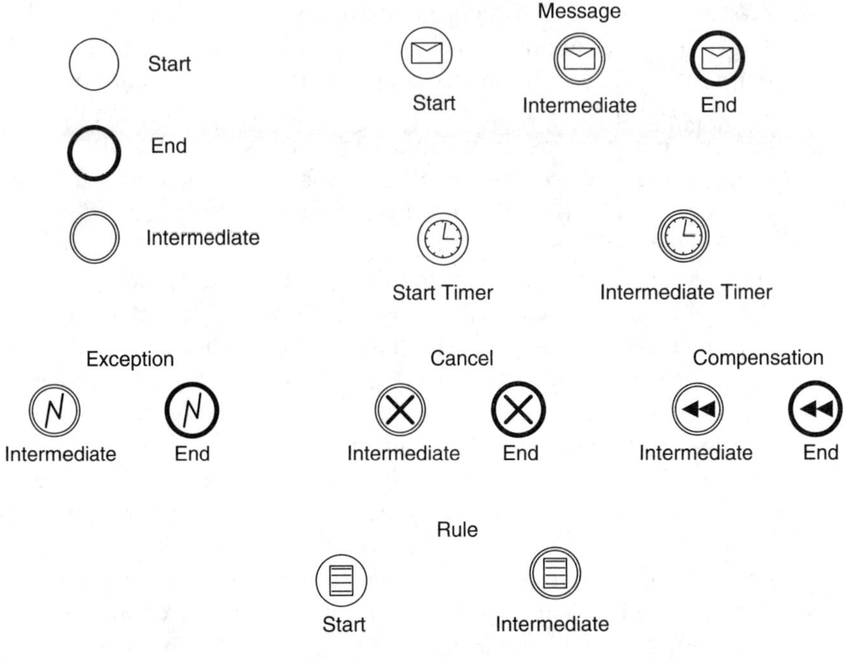

Figure 5.43 Event types in BPMN

task that will do the compensation (e.g., notify managers or send e-mails; undo effects of database update) (Figure 5.44). Events are quite ubiquitous in BPMN diagrams. For example, events could set alarms (service levels), cause selections (e.g., gateway branch), implement process breaks, process faults, and process termination.

- Atomic activities or tasks: These are the core building blocks of processes, and this chapter has already mentioned several examples of activity nodes, which are basically rounded rectangles.

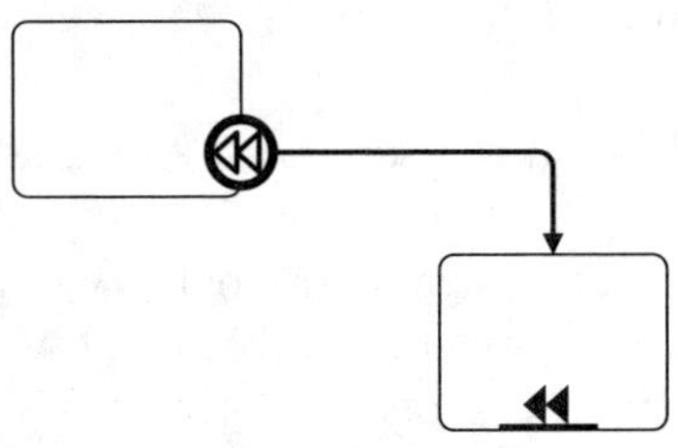

Figure 5.44 Compensation event and activity

- Subprocesses: BPMN provides several options for designing subprocesses. The most common shape is the collapsed subprocess. There can also be expanded subprocesses in a rectangle. Figure 5.45 shows the notation for a subprocess. Looping of subprocesses also can be visually indicated or be used with activities. For instance, to process each item in a purchase order, you will have a loop and execute the subprocess for each item. Figure 5.46 illustrates a looping subprocess.
- Gateway controls: Section 5.3.6 discussed split and join and decision splits. Gateways are used to implement these parallel and decisioning controls (Figure 5.47). The XOR means there will be a fork, and only one of the alternative paths emanating from the diamond shape will be selected. The inclusive OR means several alternative branches could be selected. The parallel gateway indicates AND or parallel split. The branches emanating from the parallel AND will execute in parallel. For example, in an employee new hire application there can be an AND split to check the references and the employment history in parallel. These are two different activities that could be handled by different participants (human or system) in parallel. Then a rendezvous (AND join) can proceed with the next activity only if the two activities are completed (references and employment history). One interesting aspect of BPMN is the event-based forking or branching. The branching will happen based on the event that occurs at the gateway. For instance, two alternative messages could cause the branching to the corresponding path or a timeout. This will be indicated using BPMN event-based gateway notation (Figure 5.48).
- Sequence flow: These are typically represented through arrows from one node to the other and can be conditional. BPMN introduces several types of sequence flow arrows; the most popular of these is the solid directed arrow used in most of this chapter's examples. Figure 5.49 shows how the connections through arrows could be categorized. Conditional flows are used in decisioning. The message flows are used to capture message communications potentially involving multiple trading partner processes. Associations are used for introducing comments or data flows between tasks. For the

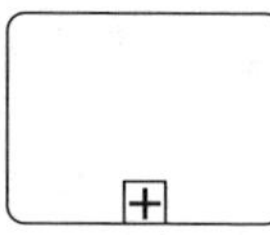

Figure 5.45 Collapsed subprocess

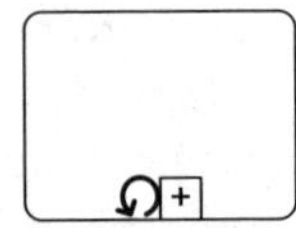

Figure 5.46 Looping subprocess

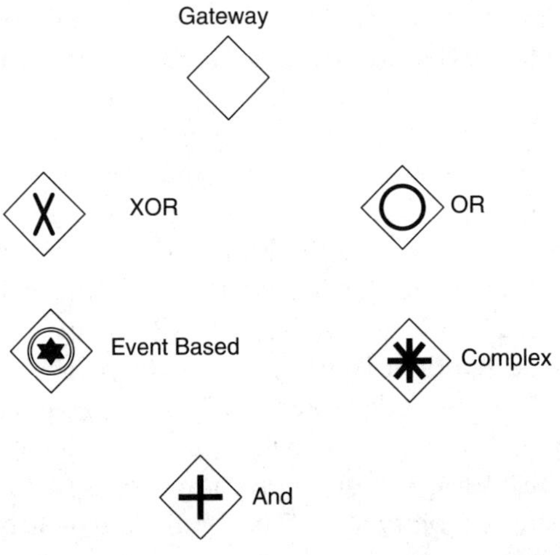

Figure 5.47 BPMN gateways

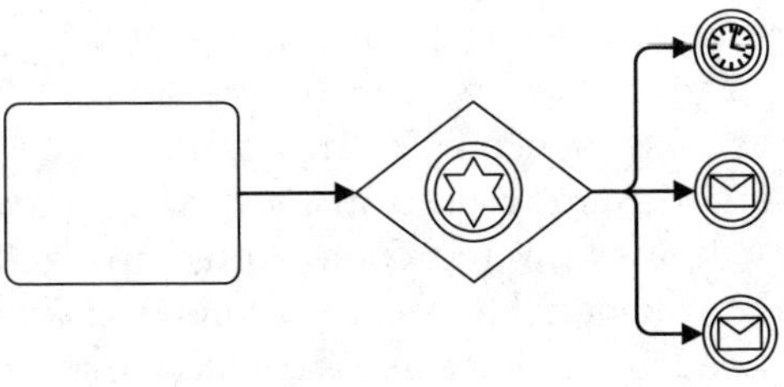

Figure 5.48 BPMN pick branching based on events

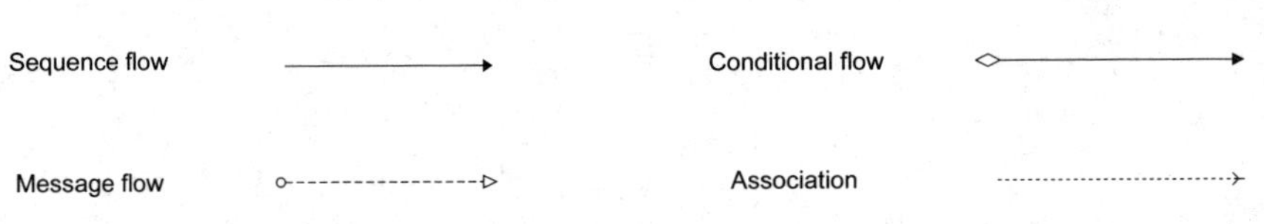

Figure 5.49 BPMN connections

sequence flows, the names, condition, and the default are typically used in conjunction with the OR gateways. For example, if the branching conditions emanating from a condition gateway include high risk, medium risk, and low risk, these will appear on the sequence flow arrows as illustrated in Figure 5.50. Figure 5.51 illustrates a process in BPMN for contract approval. As illustrated, the contract is received via e-mail. It is prepared by procurement to submit to the business and legal for approval. If it is rejected, an e-mail is sent to the provider. If accepted two subprocesses execute in parallel: one for business and financial approval and the other for legal approval. After both of these subprocesses have completed, the service or product is procured.

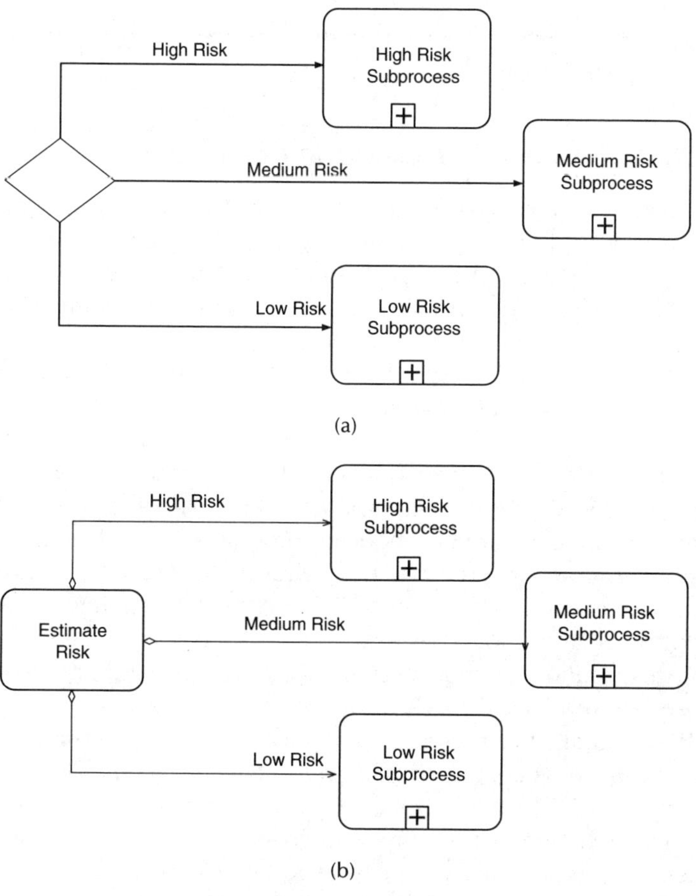

Figure 5.50 Sequence flows: (a) OR gateway followed by decisions sequence flows; (b) decisioning sequence flows

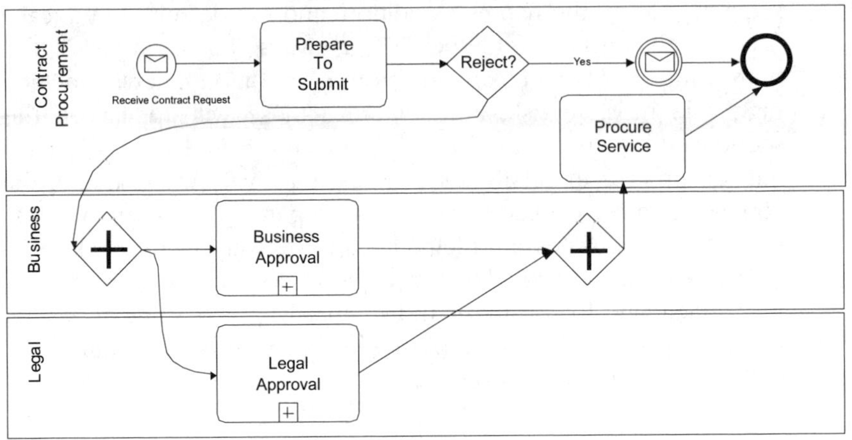

Figure 5.51 A BPMN example

5.6.2 XML Processing Description Language

XPDL supports a schema to define processes in XML. XPDL makes it possible to define a process template through a graphical Integrated Development Environment (IDE) tool and then to deploy the template, potentially on different tools. One of these tools could be a simulation engine. Of course, the workflow defined by XPDL is eventually executed by a process engine.

Currently XPDL is in its second version, XPDL 2.0, which is compatible to XPDL 1.0. XPDL 2.0 attempts to provide support for BPMN. As noted previously, BPMN provides a graphical notation for processes. Processes defined with BPMN shapes can be useful for capturing and documenting processes in service oriented enterprises. The goal of business process management is the execution of modeled processes. Actually some systems can import, for instance, Visio diagrams with BPMN stencils for execution. An alternative approach is to use XML as the interchange mechanism between various BPM tools. For example, one tool can be used to create BPMN processes and to export it in an XML format, and then another tool can be used to import it.[12]

The BPMN goal is to provide a graphical notation to facilitate human communication between business users and technical users of complex business processes. The XPDL goal is to provide a XML file format that can be used to interchange process models between tools. So some tools allow you to design in BPMN and then export XPDL. Figure 5.52 illustrates how XPDL can be used in conjunction with BPMN or other graphical notations. The figure illustrates two fundamental functions in business process management: graphical modeling and execution.[13]

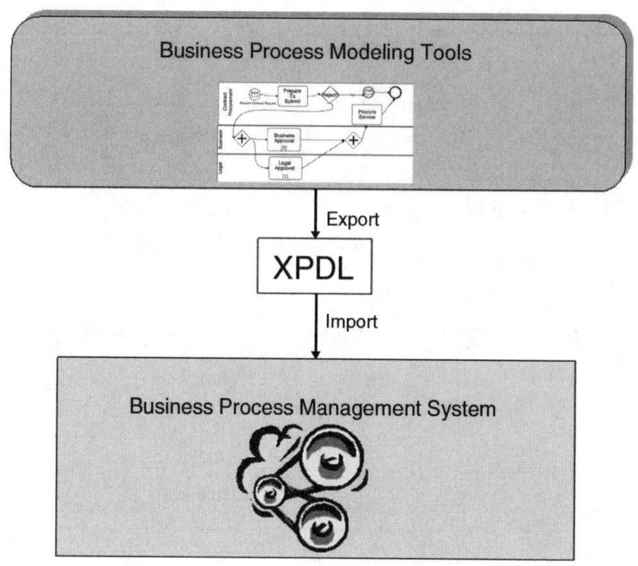

Figure 5.52 XPDL in process definition interchanges

The XPDL 2.0 is consistent with the BPMN metamodel. This facilitates the generation of XPDL definitions from the BPMN diagram. Figure 5.53 illustrates part of the XPDL metamodel. A number of these elements in XPDL directly support BPMN. Examples of XPDL elements that have been introduced to support BPMN include event, gateway, pool, lane, associations, and artifacts. The events are subtypes of activities and are used to support BPMN's event activities. Pools and lanes delimit flows executed by participants as well as message exchanges between flows. Message flows are used to represent communication between processes, based on WSDL protocols. Associations and artifacts are used to document the process definitions. Associations and the artifacts to which they connect provide additional information for the reader of a BPMN diagram but do not directly affect the execution of the process.

5.6.3 Business Process Execution Language

The Business Process Execution Language was developed primarily by IBM and Microsoft, combining various features of their standards (i.e., WSFL and XLANG, respectively).[14] In April 2003, WS-BPEL was submitted to the OASIS consortium. Soon afterward, many companies started to support and promote WS-BPEL as the Web services process standard. The official version is BPEL4WS version 1.1, and a number of BPM products support it more or

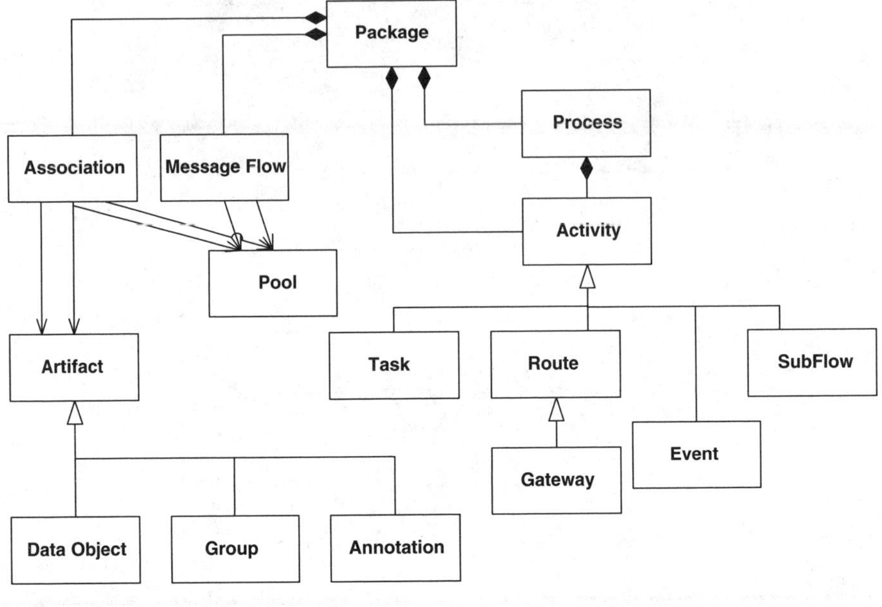

Figure 5.53 Part of XPDL metamodel with some BPMN elements

less—some with their own proprietary extensions. The OASIS WS-BPEL TC plans to release the 2.0 version of the standard in 2006.

5.6.3.1 WS-BPEL and WSDL

WS-BPEL uses WSDL extensively to implement the orchestration of the services. The service interfaces are defined through WSDL. Therefore for the actual service invocations as well as the invocation of the process engine that executes the process, WS-BPEL relies on WSDL. When services invoke one another, the operations of the invocations are defined in WSDL. WSDL defines the operations and WS-BPEL orchestrates them. In fact, WS-BPEL extends WSDL to facilitate the linking between partner service invocations. So in the WS-BPEL specification, you are dealing with the definition of processes, as well as extensions of WSDL to support message exchanges between participants (partners) in the process. There is one designated role that is actually running the process. Other partners are either calling the executing process or being called.

As we saw in Chapter 3, WSDL defines abstract types, the messages, the operations, and the portTypes. WSDL also specifies the concrete bindings and services (how and where to invoke the operations).WS-BPEL uses WSDL's abstract constructs and extends WSDL through a number of new elements including *partnerLinkType,* providing a mechanism to track the stateful context of conversations among otherwise stateless Web services. Partner links are used to capture relationships and dependencies between partners. A partner link specifies the roles and the port type for each role. Here is an example from the WS-BPEL specification:

```
<partnerLinkType name="purchaseLT">
  <role name="purchaseService">
    <portType name="pos:purchaseOrderPT"/>
  </role>
</partnerLinkType>
```

These partner link types will then be used in various WS-BPEL process definitions. More specifically, WS-BPEL will specify:

- *Partner Links*: Which will reference the partnerLinkType by name, the role of the partner that is executing the process (e.g. for receiving messages), and the partner service's role (e.g., for invocations). Partner links are then used in activities that receive, invoke, or reply to requests.
- *Port Types and Operations*: A WS-BPEL process provides the composition of Web service operations within activities. Therefore, WS-BPEL uses port types and operations within these port types to denote these services that are called within the process. The port types and operations are defined within WSDL documents.
- *Properties*: Within WSDL you also define properties (this is an extension of WSDL), and then associate them with WSDL message parts. Properties are very useful in uniquely and globally identifying process instances (e.g., for associating messages).

In WS-BPEL process definitions, the WSDL documents are defined via namespaces and then referenced throughout the WS-BPEL process definition elements. You will often see the same WSDL document used to define the port types and operations that are supported by multiple partners and processes.

5.6.3.2 Process

The <process> element is the root or top level element of a WS-BPEL process definition.

```
<process name=" ...">
  <partnerLins>
    ...
  </partnerLins>

  <variables>
```

```
    ...
  </variables>

  <correlationSets>
    ...
  </correlationSets>

  <faultHandlers>
    ...
  </faultHandlers>

  <eventHandlers>
    ...
  </eventHandlers>

          ... top activity

</process>
```

The process can describe partners, variables, correlations, compensation handlers, event handlers, and fault handlers. The process will have a top activity which could be a <sequence> or a <flow> or another activity type discussed in the following sections. The other components are optional, but every process must have an activity.

An engine executes the process and then this process will likely invoke other services; after all the process is *orchestrating* several services. A general form of a process in WS-BPEL consists of the components shown in Figure 5.54 and described below.

The <receive> (1) can create an instance of the process.[15] The engine receives the request, creates the process instance and then executes a flow of activities (often in a <flow> element). Now upon receiving the request, the process also uses input values from the request (which is presented in the requestInfo variable in the diagram). These values are then used by the <invoke>. Upon completion of the request, the steps in the process will be providing values to other variables (such as the responseInfo) to return to the client.

While processing the customer or client request, the process might <invoke> (2) other Web services, which in turn could instantiate other processes, and so on. The figure illustrates such an <invoke> of a service provider. Once all the results are accumulated and combined, the process then sends a <reply> (3) to the requesting customer or client. This reply corresponds to the <receive> element. This is a simple, general form and scenario used by many WS-BPEL processes. This <receive>, potentially <invoke>, and then <reply> provides an example of synchronous process

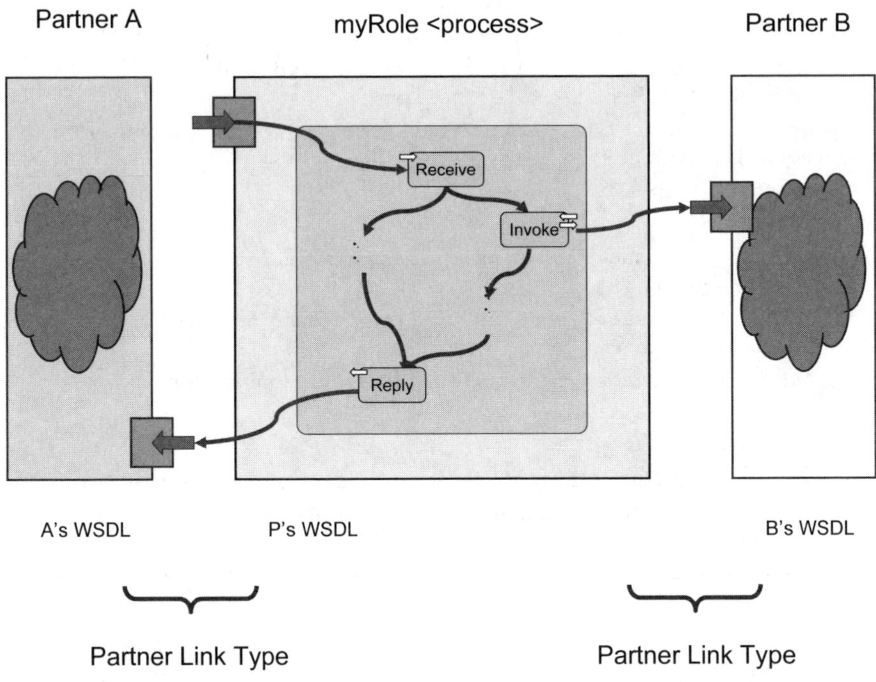

Figure 5.54 Receive, invoke, and reply within a process

operation: The partner that called the <receive> and the created process instance will block until the process engine returns the result through <reply>. The other option is to have an asynchronous process operation. Here instead of a <reply>, an <invoke> will be used to call the client to provide the response. The advantage of the asynchronous is that the caller can continue with its own processing without waiting for the process engine's response. The disadvantage is that the caller has to expose a service interface to get the response from the process instance.

The following is a sample WS-BPEL involving a buyer, a seller, and shipper. It uses the synchronous <receive>/<reply>.

```
<process name="salesProcess" suppressJoinFailure="yes"
targetNamespace="urn:salesprocess.pegasamples.
bpelsalesRequest_1.sales"
xmlns="http://schemas.xmlsoap.org/ws/2003/03/business-process/"
xmlns:bpws="http://schemas.xmlsoap.org/ws/2003/03/business-process/"
xmlns:lns="urn:salesprocess.resources.wsdl.bpelsalesRequest_1.sales"
xmlns:xsd="http://www.w3.org/2001/XMLSchema">
  <partnerLinks>
```

```
    <partnerLink myRole="salesService" name="buyer"
partnerLinkType="lns:salesPartnerLinkType"/>
    <partnerLink name="seller" partnerLinkType="lns:
    salesLinkType"partnerRole="seller"/>
   <partnerLink name="shipper" partnerLinkType="lns:shipmentLinkType"
partnerRole="shipper"/>
  </partnerLinks>
  <variables>
    <variable messageType="lns: salesApprovalMessage"
    name="request"/>
    <variable messageType="lns:confirmShipmentMessage"
    name="shipment"/>
    <variable messageType="lns:errorMessage" name="error"/>
  </variables>
  <faultHandlers>
    <catch faultName="lns:salesProcessFault" faultVariable="error">
      <reply faultName="lns:unableToHandleRequest"
      operation="request"
partnerLink="buyer" portType="lns:salesServicePT" variable="error"/>
    </catch>
  </faultHandlers>
  <sequence>
    <links>
      <link name="receive-to-shipment"/>
      <link name="shipment-to-reply"/>
    </links>
    <receive createInstance="yes" operation="request"
    partnerLink="buyer"
portType="lns:salesServicePT" variable="request">
      <source linkName="receive-to-shipment"/>
    </receive>
    <invoke inputVariable="request" operation="sale"
    outputVariable="sales"
partnerLink="seller" portType="lns:saleApprovalPT">
      <target linkName="receive-to-shipment"/>
      <source linkName="shipment-to-reply"/>
    </invoke>
    <reply operation="request" partnerLink="buyer"
    portType="lns:salesServicePT"
variable="shipment">
      <target linkName="shipment-to-reply"/>
    </reply>
  </sequence>
</process>
```

5.6.3.3 *Variables*

WS-BPEL uses the <variables> element to store process state as well as values of messages exchanged between Web services receives, invocations, or replies. For instance, when a process is instantiated, the input arguments to the receive will be stored in variables (e.g., student number, purchase order number, amount) that may be used in subsequent Web services calls. The type of variable is determined by a message type. The message type definition will be from a WSDL. Here is an example of variables.

```
<variables>
    <variable name="input"
      messageType="tns:initiateFinancialAidRequest"/>
  <variable name="crInput"
      messageType="crs:processStudentInfoRequest"/>


  ...
</variables>
```

These variables and the values they hold will persist for the lifetime of the process instance. BPEL also provides an activity called <assign> to manipulate variable values and to assign values from one variable to the other. Here is an example of <assign> and its <copy> child element.

```
<assign>
    <copy>
      <from variable="input" part="parameters" query="//SSN"/>
      <to variable="crInput" part="parameters"
         query="/processStudentInfoService/ssn"/>
    </copy>
</assign>
```

5.6.3.4 *Activities*

A process is a collection of activities, which are the building blocks of processes. These activities are either basic or structured. Basic activities include Web service operation invokes, receives, or replies. Structured activities are built from other activities—basic or structured. Activities are the building blocks of the process. Most processes will have a structured activity that contains multiple other activities (Figure 5.55).

The following sections provide brief descriptions of some of the basic and structured activities.

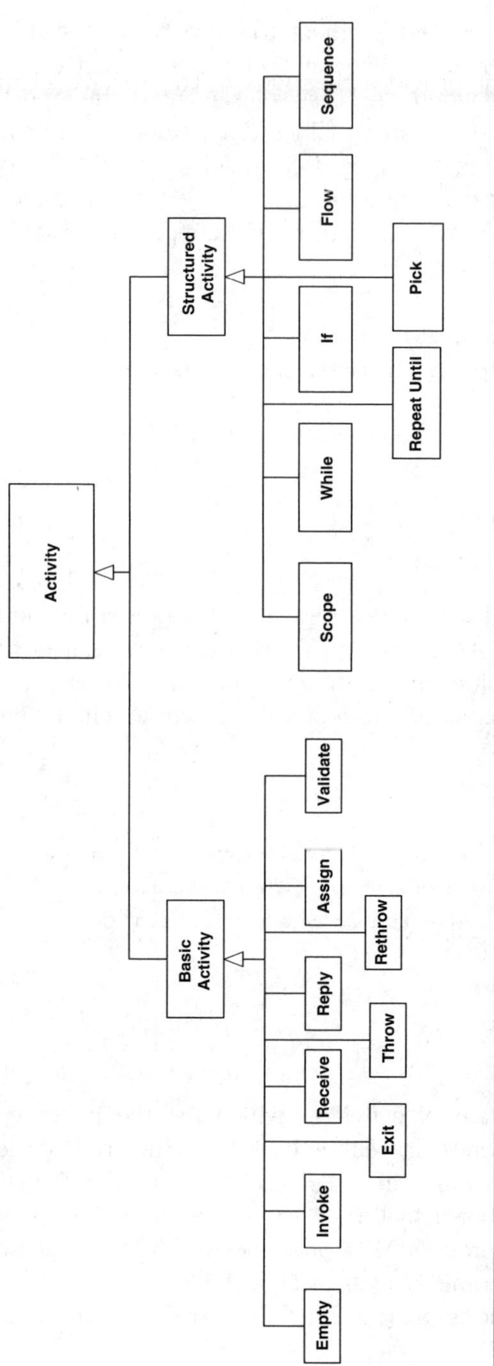

Figure 5.55 Basic and structured activities

5.3.6.5 Receive, Invoke, and Reply

As indicated already, processes can start with the receive element, or with <pick>. The receive element provides the input for a WSDL operation, and then the reply element provides the output. The receive element has a createInstance attribute. If the value of this attribute is yes, a process instance will be created by the engine. Other attributes of <receive> include the partnerLink, portType, and operation as well as the variable. The reply element corresponds to the output of the WSDL operation. The same receive could be associated with several replies in a WS-BPEL process. The actual decision on the particular reply will depend on conditions in the process instance. For example, there could be branching with different message reply content. Depending on the branch in the process instance, one or the other reply will be executed at run time. Between the <receive> and <reply>, there could be several invocations of Web services through the invoke element.

5.6.3.6 Structured Activities

WS-BPEL contains a number of structured activities that define the flow in the run-time ordering of the activities within a WS-BPEL process. These include the following:

- <sequence>: With sequence the activities are executed in the listed sequential order:

  ```
  <sequence standard-attributes>
  standard-elements
  activity+
  </sequence>
  ```

- <if>: The if element supports conditional branching. If can contain nested <elseif>s. The one activity whose branch is true is chosen to execute.
- <flow>: The flow element contains activities that are executed concurrently. The links in the flow element indicate the synchronization dependencies between activities. The link provides the control flow support and has a source and a target, which are specified within those activities' definitions. Figure 5.56 illustrates a <flow> with three sequences. Although the transcript, reference, and financial services can execute in parallel, there is a control link dependency between the service that gets references and the one that prepares a transcript and a reference report.
- <pick>: The pick element captures event handling. When an event happens, the pick indicates the activity that will be executed to handle that event. This element also supports alarms.

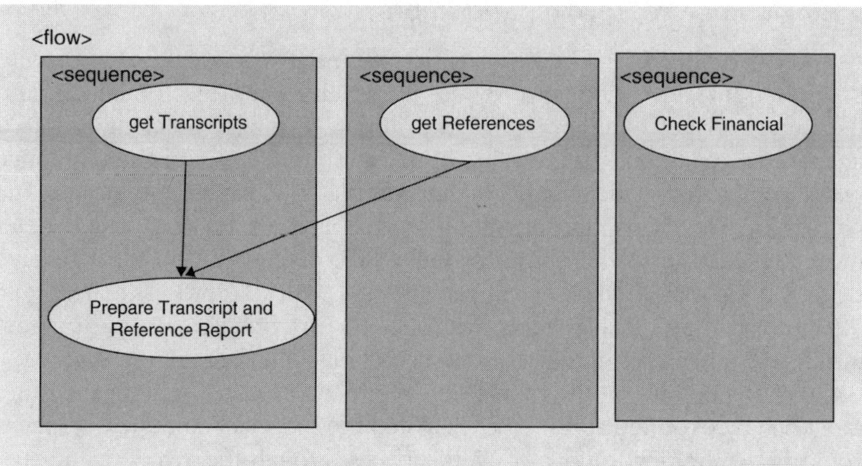

Figure 5.56 Example of a <flow> with three sequences

- Iterating activities: WS-BPEL also has a number of looping constructs very similar to what is found in procedural programming languages. These iteration and looping elements include the following:
  - <while>: The while semantics are similar to while looping in programming languages. The statements in the body of the loop continue executing until the Boolean expression is no longer true.
  - <repeatUntil>: This structured activity will have an activity over which it will repeat in a loop until a condition is satisfied.
  - <forEach>: This will have a counter and repeat the iteration from the start to the final value of the counter.

5.6.3.7 Correlation Sets

All WS-BPEL process instances will be receiving or invoking the operations on the specified ports. The port and the binding are not sufficient to identify the particular instance of the process. There must be an additional mechanism to allow receiving, replying, and invoking messages that all pertain to the same process instance. WS-BPEL achieves this through the support of correlation sets, which consist of one or more message properties that identify the particular process instance. For one process definition, there could be hundreds or even thousands of process instances—perhaps all executing concurrently. As illustrated earlier, in most cases the message exchanges between partners should be performed in the context of the same process instance. The ports of Web service operations cannot distinguish between process instances. This is where correlationSets come into the picture. Through property values, they can correlate Web service invocations to be bound in the context of the same process instance. The correlationSets element specifies all the properties used to correlate process instances.

5.6.3.8 Scopes

WS-BPEL has the notion of scopes and <scope> element. The concept is very similar to structural scopes in programming languages. A scope can define local variables. Scopes can have event handlers, which can respond to messages or alarms. Scopes also define fault handlers and compensation handlers. A scope can contain structured (e.g., a <flow>) and nested activities within it. One of the most important benefits of having scopes is the notion of compensation handlers. Compensations are discussed in more detail in Section 5.6.3.10.

5.6.3.9 Fault Handling

In any business process, occasionally situations will arise where exceptions or faults occur. The WS-BPEL standard provides a fault handling element, which executes an activity in response to faults that could potentially occur in the executing scope or process instance.

5.6.3.10 Compensation

The WS-BPEL processes can be long-duration processes, potentially involving many partners and activities. As noted earlier in this chapter, in traditional transaction systems, transactions typically have atomic, all-or-nothing semantics. This atomic transaction support and all the ACID properties of transactions are appropriate for short-duration transactions in DBMSs, messaging systems, or EAI. In long-duration business transactions, however, a more reasonable approach is to provide a more flexible transaction model with less stringent requirements for atomicity as well as isolation levels between transactions.

The WS-BPEL approach is to use compensation activities to undo the effects of completed steps. Inside a fault, for instance, an explicit <compensate> element can be used to invoke a named scope's compensation handler to undo work that previously completed successfully.

One of the most common usages of compensation is for a parent scope to invoke the compensation handlers of its child scope. For example, if a credit card was charged in a nested scope for a purchase and then there was a problem and the purchase is to be cancelled, the compensation is to credit the account with the charged amount.

5.6.4 WS-CDL

WS-CDL is sponsored by the W3C consortium. Whereas WS-BPEL processes are executed by a process engine, choreography, as discussed in Section 5.3.9, focuses on the dance involving potentially multiple process engines, or even component implementations. Choreography captures the collaboration between the participating process implementations. Figure 5.57 illustrates the same processes in Figure 5.6, but now there is a higher-level choreography definition involving the participants, or partners.

The fundamental concept in WS-CDL is the notion of interactions. Figure 5.6 shows several roles: buyer, seller, shipper. As illustrated, these

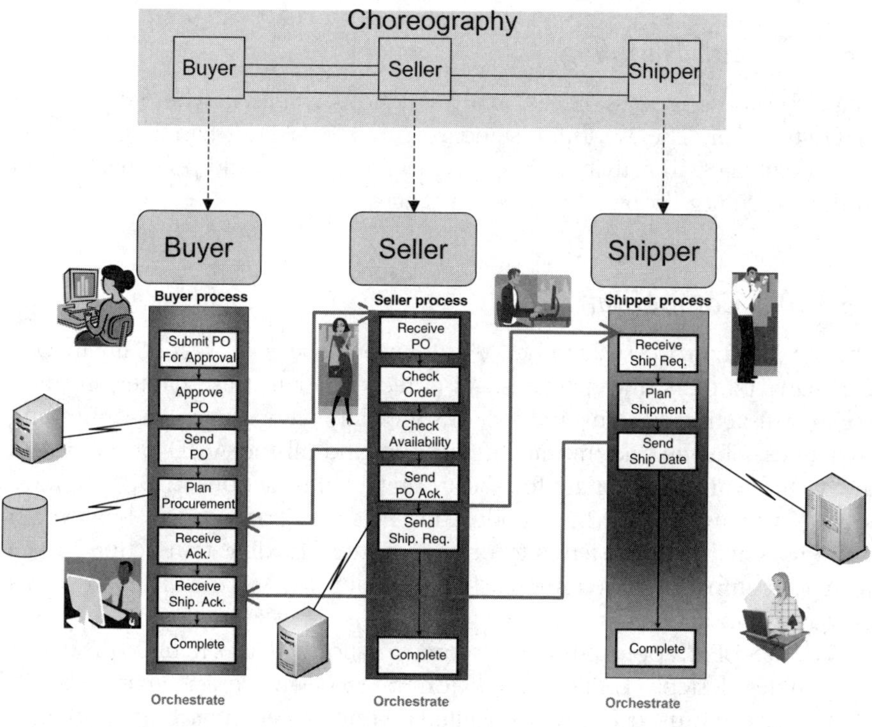

Figure 5.57 Choreography example

roles will be interacting, and WS-CDL captures the ordering and messaging sequencing of the interactions between the roles. WS-CDL provides a holistic view in terms of the roles, message exchanges, and overall interactions between the participants. Figure 5.57 shows the aggregate interaction and sequencing of the exchanges between the participants, not the individual processes executed by each participant. So in a sense what is at the top provides the roles and what they are exchanging—that is, the information or the messages—and the communication parameters.

The roles and their exchanges are handled by implementations, which could be realized through WS-BPEL or other process or component technologies. Each orchestration will define the sequencing of the operations in their respective execution engines. WSDLs define the partner links, operation signatures, and service bindings. Assuming the buyer, seller, and shipper are each deployed on a BPM process engine, there will be process definitions (e.g., WS-BPEL) and operation definitions and bindings (e.g., WSDL) for each partner. WS-CDL brings it all together in a super choreography process so that the individual processes deployed at the partners can interact according to the interaction activities and messages defined in the WS-CDL file. It is not that the details of the internal orchestration processes are not specified for each role; rather, the focus in WS-CDL is on the exchange occurring between the participants. More specifically a WS-CDL file will define:

- The role types and roles of each participating partner: Each of the participants—buyer, seller, shipper—will play a role. For example, the following is the seller role type:

  ```
  <roleTypes name="Seller">
    <behaviors name="SellerService"
    interface="purchaseOrderPT" />
  </roleTypes>
  ```

- Relationships: For example, there will be a relationshipType defined for the buyer–seller relationships using the role types.
- Choreographies, interactions, and channels: WS-CDL includes a <choreographies> element that aggregates the participant's exchange activities and the interactions between the partners. Interaction provides information about the type of the exchange (e.g., one way, request/response). The communication pipe is represented through channels, which are the links between partners. Interestingly, these channels can be passed around between various role types. Information—called tokens—is communicated in these channels, which are points of contacts between the participating partners.

- Control structures and activities: Choreography, as its name suggests, also defines the control and ordering of the activities. Similar to other process flow definitions, sequential and parallel ordering of activities can be defined, as well as selection and choices. Within the activity element, the particular operation that needs to be invoked is specified.

5.7 Summary

This is one of the most important chapters of the book. This is where business and IT come together to model business procedures, business policies, information, and integration models. These models will result in automated or digitized processes and business rules. Participants of these business processes will include humans, back-end systems, and trading partners.

Increasingly, a division of labor is being witnessed in the execution of a process. The microflows that are short duration and that involve systems or trading partners can be executed in the enterprise service bus. The overall business process is executed in the process and rule engine of the BPM suite. This is important. At one level are infrastructure, transportation, and integration support through the ESB. At another level are the business processes that provide comprehensive end-to-end support from business rules and process modeling to execution, monitoring, measurement, and improvement.

The servicing works both ways. Clients of the BPM system or suite can also be invoked through the ESB. That is, BPM is also a service provider: business rules, specific flows, or entire application functionality could be published and invoked as a service.

This chapter provided a primer on BPM. A business process needs to model the process data (i.e., information model), the flows, the business rules, the organizational model, and the integration. The chapter also focused on the metamodel of process flows.

Also discussed was an overview of the BPM methodology for continuous improvement. This methodology should be embedded and used in conjunction with the service oriented enterprise maturity model described in Chapter 2. It is an iterative and continuous improvement approach.

Finally, a number of standards were highlighted in BPM within three categories: (1) process modeling notation; (2) process definition (i.e., XML); and (3) process execution. These standards continue to emerge. Unfortunately, currently widely accepted standards do not exist to clearly delineate the ESB layer, microflow process execution, and the higher BPM layer of business processes. More importantly, BPM standards should include as part of the core process standard the standardization of the business rules that actually drive the processes.

Notes

1. As indicated in http://www.bpminstitute.org/articles/article/article/business-and-it-alignment-is-it-for-real.html, other strategies can be used to align IT and business through BPM. These include measurable strategies and tying performance indicators to executing processes; unification of processes and policies—that is, having the business rules drive the processes in the context of one unified BPM suite—execution solution frameworks that focus on the specific business objects of the solutions; and the aforementioned accessible platform to business and IT.
2. Also called a task in some BPM systems.
3. *System* is a very generic term: It can represent back-end applications such as SAP, PeopleSoft, or Siebel; a component such as an Enterprise Java Bean (EJB) or a Common Object Request Broker Architecture (CORBA) component; or an executable program with an application interface—C# program or a Java program. It could thus be a homegrown and internally developed system or commercial software.
4. An overloaded term used in conjunction with activities and processes is manual. Depending on the context, manual could mean carried out by a human participant or that the entire process is not enacted by an underlying process management system.
5. The UML standard has syntax and some semantics for object constraints, called Object Constraint Languages (OCLs). But that is not complete, nor is it that usable or applicable in business contexts.
6. http://www.microsoft.com/technet/prodtechnol/biztalk/biztalk2004/planning/bpm-solution-overview.mspx.
7. The time when the invoice should be sent could be specified in a service level agreement between the trading partners.
8. The Workflow Reference Model-reference TC-1003, January 1995. Can be obtained from www.wfmc.org.
9. http://www.bpminstitute.org/articles/article/article/developing-a-bpm-reference-architecture.html. "Developing a BPM Reference Architecture," by Bill Chambers, principal analyst, Doculabs (www.doculabs.com). Also see http://www.bpminstitute.org/roundtables/past-round-table/article/building-a-bpm-reference-architecture-a-strategy-for-enterprise-agility/news-browse/1.html
10. An alternative is becoming increasingly important in BPM: the use of monitoring agents that can use declarative rules to decide what to monitor and analyze. Agents can also inform the parties (i.e., IT or business) that need to be involved in responding to the outliers. With this option, businesses can author rules that determine what the agent should watch for and what actions need to be taken if there are potential bottlenecks to be avoided, exceptions to be handled, or events to be responded to.
11. The ebXML and RosettaNet standards focus primarily on B2B process integration and are much less popular than either WS-BPEL or XPDL.
12. This is a theoretical approach that is yet to be proven in large-scale adoption of the alternative standards. First, there is the problem of less precision

between versions of the graphical and XML standards—typically, these are developed by different standardization bodies. Second is the problem of the semantic gap between various tools, especially business process analysis tools, which focus on modeling, and BPM systems, which can provide both modeling and execution.

13. Increasingly the same BPM suite is providing both functions. This means that exchange formats between various tools are becoming less important.
14. WS-BPEL was originally (and sometimes continues to be) called BPEL4WS for Web services 1.1—for Web services. The upcoming version will be named WS-BPEL 2.0.
15. There is actually an attribute createInstance. If the value is Yes, then a process instance will be created by the receive. Process instances can also be created through the <pick> element.

Chapter 6

Service Quality and Management

Business and IT: Quality of service (QoS) is critical to the success of any service oriented deployment. QoS here is defined in terms of security, reliability, and performance. Each aspect of QoS is essential. There are many moving parts and vulnerabilities when deploying SOA infrastructures. Typically, QoS will be as strong as the weakest link. There will be underlying networking infrastructures, enterprise service buses (ESBs), database management systems (DBMSs), application servers, and business process management (BPM) systems, each with its own QoS features and requirements. Furthermore, it is also necessary to map the QoS stacks with those of trading partners. This is easier said than done. Mapping QoS layers cohesively within the enterprise is complex enough. There are many components where security could be compromised, reliability could be illusive, or there could be unrealistic performance goals—often discovered through after-the-fact deployments. QoS is essential in service oriented information connectivity over supply chains, with mission critical transactions carried through service interactions.

IT: This chapter provides an overview of the critical factors involved in QoS. It also highlights all the key components that need to be analyzed for security and reliability and benchmarked for performance. Most of the discussion on standards is Web services (WS) focused for obvious reasons. Security, reliability, and performance should not be added as afterthoughts. Please consider analyzing carefully the QoS features of the components and how they map to one another, especially over extended enterprises. Furthermore, it is essential to have built-in redundancies and replications in the deployment of service infrastructures. This chapter does not cover redundancy issues in detail, even though they are alluded to. The QoS considerations discussed here should be developed in conjunction with overall recovery, non-interruption of production or service, and built-in redundancy solutions.

Business: Most of this chapter is quite technical, so you can skip over it. However, it is important to appreciate the importance of QoS. Often businesses focus on functionality and the look-end-feel of applications developed and deployed by information technology (IT) without appreciating the complexities involved in QoS support (i.e., the invisible and sometimes expensive parts of the implementation). In a service oriented application security, reliability, and acceptable performance are sometimes more difficult to implement than the required functionality. What this chapter provides is just the tip of the iceberg. QoS support should be part of the requirement specification of any service oriented solution. Though it is true that this is driven by IT, there are tremendous ramifications on the overall success of service oriented projects.

6.1 Introduction

> IT not only needs to deliver more effective business applications and solutions, but it needs to do so more efficiently, with fewer problems, faster, and with reduced budgets.
>
> **David A. Kelly**

Chapter 5 discussed business process management. Services can be composed, orchestrated and choreographed. BPM is particularly important for business owners. It is important to monitor and to measure the key performance indicators (KPIs). If there are problems with some KPIs, the situation needs to be remedied—perhaps activating additional processes or increasing the monitoring and control capabilities of the solutions. The as-is processes need to be changed and continuously improved with to-be processes. In most situations change is the guiding principle. Occasionally there will be solutions that will be stabilized for long periods of time. This *improvement* life cycle for business projects includes measurable leading and lagging performance indicators, which are typically associated with underlying processes. Service orientation is about continuous improvements for the business objectives and goals.

But to be able to support the processes, it is necessary to manage the underlying component services and the overall infrastructure to make sure the performance, reliability, and security of services are on par with business goals. The process implementation experience and success will be determined by the performance responsiveness, reliability, and security of the services. Quality of services is essential for the success of business process deployments. The trend in the implementation of the services is typically through business process management solutions. In other words, what is published as a service is in fact a BPM solution, built and hosted in the BPM container. However, there are service implementations through ground-up component implementations (e.g., implementing services as Enterprise Java Beans [EJB] components). Services are also provided through exposing current enterprise information system (EIS) interfaces or even legacy applications through standard interfaces.

Service management is also essential. To support all the advantages of automated business rules and processes, a secure, reliable, high-performance service platform is needed. The relationships are illustrated in Figure 6.1. At the top level are the KPIs and overall objectives; the business processes support these objectives.

Once individual services are developed and deployed, the production environment needs to consider several crucial issues for the success of the service application. One of the top priorities in taking a project to production is quality of service. The management of services is also essential to make sure the quality of the services in terms of availability, security, and overall performance is monitored, measured, and sustained.

So this chapter focuses on quality of service and the management of services. Quality of services covered here includes service level performance, reliability, and security.

6.2 Defining Quality of Service

> On the Internet and in other networks, QoS (Quality of Service) is the idea that transmission rates, error rates, and other characteristics can be measured, improved, and, to some extent, guaranteed in advance.
>
> **www.whatis.com**

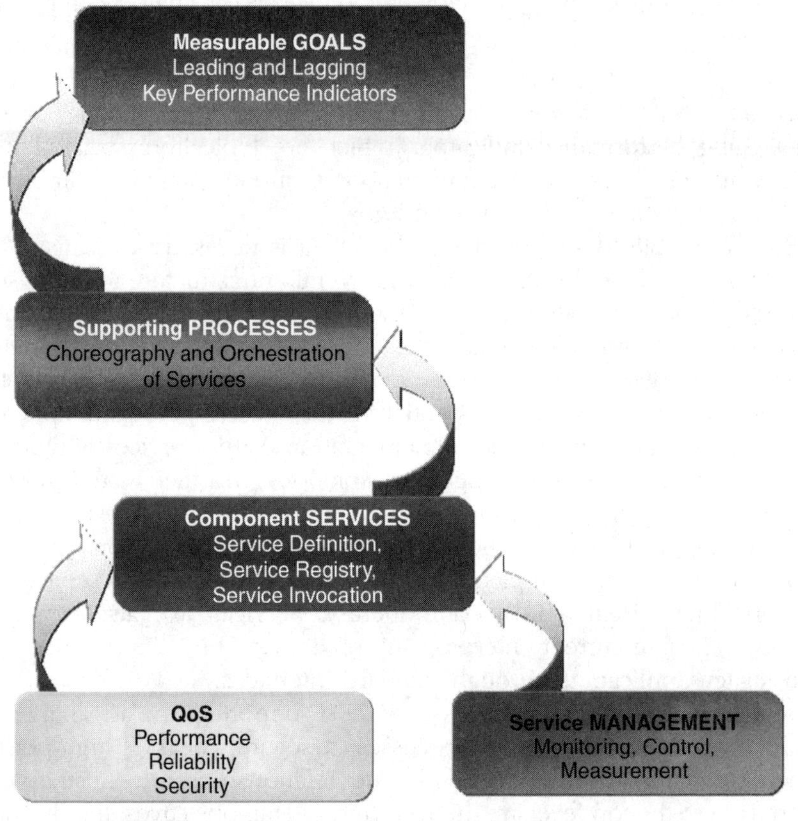

Figure 6.1 QoS and service management supporting business objectives

There are many alternative definitions of QoS, and the term conjures up various connotations depending on the context of its usage. Whatever the scope and the dimension of QoS, it is always associated with reliability and performance of the service. It also involves secure communications and transmissions. QoS is perhaps the most obvious, yet least appreciated, feature of services. It is essential for service oriented enterprises (SOEs): The more the focus is on quality of the service, the better the various communities can be served, especially customers and partners.

The quality culture is becoming pervasive in a number of domains. In the West, a high quality of services in telecommunications or electricity is commonplace and expected. In networking architectures quality is defined, for instance, as follows: "a generic term which takes into account several techniques and strategies that could assure application and users a predictable service from the network and other components involved, such as operating systems."[1]

The network, whether it involves digitization or analog communications, needs to guarantee an end-to-end quality of service. It is as strong as its weakest link or hub. Customers will hold the end-service provider responsible for the ultimate quality of the service, even though the service interruption could have been caused by another intermediary on the end-to-end service network. Cisco[2] characterizes several levels of service. Best effort services focus on connectivity alone. Internet connectivity cannot be guaranteed by default. At the other end of the spectrum are guaranteed services. This assures that enough resources and redundancies are built into the network to guarantee uninterrupted service.

All of these QoS definitions are used primarily in conjunction with networking infrastructures. There is strong emphasis on reliability, availability, and performance. In service orientation it is necessary to rely on the underlying networking infrastructure to guarantee QoS commitments.

6.2.1 QoS in Service Orientation

> Application integration lets us make our systems work better. It lets us reduce costs, increase efficiency, and improve quality. Web services help us do integration.
>
> **Anne Thomas Manes**

Service orientation is about integration: invoking local and remote services, orchestrating these services, and publishing them as composite services. In all these interactions QoS is essential. There is no single agreed-on definition of QoS for service orientation. As is true of QoS for networking infrastructures, reliability, availability, and performance are important for services. But QoS for services also focuses on features such as security, which is critical, especially to virtual or extended enterprise interoperability.

Some industry observers have even suggested that the lack of robust security standards and solutions is the main impediment to pervasive adoption of Web services[3] throughout the extended enterprise. As a result, the largest portion of this chapter is devoted to a discussion of security in Web services. Other important QoS topics such as performance and reliable messaging are covered as well.

Some QoS stacks for Web services are quite extensive and include many dimensions of quality. Quality in the context of service orientation relates to the overall business transactions carried out between collaborating trading partners who are accessing each other's services, as shown in Figure 6.2.

This chapter focuses on performance, reliability, security, and system management. So QoS of services is defined as QoS = Performance + Reliability + Security.[4]

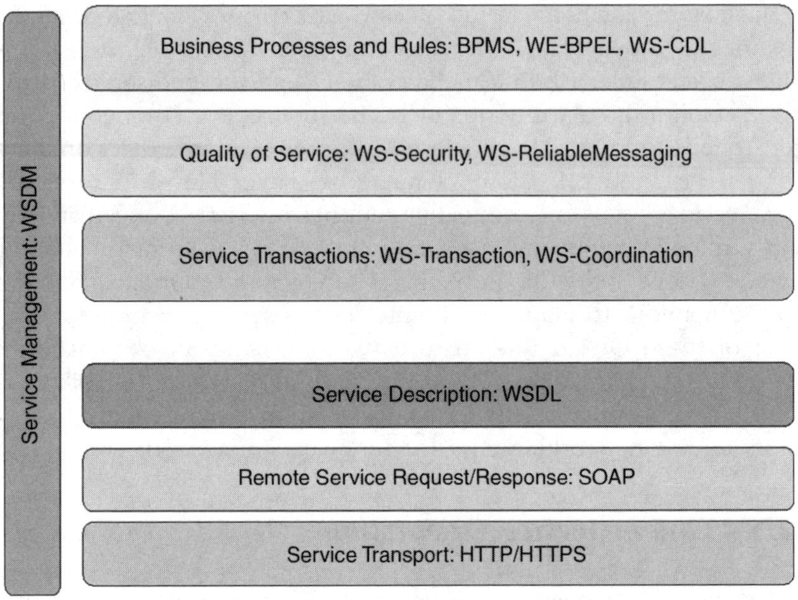

Service Management: WSDM

Business Processes and Rules: BPMS, WE-BPEL, WS-CDL

Quality of Service: WS-Security, WS-ReliableMessaging

Service Transactions: WS-Transaction, WS-Coordination

Service Description: WSDL

Remote Service Request/Response: SOAP

Service Transport: HTTP/HTTPS

Figure 6.2 Relationship between Web services and QoS stacks

Most will agree that performance and reliability are essential ingredients for quality of service. Perhaps security is less obvious. The year 2005 witnessed one of the most dramatic compromises of MasterCard:[5] About 40 million credit card accounts were compromised by hackers through an online security breach. This came on the heels of another scandal where the storage device that had stored potentially thousands of customer accounts was lost. Similar incidents have shaken customer confidence in e-business-oriented services.

The credit card scandal was more serious. This type of security concern is definitely a quality of service issue: Customers would like to be assured that their personal accounts are not compromised. The implications are tremendous and unacceptable. If customers have a choice, they will always select the service provider with the best security quality, even at a higher cost for the services. Security is an essential component of quality of service.

The following sections present standards and solutions in providing quality of service:

- Performance and benchmarking: Performance is a critical element for service invocations. Some applications have throughput and response time requirements that might prove to be challenging for deployments that are services-centric. Performance is one of the most obvious factors in determining the usability and quality of a service application. Pressing on a link or a button on a browser ends up accessing multiple components, platforms, and systems in the round-trip service request/response interaction. Service invocation needs to be analyzed holistically to make sure the performance of each element in the service round trip is on par with the response time and throughput requirements of the service invocation.

- Reliability: Reliability deals with the delivery of messages and service invocations. There is always the possibility of failure, and as mentioned already, there are multiple possible points of failure in the service request/response round trip. The failure can happen in the component that implements the system, in the overall business process engine, in the enterprise service bus, in the underlying application server software, in the overall operating system that supports the services, and of course in the communication networks. Reliability and handling failover are essential in any mission critical deployment. It is of course critical for the quality of the service.
- Security: In any enterprise application security is critical. The two fundamental components of security are authentication and authorization. The service invocations need to be protected from various types of security threats including viruses and malicious attacks. In Web services the emerging standard is WS-Security. Furthermore, there are a number of standards in eXtensible Markup Language (XML) for security. Among the key XML security standards are XML Signature and XML Encryption. Security Assertion Markup Language (SAML) is another security standard that is becoming popular for Web services.
- Management: The focus here is on system-level management capabilities. A service oriented enterprise monitors all its outbound and inbound service calls. It measures the performance of its services deployed on various platforms. Management can also include the registration of services and their availability. Management supports performance analysis and tracking of service exchanges.

The focus in this chapter is on these four areas from a system and platform perspective. First the chapter expands on service performance and benchmarking, identifying the various factors that could potentially cause performance bottlenecks. This is the focus of Section 6.3. In the service request/response intersections you have XML/SOAP message formats; the communication over the Internet; Web servers; and ESB, BPM system, and DBMS servers. Section 6.4 focuses on service reliability, especially reliability of service messaging. Section 6.5 explains various security standards, especially SAML and WS-Security. Finally, Section 6.6 will concentrate on management for services.

6.3 Services Performance and Benchmarking

> Generally speaking, benchmarks aren't just about bragging rights. Server performance testing plays some extremely important roles in today's IT departments. Benchmarks help to ensure that system performance meets expectations.
>
> **Stephen J. Bigelow**

A number of dimensions influence the overall performance of Web services. The various elements in the Web services QoS stack are interrelated. Performance involves the interaction, reliability, and security of services. It could also potentially involve management overhead. For instance, if a message from a source to its destination and back goes through several intermediaries for security or reliability, this will obviously affect the overall response time of the service invocation. Furthermore, the performance of services depends not only on the technology stack of service implementations but also on the application server, the BPM system, the DBMS, and the enterprise service bus deployed at the provider site. Performance needs to consider the end-to-end interactions from service requestor to service consumer.

Most of this chapter's concentrations and issues are related to XML and, more specifically, to SOAP over Hyptertext Transfer Protocol (HTTP), with Web services standard technologies. Other technologies could be and are often used. For example, SOAP messages can be communicated over Java Message Service (JMS). More compact and efficient messaging standards can also be used, including programming language (i.e., Java or C#) and local and remote service component invocations. But by and large XML-based Web services is becoming the de facto standard in service oriented deployments. There are challenges, though.

Section 6.3.1 discusses networking and Section 6.3.2 delves into the performance issues related to XML. The verbosity of XML has a direct influence on the performance of Web services applications. The following section discusses the performance implications of SOAP messaging. A message sent from a service requestor to service provider goes through several steps: (1) parsing the XML message; (2) marshaling and unmarshaling the message; and (3) potentially traveling through security and reliability intermediaries. Section 6.3.3 discusses SOAP performance.

6.3.1 Networking

Service oriented enterprises rely heavily on networking, both for connecting intranet within the enterprise as well as partner integration and access. Several layers in a network allow communication between servers that host services. The Transmission Control Protocol/Internet Protocol (TCP/IP) is perhaps the most popular protocol in service oriented architectures (SOAs). It was

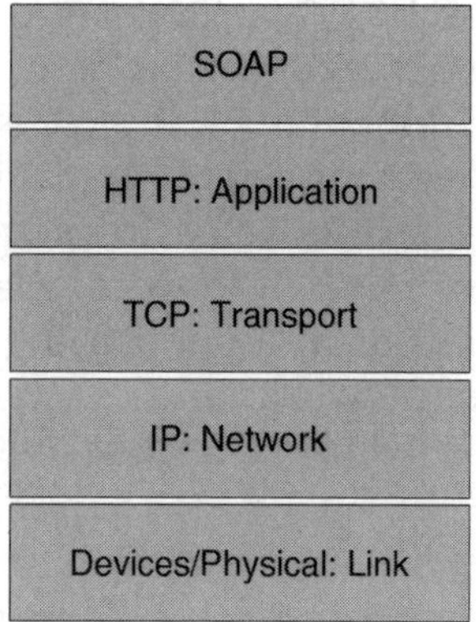

Figure 6.3 Layers of a network architecture

designed by the U.S. Department of Defense for their ARPANET wide-area network. ARPANET was the predecessor of the Internet protocol. Figure 6.3 provides a high-level illustration of the network layers and technologies.

At the lowest layer are the devices and device drivers. This is the link layer, and it is the hardware base of the network. In networking jargon *nodes* are being connected that could be servers hosting services or other devices such as database servers. The next layer is the IP. Information communicated across the Internet or intranets using Internet technologies is organized into packets. The IP protocol implementations are responsible for communicating between networks. IP is sessionless or connectionless. The packets in IP consist of an IP header and the data they contain. The IP layer does not concern itself with the sequencing or the reliability of the packet transfers. That is where the TCP comes into the picture. Requestors and providers establish connections through the TCP layer. The reliability of the communication is also supported through TCP. The SOAP message will be carried within the HTTP message. As noted in Chapter 4, other technologies could be used (e.g., SOAP could be sent through JMS messages). However, HTTP is the most popular protocol over the Internet and intranet networks within the enterprise. SOAP and HTTP were discussed in Section 3.5.2.[6]

IT: The building block and foundation of any network is the local area network (LAN). A LAN is a group of servers connected together and configured through one of the popular network topologies: the star, ring, hierarchical, and—increasingly the most popular—the bus. The Ethernet network that uses the bus topology is the most widely used networking infrastructure. An Ethernet network connects multiple network service nodes and stations at intervals over one long main cable. The Ethernet has evolved over the past 25 years to provide the most robust technology to connect LANs. In terms of the performance of the Ethernet, it has been constantly improving. Originally it began with 10 Mbps Ethernet networks and evolved into 100 Mbps and 1 Gbps; now the more robust Ethernet networks carry 10 Gbps Ethernet networking.[7]

6.3.2 XML

Performance of services is critical and will continue to be a key QoS parameter in selecting and deploying Web services applications. Increasingly services are XML in action. In other words, they inherit all the extensibility and advantages of XML. By the same token, they also inherit all the performance-related issues associated with XML. XML messages are elegant and even human-readable. On the other hand, compared to cryptic text or even better binary representation of information, they are rather verbose. Consider the representation in Figure 6.4 of four integers, where each of the two integers represents the coordinates of a point. The four integers represent a rectangle. If 32 bits are used to represent an integer, the total space requirement will be of the order of 32 × 4 = 128 bits, or 16 bytes. Of course, if this were a

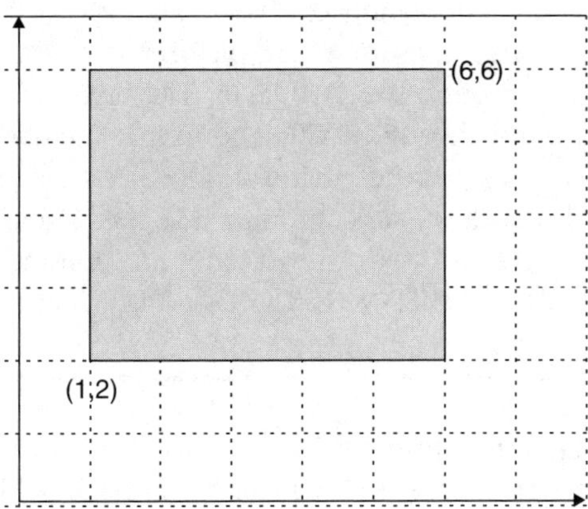

Figure 6.4 Rectangle

message or an object sent over the wire, there would be some overhead. But nevertheless, it is a rather compact representation of data.

Now here is the same rectangle in XML.

```
<Rectangle>
      <LoweLeft>
           <X>1</X>
           <Y>2</Y>
      </LoweLeft>
      <UpperRight>
           <X>6</X>
           <Y>6</Y>
      </UpperRight>
</Rectangle>
```

This representation in XML, although clear and elegant, is about 133 bytes. Not only is the space allocated to XML messages or documents much larger, but there is also the overhead of parsing the XML to make sure it is well formed. And, of course, sometimes it needs to be validated against a schema. Validation is much more complex than just parsing the XML to make sure it is well formed—it takes longer.[8]

All this translates into additional overhead. This has been, and continues to be, one of the main reasons some application domains that process very large volumes of transactions use their own proprietary formats and shy away from Web services. Over the past several years XML parser technologies have been getting much better. But still, Web service implementations will have a hard time competing with proprietary or binary object representations over the wire. The verbosity of XML, despite its advantages, will remain a serious bottleneck for Web service performance in the foreseeable future.

Another disadvantage of the relatively larger sizes of XML messages is the persistent storage of messages in message repositories. This is often necessary, especially for reliable message delivery. Even though storage devices are becoming relatively inexpensive compared to other representations such as binary messages, the size of XML messaging repositories could be considerable.

IT: There are some approaches and attempts to improve the performance bottleneck, resulting in better and more improved performance in XML processing, especially in distributed SOA. One of these is the binary XML. For instance, there are a number of XML binary standards, such as XML Binary Information Set (XBIS) (http://xbis.sourceforge.net/). XML binary proposals have shown both processing as well as size-reduction advantages. The XBIS maintains the overall canonical structure of XML. XBIS documents can be processed piecemeal. There are other alternatives such as XMill (http://www.liefke.com/hartmut/xmill/xmill.html), which takes a conventional compression approach—always an alternative while sending XML data over the wire. In any case, for now none of the nontext-based conventional XML encoding or binary representation techniques have found wide support and adoption in the industry. Since XML, especially with SOAP and other emerging options such as Representational State Transfer (REST) and Asynchronous JavaScript and XML (AJAX), is so ubiquitous, it is unlikely an alternative format will gain popularity without wide acceptance by infrastructure standards and vendors alike.

6.3.3 SOAP Performance

The previous section discussed the performance of raw XML. Most Web services approaches and standards are XML based. Perhaps the most important of these standards is the SOAP standard. WSDL specifies the message style. For message style there is document and remote procedure call (RPC). Here are brief explanations of these styles (also see Section 3.4.9).

- Document: With this option, there is no explicit formatting for the operation or procedure call within the <soap:body> element of the SOAP message. The sender and receiver agree on the content of the parts of the message contained in the <soap:body>.
- RPC: Here the <soap:body> contains the structure of the method invoked (or its return), including the method name and its parameters.

Therefore, the fundamental difference is that with the document style, the XML contained in the body is passed on to the receiver who is responsible for parsing and processing the request/response message. With the RPC, the SOAP engine parses and invokes the deployed service implementation. With document-literal,[9] the SOAP engine hands the XML in the body that is then parsed by the implementer of the service, which in turn calls the required service method on invocation. RPC tends to be easier for the developer. However, as many studies show,[10] the SOAP document-literal approach tends to provide better performance, especially under heavy

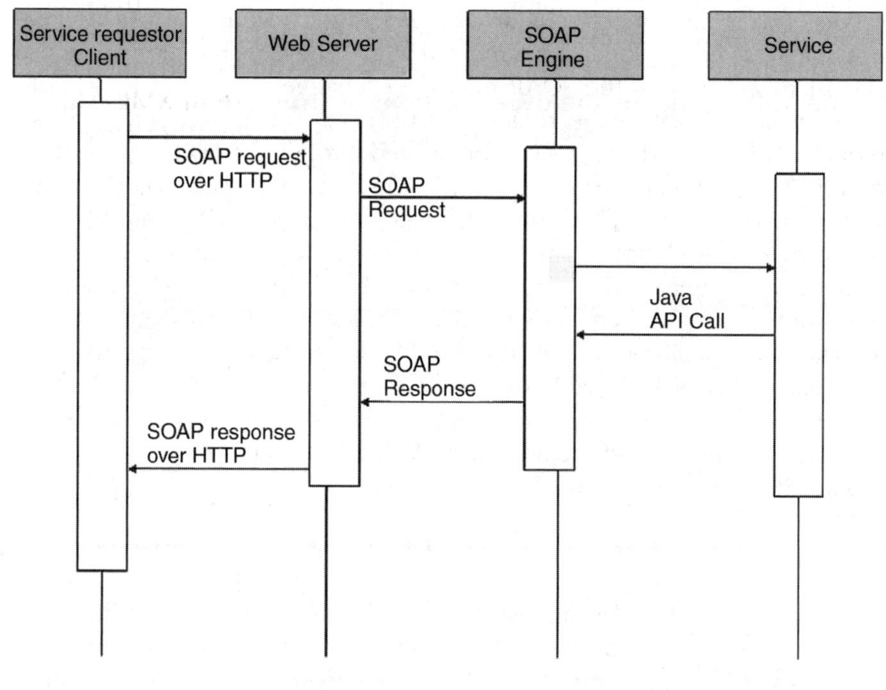

Figure 6.5 Sequence diagram for SOAP request/response

user loads. Therefore, for service oriented applications document-literal is the preferred choice.

Several objects are involved in the request trip from the client to the server and back. Figure 6.5 illustrates this sequence of calls. In most typical SOAP applications, a client invokes an application programming interface (API)—sometimes called a client proxy of the services—in an object-oriented language such Java or C#, as noted previously. The API implementation generates a SOAP request, which in turn is sent through HTTP from the client as a request. On the server side, the HTTP is received, and a SOAP engine is invoked, typically via a servlet. The SOAP engine object represents any service or server that takes a SOAP message, parses it, validates it, and then invokes the appropriate server through a programming language API call. This engine then translates the SOAP request to a service call. The service is deployed on the SOAP server, so the SOAP engine knows which service to invoke.

With the SOAP layer in between, the requestor and provider operate through a request/response model that enables them to use different object-oriented (or other) languages. For example, a C# client can invoke a Web service that is implemented as an EJB component. Similarly, a Java client can invoke a service that is implemented in C#. The actual request/response is carried out through the SOAP message exchanges.

A client API call to the remote Web service is mapped onto a SOAP request. This SOAP request is communicated through the HTTP packet with an HTTP message header and is sent to the remote service's HTTP server, with a uniform resource identifier (URI) pointing to the SOAP processes of the Web services platform. The HTTP server then delivers the SOAP message to the SOAP engine, which in turn parses the SOAP message, locates the deployed service, and converts the SOAP call to an API call.

Therefore, similar to other distributed systems, there is an unmarshaling and marshaling of serialized SOAP calls to and from the client and server of the Web service. SOAP is the intermediate marshaling and unmarshaling language for the remote method calls. With HTTP in the request/response model, SOAP should use the POST method.

IT: The accessibility, reliability, and availability of the quality of service translate to service level agreements (SLAs) between trading partners that have a service requestor and service provider relationship. An SLA involves the response time of the service.

Synchronous service requests could be measured in terms of microseconds to receive a response from the invoked service. An asynchronous request means the partner guarantees to respond within a prescribed period of time. For asynchronous service requests, the SLA could specify seconds, minutes, hours, or even days. Typically, these requests involve business transaction agreements. For instance, if a purchase order is submitted to a seller, the seller should guarantee to respond within a specific period of time—usually measured in a few days—indicating that the order is accepted and will be fulfilled. The SLA for response time of synchronous Web services requests as well as SLAs for business transactions are both critical to guarantee the overall quality of Web services applications.

A concept also associated with SLAs is availability of the service. Here the agreement specifies the boundaries of down time for the service and the maximum allowed amount of time it will take for the service to become operational. This requires the service provider to have an application server environment that supports fault tolerance and has redundancies built in to be able to provide the required availability to its service requestors. Most application servers have clustering technology that allows the application builder to deploy a farm of servers, such that if any one server goes down the requests processed by the failing server could be redistributed to the others. Furthermore, when either the failing server or a new server is introduced to the cluster, application server's clustering mechanism will redistribute the request and will attempt to achieve an optimal load balancing between the servers. This fault tolerance of the servers in the service provider's back end is essential for availability and response time, since clustering also helps improve the performance through increased parallelism.

6.3.4 Multi-Tier Architecture

Availability and the service level response time of services depend on several critical factors: the performance of the service implementation; the middleware that hosts or communicates with the service; the application service and deployment platform; and the availability and performance of the networking communications, including the Internet as a whole.

Figure 6.6 presents an example of a simplified end-to-end architecture from a service requestor to provider. The requestor can involve several components, eventually moving through the Internet cloud to the HTTP server of the service provider. The access is through the external firewall of the service provider. Between the external firewall and internal firewall is called the demilitarized zone (DMZ). In this illustration, the request goes to the business process management system through an ESB compliant

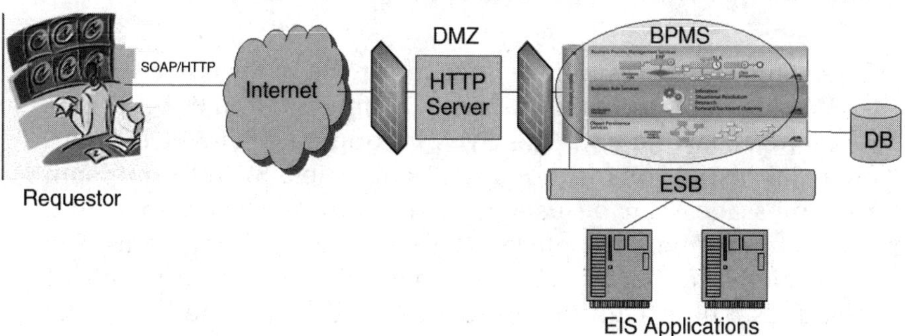

Figure 6.6 Simplified end-to-end service request/response

service component (e.g., a binding component). The persistent process data is stored in a DBMS. The BPM system can also access back-end EIS systems to obtain enterprise application data also through the ESB.

Enterprise exception management: This factor should not be overlooked. Most organizations have isolated networks behind their internal firewalls. The performance of these networks relies primarily on the performance of the Ethernet. The past few years witnessed hostile attacks on the Internet. For instance, an e-mail virus could generate enormous amounts of messages that could potentially swamp the Internet. Sometimes specific Web sites are the target of attacks.

Those who have been involved in software know that the difficult and more challenging issues deal with the exceptions and boundary cases—not the happy path of the call sequences. This is particularly true in service oriented enterprise applications. Handling exceptions is critical for service quality. Business process management, the core and heart of service oriented enterprise architectures, provides an ideal platform to automate not only the happy paths but also the exception handling paths in various end-to-end straight-through processing business transactions. In financial transactions, for instance, between 3 and 5 percent of payments are erroneous. These need to be investigated and resolved. Manual exception management is labor intensive and error prone. Automated BPM solutions can greatly improve the overall quality of exception processing. A BPM platform can (1) capture the settlement rules directly; and (2) provide the process automation involving back-end accounts, human operators, and bank-to-bank transactions.

One standard that is quite effective for the latter is the Society for Worldwide Interbank Financial Communication (SWIFT) protocol (www.swift.com). The SWIFT cooperative involves 7,800 financial institutions in about 200 countries. SWIFT compliant XML messages can be used to communicate between banks, such as between a beneficiary bank and a remitting bank. The SWIFTNet is a TCP/IP network that reliably supports SWIFT messages. The exception could be raised by a beneficiary of a payment. If the beneficiary's bank cannot apply the payment—hence the exception—this will be communicated as a bank-to-bank SWIFT message over SWIFTNet. So the bank-to-bank transactions and the investigation of the payment between payer and payee organizations could happen in real-time. Both enterprises could involve human participants and back-end applications in the overall end-to-end exception handling transaction.

6.3.5 Internet Performance

The Internet is a network of networks. A plethora of sites and tools specifically target Internet performance.[11] For example, the Internet Traffic Report[12] monitors the Internet traffic across the world and then provides a number between 0 and 100 that summarizes the performance and reliability of the Internet per continent. Figure 6.7 shows indexes for North and South America, Europe, Asia, and Australia.

A high number indicates fast traffic. The number is calculated through pinging the router and then comparing its response time to the response times from the previous seven days.

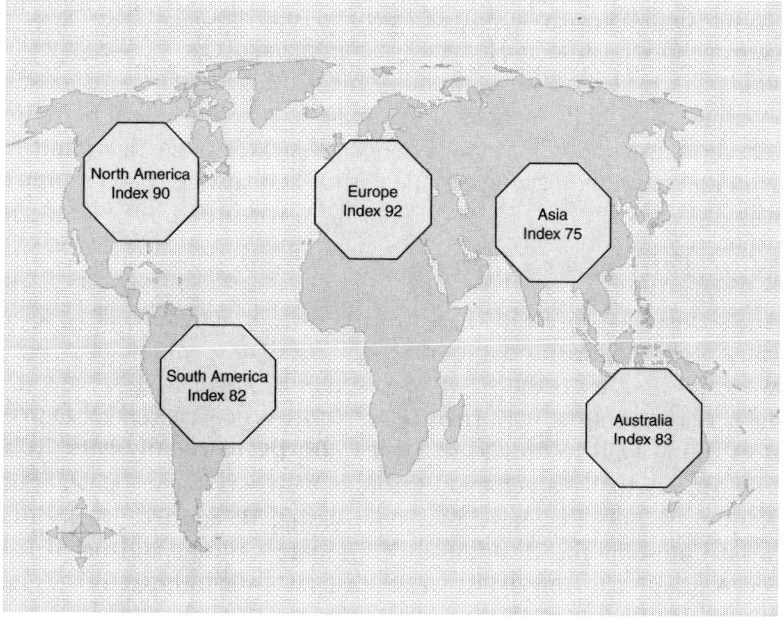

Figure 6.7 Internet traffic report worldwide

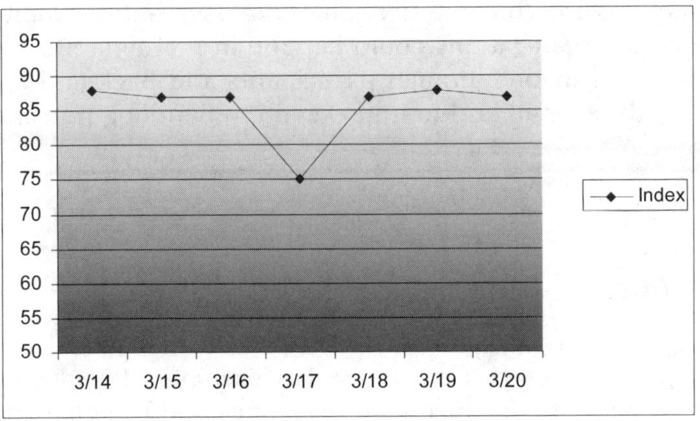

Figure 6.8 Traffic index values over a period

Gathering index values can help administrators compare the performance of the Internet over a period of time. For example, Figure 6.8 shows index values from March 13 to 20. As illustrated there was a problem on March 17. Traffic performance measurement is important when one considers the Internet as the deployment platform of business-to-business (B2B) service interactions or the infrastructure for the programmatic access of Web sites.

Reliability is also an issue—another measure is the number of lost packets. Web services implementation technologies, as illustrated in Figure 6.6, are attempting to address some of these issues through providing robust measurement and monitoring capabilities to Web service-based transactions.

6.3.6 Web Server Cluster

Requests will be submitted over the Internet or intranet networks using Internet technologies, and the protocol used to communicate between browsers and servers is the HTTP Web server protocol. Web servers receive all the service requests. Performance of Web servers is essential. One of the most efficient ways to handle heavy request loads to Web sites—whether internal or external—is achieved through Web server clusters. A cluster is a group of servers that have the same virtual IP address. This virtual IP address represents the IP address of the entire cluster and not a specific server. A load-balancing dispatcher then uses an algorithmic invocation of servers to send requests appropriately to servers in a group to achieve the best throughput and response time from the cluster. The load balancer handles the virtual IP to physical IP mapping. This might involve rewriting address headers to reference the specific server in the cluster.

Several alternative load-balancing algorithms could be used to achieve the desired parallelism in a cluster. For example, a round-robin algorithm dispatches requests to each server in a prescribed order, so request 1 will go to the first server; 2 to the second server; and n to the nth server. If there are n servers, request $n + 1$ will go back to the first server, and the cycle continues. Other algorithms include dispatching based on random selection and dispatching based on server load.

As illustrated in Figure 6.9, many devices will be submitting requests to the server cluster. Clusters are used extensively in high-volume Web server request processing. The servers involved in the cluster can run independently of each other. One big advantage of the cluster is the ability to add servers without interrupting the operation of the server group. Another advantage is the ability to handle a failover: If one of the servers goes down, the others are able to pick up the load without interrupting the service of the cluster.

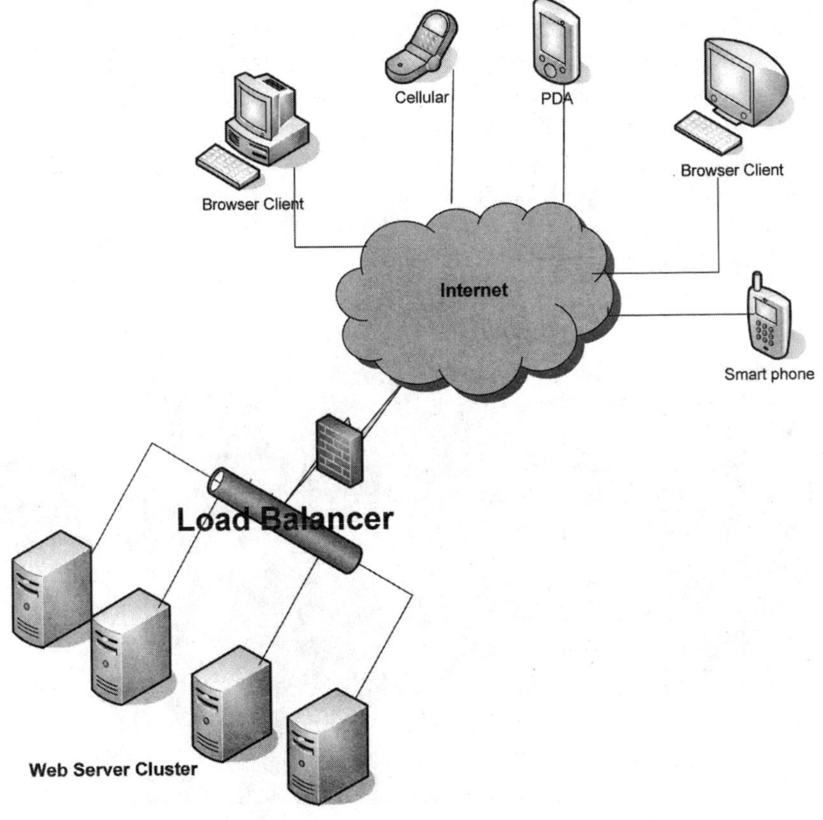

Figure 6.9 Web server cluster

6.3.7 Application Servers

Each service is implemented by a program or component that is typically deployed in an application server or accessed (the "or" is not exclusive) through an enterprise service bus. This is the service implementation. It is important to realize that highly reliable, high-performance, and secure service implementations depend on the underlying implementation of the service. Typically, the implementation of the services uses component technologies. Components have descriptors that capture deployment and execution features of the components, separate from the component's implementation. For example, a component might be executed with strict transactional features or with tight security controls. These and other types of descriptions are deployment properties that can be set independent of the component's implementation.

The traditional Java 2 Enterprise Edition (J2EE) application server contains two main categories of containers: the Web container and the EJB container. In a strict model–view–controller model, the servlets executing in the Web container provide the controller functionality. The EJBs provide the business model functionality, and the views are delivered through Java Server Pages (JSPs). Figure 6.10 illustrates a high-level traditional J2EE architecture, with the Web container and the EJB container. These two containers could be deployed in the same physical server and the same Java Virtual Machine (JVM). Alternatively, each container could be deployed in a different JVM. Typically, the former is more efficient. The clients of the EJB containers can access the business logic of the container either through the servlet or

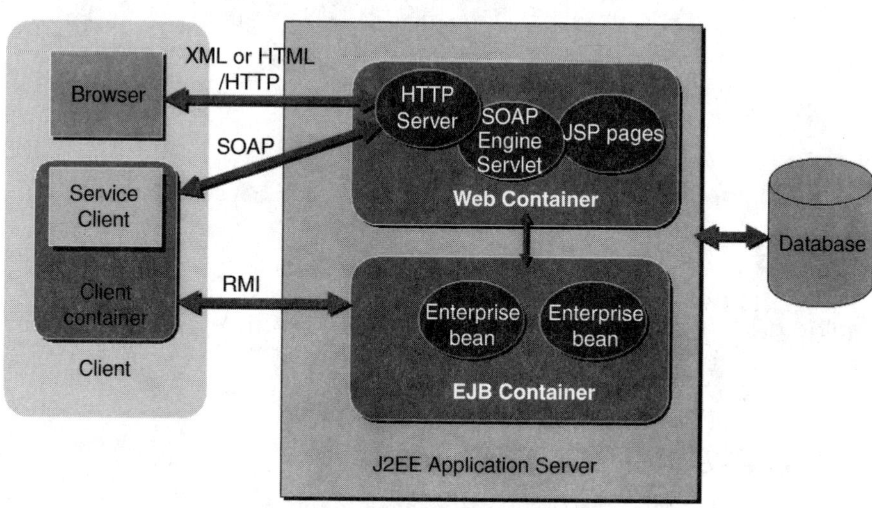

Figure 6.10 Multi-tier J2EE application server architecture

through clients of the component. The clients could invoke the component either through a local or remote interface.

The Web services interfaces of clients could go through the SOAP engine through its servlet and could potentially access the service as a business component (e.g., an EJB). The other option is to go directly to the component implementation through a SOAP message, over a messaging transport such as JMS. In either case it is necessary for the SOAP message to be marshaled and unmarshaled to and from the implementation (e.g., Java) of the service.

6.3.7.1 BPM Systems, ESBs, and Application Servers

Service implementations could be implemented and deployed in an application server. BPM software could be implemented and deployed as components in an application server. Several EJB types could implement the engine functionality of a BPM system. The same is true of ESBs, which could be implemented as components and deployed in a components container. Alternatively, the ESB could implement its own potentially proprietary container approach and could provide the component and container technology without relying on the container technology of the application server.

Both BPM systems and ESBs could leverage the component model including the security, transactional, reliability, and performance advantages of the application server. In addition, the BPM systems could allow composition of services and publication of orchestration, together with all the business rules that drive them as an aggregated component service, with a component interface. So potentially BPM systems not only can have generic component interfaces to the engine but also can potentially automatically generate and deploy components in the application server's enterprise tier. For instance, there might be a service that checks quotes and another that changes currency. A composed service can call these two services in order and be deployed as a component with a Java or EJB[13] client interface. This of course is in addition to the Web service interface. The key point here is that the BPM system is potentially deployed in the EJB container, and in addition the application layer EJBs (or components) are generated and deployed in the application server dynamically. So the application server performance is critical in the overall performance of services.

6.3.7.2 Benchmarking Application Servers

There has been some performance evaluation and benchmarking of application servers. The performance tuning of application servers is rather complex and involves several factors, including the implementation and optimization of the services deployment model, such as if EJBs are used to implement the business logic or if Java is invoked through servlets without EJB containers. ECperf[14] was one of the more popular performance benchmarks that was used to measure the scalability of EJB containers.

Another organization that has developed an application server benchmarking standard—called SPECjAppServer—is the Standard Performance Evaluation Corporation (SPEC).[15] This nonprofit organization, which has approximately 60 member companies, concentrates on performance standardization and benchmarking. The SPECjAppServer benchmark measures the performance of J2EE application servers.

IT: Benchmarks are tricky. Microsoft has either published or has endorsed several benchmarks that demonstrate the advantages of .NET over J2EE. One of the more recent benchmarks comparing the two alternative application servers in 64-bit servers is described at http://www.theserverside.net/articles/showarticle.tss?id=NET2BMNov64Bit. Other comparative performance evaluations can be found at http://www.gotdotnet.com/team/compare/default.aspx.

Another earlier extensive benchmarking study, which caused some commotion when it first came out, was carried out by The Middleware Company starting in October 2002. The study provided a comparison between the .NET and J2EE platforms. The Middleware Company discontinued in November 2004, and other organizations such as TheServerSide took over publishing analyses and benchmarks of application servers.

The Web services benchmark was analyzed in two scenarios. In one scenario, the SOAP-over-HTTP message was sent directly and was measured in the benchmark. In the second scenario, the user request was submitted via a JSP request in J2EE and an Active Server Page Framework (ASPX) request in .NET. Two Web servers are involved—one for the Web service and the other to receive the JSP or ASPX request and to return a HyperText Markup Language (HTML) page to the user.

The result shows .NET supports higher throughput, especially for larger populations of users. Needless to say, those in the J2EE camp have often disputed the validity of these results and have raised questions especially on the coding of the pet store example and its deployment.[16]

Benchmarking is controversial. The companies whose products do not perform well question the validity of the benchmark, and it is always difficult to get a fair comparison using similar coding and deployment parameters for entirely different platforms. That was the case when Middleware Company's study was published.

Such questions about the validity of benchmarking by those who favor one platform or product are understandable. However, benchmarking is important if an organization is considering deploying a Web services application. Benchmarking is only one dimension; others include the security and reliability of the application server. However, it is an important concern in production environments. Often the success and failure of an enterprise project depend on achieving the desired performance throughput for the application. Benchmarking can help determine the best architecture and server solution to achieve the performance goals.

6.3.7.3 Application Server Clustering and Scalability

Clustering is a critical feature that supports high-performance scalability as well as reliability and failover. A variety of cluster architectures could be used to enhance the performance of service solutions, especially through parallel processing. We are often satisfied and impressed with the response time of our interactions when submitting a Web server request to a popular Web site. Actually, behind the scenes are hundreds and sometimes thousands of servers working to satisfy the requests through load balancing[17] and parallelism. Redundancy is also used extensively to handle failed servers and to maintain the response times within acceptable boundaries.

One key feature of scalability support is the ability to serve increasingly higher numbers of client requests (i.e., request load) through adding additional servers. The underlying scalability support should make this migration to larger number of servers as seamless as possible. This is a tall order, but in the presence of high loads it is critical.

One of the more recommended cluster architectures involving application servers behind the protected firewalls within the enterprise involves a load balancer and a cluster of servers. There are typically two firewalls: an external and an internal firewall. Figure 6.11 illustrates the internal firewall. The figure illustrates a basic parallel architectural pattern involving Web and EJB containers deployed on the same JVM and on different physical servers. The advantage of this architecture is relative simplicity of deployment as well as scalability and failover. Typically, additional servers can be added without interruptions or performance degradation. Also, if any of the servers go down, the others will pick up the load.

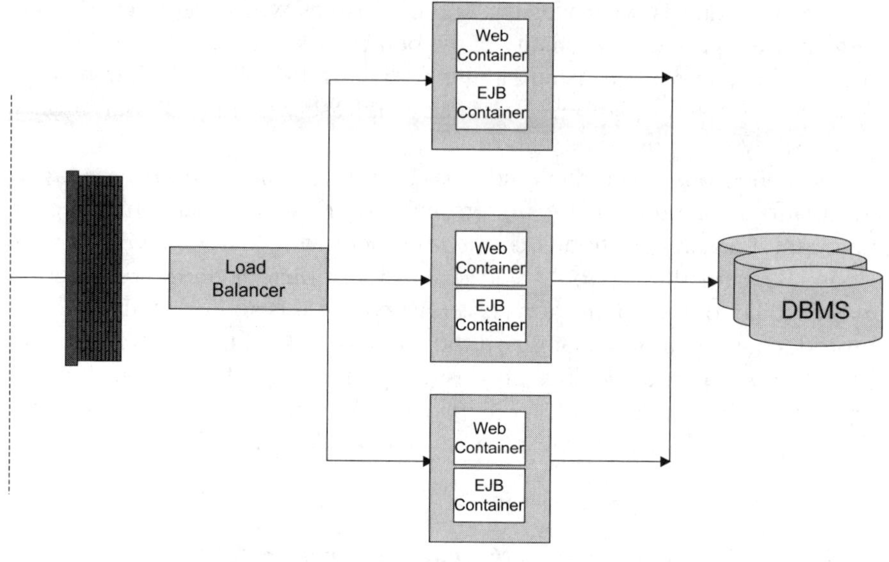

Figure 6.11 A clustered architecture: vertical scalability

6.3.8 Business Process Management Systems

BPM systems are a relatively new technology. Not surprisingly, there are no benchmarks conducted by independent third parties, comparing the throughput and response time of BPM system under heavy transactional access loads. As stated earlier, this is difficult to obtain even for the relatively more mature application server products. In fact, the overall performance of a BPM system depends on the performance of two critical platforms:

1. The application server: BPM systems can be deployed entirely in a server component container tier (e.g., EJB components in J2EE) or entirely in the Web container tier, or using a combination of the two.
2. The DBMS: all BPM system artifacts (e.g., processes, rules, integration) as well as the process data of executing process instances. So the DBMS is used to store both the application source and the data and events generated and manipulated by the applications (Figure 6.12).

The BPM system should leverage the application server clustering and the DBMS clustering. However, specific performance-related features are

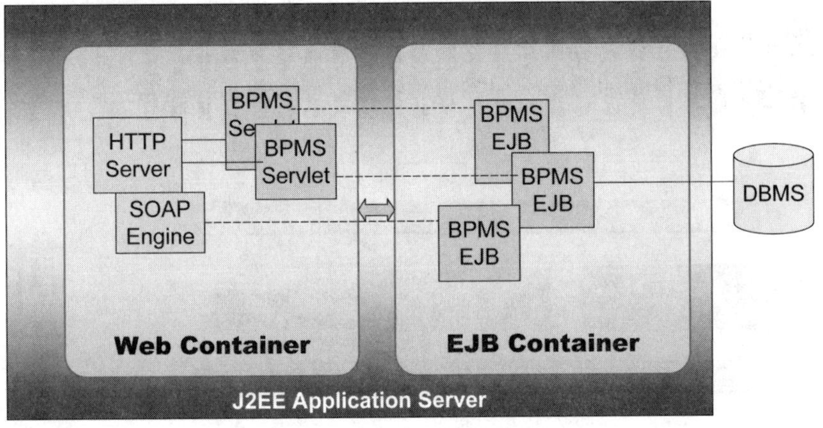

Figure 6.12 BPM system in an application server

specific to the BPM system. In particular, the BPM system is the touchpoint for the users and needs to provide optimal response time and throughput for large numbers of user transactions. More specifically, it needs to be scalable, allowing more servers to be added while maintaining the performance goals of the BPM system solution. The BPM layer uses an underlying DBMS to store process data. For example, if the application is a procurement process, all the requested items as well as the status of the procurement processes will be stored in an underlying relational DBMS.

IT: The following figure illustrates a BPM system benchmark from Pegasystems Inc.,[18] deployed over a multi-tier distributed architecture. The benchmark emulated more than 31,000 concurrent users. The processes included flows and business rules. More than 310,000 business rules are executed per second. This type of benchmark illustrates the importance of a highly optimized BPM system, leveraging the parallelism in the underlying application server clusters and the parallel execution of DBMS queries and updates. More than 24 million processes were completed in an eight-hour period.

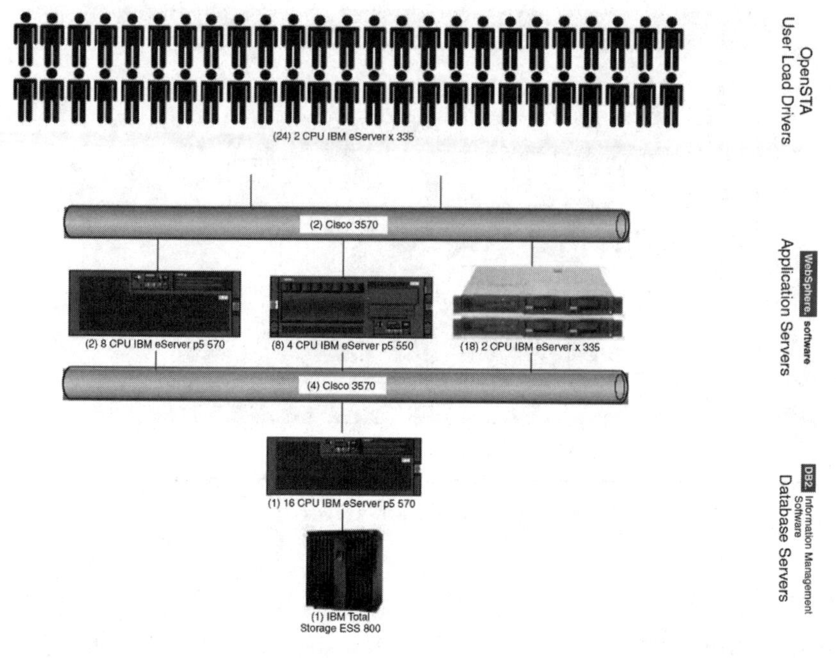

6.3.9 Database Management Systems

Database management systems are essential in any service deployment strategy. DBMS performance is critical. Many factors need to be considered in optimizing the performance of database management systems. These issues include normalization and denormalization, indexing, and the DBMS engine. DBMS software implements transaction, concurrency, recovery, query optimization, and buffering strategies, each of which could have a huge impact on the performance of system applications.

In general, the performance of the database server has two components: (1) the performance or response time for the execution of standard operations using a prescribed database server workload and configuration; (2) the database server's throughput, or the total amount of work a particular server can perform as its workload changes. Generally, the overall performance of a database server, as noticed by any one user accessing it, will degrade as the workload or the number of users accessing it increases.

The performance of DBMSs—and in fact other container or server software—can be monitored or measured in two ways. First, a staging server can be used to perform the accesses, updates, and tasks needed using the exact table schemata, configuration, and access patterns of the application. This is ideal, since completing the task will give you a good idea about the expected performance of the implementation—especially of the DBMS. The second approach of measuring performance is with standard benchmarking. Though benchmarks may be quicker and cheaper, their results may be less accurate or less indicative of the performance that may be achieved using actual data in real workload environments.

DBMSs are relatively mature technologies, and a number of benchmarks have been developed to measure their performance. The most famous of this is sponsored by the Transaction Processing Performance Council (TPC).[19]

TPC has three benchmark specifications: TPC-A, TPC-B, TPC-C. The most popular of the benchmarks is the TPC-C, which consists of five online transactions:

1. New-order: enter a new order from a customer
2. Payment: update customer balance to reflect a payment
3. Delivery: deliver orders (done as a batch transaction)
4. Order-status: retrieve status of customer's most recent order
5. Stock-level: monitor warehouse inventory

This is not a typical service-based transaction, but measuring the performance of database management systems against TPC-C provides a good indicator of the overall performance level of DBMSs.

Database management systems also can operate in highly parallel and clustered architectures. Today, servers have multiple central processing units (CPUs), and modern database management systems leverage the parallelism of these super servers through advanced query processing algorithms. Anytime an application is input/output (I/O) bound—and many are—the parallelism in the DBMS as well as the underlying storage disk farms could be leveraged to achieve the required transactional throughput. The database tables are mapped onto underlying physical hard disk clusters. Clustering supports both scalability and availability. DBMS servers can utilize the following:

- Horizontal partitioning of database tables: Here the same database table, such as a customer database table or an order database table, is partitioned into subtables. For example, a table of 100 million rows can be partitioned into 10 tables, where each table contains 10 million rows. The partitioned tables could be distributed to different servers and hard disks. Through this parallelism, the performance of queries and overall throughput of database transactions potentially could be increased substantially.
- Vertical partitioning of dataset tables: With vertical partitioning, the tables are partitioned by columns. For example, social security numbers or account balances might be partitioned in a separate vertically partitioned table. To reconstruct the table, it is also necessary to have the key of the table with each partitioned collection of columns.

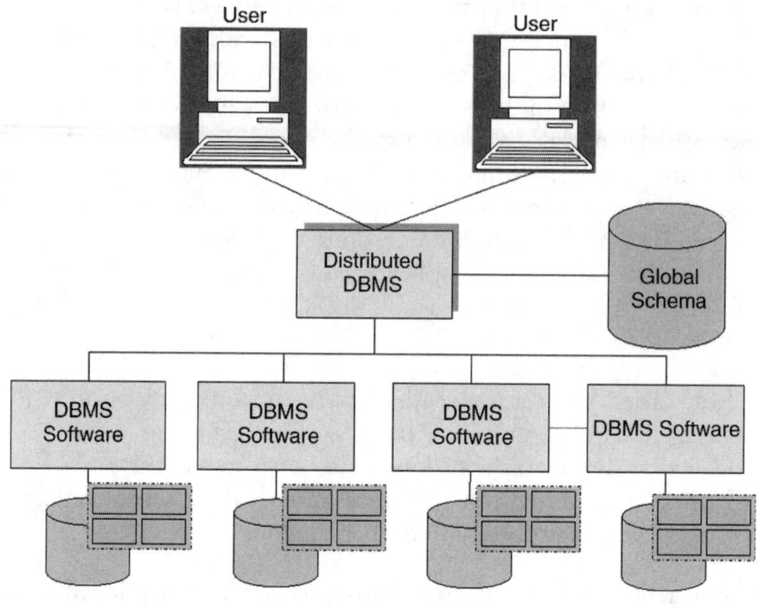

Figure 6.13 Distributed database architecture

Given the partitioning of database tables, the query optimizers of the DBMS can generate optimal execution plans in processing user queries. These algorithms utilize the multiple CPUs of the underlying parallel system that deploys the DBMS as well as the distribution of the tables among parallel disk clusters. Figure 6.13 illustrates a typical distributed database architecture with vertical or horizontal segments managed across a database cluster. From the perspective of the end-user, the details of the horizontal or vertical partitioning is completely hidden. The distributed database schema keeps track of the various segments and conducts the appropriate query optimization submitting subqueries to the individual DBMSs.

Another technique used to provide not only performance but also recovery and resiliency of database management systems is replication. Here the same logical table or database is stored and maintained in multiple replicated tables or databases. In fact, replication and mirroring of mission critical data is one of the safest ways for guaranteeing resiliency, especially with catastrophic failures where entire DBMS servers go down. Replication also helps performance. If some database tables are mostly read and are infrequently updated, replication can provide tremendous advantages and more scalable implementations in the presence of high-volume transactions.

6.4 Service Reliability

> The loss of their [businesses] information systems means loss of the business. As compared with other redundancies, keeping redundant databases with shadow transactions and redundant application systems is relatively inexpensive given the potential damage from loss of data or the information technology infrastructure.
>
> **Yossi Sheffi**

Reliability is critical for service orientation. The various trading partners need to be assured of the reliability of their message exchanges. In some ways, reliability of messaging is one of the most important requirements for the QoS of services. Service security, transactional exchanges, and business process management all need reliable message exchanges.

The previous section illustrated the various components and technologies that get involved in service oriented architectures. Each of these components needs to support reliability. Often the reliability is supported through built-in redundancies such as mirroring or replication. For example, as illustrated in Figure 6.14, within a cluster supporting reliability and failover, if one of the servers goes down the other servers take over to continue handling client service requests.

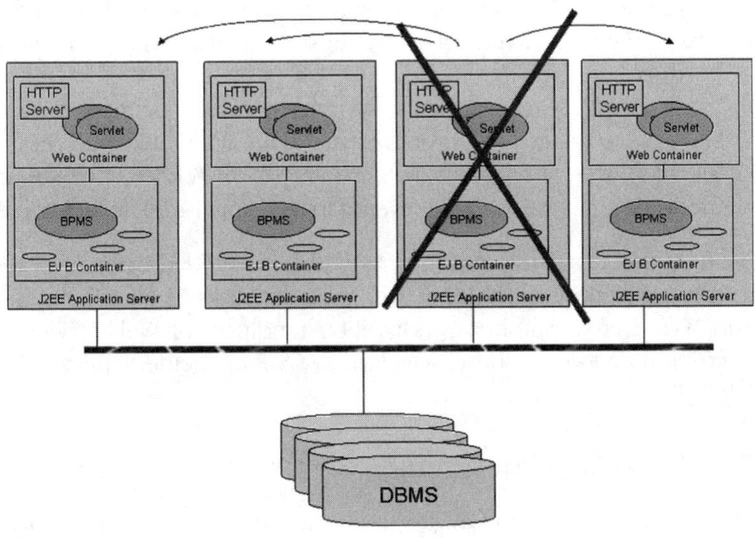

Figure 6.14 Failover in application server clusters

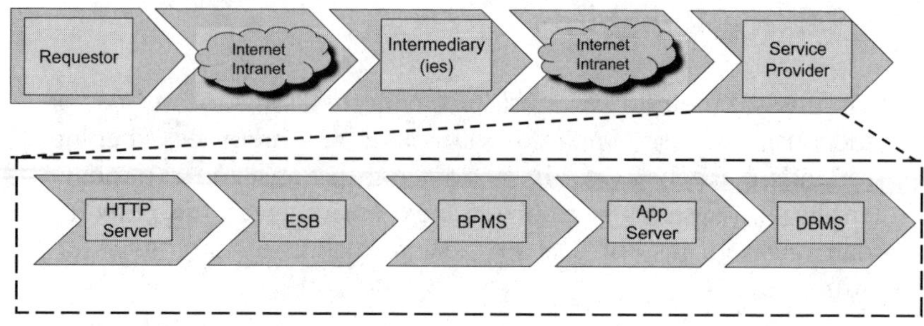

Figure 6.15 Message from requestor to provider

6.4.1 Reliable Messaging

Services are about sending and receiving messages over reliable platforms and servers. From its original client request to the final destination, a message goes through several hoops. The notion of a weakest link definitely applies here. It is necessary to achieve end-to-end reliability. Figure 6.15 provides an illustration of the overall journey from a requestor to a service provider.

In terms of the delivery of messages from a source to destination, here are several types of assurances. These assurances are from the WS-ReliableMessaging standard, which is discussed in the next section.

- AtMostOnce: The message will be delivered once without duplication. It is possible that some messages may not be delivered.
- AtLeastOnce: Delivery of every message is guaranteed. There could be duplications.
- ExactlyOnce: This combines the two previous delivery assurances. Here the message will be delivered and it will be delivered only once.
- InOrder: This applies when there are several ordered or sequenced messages that need to be delivered in the same order as they were sent.

These categories of service assurances will be provided and supported by typical message-oriented middleware, such as IBM's MQ Series messaging platform. There are a number of reliability standards for Web services. Here is a discussion of two of these standards: WS-ReliableMessaging (RM) and WS-Reliability.

6.4.2 WS-ReliableMessaging

WS-ReliableMessaging is an OASIS standard protocol[20] that allows messages to be delivered reliably between distributed applications in the presence of software component, system, or network failures. The basic model of WS-ReliableMessaging is described as follows:

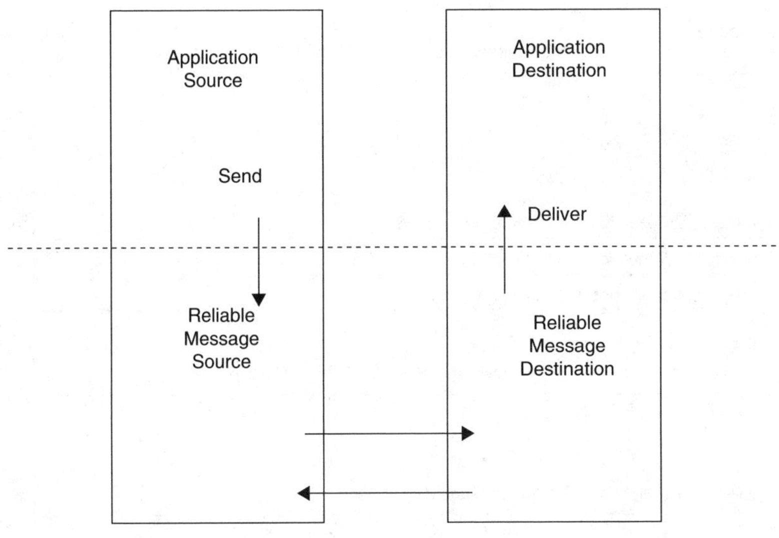

Figure 6.16 Transmit and acknowledgement

1. The source node sends a Web service message with a WS-ReliableMessaging header.
2. The destination node receives the message and sends an acknowledgement message to the source (Figure 6.16).

The RM Source and RM Destination are called endpoints. According to the RM standards, endpoints are addressable entities that send and receive Web services messages.

There are handshaking and delivery assurances involved in implementing WS-ReliableMessaging protocol between two endpoints. The endpoints implementing the reliable delivery must guarantee the policy assurances and raise exceptions when they are violated.

The source and destination involved in reliable messaging exchanges follow a protocol. This protocol can involve retransmission of messages until all the messages pertaining to the same message sequence are sent from source to destination (Figure 6.17).

6.4.3 WS-Reliability

WS-Reliability is another standard that uses SOAP headers to provide guaranteed delivery of Web services messages. The WS-Reliability standard provides the schema that can be used for conforming messages in reliability header blocks. It also provides an HTTP binding specification and fault handling messages.

Figure 6.18 illustrates the messaging model with WS-Reliability. So in

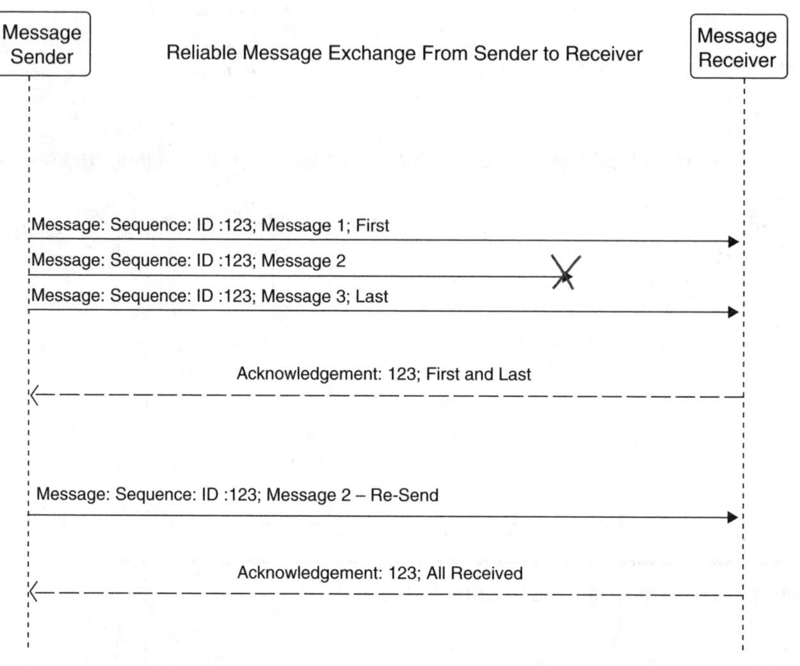

Figure 6.17 Reliable message exchange between source and destination

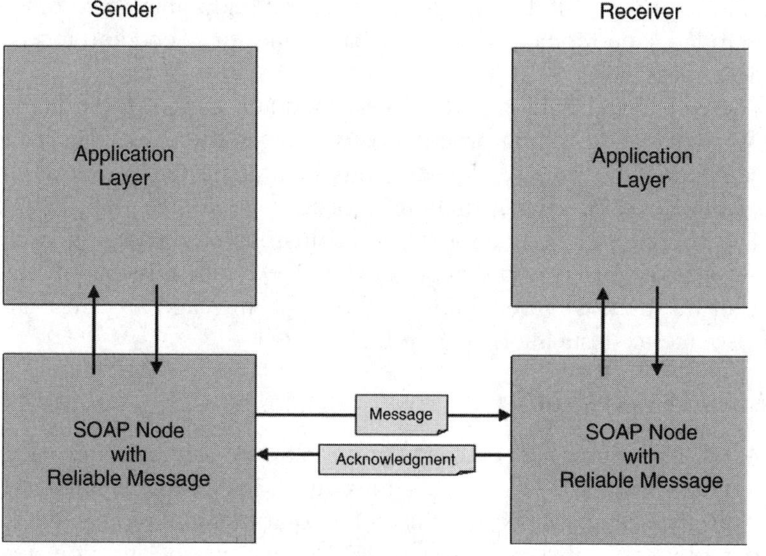

Figure 6.18 Reliable message exchange protocol

the request/response exchange with WS-Reliability, there is a message with a reliability header block and an acknowledgement. In the SOAP header, the reliable message sent by a requestor will specify the source, destination, message ID, timestamp of the message, and request for acknowledgement. The returned acknowledgement message header will indicate the message ID, timestamp, and source/destination identification. The WS-Reliability also supports QoS message exchange patterns. For instance, guaranteed delivery means the message will be delivered but could be delivered more than once. The duplicate elimination exchange, on the other hand, will ensure the message will be delivered at most once.

6.5 Service Security

As noted in previous chapters, XML is the foundation of Web services, so XML standards are critical for the effective functioning of Web services. There are several XML security standards.

Authentication and authorization are the two concepts underlying all security standards. Authentication addresses who is accessing the service. It deals with verifying the identity of the agent requesting a service, usually through a unique log-in and password mechanism. Authorization addresses what the access privileges are of an authenticated service requestor, agent, or user. For example, authorization can control service management—making services available—as well as specific types of operations offered by services.

The main focus in this section is XML and Web services-based security protocol. It should be emphasized that application servers, ESBs, and BPM systems all leverage and provide their own layers of security. For instance, a BPM system can use a single sign-on security server and can rely on underlying secure HyperText Transfer Protocol (HTTP) or WS-Security implementations, yet it provides its own higher level of authorization and authentication.

6.5.1 Security over HTTP

Before discussing XML security standards, it is important to review the common security strategies over the most popular transport protocol: HTTP. It is possible to convey user name and password over a basic HTTP protocol exchange. A more secure, popular mechanism on the Web is the Secure Sockets Layer/Transport Level Security (SSL/TLS). SSL was originally developed by Netscape and is currently in version 3; TLS is the successor protocol to SSL.

TLS provides encryption—not simply American Standard Code for Information Interchange (ASCII) communication—of authentication information.

Before using the protocol, a Web site must set up TLS by completing the following steps:

1. An encryption key pair must be generated and a request made for an authentication certificate. Authorities such as Verisign will handle the request. The authentication certificate must be installed on the Web server. Once these steps are completed, the TLS software will handle the secure and encrypted authentication.
2. After TLS is installed, the server will generate digital signatures for every access through SSL. These signatures prove the authenticity of the server.

TLS sits on top of the TCP/IP protocol and can be used with many application-level protocols, such as File Transfer Protocol (FTP). When the SSL/TLS protocol is used, the Web site will have a URL starting with https (versus http). URLs are often seen with https when a purchase is made over the Web or when a secure Web site is accessed. It is the most pervasive security mechanism over the Web, and essential when submitting sensitive information, such as social security or credit card numbers, over Web sites. The same applies to Web service accesses. If sensitive information is passed along in messages to remote Web services, https protocol is the minimal security protection that must be used in the request/response message exchange.

6.5.2 SOAP Intermediaries

SOAP messages can travel through several intermediaries to their final destination. An intermediary node is both a receiver and sender of a SOAP message. SOAP intermediaries can process security and reliability portions of a SOAP header.

The intermediary architecture works as follows. There is a sequence of nodes through which a SOAP message travels on the way to its final destination, the service provider (Figure 6.19). This was demonstrated in Section 4.4 on distributed service integration. Each of these nodes might do some processing of the message. Typically, the nodes will use header blocks addressed to them.

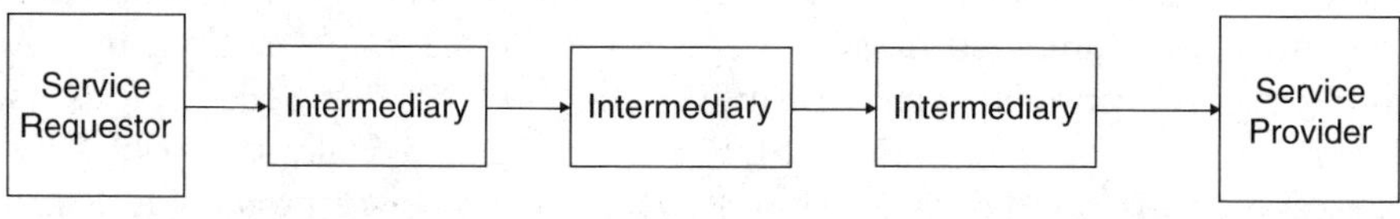

Figure 6.19 Intermediaries through which SOAP messages travel

Table 6.1 Roles of SOAP Nodes

Short Name	*Name*	*Description*
next	"http://www.w3.org/2003/05/soap-envelope/role/next"	Intermediaries and ultimate destination must support this role.
none	"http://www.w3.org/2003/05/soap-envelope/role/none"	SOAP nodes must not support this role.
ultimate receiver	"http://www.w3.org/2003/05/soap-envelope/role/ultimateReceiver"	Role must be supported by ultimate receiver.

Therefore, even though the request in the body of the SOAP message is targeted to the provider, sub-elements in the header of the SOAP message will be processed by the intermediaries.

As specified by the SOAP standard, SOAP nodes have roles. The standard identifies three roles: next, none, and ultimateReceiver, described in Table 6.1. There is one ultimateReciever node; the rest are intermediary next nodes.

6.5.3 OASIS and the World Wide Web Consortium Standards

Two organizations are responsible for the ratification of XML security and other QoS standards: OASIS and the World Wide Web Consortium (W3C) (Table 6.2).[21]

Typically, the W3C organization is responsible for core XML, HTML, and related standards. For instance, besides XML and HTML, the XML schema as well as SOAP and WSDL are W3C standards. OASIS also hosts many important schemata that typically use and build on the W3C standards. Examples include Universal Description, Discovery, and Integration (UDDI), Business Process Execution Language (BPEL), and, of course, SAML, WS-Security, and eXtensible Access Control Markup Language (XACML).

Table 6.2 Organizations Responsible for XML Standards

W3C Standards	*OASIS Standards*
XML Encryption	SAML
XML Signature	Web services Security (WS-Security)

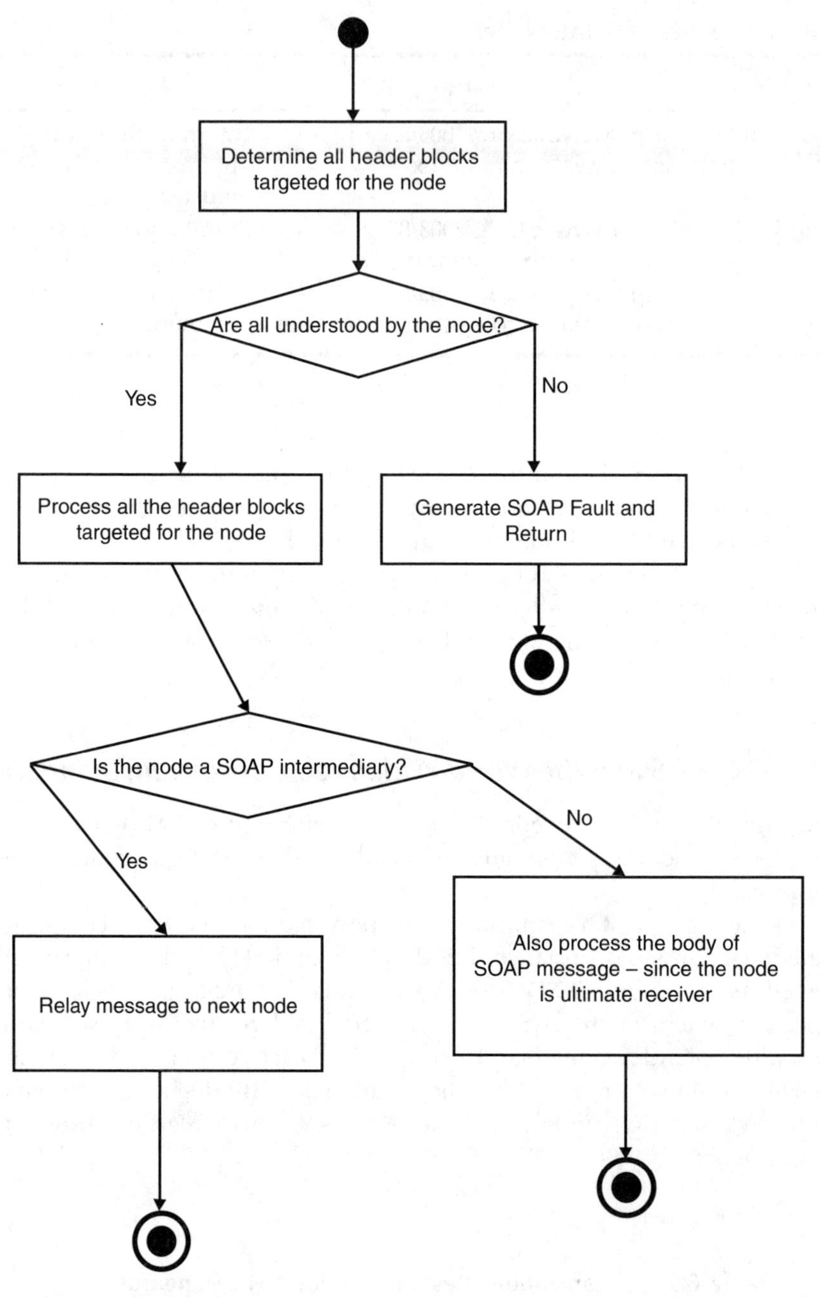

Figure 6.20 SOAP processing model

6.5.4 XML Encryption

In 2001, the W3C and the Internet Engineering Task Force (IETF) developed a standard for encrypting XML documents.[22] The XML Encryption protocol and standards provide the rules used to process raw data into encrypted XML as well as the rules to cipher encrypted data back into raw data. XML Encryption allows portions of an XML document to be encrypted; other parts of the document can be nonencrypted or open.

The mission of the W3C and IETF is to "develop a process for encrypting/decrypting digital content (including XML documents and portions thereof) and an XML syntax used to represent the (1) encrypted content and (2) information that enables an intended recipient to decrypt it."[23]

Following is a simple example of an unencrypted XML document:

```
<?xml version='1.0'?>
  <PaymentInfo xmlns='http://example.org/paymentv2'>
    <Name>John Smith<Name/>
  <CreditCard Limit='5,000' Currency='USD'>
    <Number>4019 2445 0277 5567</Number>
     <Issuer>Bank of the Internet</Issuer>
     <Expiration>04/02</Expiration>
  </CreditCard>
</PaymentInfo>
```

Using XML Encryption, part of the document can be encrypted as follows:

```
<?xml version='1.0'?>
  <PaymentInfo xmlns='http://example.org/paymentv2'>
    <Name>John Smith<Name/>
    <EncryptedData Type='http://www.w3.org/2001/04/xmlenc#Element'
      xmlns='http://www.w3.org/2001/04/xmlenc#'>
      <CipherData><CipherValue>A23B45C56</CipherValue></CipherData>
    </EncryptedData>
  </PaymentInfo>
```

The core element in the XML Encryption standard is EncryptedData. The entire XML document or elements within the XML document can be encrypted using EncryptedData. The content within the EncryptedData element is the cipher data. The original raw elements get replaced with encrypted data delimited by EncryptedData.

6.5.5 XML Signature

XML Signature[24] is another security standard that allows all or part of an XML document to be digitally signed. XML signatures can be used to ensure that the XML document content has not been tampered with or modified.

The standard specifies how to process XML digital signatures. More specifically, the XML Signature specifies a CanonicalizationMethod and a SignatureMethod. These are defined as follows:

- CanonicalizationMethod: It is possible to have the same XML document content but a different order or form of the elements or attributes of the document. This will cause the XML signatures to be different. Canonicalizaiton takes care of this discrepancy and signs the canonical form of the document.
- SignatureMethod: This option allows you to specify the algorithm for generating and validating signatures. For instance, DSA stands for the Digital Signature Algorithm, PKCS1 is for the RSA algorithm, and so on. These algorithms are specified through their URIs.[25]

6.5.6 Security Assertion Markup Language

SAML is an assertion markup language that supports authentication and authorization. SAML 1.0 was first adopted in 2002. In September 2003 OASIS ratified SAML 2003 and in March 2005 SAML 2.0 became a standard.[26]

SAML supports the notion of SAML Authorities. These authorities provide assertions that are trusted. These assertions in turn are used by service providers to grant usage authority for a Web service.

SAML specifies three different types of assertions for different purposes:

1. Authentication Assertion describes how and when a subject has been asserted.
2. Attribute Assertion specifies that a subject has a number of attributes—A1, A2, ..., An with values V1, V2, ... Vn.
3. Authorization Assertion asserts the authorization of a subject for resources.

6.5.6.1 How SAML Works

The SAML algorithm involves authentication authority and policy enforcement. User applications must communicate with an authentication authority to obtain the assertions.

Figure 6.21 shows SAML in action, using different assertions and using XML to encode authentication and authorization information. The following are the key steps highlighted in the figure. A user application provides authentication information (i.e., log-in and password) to the SAML authentication authority. This authentication authority generates the SAML assertion—a SAML token. The application accesses a request or resource using the token. On the service provisioning side, a policy enforcement point (PEP) intercepts

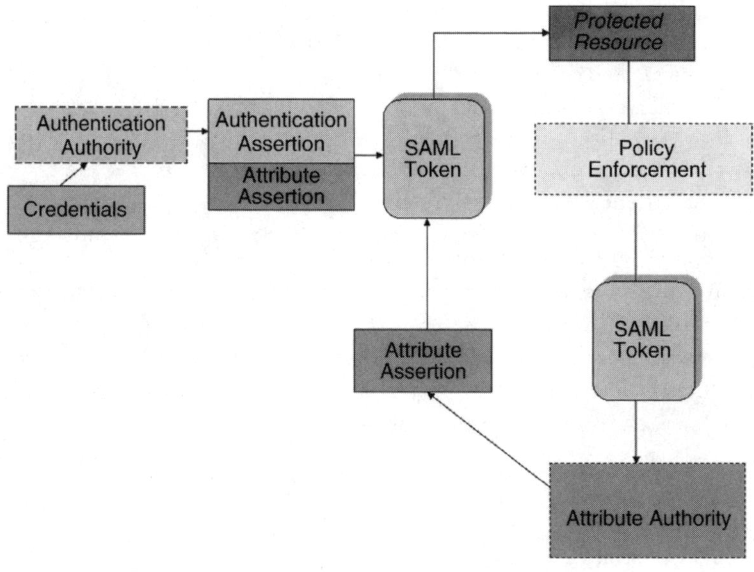

Figure 6.21 SAML in action

the request to determine access or authorization; here again, a SAML token is used. If the authorization is to be granted, the attribute authority generates an attribute assertion, and this assertion is attached to the SAML token.

Here is an example of a message exchange involving SAML. Suppose a user logs into an e-learning Web site with her log-in and password and is authenticated. Later, when the waitlist Web service is used, she does not need to log in again. Instead, she can request the Assertion Issuer to send the authentication assertion. This can be attached to the header of the SOAP request sent to the waitlist Web service. That service, on receiving a SOAP request, checks to determine if the assertion is present in the SOAP header.

The following illustrates a request and response with SAML:

SOAP Generated for the Request

```
<?xml version="1.0" encoding="UTF-8"?>
<soapenv:Envelope xmlns:soapenv="http://schemas.xmlsoap.org/
soap/envelope/"
xmlns:xsd="http://www.w3.org/2001/XMLSchema"
xmlns:xsi="http://www.w3.org/2001/XMLSchema-instance">
  <soapenv:Header>
    <saml:Assertion AssertionID="4vMruW3qprimQgVgRGUHow22"
    IssueInstant="2003-08-04T20:16:37Z" Issuer="https://www.
    signsecure.com"MajorVersion="1"
MinorVersion="0" xmlns="urn:oasis:names:tc:SAML:1.0:assertion"
xmlns:saml="urn:oasis:names:tc:SAML:1.0:assertion">
```

```
        <saml:Conditions NotBefore="2003-08-04T20:16:37Z"
        NotOnOrAfter="2003-08-04T21:16:37Z">
         <saml:AudienceRestrictionCondition>
           <saml:Audience>https://my.signsecure.com
           </saml:Audience>
       </saml:AudienceRestrictionCondition>
      </saml:Conditions>
      <saml:AuthenticationStatement AuthenticationInstant="2003-
      08-04T20:16:37Z"
AuthenticationMethod="urn:oasis:names:tc:SAML:1.0:am:password">
       <saml:Subject>
         <saml:NameIdentifier>Alice</saml:NameIdentifier>
       </saml:Subject>
       </saml:AuthenticationStatement>
    </saml:Assertion>
  </soapenv:Header>
  <soapenv:Body>
    <ns1:getWaitlistPos
soapenv:encodingStyle="http://schemas.xmlsoap.org/soap/encoding/"
xmlns:ns1="urn:xmlcourse-waitlist-info">
       <strStudentId xsi:type="xsd:string">123-45-6789</strStudentId>
    </ns1:getWaitlistPos>
   </soapenv:Body>
</soapenv:Envelope>
```

The following is the response to the service call:

```
<?xml version="1.0" encoding="UTF-8"?>
<soapenv:Envelope xmlns:soapenv="http://schemas.xmlsoap.org/soap/
envelope/"
xmlns:xsd="http://www.w3.org/2001/XMLSchema"
xmlns:xsi="http://www.w3.org/2001/XMLSchema-instance">
   <soapenv:Body>
     <ns1:getWaitlistPosResponse
soapenv:encodingStyle="http://schemas.xmlsoap.org/soap/encoding/"
xmlns:ns1="urn:xmlcourse-waitlist-info">
       <getWaitlistPosReturn xsi:type="xsd:int">3 </getWaitlist
       PosReturn>
     </ns1:getWaitlistPosResponse>
   </soapenv:Body>
</soapenv:Envelope>
```

6.5.7 WS-Security

According to the WS-Security specification, this standard “describes enhancements to SOAP messaging to provide quality of protection through message integrity and message confidentiality.” The WS-Security[27] specification defines how to attach and include security tokens within SOAP messages. A Web service can require that an incoming message prove a set of claims (e.g., name, key, permission, capability). These are essential parts of a message for authentication and authorization. The aggregation of the claims information required for a message exchange is called a policy.

The following is an example of this element, which appears in the SOAP header:[28]

```
<S:Envelope xmlns:S="http://www.w3.org/2001/12/soap-envelope"
            xmlns:wsse="http://schemas.xmlsoap.org/ws/2002/04/
            secext">
    <S:Header>
            ...
          <wsse:Security>
            <wsse:UsernameToken>
              <wsse:Username>Zoe</wsse:Username>
              <wsse:Password>ILoveDogs</wsse:Password>
            </wsse:UsernameToken>
          </wsse:Security>
            ...
    </S:Header>
    ...
</S:Envelope>
```

If a request is made for a specific operation or method, the requestor can associate security tokens that capture the claims for the operation or action. Security tokens can be SAML assertions, X.509 certificates, or Kerberos tickets. In addition to the requestor and Web service provider, there are security token service providers, which act as brokerage houses, issuing security tokens and verifying claims.

Figure 6.22 illustrates a service requestor communicating with a service provider involving security tokens and policies. Several other supporting standards support the WS-Security framework. This section briefly describes two of these standards that are also supported by OASIS: WS-Policy and WS-Trust.

1. WS-Policy[29] describes "the capabilities and constraints of the security (and other business) policies on intermediaries and endpoints (e.g., required security tokens, supported encryption algorithms, privacy rules)."[30] The specification was originally developed in December 2002 by Microsoft, IBM, BEA Systems, and SAP. WS-Policy defines policy assertions that are individual security preferences (for instance, using Kerberos security tokens). Policy expressions can include a group of policy assertions.

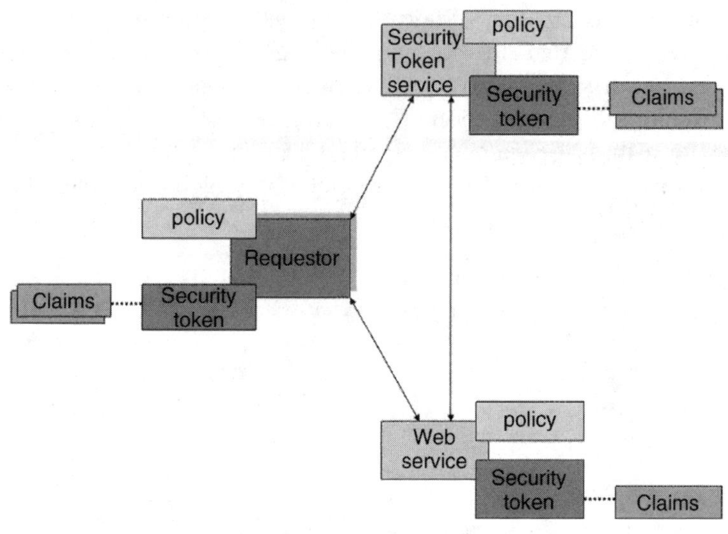

Figure 6.22 Security tokens

- The following is a simple example that includes a top-level policy expression element. This example also illustrates one of the options that policy provides: ExactlyOne policy, which indicates that exactly one of its child element policies must be satisfied (other options are All and OneOrMore):

```
<wsp:Policy xmlns:wsse="..." xmlns:wssx="...".
  <wsp:ExactlyOne>
    <wsse:SecurityToken wsp:Usage="wsp:Required">
      <wsse:TokenType>wsse:Kerberosv5TGT</wsse:TokenType>
    </wsse:SecurityToken>
    <wsse:SecurityToken wsp:Usage="wsp:Required">
      <wsse:TokenType>wsse:X509v3</wsse:TokenType>
    </wsse:SecurityToken>
  </wsp:ExactlyOne>
  <wssx:Audit wsp:Usage="wsp:Observed"/>
</wsp:Policy>
```

2. WS-Trust: The WS-Trust specification addresses the "characteristic that one entity is willing to rely upon a second entity to execute a set of actions and/or make a set of assertions about a set of subjects and/or scopes."[31] This specification was released in December 2002 by Microsoft, IBM, Verisign, and RSA Security. As its name suggests, WS-Trust captures the protocols for issuing security tokens and

managing trust relationships between trading partners. The WS-Trust protocol involves the exchange of security credentials between two parties. Usually trust engines on the sender and receiver sides exchange security tokens. These security tokens are then analyzed by a trust engine. There are several activities performed by the trust engine, including verifying if the security token claims comply with the policy.

6.6 Services Management

As an industry or technology sector evolves, the applications, artifacts, practices, and entire life cycle of the domain will require management. The more popular a domain, the more pervasive the management needs. Once a service is deployed it is necessary to monitor and to mange its performance and life cycle. Management in any sector is a sign of maturity. Databases, documents, and business process systems all went through the same life cycle and became management systems—database management, document management, and business process management systems. A similar evolution is occurring in service orientation. As these services become increasingly popular and address standardization for loosely coupled integration and interoperability, the need to manage the services becomes essential. Services management and standards are being addressed through a number of initiatives.

Despite some shaky starts and persistent criticism by skeptics as being simply a fad, service orientation is becoming pervasive. Services are penetrating the bloodstream of IT organizations. SOA is becoming a foundation for loosely coupling, integrating, and accessing existing business objects or applications. Service orientation is integrating organizations and providing new and emerging business opportunities. So it is not surprising to see standards, products, and solutions for managing services.

Service management is primarily a technical system or infrastructure issue. The business managers are concerned about their specific business metrics such as bottom-line sales, customer satisfaction, customer retention, relationship with partners in joint ventures, and smooth operation of the supply chain. Business performance management is covered in Chapter 7.

IT managers, on the other hand, are interested in technology measures such as the throughput of the message exchanges, the response time of the various categories of middleware deployed in the enterprise, security leaks, and resiliency for 24/7 operations. This section focuses on the system management of service deployments.

There are two important and interrelated dimensions in managing services:

- System management: A number of system management features were described in earlier sections. Monitoring is perhaps the most important system management feature. Monitoring spans the execution and performance of deployed Web services. Lower-level temporal SLAs could also be supported. System management can also include support for diagnostics, exception processing, alerters, and in general, exception handling at the systems level. Since the Web service invocations are monitored, this dimension can also include audit trails and analysis of Web services performance. Other potential features, especially for established and popular Web services, include account management (i.e., metering and billing support).

- Life-cycle management: Services, like any other software, are designed, implemented, debugged, deployed, and refined in versions over time. In some cases, Web services are deprecated and taken off line. Life-cycle management deals with the entire life cycle of the Web service, providing the tools and capabilities for Web service developers and owners to efficiently manage Web services development and deployment.

6.6.1 Service Oriented Management

Web services management refers to the management capabilities offered to enterprises implementing service oriented architectures—in other words, service oriented management. SearchWebServices defines SOM as follows: "Service oriented management (SOM) is the operational management of service delivery within a service oriented architecture (SOA). The primary objective of service oriented management is to provide a differentiated service delivery capability during operation, using business objectives to drive system behavior."[32]

Service oriented management is at the intersection of service delivery, system-level reliability, security, performance metrics, and business metrics that satisfy business objectives. For example, a manufacturer and shipping trading partner could agree on a response time and transaction load measure as business objectives (e.g., ship within one day of receiving an order and process 10,000 orders a day). The underlying services implementations on the system side must guarantee these business objectives. Management in this case implies real-time performance monitoring and measuring of the service traffic.

The overall context of management is the service oriented enterprise, involving many organizations operating as an aggregated unit, with all interactions conducted via Web services. The key resources that must be managed include Web services, Web service processes, and partner relationships.

- Services Building Blocks: At the lowest layer of the management taxonomy are the individual Web services being managed. There are a number of alternative approaches to managing the actual invoked services. Management in this context deals with the overall response time, uptime of the service, reliability and security of the service, handling of exceptions and faults, and overall throughput of the service.

- Enterprise service bus: As Chapter 4 demonstrated, the ESB handles message transformations, transport mappings, message routing, and security and reliability for the overall service infrastructure. ESBs also provide management and monitoring portals for the various services managed by the ESB.
- Business processes: In addition to individual services, the processes compose services and involve human participants. Chapter 5 discussed the various functionalities and capabilities of BPM systems. The interfaces, business rules, and actions on processes involving orchestration of services can be published as services. BPM system platforms typically provide both business activity monitoring as well as system-level performance monitoring capabilities and portals. The business process management layer is on top of the ESB.
- Partner relationship management: Service orientation involves partners. Typically, one service invocation will invoke another service. Several partner organizations could be involved in supporting these services. These partners will have various compliance, service level, quality, security, and performance agreements. The partnership relationship, therefore, becomes essential. The Web service deployment in extended enterprises is not just a matter of informational access. It also involves programmatic access to processes within organizations. The partners involved must rely on each other in secure and high-performance deployments.

These four layers of manageability are illustrated in Figure 6.23. Going back to the definition of SOM, we can see that objectives of service oriented enterprises involve trading partners as well as all the other communities served by the SOE. The management spans multiple organizations executing processes across their enterprises and invoking services through the ESBs potentially across continents.

6.6.2 System Management and Monitoring in Application Servers: JMX

Application servers can be containers for ESB and BPM components. Application servers often include some monitoring capabilities. For instance, J2EE application servers have the Java Management Extension standard, and open technology allows deployed components to be managed and monitored in an application server. Since it is standards based,

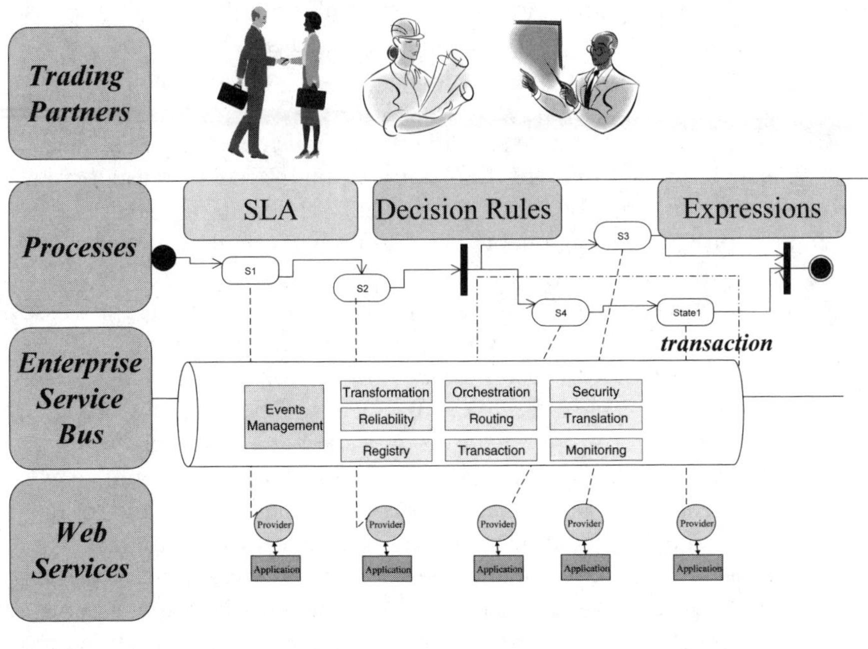

Figure 6.23 Hierarchy of managed resources

JMX compliant system management provisioning solutions (e.g., Tivoli, HP Open View) can be used to monitor the deployed services. Figure 6.24 illustrates the JMX architecture. The JMX Administration Console provides a graphical interface through connectors and adaptors. The MBeans do the actual monitoring of the resources (i.e., the application or service implementations). The MBean Server is the container of the MBeans and manages the MBeans.

At the bottom are the resources that actually implement the services. For example, BPM system engines can be treated as resources, and so can application specific layers that use the BPM system engine, such as procurement, accounting, or compliance services.

6.6.3 Web Services Distributed Management

A number of organizations are now pursuing Web services management standards, solutions, frameworks, and products. One of the more interesting efforts is the Web Services Distributed Management (WSDM) Technical Committee (TC) of the OASIS consortium. This group was created in March 2003. The group's charter is as follows: "To define web services management. This includes using web services architecture and technology to

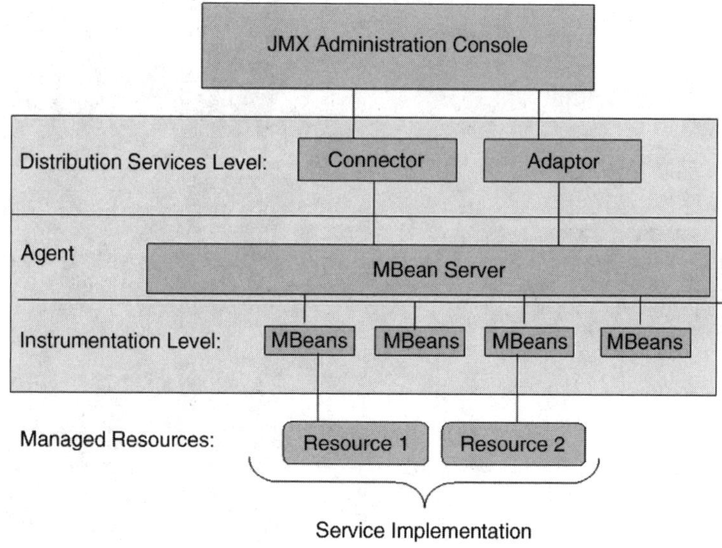

Figure 6.24 JMX architecture

manage distributed resources. This TC will also develop the model of a web service as a manageable resource. This TC will collaborate with various evolving activities within other standards groups."[33]

The WSDM focus therefore is on managing both various resources over networks through standardized Web service interfaces and management of Web services. The former is called Management Using Web Services (MUWS). The latter is called Management of Web Services (MOWS). So WSDM specifications can be used to manage heterogeneous and distributed resources using standard Web services technologies. WSDM can also be used to manage deployed Web services.

The approach of using Web services for management makes a lot of sense. Web services are excellent in loosely coupling heterogeneous systems over distributed networks. Therefore, they are a prime candidate for also managing these resources through Web services technologies. For a resource to be managed through Web services, it must provide a WSDL implementation and what the TC calls manageability endpoints. Figure 6.25 illustrates an MUWS compliant manager accessing various resources that provide Web services-based interfaces to be managed by the manageability consumer.

Note that the notion of resource is quite flexible. A resource can be an application deployed over the network in application server, a server, a storage device, network devices, or even a peripheral such as a printer. System

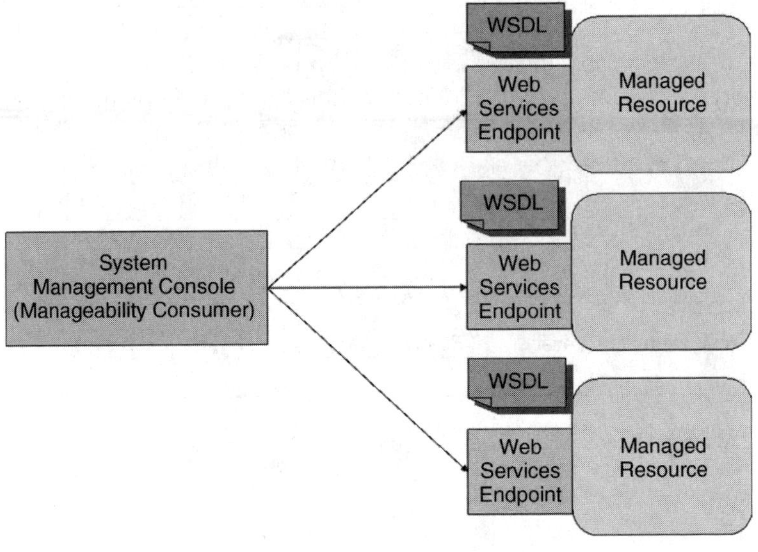

Figure 6.25 Resources managed through Web services

management software and portals provide visual monitoring capabilities to resources deployed over the network. A resource can also be a Web service.

Therefore, the same models and principles of MUWS also apply to Web services: Service interfaces could be used to manage services. There are two approaches in managing the endpoints of the service. A single endpoint can be used for both the service interface invocations and the management services. In this management pattern, the WSDL interface specifies the endpoint both for the core service operations and the manageability interfaces. The advantage of this approach is simplicity: one endpoint for both operational and manageability features. The disadvantage is single point of failure, as the function and service management are not separated.

The alternative is to have a separate endpoint and interface for managing the services. Under this management pattern, a separate endpoint and interface handles the management of the service. So there are two endpoints: one for the Web service application functions and the other for the management functions.

6.7 Summary

This chapter first discussed the performance issues and requirements for Web services. Performance is often captured in service level agreements between trading partners. These SLAs specify response time, throughput, and availability parameters. This chapter defined quality of service as QoS = Performance + Reliability + Security. All the layers that make up a service oriented architecture and all the components that influence performance, reliability, and security were identified here. Service implementations are complex, and an end-to-end invocation of a service invokes many different components. The chapter discussed the performance related issues as well as benchmarking of all these essential components that get involved in a services journey from invocation to response.

The chapter also discussed security and reliability of services. Several XML standards address security, such as XML Signature, XML Encryption, SAML, and WS-Security. For the reliability the main standard is WS-ReliableMessaging.

The last section of the chapter discussed management of services. Service management involves management of the service building blocks, of the processes that compose services, and of the participants or trading partner relationships that get involved in services. The chapter described the Web Services Distributed Management standard that uses services to manage resources, including other Web services.

Notes

1. http://archive.dante.net/sequin/QoS-def-Apr01.pdf
2. http://www.cisco.com/
3. This has been mentioned elsewhere, but often the focus is on Web services. This is not to exclude other technologies that are also essential and are used for service orientation. Examples here include messaging middleware (MOM), EAI, and application servers. These platforms also provide QoS support. MOM, for instance, provides reliable message deliveries. However, these platforms typically operate within the secure firewalls of the enterprise. Service orientation is about connecting different enterprises and aligning their QoS features. Furthermore, the trend is to have more standardized interfaces and solutions over the middleware platform, and hence the emergence of the ESB as the middleware providing both the QoS support of traditional middleware while at the same time being open and standards based.
4. There could be other definitions and differences of opinion as to what should or should not go in QoS definition for services. For instance, some consider security outside the scope of QoS. Transaction support could also be considered as part of QoS. These are valid considerations. We covered transactions in Chapter 4. Considering it as an integral part of QoS is an interesting alternative. Each of these dimensions, security, reliability, performance, and transactions, are critical for service orientation. We prefer to include security and exclude transaction in QoS because transactions in service orientation are involved in a distributed services context and hence more appropriate for distributed service oriented architectures. Security on the other hand is critical for the service consumer experience: it will not be acceptable to have

service implementations that compromise security. Hence, we associate it with quality of the service.

5. http://www.washingtonpost.com/wp-dyn/content/article/2005/06/17/AR2005061701031.html
6. There are several limitations of the HTTP protocol when it comes to scaling and parallelism. There are alternatives such as sending SOAP messages over other protocols including MQSeries, JMS, and Common Object Request Broker Architecture's (CORBA) Internet Inter-ORB Protocol (IIOP). The one thing, and perhaps the most important, going for HTTP is its ubiquity and availability. It is not necessary to buy expensive proprietary systems such as MQSeries (IBM) or CORBA implementations, which are difficult to manage and to maintain. Furthermore, given the emergence of the ESB, now there is no need to worry about the transport protocol: The ESB can do the transformation and translations. Applications need to worry about standards-based communications between service providers and consumers: ESB can take care of the protocol translations and transformations, taking into consideration the performance, reliability, and security requirements.
7. Another factor in the overall performance is the network cabling used as the physical medium that connects the server over the network. Technologies here include Unshielded Twisted Pair, Shielded Twisted Pair, Coaxial Cable, and Fiber Optic.
8. It is not uncommon to see advanced enterprise applications ignore validation and deal with errors or exception handling when they encounter unexpected elements while parsing the XML message.
9. In addition to the messaging style, another choice must be made: the encoding. Here there are two main choices: literal or SOAP. SOAP encoding specifies how object graphical structures are serialized. Literal, on the other hand, specifies a World Wide Web Consortium (W3C) schema for serialization. SOAP encoding is typically used with RPC. Literal (more specifically, document-literal) has proven to perform better.
10. See, e.g., http://www.informit.com/articles/printerfriendly.asp?p=177376.
11. See http://www.slac.stanford.edu/comp/net/wan-mon/iepm-cf.html for a listing of some of the projects and tools for Internet performance monitoring.
12. http://www.internettrafficreport.com
13. EJBs assemble Java classes that implement the business logic. There are several types of EJBs. The most important of these are the stateless session beans. Other EJB types include message-driven beans and entity beans. Besides the bean implementation of the core business logic, EJBs also include a deployment descriptor, which is an XML file that specifies the various interfaces of the EJB package as well as the EJB type (i.e., stateful, stateless) and its security and transactional characteristics (bean managed or container managed). An EJB type could make a huge difference. Typically the best bet, or best performance, is from stateless session beans.
14. ECPerf's results, as of the publishing of this book, are a bit dated. Nevertheless, the benchmark toolkit can serve as an effective measure of the performance of application servers. See http://ecperf.theserverside.com/.
15. http://www.spec.org/benchmarks.html

16. See, for example, http://www.eweek.com/article2/0,3959,1081054,00.asp.
17. A *load balancer* is an important technology that combines hardware and software capabilities and algorithmically (such as round-robin) distributes client requests to a farm or cluster of servers.
18. The original paper can be requested from http://www.pega.com.
19. http://www.tpc.org
20. http://xml.coverpages.org/WS-ReliableMessaging200502.pdf
21. The Web sites for these organizations can be found at http://www.oasis-open.org/ and W3 http://www.w3.org.
22. The standard is presented in http://www.w3.org/Encryption/2001/.
23. From the W3C XML Encryption Working Group mission statement, http://www.w3.org/Encryption/2001.
24. The XML Signature standard is specified at http://www.w3.org/TR/2002/REC-xmldsig-core-20020212/.
25. The URI for DSA is http://www.w3.org/2000/09/xmldsig#dsa-sha1 and the URI for the RSA algorithm is http://www.w3.org/2000/09/xmldsig#rsa-sha1.
26. For SAML specifications, see www.oasis-open.org/committees/security/.
27. http://www.oasis-open.org/committees/tc_home.php?wg_abbrev=wss. In April 2004, the Organization for the Advancement of Structured Information Standards ratified the WS-Security standard. http://xml.coverpages.org/ni2004-04-08-c.html.
28. From the standard found at http://schemas.xmlsoap.org/specs/ws-security/ws-security.htm.
29. http://www.oasis-open.org/committees/download.php/15979/oasis-wssx-ws-securitypolicy-1.0.pdf
30. The WS-Policy statement can be found at http://msdn.micr osoft.com/webservices/default.aspx?pull=/library/en-us/dnglobspec/html/ws-policy. asp.
31. http://msdn.microsoft.com/webservices/default.aspx?pull=/library/en-us/dnglobspec/html/ws-trust.asp
32. http://searchwebservices.techtarget.com/sDefinition/0,,sid26_gci929186,00.html.
33. http://www.oasis-open.org/committees/wsdm/charter.php

Chapter 7

The Service Oriented Enterprise

> Don't push your way to the front; don't sweet-talk your way to the top. Put yourself aside, and help others get ahead. Don't be obsessed with getting your own advantage. Forget yourselves long enough to lend a helping hand.
>
> **Philippians 2:3–4, *The Message***

7.1 Introduction

We have now come to the most important chapter of the book. All the previous chapters presented different aspects of the service oriented enterprise (SOE). Here the organizational performance and cultural aspects of service oriented enterprises are summarized and examined more in depth. Elements of the service oriented enterprise have been around for quite some time. It is now that a number of key business models as well as enabling technologies are coming together to realize the service oriented enterprise.

Quite a bit of time was spent in this book on technology. Compared to issues, models, and implementation of service oriented cultures, it is easier to focus on technology. Also, it is important to understand the underlying components of the technology. Think of an office building: Technology makes it possible to construct efficient, networked, and highly intelligent buildings, but what makes an enterprise successful are the people and the culture of its organization.

Service orientation is about a service culture.

Serving is praised as a virtue, yet it seems much more difficult to realize it in practice. Inspiration and goose bumps well up when stories are told of unselfish sacrifice and service for noble causes: in social service, in politics, in religion, and—why not—even in the military. However, there is a flip side. Our culture sometimes places the wrong emphasis when it rewards greed, aggrandized egos, and cut-throat approaches in climbing the corporate ladder. In a flattened world, we cannot afford to reward selfish ambitions. The service culture sees the success of customer, shareholder, employee, and partner as essential requirements to fulfillment. It is service oriented. In a service oriented enterprise, greed is not good.[1] Success is a side effect, not the focus. Success is not just about finances; it is about how well others are served and elevated. A service oriented culture means our main function and purpose is found in serving others: helping them achieve their potential.

7.1.1 Technology Is the Enabler

An examination of a service oriented enterprise reveals three fundamental layers (Figure 7.1). At the foundation is the service oriented architecture (SOA) components, including the infrastructure guaranteeing service, quality of service (QoS) as well as the enterprise service bus (ESB) for intra- and inter-enterprise connectivity. As Chapter 4 demonstrated, the ESB provides connectivity between various systems and trading partners using standard integration interfaces, especially Web services.

Service orientation is about leveraging technologies—especially ESBs and business process management (BPM) systems—while realizing continuous performance improvements.

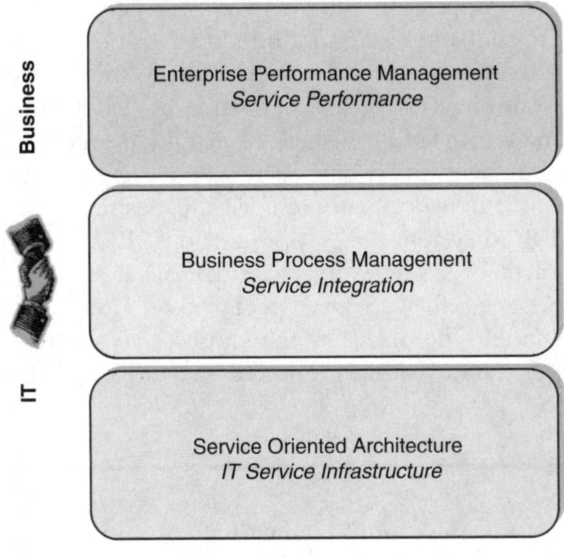

Figure 7.1 Service oriented enterprises

At the top is enterprise performance management (EPM). Here is where the overall performance of the organization, service contracts, trading partners, and organizational interactions are dealt with. This is where different departments within an organization—and in fact different organizations—are brought together to realize business goals. For instance, parts manufacturers and assemblers can participate in a value chain involving many companies. Each on the chain adds value toward the ultimate product. Organizationally each department internally is a service department at its core—offering services to various functions in the organization. Products are services offered to customers, trading partners, or distributors. In fact, the service oriented enterprise assembles services and publishes them as composite applications.

Business process management is the middle layer of the SOE architecture. It brings business and IT together. What is a business process? As Chapter 5 illustrated, a BPM system models and executes the interactions among human participants, systems, and trading partners. Business process is not just about flowcharts and pretty workflow diagrams. These are important, but not sufficient. The flowchart, or the flow, is only one aspect. Traditional workflow does a good job at guiding the work through the process but is often weak at integrating enterprise business policies, or rules, to interact with existing services, to complete work more efficiently, to reduce manual processing, and to manage enterprise as well as business-to-business (B2B) integration guided by business agreements. Agile enterprises are those that let the system manage the policy governance. Business rules engines (BREs) are becoming an essential component in the overall architecture solution stack of extended enterprises. However, these rule engines need to be part of the same system that also manages the processes. In other words, to achieve the desired agility, businesses need a unified BPM system that supports robust BPM and BRE functionality in the context of a single object model and a single system. Procedural (i.e., process flows) and declarative (i.e., business rules) programming should be used in tandem, with the rules driving the processes and executed within the same system to realize the best platform for agility.

Business and IT Governance: The Sarbanes–Oxley Act of 2002 is now levying an enormous amount of complexity on enterprises, requiring them to document in detail their business transactions and internal operations. In response, many companies are introducing checks and balances as well as auditing of their operations to track their documents, business dealings, and transactions and maintaining a comprehensive paper trail of their activities. Compliance with the act and other regulatory requirements could have an interesting side effect. Even though we cringe when we hear of government regulations, we should remember that not too long ago during World War II, it was precisely a push from Franklin D. Roosevelt in the military and civilian government that resulted in massive adoption of the punched card that started the initial phases of digitization and automation, with tremendous financial benefits for the military and civilian sectors, to say nothing of the enormous profits generated for companies such as IBM. If the Sarbanes–Oxley Act compliance results in digitization and automation of internal financial and information technology (IT) processes, as it probably should, the result could also be dramatic for the enterprises that support governance through service oriented platforms, especially BPM. Interestingly enough, because the act is designed to ensure that corporate policies are followed, the weakest link is actually the individual (i.e., human participants), who needs to understand the policies and to decide if a particular transaction is, for example, of high, medium, or moderate risk. For instance, if an employee is deciding whether a particular business transaction is at risk—potentially violating a corporate legal policy—the flow will stop at either that employee's manager's inbox or with corporate legal counsel. Consequently, the overall performance of the system and the ability to change is dependent on its human participants and is limited by activation of processes—making sure the work actually gets to the next inbox. Without automating the policies and the business rules encoded in the Sarbanes–Oxley Act, this approach simply will not scale. Instead, the system should be allowed to assist with policy conformance. Just as success was achieved in automating and digitizing the processes (i.e., the flows), the rules also need to be automated and digitized. Otherwise, the process will be slowed by employees who either have the rules in their heads or who hold them in volumes of documentation.

The infrastructure layer supporting the business processes and carrying out all the connectivity, transformation, and QoS functions for service exchanges is the SOA layer, with ESBs as the key enabler for service architectures. With this robust three layered architecture, service orientation provides the ability to loosely couple applications, trading partners, and organizations and to connect them via service calls. The coupling is often achieved through discovery. Furthermore, independent services can be composed in processes to provide even greater value than the sum of component services. Service orientation enables internal as well as external trading partners to participate in distributed applications. Each party complies with agreed-on protocols and carries out its part in the overall execution of processes involving services from diverse organizations. The processes here are microflows typically involving only system or trading-partner service accesses. BPMS processes use the standards-based ESB transformation primitives as well as these micro-integration flows to create comprehensive business processes involving both human as well as system (i.e., back-end applications or trading partner) services. The enterprise implements its horizontal and vertical applications primarily as BPM applications. Business performance management is then enacted to make sure various business goals and service metrics are continually measured and monitored.

7.2 Service Oriented Organization

Serving customers: Newegg.com is an interesting e-market company that brings together manufacturers of computer hardware and software as well as home electronics with mid-market consumers. Newegg focuses on serving the customer. It has a huge collection of products at its Web site that could be purchased online. Here is a quote from its Web site: "We view every customer as a customer for life and instill this philosophy in our employees to assure the complete satisfaction of every shopper." Newegg employees spend a considerable amount of effort and time making sure customer questions are answered and that customer service is first class. They typify service especially by focusing on the customer. One aspect of this service is the responsiveness to customer inquiries or service. Increasingly, companies like Newegg are providing real-time customer service via their Web sites. In some ways, focusing on the customer helps serve shareholders and of course the employees as well.

Serving employees or associates: For a completely different and almost a textbook case illustrating organizational culture, consider WL Gore and Associates (http://www.gore.com). This culture does not even call their workers employees; rather, those hired are associates. These associates have sponsors, not supervisors or managers. The associates together with their sponsors search and find projects based on their interests. Innovation is encouraged. WL Gore and Associates has an employee-focused culture that helps foster a highly motivated workforce that innovates. The company has now 6,000 associates and an annual revenue of $1.5 billion.

Serving shareholders and employees as well as customers: Toyota (http://www.toyota.com/) is another interesting company that has created a culture of excellence in what is called lean manufacturing. Toyota emphasizes controlled processes, which are changed continuously involving the participants in these processes. The improvements in Toyota processes involve employees even at the lower levels of the enterprise echelon. This is important and definitely a service oriented enterprise culture.

A service oriented enterprise is an extended, virtual, real-time, and resilient enterprise. The essential characteristics of an extended enterprise are its involvement and ability to realize straight-through processing of a number of organizations to deliver goods and services to customers. Extended enterprise is about connectivity between various service providers and service requestors. Therefore, a service oriented enterprise achieves the delivery of the supply, or value, chain. As mentioned throughout this book, service orientation deals with loose coupling. An essential feature of loose coupling is the idea that services can be developed independently and then integrated with minimum or no dependency of the bindings between various platforms that support the services. Therefore, a service oriented enterprise facilitates the integration of loosely coupled services yet at the same time appears aggregated—as a functional whole. With aggregation, various applications, repositories, and even roles or organizations appear to be well integrated, providing an essential service. For instance, a production or development effort could involve many applications and different groups from potentially geographically distributed organizations. The applications need to be invoked in a particular sequence or process flow. The output of one application, such as the blueprint of a product component, needs to be the input of another application, such as an automated manufacturing plant. The data type exchanges between the various applications need to be consistent. Similarly, the different groups involved in the ultimate objective need to be part of the same production, testing, certification, and manufacturing calendar.

The term *virtual corporation* was coined by an executive at DEC named Jan Hopeland, who claimed that we are entering an age where we need to very rapidly respond to demands by creating organizations dynamically. The concept was popularized in *The Virtual Corporation* by William H. Davidow and Michael S. Malone. The idea was that as the 21st century approached, there will be demands on organizations to quickly and globally deliver customized products. In fact, there is even the vision that not only would the product be high quality and produced rapidly, but it would involve the customer in its design. Of course, information technologies are going to be needed to achieve a virtual organization. So the essence is to concentrate on the needs of the customer—the essence of the business—and then realize the greatest flexibility to achieve it. Everything else is secondary. So in its original conception, the notion of a virtual organization or virtual corporation was the idea of creating very flexible and dynamic organizations that can rapidly (or more appropriately, serve) satisfy the demands of a community (customers, trading partners, and even employees and shareholders). And there are methodologies, or step-by-step strategies, as well as tools and software to construct a virtual organization. Enterprises are becoming transparent and are actually exposing their inner processes: how they manufacture, deliver services, or realize governance. An organization that opens up its processes and is transparent inspires trust by its customers and trading partners alike. In fact, it also indicates confidence. Imagine a company sharing its processes for quality improvement with its competition.

How about real-time enterprises? They are related to the extended and virtual enterprise dimensions. Here is the notion of on-demand enterprises. Real-time means change can be responded to in real-time. It also means the organization can come together whenever needed. This is similar to virtual enterprises. The main difference is the scope of the projects. In general, real-time has shorter duration projects. A good example of this is a network of consultants that can come together whenever there is a need. In e-business it could be a network of organizations with specific roles that could come together to satisfy a particular request for a customer. E-marketplaces also can result in the creation of virtual enterprises once the trading partners discover each other. The e-marketplace portals for B2B trading between organizations provide many potential partnerships. These can be enacted once the partners agree on the pricing and the terms of the agreement in real-time.

Last, in the midst of the uncertainties we face in the 21st century, there is the resilient enterprise. A resilient enterprise has established policies, detection mechanisms, practices, and redundancies that enable it to recover from disruptions and recover service provisioning. Resilient enterprises focus on exception handling and recovery, not just the "happy path" of business processes. Resiliency is essential in service orientation: the enterprise does it best to plan for unexpected disruptions in its service offerings. If an earthquake disrupts a supplier, the enterprise has predetermined alternative supply channels. If a disaster hits an information center, the enterprise has built-in mirroring of data and applications and can recover immediately and be back online. In resilient enterprises, the protection and recovery processes have to be preplanned and put into effect and tested.

Service enterprises are dynamic: partners could change; market conditions could change; new technologies could emerge in real-time. The service enterprise should take change into consideration in all its endeavors: in its organizational infrastructure and in the service oriented technologies it uses to realize its business goals. For instance, the objective could be a financial transaction involving financial institutions, custodians, brokers, contractors, legal entities, and clearing. The particular selection of a financial institution that provides a product or a service or the selection of the service could be dynamic. It could depend on price, availability, or benefits. Thus, financial processes such as purchasing securities could involve different organizations depending on the parameters or requirements of the transaction. Interfaces could also change. For instance, if a particular eXtensible Markup Language (XML) vocabulary is used for the process, the vocabulary could undergo iterations and changes, such as various versions. Exchange choreographies could also change. The only constant is change. The agility required to adapt to these changes dynamically is part of the very nature of the service oriented enterprise.

7.3 Service Orientation by Example

> O Divine Master, grant that I may not so much seek to be consoled as to console; to be understood, as to understand; to be loved, as to love; for it is in giving that we receive, it is in pardoning that we are pardoned, and it is in dying that we are born to eternal life.
>
> **St. Francis of Assisi**

Service orientation is a state of mind. If organizations develop a culture of service, everyone benefits. Is this new? Haven't commercial organizations been promising and delivering services for centuries? Yes, the notion of service orientation is not new. In fact, most commercials emphasize this customer and service oriented attribute of the company that is promoting the product. Reality, though, is something else. It is one thing to express service orientation in brochures and commercials, but it is quite another to actually be a service oriented company.

Some trends and cultural changes, however, are coming together at an increasing pace to give birth to this new type of service oriented enterprise. The focus of this section is the attributes of service orientation as a corporate culture, or as a virtue, so to speak.

Enterprises are about people, not about finances or making the revenue forecasts at all cost. Doesn't this contradict and go against everything we have learned in a "go and get them" culture? It does, and it will. Many times executives try to cut corners to make the numbers look good. After the fiasco with companies such as Enron and WorldCom, it is interesting to note how Congress is trying to legislate ethics. The first requirement in any organization is that its leaders are committed to integrity and to becoming servant leaders.

The term *leader* here means both the business as well as IT. A servant approach and philosophy is essential for service oriented enterprises. Recently, a great deal of discussions have taken place on servant leadership. A number of key servant leader qualities are summarized in Table 7.1.[2]

When dealing with service orientation, the focus is often only on the technology; however, it is important to realize that it is about the people as well.

Servant leadership sets the tone and modus operandi of the enterprise. The servant leadership example will inspire the employees of the enterprise

Table 7.1 Qualities of a Servant Leader

Focuses on Serving	Servant leaders' primary focus is to serve, not to lead. Servant leaders do not try to impose their opinions or approaches on others. Instead, they attempt to serve needs, wants, and aspirations of the people they manage or serve. The pyramid is reversed. At the top are the people or organizations being served. The leader is at the bottom. As Robert Greenleaf stated, "It begins with the natural feeling that one wants to serve first. Then conscious choice brings one to aspire to lead. The difference manifests itself in the care taken by the servant to make sure people's highest priority needs are being served."[3]
Sharing Vision	Servant leaders share their vision with employees, customers, and other communities they are serving. Workers know what part they are playing in a big picture.
Decisioning with Involvement	Servant leaders try to involve their workers, partners, and customers in their day-to-day decision-making processes. The goal is to serve the various communities and not to impose one's approach or priorities on others.
Teamwork Approach	Servant leaders believe in and promote teamwork in which each member contributes and collaborates for a common goal.
Building Relationships and Communities	Servant leaders attempt to build communities and to prioritize relationship building. Servant leaders realize that if workers and partners like and enjoy each other, the productivity and quality of work will greatly improve. Servant leaders believe in and emphasize relationship building and relational leadership.
Mentoring and Development	Servant leaders are committed to mentoring their employees and focus on their professional development. Servant leaders are also keen to making sure partners and customers are also mentored and trained in their products they offer—to help them realize the best benefits on the servant leader's offerings.
Encouragement Focused	Servant leaders are positive leaders. They constantly appreciate and encourage their employees as well as other communities that they serve. Credit is always given when credit is due—with strong emphasis on building up.

Table 7.1 Qualities of a Servant Leader (Continued)

Balanced Perspective	Servant leaders realize work is just a means to produce income, not an end in itself. Servant leaders believe in and promote a balanced perspective on life and priorities.
Practical and Rational	Servant leaders prefer to focus on exceptions and needs versus legalism. They take a practical approach when it comes to providing the right resources for their employees and communities they serve so that each can best carry out their responsibilities. Servant leaders are rational with reasonable expectations and priorities.

and help them learn and practice the same qualities within their own groups. Servant leadership also helps promote sustainable business practices when dealing with customers or partners. Ideally the servant leader's passion will be contagious and encourage other organizations to emulate a similar leadership culture.

7.4 Business Performance Measurement[4]

> To be effective in a global economy with rapidly shifting market conditions and quick and nimble competitors, organizations have to be able to adapt constantly their priorities and have to put their resources where they can create most value for customers and shareholders.
>
> **Juergen H. Daum**

There are two interrelated BPM acronyms. One designates the automation and digitization of processes—that is, business process management. The other expands on the performance of business process management—that is, business performance management. Business process management systems typically include business process activity monitoring and performance capabilities. Business performance management can in addition include monitoring and analysis of applications from a variety of sources: business processes, enterprise resource planning applications, customer relationship management systems, or any commercial as well as home-grown applications.

A number of mechanisms come into play when analyzing or monitoring the performance of processes. But first this notion of performance of processes needs to be explained further. In fact, although the overall performance of a process is critical, it is only one piece of the performance management puzzle. Here a deeper analysis is provided as to what is being measured; then the how and when dimensions of performance measurement will be explained in greater detail.

The concept of the *management cockpit*[5] is used to explain what is going on with performance management The intention is to use the cockpit as a concept and example and to drive a critical point: Managers at all levels need to continuously monitor, control, measure, understand, and analyze their processes. In a cockpit are dials, which measure the performance indicators. For aggregate views or measurements, graphs and charts are used. Typically, the cockpit should be customized and the decision made as to what are the measures or performance indicators and charts or graphs needing to be observed.

The management cockpit model takes this to its logical conclusion and allows real value to be extracted from the enterprise's process data. The managers are in the driver's seat and can technically drill down and analyze the data from a variety of sources. The drilling down allows managers to trace from higher-level abstractions down to lower-level operations and even to individual operators. For instance, there can be a measure of the current sales booking. This could be a number of the current bookings for the quarter. Then from this measurement you can drill down to bookings per region: East Coast, West Coast, Midwest, and South. You can further drill down to the state level and then to individual counties and then to the accounts of the current process status involving sales executives for the county. The ability to have processes and business rules connected to finance applications via service calls enables the managers to implement controls over the critical processes.

In addition to the visual and graphical representation of the performance indicator, agents can be associated with measures or critical limits, and processes can be proactively activated when certain values fall below specification limits (Figure 7.2). For example, a rule might be defined stating that an e-mail should be sent to the sales manager and the sales vice president if within two weeks of closing the quarter and the quota of a sales person is less than 50 percent of the allotted bookings. In other words, the management cockpit provides both a visual representation of the enterprise's performance and also a portal where the exception or control processes that need to be fired based on business rules are specified.

This section focuses on what is being measured and monitored by managers at all levels within the enterprise. Using proven methodologies such as balanced scorecard, service oriented enterprises can view their service organizations through a number of different and complementary perspectives. Monitoring and managing business processes are first discussed. Then the section delves into two types of analysis: one based on

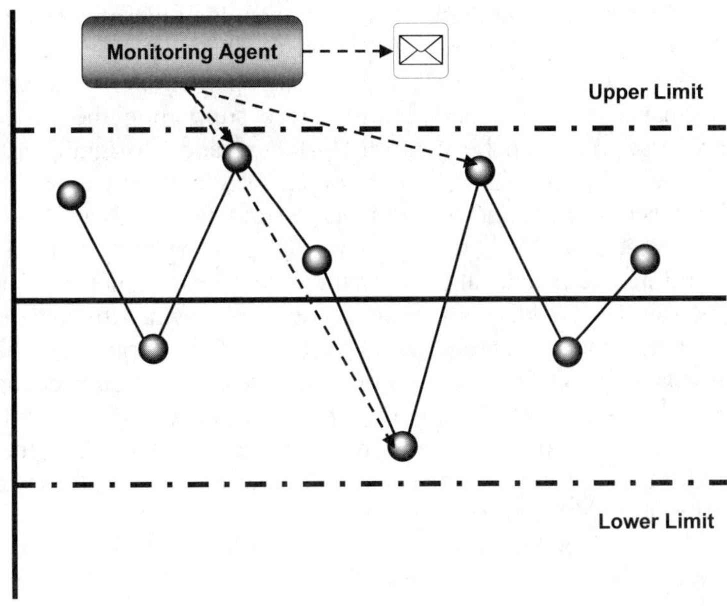

Figure 7.2 Monitoring specification limits

historic data and the other involving real-time business monitoring of business events.

7.4.1 Monitoring Business Processes

Chapter 6 showed how management standards and system management tools can be used to monitor, measure, control, and manage services. System management tends to deal with lower-level system-related performance monitoring of various resources deployed over the service oriented enterprise's networks. This is of course important. However, performance monitoring and control should also include the higher-level business measures. A business is the aggregation of its procedures and policies. Using a BPM platform to automate enterprise procedures, all process events, such as creating a new process instance, assigning a task to a participant, completing a task, completing a process, violating a service level agreement, waiting for a pending or suspended activity, receiving a service call from a partner, and just about every single action associated with processes could be audit trailed. This provides real-time auditing and process management capabilities. Depending on the process owner—business or IT—the managers could graphically monitor real-time data of the processes they care about.

With BPM activity monitoring, managers examine the status of business processes. Real-time access can be gained to all the processes, specific process instances, human participants, trading partner performance, and the performance of the overall infrastructure supporting the processes. These processes also can be controlled—for instance, assigning tasks of participants who are not performing to others. Key performance indicators (KPIs) can be connected, and performance-related measures can be defined for the processes. Business rules can be defined that will automatically monitor and act when critical performance measures are not on par with business goals. The cockpit for digitized processes provides the main mechanism for managing the enterprise, allowing to drill deeper from higher-level measures to details of executing processes, introducing changes if necessary. This is similar to monitoring the performance of any automated machinery, from automated manufacturing plants or monitoring feeds in automated transit systems: with real-time monitoring of stations, switches, rail cars, bridges, and tunnels.

The advantage of business activity monitoring by a BPM system is that the data presented and analyzed is real-time. Figure 7.3 illustrates various types of charts and graphs that can be used to monitor the

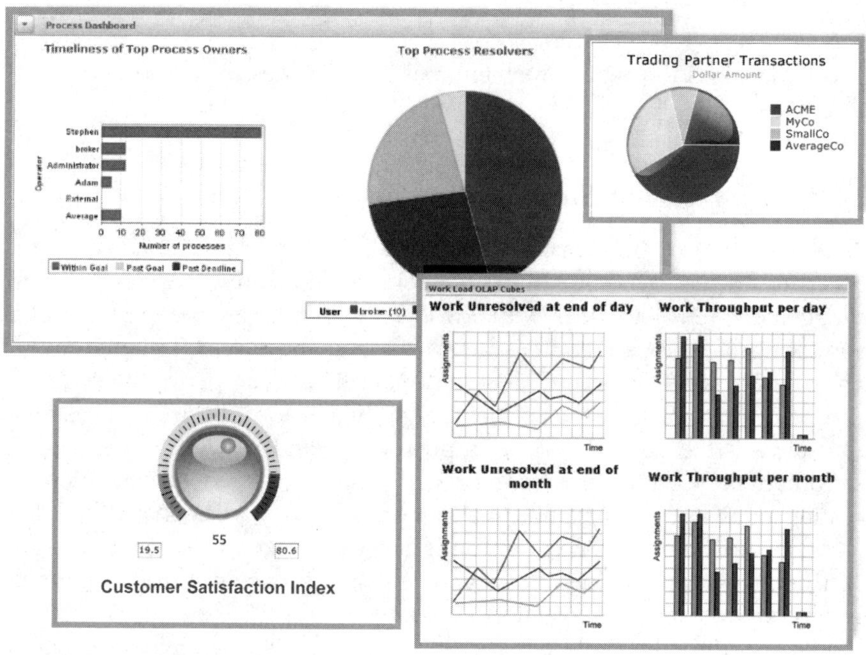

Figure 7.3 Business performance monitoring dashboard

processes. Graphical performance charts in a performance management portal could be live: You can drill down to executing processes and take action on the spot. Business rules also can be defined to handle any type of performance deficiency.

Reports can be monitored and run on the events of operational processes. Examples here include the start of a process, the assignment of a task, the reassignment of tasks, completion of tasks, termination or completion of processes, and other types of events that change the state of processes. The business stakeholder can drill down any of these events through business process activity monitoring (BPAM) interfaces and can take the appropriate actions. The stakeholder can also run reports to gain a better graphical understanding of the process performance trends. The real-time monitoring hand can enable the managers as well as the BPM system to take remediation or corrective actions in real-time, as they happen.

For a much deeper analysis of trends, business process performance uses data warehouses, discussed in the next section. Unlike the business process activity monitoring that operates primarily on the source process event data, with data warehousing the process data goes through a transformation and then through subsequent analysis using business intelligence tools.

7.4.2 Business Intelligence

> Those who cannot remember the past are condemned to repeat it.
>
> **George Santayana**

> Most companies in most industries have excellent reasons to pursue strategies based on analytics. Virtually all the organizations we identified as aggressive analytics competitors are clear leaders in their fields, and they attribute much of their success to the masterful exploitation of data.
>
> **Thomas Devenport**

As illustrated in Figure 7.4, performance focused enterprises create a common repository called the data warehouse that collects data from various applications, including online transaction processing (OLTP) applications, enterprise resource planning (ERP) applications, and increasingly BPM applications.

A business intelligence tool can help to drill down and analyze the data. It helps in understanding (i.e, the why) the information. Queries can be run on your data warehouse database. The results of the queries can be displayed in various visual or graphical formats. In addition to the back-end enterprise applications, process data—generated from the BPM system—can also be fed to the enterprise performance management (EPM) tool. The data warehouse

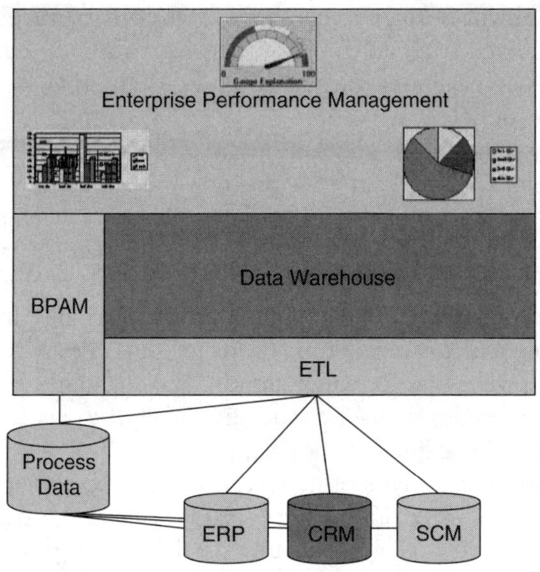

Figure 7.4 Enterprise performance management data sources

can be analyzed through online analytical processing (OLAP). The OLAP approach provides a higher-level analytical interface to the data, which is easier to be manipulated by business users—easier than, for instance, ad hoc Structure Query Language (SQL) querying.

OLAP techniques can extract and analyze data through a number of dimensions and measures, providing a multidimensional analysis of the data. The dimensions are used to categorize the data. The measures then provide measurements over the dimensions. For example, in a BPM application process type and enterprise department could be defined as dimensions. Then process completion time can be defined as a measure. Once the data is gathered along these dimensions for the specific measures, it can be displayed in an analysis tool such as an Excel spreadsheet. A business user can then slice and dice the data and can use alternative graphics to understand the significance of the measures along the dimensions. For instance, an OLAP tool can analyze process data, where the process data gathers information from a variety of sources (e.g., ERPs, OLTPs). Figure 7.5 illustrates process completion cycle times and compares performance of processes for credit card and loan processing. It is possible to extract the OLAP data into a spreadsheet and to conduct the pivot table analysis within the familiar Excel spreadsheet. Of course ad hoc queries can be conducted using various querying tools—or if you are really adventurous, using SQL queries directly.

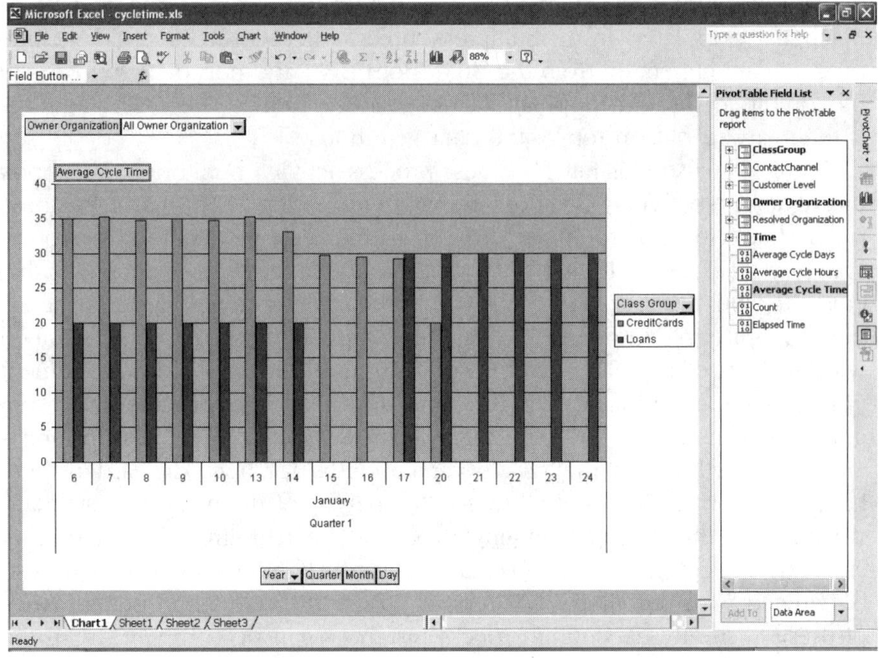

Figure 7.5 An OLAP cube for process completion cycle times

In going from the data sources (e.g., OLTP, ERP) to the data warehouse, typically there is some extraction and transformation, which is achieved through an extraction, transformation, and loading (ETL) tool. Data is extracted from the sources. The extraction starts with querying to extract data from the sources. Then the data is transformed into a common schema and is loaded into the data warehouse. Why the transformation? Transformation and mapping onto the common schema is essential when dealing with multiple applications. For example, the same customer information (e.g., customer ID, customer location, customer address) could have different representations. One application might spell out the state of the customer (e.g., Massachusetts), and another might just use an abbreviation in uppercase letters (e.g., MA), and yet a third application might use a lowercase abbreviation (e.g., ma). The goal of the transformation is to map the data into a common data warehouse that will then be used for analysis. The data can also be combined from various sources into the data warehouse data tables. Furthermore, transformation is often followed by cleansing the transformed and normalized data. Cleansing is needed to eliminate duplicates.

Figure 7.4 illustrates a performance management portal, with various sources feeding the data warehouse: ERP, customer relationship management

(CRM), and supply chain management (SCM). So the warehouse contains a schema populated from multiple sources. These sources could include process data generated from the BPM. Both BPM and non-BPM sources can be combined through populating a common schema. The online analysis is then carried out on top of the data warehouse.

Figure 7.4 also illustrates business process activity monitoring. This book distinguishes between business activity monitoring (BAM) and business process activity monitoring in that the former can monitor events from a variety of sources, including BPM, whereas the latter focuses on events that emanate from the state transitions within the BPM system. In a performance portal monitoring and control of real-time process data could be combined with analysis of the data warehouse. The same performance management portal can view historic trends charts and real-time process execution graphs. For instance, an OLAP chart will show how many process instances are completed within the past several months for a credit card dispute handling process. This will allow for an analysis of the mean and standard deviation of the dispute handling process. The real-time performance of currently executing process instances that are handling disputes can also be viewed with real-time BAM reports. Then, the status and performance of these currently executing process instances can be compared with the historic trends of credit cart disputes executions from the OLAP charts. The side-by-side comparison of historic and real-time data enables one to be proactive in improving the overall performance of applications.

7.4.3 Business Activity Monitoring

> There's a global cloud of business events flowing through the IT layers of any enterprise. These events flow from all four corners of a distributed event-driven enterprise, as well as from outside partnering enterprises.
>
> **David Luckham**

A BPM system provides out-of-the-box business activity monitoring for the events that happen through the enactment or activation of processes. The following are examples of events in a procurement process:

Start the process (e.g., to procure a computer for John)
Approve the procurement request (e.g., by John's manager)
Submit the order to approved vendor
Deliver merchandise (e.g., John's computer)
Complete and close the request

A more general BAM approach is to correlate events from any source—not just processes—and to serve as the main mechanism for event

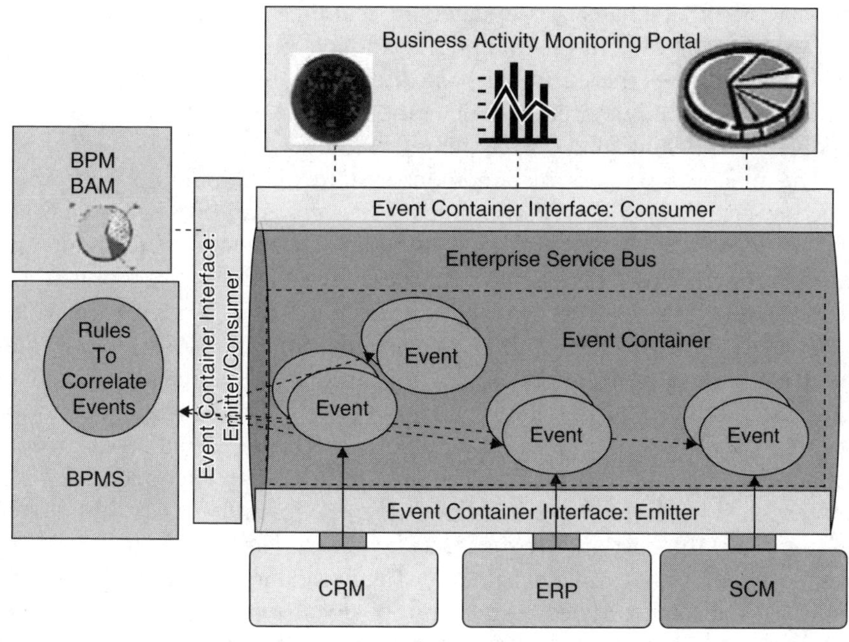

Figure 7.6 BAM architecture

monitoring. The monitoring of the events could take several forms: speedometers (or dials), line graphics, pie charts, or just tables. Figure 7.6 illustrates a business activity monitoring architecture. There are two types of actors for events. Event producers, or emitters, generate the events. Event consumers read and process the events. In the figure the events are managed by the event container, within the ESB. So here the assumption is made that the event management is done within the ESB. There are other viable options, such as handling the event management within a BAM server component or the business process management system, separate from an ESB. In any case, the event container processes the events in their normalized formats. It provides and supports the consumer, emitter, and the administrative management of event interfaces.

Depending on a particular implementation of the event container, events will have attributes that will describe the time, application, reason, and priority of the event. Figure 7.6 illustrates back-end applications such as CRM, SCM, or ERP systems emitting events. So these applications produce events. As indicated earlier, the business process management system also produces events. At the top of the diagram is the BAM portal. The processing of these events can be in real-time. For example, if a dial is measuring some aspect connected to event measurements, when new events are generated the dial or other charts are updated in real-time. Most important, event actions often involve firing exception handling processes. For instance, if the event indicates the customer has canceled an order, an exception handling process could be fired to contact the customer, report on the customer complaint, and strategize on retaining the sales.

The business process management system plays multiple roles. BPM processes can produce events so the BPM system is an event emitter. Some of the events of a BPM include assigning a task to a participant and receiving a request that starts a process. BPM suites also contain the business rule engine. The correlation of the event can be performed within the BPM system. This means the BPM system is an event consumer. Finally, the BPM system typically has its own management portal that provides real-time monitoring capabilities primarily for its own process application events. The BPM system can potentially correlate events from various sources.[6] For example, it might be desired to fire off an exception handling process if (1) the shipment has been delayed for more than the allotted 48 hours; (2) the customer request has become critical; or (3) the customer has more than two complaints already. The correlation of these three events and customer context is combined in a business rule. Figure 7.6 illustrates both a BPM system-specific BAM portal and a BAM portal that is external to the BPM system.

7.4.4 Balanced Scorecard

So far the emphasis and discussion on performance monitoring, and especially BAM, has been primarily technical, concerned with the components of the technology platform. This section is about *business* performance management. The various measurements need to be tied to business goals. It is necessary to have a management discipline to measure and tie the various performance management measures to indicators that reflect current as well as future sustained performance objectives. This is where the balanced scorecard methodology comes in. Balanced scorecards can be used in conjunction with business activity monitoring or business intelligence analysis.

The balanced scorecard first appeared as a paper in the *Harvard Business Review* (1992) by Robert Kaplan and David Norton. The title of the paper was "The Balanced Scorecard—Measures that Drive Performance." The balanced scorecard approach identifies four areas for organizational performance monitoring and measurements:

- Financial: This deals with the financial objectives and measures of the organization. These financial objectives could have several aspects. The most obvious is revenue growth. This growth in revenue can have objectives in gaining market share, increases in number of customers, increase in sales revenue, and new market products or strategies. Another aspect of the financial is management of the budgets and cost reduction in the various departments of the organization: product development, marketing, operations, and sales.

- Customer: Enterprise products and services target specific market sectors or customer types. Several measures help the success of the enterprise in this area. The customer is identified by the percentage of market sector by specific products. But more importantly, customer-related goals and measures deal with customer satisfaction and retention. The number of customer complaints (or compliments) is one objective measure that could be used to assess customer satisfaction. The number of new customers is another measure in this area. Others include the number of inquiries and the ratio of closed sales to inquiries.
- Internal business processes: These processes are used to support the business goals. All business processes are included here, reflecting the organizational structure of the enterprise. The more obvious units here include product development, service delivery, customer call center front-office processes, logistical back-office processes, and delivery processes. Internal business processes support all the operations of the business.
- Learning and growth of employees: Morale and success of employees with fair reward systems have a direct bearing on the overall performance of the organization. Happy and satisfied employees deliver better and superior products and services. In addition to employee satisfaction and productivity, Kaplan and Norton also identify IT motivation and alignment. Here also one could define several measurable indicators such as employee turnover.

The key contribution of the balanced scorecard is that it is a holistic and balanced approach to measuring the overall performance of the enterprise compared to traditional measures such as revenue, share value, or earning per share. More importantly, the balanced scorecard with its focus on customers and employees as well as shareholders provides very much a service oriented approach to measuring performance. The enterprise can view itself as a service oriented enterprise attempting to serve various communities through measurable results (Figure 7.7).

What makes balanced scorecards especially relevant to service oriented enterprises is the holistic balance involving various communities served by the service oriented enterprise. More specifically:

- The financial perspective focuses on serving the shareholders primarily but also the employees of the enterprise. Financial perspective also has implications for the partners, government, and community.

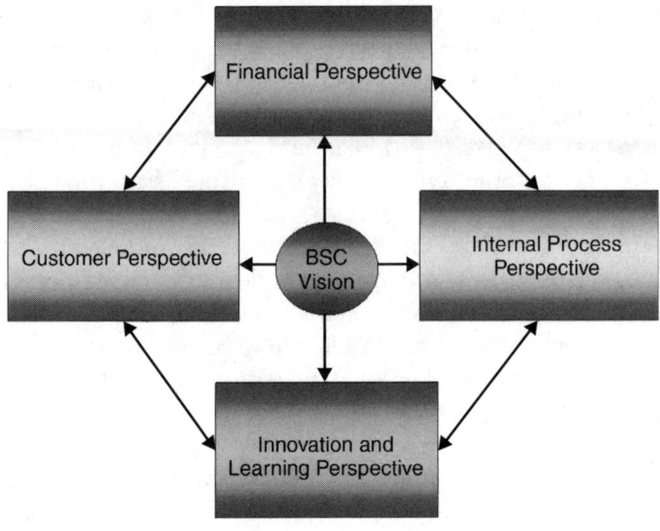

Figure 7.7 The balanced scorecard

- The customer perspective is obvious and focuses on the customer. But happy customers will have a positive influence on the financial measures (i.e., shareholders) as well as the employees.
- The learning and innovation perspective focuses primarily on the employees but also has implications for the other communities such as the customers and the partners.
- The internal processes are the least obvious but perhaps the most important. As business flows and rules are improved and automated, all the various constituents are served. More specifically through business process automation, enterprises will spend less effort and money operationally. Also through BPM, suppliers and providers will both be served better, in the straight-through processing supply and value chains. Automation in human resources and other IT operations will improve employee productivity. Business processes and rules also provide opportunities for innovation, allowing invention of new processes and business rules for operational or production innovation.

In the balanced scorecard, and for each perspective, there will be:

- Objectives: What is being improved
- Measure goals: The quantitative performance indicator targeted for improvement. The is the actual value of the measure, for instance.
- Processes: These are the processes that will either be automated or improved to achieve the objectives and their measurable target values.

Table 7.2 Balanced Scorecard Perspectives

Perspective	*Objective*	*Measure Goal*	*Process*
Financial	Increase revenue	20 percent	New market initiative
	Decrease cost	10 percent	Automate customer relationship process management
Customer	Increase customer satisfaction	25 percent decrease in customer complaints	Streamline complaint processing rules and processes
Internal Process Perspective	Accelerate employee Promotions	Increase employee retention by 10 percent	Automate performance management processes
Innovation and Learning Perspective	Train employees on latest technologies for enablement	Achieve 70 percent certification on product by customer support	Implement process to automate delivery of e-learning courses

Table 7.2 contains some examples of processes that could either be enacted or improved in each of the perspectives.

The fourth column of Table 7.2 indicates the processes that are automated for each perspective objective. Many other processes might be supporting each of the objectives. To achieve the measurable results, there needs to be a mechanism where continuous improvements can be evaluated objectively. The next sections expand on two alternative yet complementary quantitative mechanisms for improving performance: activity-based costing and Six Sigma.

7.4.5 Activity-Based Costing

One technique increasingly being used in conjunction with BPM and the balanced scorecard methodology is activity-based costing (ABC). ABC offers a substantially different and process-oriented approach to finance. In traditional financial approaches, organizations focus on budgets for each division and unit; then being within budget is always rewarded. There are also corporate financial objectives and measures. For instance, an enterprise might target a 25 percent growth in revenue. The rewards of employees are then based on achieving the corporate goals. These traditional approaches are still very much used in most organizations.

ABC views the organization as an aggregation of processes, each of which consists of activities. These activities have dependencies and are performed by units, individuals, or systems—including services invoked locally or remotely. ABC attempts to determine the cost of these activities. For instance, if the activity is performed by a person, it estimates the person hours spent on the activities. More importantly, it ties the activity to the value it provides the customer. This is challenging. It means the enterprise, and especially the leadership, needs to carefully analyze its processes and activities of these processes to potentially link each one of them to key performance values for customers.

Consider Figure 7.8, which shows the as-is process for purchase orders. Now each of the activities represented by a rectangle will potentially have the following:

- Direct costs: These are the costs of the raw materials processed at the step to carry the task. Typically in a white-collar office environment these are basic office material costs such as paper. But there might also be costs of communications, such as for teleconferencing.
- Indirect costs: These are the overhead costs. Typically, in a white-collar office environment there are costs associated per resource or employee for IT, rent, and utilities.
- Resource costs: These are typically the largest and most considerable of the costs in the context of a process. Depending on the type of tasks being performed, a resource cost will be associated with the task. For example, if an employee spends four hours searching and the cost of the employee is $100 per hour, the cost of the task is $400.

Figure 7.8 is a rather simple as-is process that nevertheless illustrates several opportunities for improvement. Before illustrating some of these, remember that this purchase order improvement is a drilled-down process improvement strategy for a key performance indicator at the balanced scorecard. The performance indicator is purchase order process cost and overall cost reduction for the financial perspective. Some opportunities to reduce the cost of this simple process include the following:

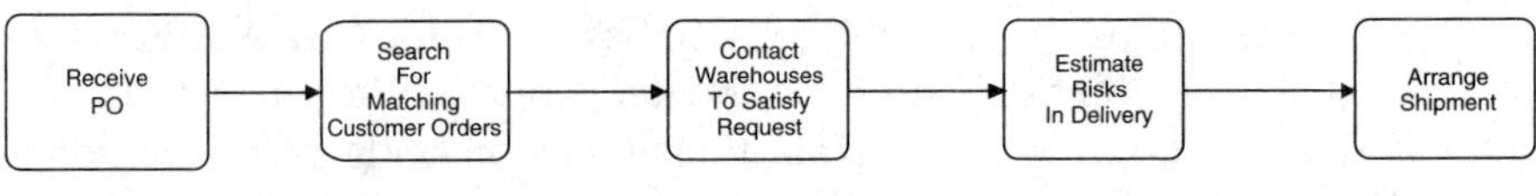

Figure 7.8 A PO process "as is"

- Reduce resource cost: The most obvious approach here is to procure with less costly resources. Outsourcing is ideal for situations where there are well-defined tasks that could easily be outsourced to resources offshore. Outsourcing has been used for just about any imaginable task. Conducting manual searches while using disparate systems, each with its own interface, is definitely a candidate for outsourcing, assuming the potential communication and security risks are mitigated. It is important to see the role of the service oriented infrastructure in improving processing. For instance, the required tasks within the context of a process could be communicated instantaneously via a Web services invocation to the outsourced organization. The organization can in turn asynchronously reply to the requestor with details of the completion time. In other words, a virtual enterprise could be created between task requestor (procurement tasks in this example) and provider while using the underlying service oriented communication and messaging infrastructure. The ideal approach is to involve internal requestor processes and service provider processes and to be able to check the status and to estimate potential risks at any point in the overall virtual process involving multiple participating enterprises.
- Policy and procedure automation: The other possibility is to reduce the amount of human involvement and to streamline the process. For example, a customer-support task, including processing an order, might involve human agents spending considerable time switching between various green screens to process the customer request. There are many opportunities to improve this, including the following:
  - Include microflows that involve integration with the underlying enterprise applications that need to be interfaced individually by the agent. This means the agent potentially interfaces with one aggregated screen the orchestration of several screens—the interface of the microflow. For instance, the warehouse search and arranging the shipment are examples of tasks that could be, at least partially, automated.
  - Associate business rules to the tasks: There are so many opportunities where business rules can be incorporated to handle the complex decisioning. For example, assessing the risk of the shipment date. In other words, whether the agent is dealing with a purchase order dispute or is attempting to make a decision as to when and how to process the request, the business rules assist the agent in decisioning. The decisioning often captured in policy manuals is digitized. This saves an enormous amount of time and effort not only for the agent but also for subsequent exceptions or error processes, as human tasks tend to be error prone.

Once these cost reductions are taken into consideration, the next phase is to design and to deploy to-be processes. The to-be process introduces cost reduction improvements over the as-is process. Improvements can be made continuously, with each iteration introducing additional optimizations or cost reductions.

7.4.6 Six Sigma

The previous sections provided an overview of the balanced scorecard management approach as well as activity-based costing. The balanced scorecard will identify measurable goals and objectives in the various perspectives. For example, a performance objective could improve customer satisfaction by 20 percent. The customer satisfaction index depends on quality of the products as well as customer service. The goals have to be translated to specific processes that need to be continuously monitored for continuous improvement. Another methodology often used in process improvement is Six Sigma.

Six Sigma has become the leading methodology by which companies manage and improve their business processes. It is borne out of work done by the Motorola Government Electronics Group in the 1980s to apply statistical methods and models to analyze process defects and subsequently to improve and to control the process. Six Sigma is a rigorous approach to identifying key process characteristics as defined by the customer, to discovering the process input or inputs that most influence that characteristic, and to implementing process improvements designed to deliver the process characteristic to the customer. Six Sigma is a framework that prescribes tasks, tools, and analytic methods to be used in different phases of the overall process improvement life cycle. One of the fundamental approaches and philosophies in Six Sigma is continuous improvement until the desired quality goals are achieved. The focus in Six Sigma is on reducing the *variations* in process performance. Quality is measured in terms of having only 3.4 defects per million opportunities: The opportunity is the measurement pertaining to a process. For example, response time to a customer request is an opportunity and so is the time it takes to produce a requirement document. In manufacturing measurements, it could be weights or sizes of parts needed for a product.

As Chapter 5 demonstrated, within an organization are three types of processes: (1) all enterprise processes and policies, documented or ad hoc; (2) modeled processes and policies; and (3) automated (executing) process and policies (i.e., business rules). The current trend is to move from ad hoc to modeling and hopefully executing processes. This provides tremendous benefit for businesses. BPM systems empower Six Sigma and help the desired sigma level to be realized more quickly if the processes are automated. Therefore, the Six Sigma methodology for enterprise performance

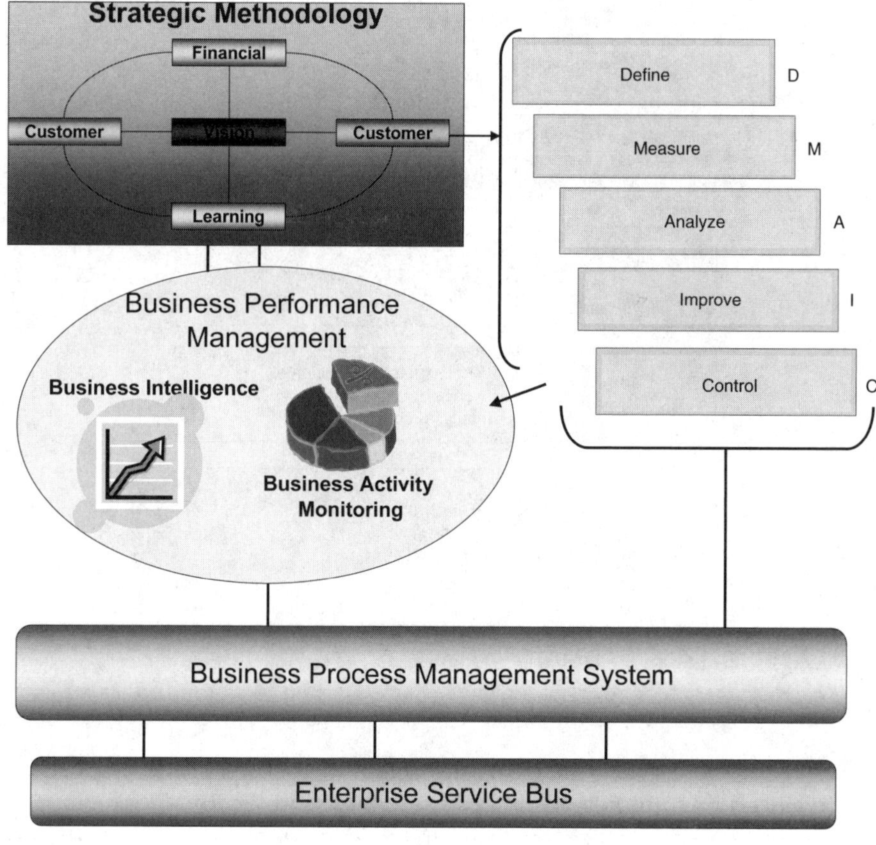

Figure 7.9 Balanced scorecard and Six Sigma

improvement gets supported with the BPM system layer, which in turn uses and depends on the SOA IT architecture.

Figure 7.9 illustrates the relationships among performance monitoring, the balanced scorecard, and Six Sigma. The performance indicators, identified for balanced scorecard perspectives, are evaluated from BPM process data. For example, assume there is a financial goal to improve invoice payment and to attempt to achieve payments within 30 days of submitting an invoice. This can be associated with a critical to quality objective in a Six Sigma project. So a balanced scorecard goal is mapped onto a Six Sigma critical to quality improvement project. The Six Sigma project will then use invoicing processes executed in the BPM and ESB and will continuously measure and improve to achieve the critical to quality goals. An underlying assumption here is that the processes managed and monitored or the

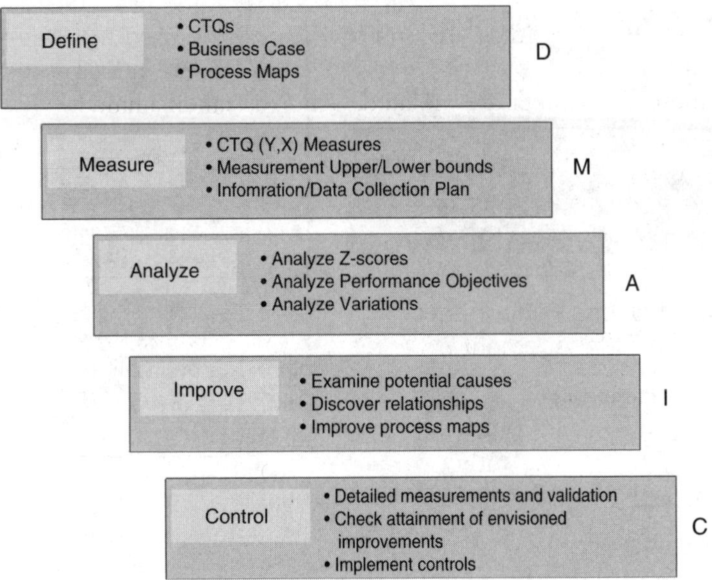

Figure 7.10 The steps in DMAIC

performance indicators targeted by Six Sigma improvement are associated with digitized and automated processes deployed in the BPM system.

Six Sigma performance projects are usually deployed with Define–Measure–Analyze–Improve–Control (DMAIC) methodology. Figure 7.10 illustrates the major phases in DMAIC. For each of the phases and steps in the DMAIC process, the underlying BPM system can be used to realize improvements in a Six Sigma project. BPM systems support procedural flow logic, declarative business rules (e.g., decision rules, constraints, expressions) and integration (e.g., ESB service integration) with back-end as well as trading partners. Furthermore, either through accessing the event repository of the process activities or through exporting to a statistical tool, the BPM system process data can be used readily to be measured and analyzed.[7]

- Define: In the define phase, critical to quality business objectives must be defined. Typically these are defined in terms of big Y's, which can depend on X's that in turn depend on small y's and x's. So expressions can be used to capture $y = f(x_1, x_2, \ldots, x_n)$ dependencies, where the y's and x's are BPM properties from the information model of the BPM system.
- Measure: The upper and lower performance specification limits are constraints on the properties of processes. These constraints can be

expressed through predicate conditions on the properties as declarative business rules. Constraint rules can be used to define upper- or lower-limit constraints. This means in an executing process when these constraints are violated, action is taken immediately. This is the power of capturing business rules in the BPM system and executing process control in real-time.

- Analyze: In the analyze phase, the target Sigma score is set and potential sources of variance are identified. The analyze phase is principally concerned with establishing both the baseline and future state performance standards. This phase investigates the sources of the greatest process variations. The analysis might discover x's that are causing the variances. These could potentially be used to implement on-the-fly activation of business process artifacts (e.g., processes, rules), depending on the critical x values.
- Improve: The measure and analyze phases are concerned with finding problems. In the improve phase, solutions are identified. Investigation, experimentation, and piloting of new solutions all fall into this phase. The starting point of the improve phase is the list of vital x's generated in the analysis phase. Operating limits are placed on the x's or input variables so that the y stays within specification. It is in this phase where the agility and flexibility features of BPM systems become apparent. BPM systems allow for quick modification of processes and the ability to set rules and reminders on processes without impacting the process flow dramatically. Because these types of improvements are quick and simple in the BPM system, they can drive huge process improvements.
- Control: The control phase is designed to implement the necessary rigor and instrumentation to ensure that the process maintains performance standards over time and mitigates the risk of process degradation. The control phase tries to keep the x's within tolerance by using appropriate controls, such as managing the risks or attempting to avoid mistakes. In this phase, plans must also be established to sustain the control of improved processes. One of the big advantages of business process management suites is the ability to actively monitor processes and the critical to quality values, sensing events as they occur and quickly responding to the events automatically. The monitoring and the events will involve expressions on properties of processes and business rules that capture the control limits. BPM systems can also use agent technologies to monitor and to control either individual process instances or aggregate values across instances of a process. The combination of process automation, business rules for the control logic and expressions, and agent technologies imply that BPM systems can dynamically and continuously control the potential risks and errors that could lead to out-of-control processes.

Process data is organized, sorted, and prepared for running through a separate Six Sigma analytical tool like Minitab. The BPM system's ability to directly export data is a tremendous enabler to support this type of work. The user can export process data from BPM to Excel and Minitab. Six Sigma Black Belts can then conduct various hypothesis testing and analysis on the exported data. Changes to processes or business rules can then be easily and immediately propagated to the live production processes, either by the business owners via business-user-friendly rule forms, or by process architects in the IT organization. Note that the BPM user (e.g., a process architect) and the Six Sigma practitioner (e.g., a Black Belt) are often the same person, which is ideal.

7.5 Solution Frameworks

Increasingly, applications are being built on top of BPM platforms. As mentioned earlier, these platforms use, elevate, and abstract the underlying service oriented architecture components such as ESBs. The idea of service composition and construction of new aggregate or composite applications is very appealing. As an example, consider independent agencies for rental car, hotel reservation, and airline reservation (Figure 7.11). Each of these could be offered by completely independent travel service companies. A fourth company can then combine these services to create yet another aggregate or composite service to carry out all the reservations for the customer. So through

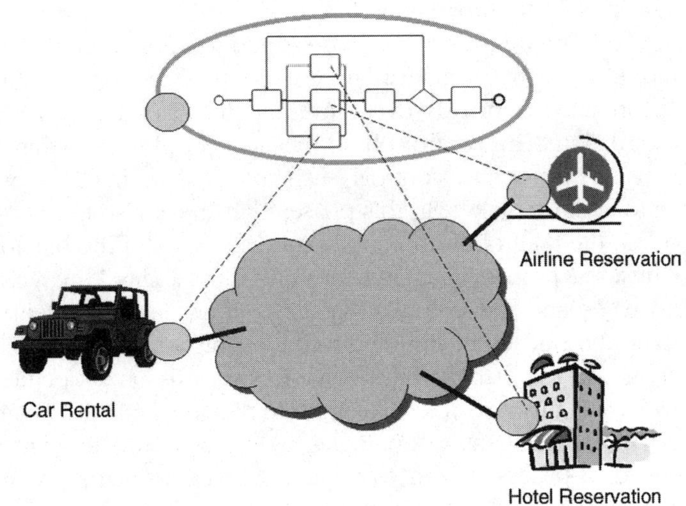

Figure 7.11 Composition of services

either a Web form or speaking to an operator, customers can provide their requirements (e.g., date, cost, type of car, type of room, flight options). This spawns a process that in turn invokes other services.

This option is always available to use existing services and to orchestrate them in processes. This results in composite business applications. Composite applications involve business flows and the business rules that drive the flows. This combined service oriented business application can then be used to generate service interfaces and deployed as a service. So services are combined, and the orchestration is published as a service. The service oriented business application therefore provides the following:

- Support of information model for the business application: For example, the reservation will contain the information model for the customer context and the specific reservation information.
- The integration and orchestration of the service invocations: The business application will integrate with the service providers involved in the solution framework. It will compose these in processes that will also involve human participants.

The overall solution, including service integrations but also human workflow and business rules with underlying information models can be packaged as a reusable framework. The intention here is to capture the best practices in a horizontal or vertical domain and to make these available as a framework to extend or to customize for a specific solution. This is illustrated in Figure 7.12. Some examples are as follows:

- Compliance solution framework
- Customer service solution framework
- Banking solution framework
- Healthcare solution framework
- Telecommunication solution framework
- Insurance solution framework
- Pharma solution framework

Compliance solution framework: Earlier we alluded to business and IT governance and compliance to Sarbanes–Oxley. One of the most difficult and costliest projects both within finance and IT is regulatory compliance. Compliance can get quite costly: In 2005 on average the Sarbanes–Oxley audit fees of S&P 500 companies was about $4.8 million. A company with a revenue of $2.5 billion or above will spend more than 25,000 person hours

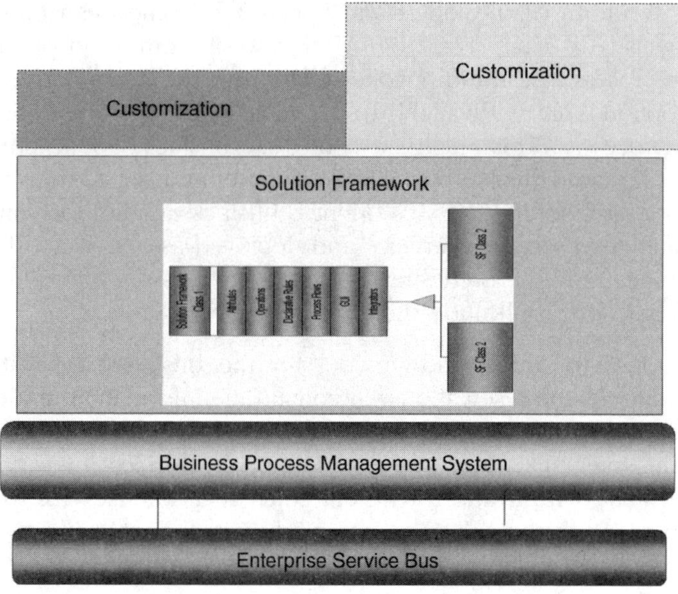

Figure 7.12 Solution framework

on Sarbanes–Oxley Section 404. Increasingly the introduction of BPM with underlying service oriented connectivity is seen as an ideal solution to automate the policies and processes of the Sarbanes–Oxley Act and compliance standards. Companies now are investing in BPM suites that can accommodate the all-important compliance rules imposed from without as well as the day-to-day operational processes. Through BPM suites, all the controls, as well as procedural flows of compliance, are kept under the close scrutiny of ongoing activity monitoring. And because the processes and business rules are separate from the application code, compliance frameworks through BPM suites can help roll out rule and process changes without altering application code anywhere. Compliance solutions based on BPM suites also leverage the EAI capabilities supported by the ESB of SOA infrastructures. For example, connectivity to underlying enterprise content management systems as well as financial and human resource systems are quite important in compliance applications.

Here are several examples of types of processes and policies that could be completely automated through the BPM suite.

Control and test management: Examples include risk assessment management, test automation, and COSO and COBIT standardized controls.

Exception management: Companies spend enormous amounts of time and effort on handling exceptions, especially and increasingly for compliance. Examples include mitigating controls; remediation workflow approval; real-time escalation, where the escalations will be handled by business rules that could be easily changed; and root-cause analysis.

Executive monitoring: Here the power and benefits of the business activity monitoring offered within the BPM suite are brought in. Examples include change tracking, change request workflow, approval routing, systems integration, audit facilitation, metrics and reporting, change approval history reports, and alerts.

In fact, each of these categories could have more specialized solution frameworks. For instance, there can be different solution frameworks for wholesale and retail banking. They will be sharing information models, processes, and rules for banking in general but then will further specialize for retail and wholesale.

Solution frameworks have another fringe benefit: They bring business and IT even closer together. As has been mentioned several times, BPM is the platform that aligns business and IT. What better alignment than alignment around solutions than just BPM platforms. More specifically, business and IT can align themselves around BPM system solution frameworks that have inherent business object models and the associated processes, business rules, usage models, and integration necessary to achieve concrete solutions. The solution framework contains not only the information models and service integration but also human task assignment and business rules. For the reservation example, human tasks include the tasks assigned to the agent for taking the reservations and approval tasks to complete the reservations. Examples of business rules include the service level agreement for responses from the various rental or reservation services, the decisioning logic to decide or to reject the aggregate reservations, and the expressions calculating potential discounts applied to customer categories.

The solution framework includes the appropriate information models and initial processes and business rules but also has pre-integrated services aggregated to provide value to the customer. BPM system solution frameworks attempt to let you have your cake and eat it too. They combine nontrivial business logic as well as process and service integration of service orientation while allowing you to customize and extend them. In other words, with solution frameworks you can hit the road quickly building and deploying applications out of the box, with little or no customization.

7.6 Service Oriented Architecture: Intelligent Technology Integration

> Service-oriented architectures (SOAs) provide flexibility and agility for organizations through their representation of business functionality as implementation-neutral, standards-based shared services. They are a natural progression in the evolution that began with the advent of XML and the emergence of Web Services.
>
> **OASIS, Electronic Business Service Oriented Architecture**

Information and programs go hand in hand. Content has been hyperorganized, or at least hyperlinked, through Web pages. Doing so has changed computer science and, in fact, has changed the world. Now we are embarking on an even greater revolution where enterprises will discover each other on demand and will create new products through service oriented architectures. The famous triangle illustration (Figure 7.13) is

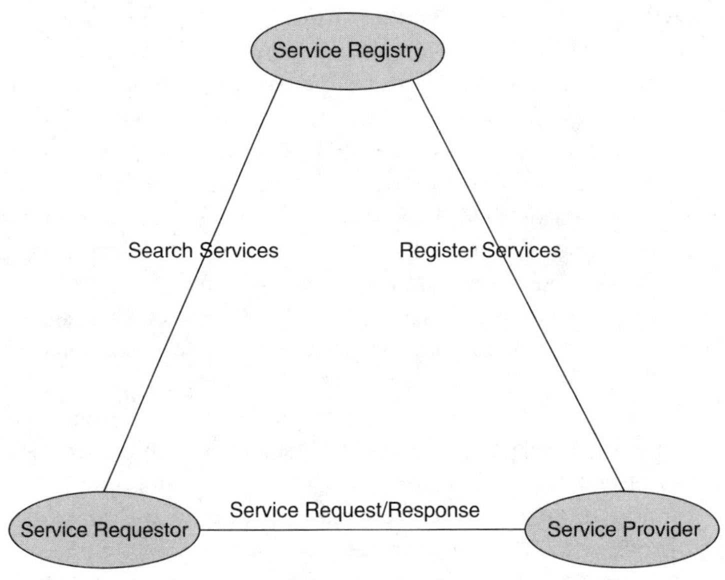

Figure 7.13 Register, search, and interact triangle

often used to depict the registration-discovery-exchange cycle in service orientation. Discovery is important in any domain. We spend quite a bit of time on the Internet with Google—we search. Typically, we search content or specific types of companies and, in fact, specific categories of services. As we move toward digitization of our processes and policies—our business rules—we now realize that computers also can discover. In fact, even though the notion of global directory services (e.g., UDDI) has not taken off as it should have, the underlying premise is correct: Allow the manual or automated discovery of services, and then go and interact with the service provider. Finding businesses and services on the Web today requires the use of a search engine or knowing the universal resource locator (URL) of the business. Currently on the Web there are no standards as to how companies organize their Web pages. Typically, they have an About company link, but every company does it differently. Also, the categorization of the products or services is ad hoc. Here again, each company will have its own way of representing the categorization of its products. UDDI improves on this chaos by providing a standard structure for companies to register information about themselves and their services. Under the UDDI standard, all registered companies will use the same elements for their contact information, standard business identification, standard categories of products, and standard mechanism to provide technical details about their services. Think of a UDDI registry as a powerful, well-organized discovery engine. UDDI benefits businesses of all sizes by creating a global, platform-independent, open architecture for describing, discovering, and integrating businesses using the Internet (Figure 7.13).

7.6.1 Looking Ahead: Intelligent Assembling of Services

The Web provides organization of content. The emerging architecture for the enterprise is providing organization of services. In other words, customers or trading partners can come to the Web site of organizations and access them programmatically. The Web hyperlinked information exists in various Web pages. The integration that emanates from service oriented invocation allows the hyperlinking of operations or functions within or between organizations. In fact, service orientation supports both. Content is also a service. But now with the linking of operations or functions that could be invoked on different systems, in different companies, the cycle is complete and doors have opened for new levels of efficiency and productivity. A huge bottleneck has been introduced even from the earliest days of computer science, and its implications are still to be grappled with. That bottleneck is programming. The vast amount of budgets in many IT organizations is trying to integrate with silos and to use custom programming to patch applications together.

This has not worked, and no matter how much is spent on programming tools, they still fall very short of the intended goals.

Does Web Services Description Language (WSDL) solve the problem? Not exactly—again, there are too many programming-level jargon and programming details to worry about. WSDL helps the definition of services. It does provide the necessary details to identify what a service does. However, at the core implementation level, it is still necessary to translate the WSDL onto a target language that implements the service. Clients need to access the services as specified by the WSDL through programming languages. So traditionally there is a programming language to programming language interaction (e.g., a C# client invoking a Java service via Web services especially SOAP layer). It is true that WSDL alleviates the language barrier in that the client can speak one language and the server can be written in another. WSDL abstracts and defines the service provider's interface, and SOAP acts as the lingua franca communicator between the two platforms—sort of a common translator. But this is still a world of programming integration or interoperability.

Enter intent-driven services and interactions. Instead of the tremendous bottlenecks created through programming, the focus should instead be on intents: Why is a particular service necessary? In what order should services with specific properties or characteristics execute? Then the power of visual and declarative programming should be used to locate and to assemble services automatically using the power of business rules. In other words, services should not be new names given to object components (if we use an object-oriented language) or Web services (if we use Web services for our implementation). For any human, organization, role, system, or trading partner we need intent-driven specifications to describe the service. Here is an example: Find the cheapest airline ticket to fly to London on March 12, 2007. This simple request could end up accessing numerous airlines or reservation systems and make price comparisons to locate the cheapest ticket. This is what is expected of travel agents. But now there are intent-driven intelligent service invocations focused on satisfying the request. This example shows interaction with one main service category: airline reservation. There can also be an intent-driven request for the entire trip including airline, car rental, hotel, recreation, etc. Services are often composed of other services. There are several intent-driven dimensions here:

- The composition or order of execution of the services—that is, the procedural intent of the services
- The constraints or the agreements that the services should satisfy no matter where they are used
- The properties that the services should satisfy—that is, the intent-driven description of the services

The intent-driven service discovery and interaction takes all these into consideration and binds dynamically to the most appropriate services to satisfy the request. Hence, the intelligence in assembling services.

Business and IT: A lot of what goes under the banner and promise of service orientation deals with distributed computing integration. Now from a technology perspective there is nothing wrong with that. Distributed computing is necessary. In fact, as CPU speeds are pushed to the limit and the proliferation of multiple CPU servers as well as distributed computing networks such as the grid are witnessed, the realization of how important it is to provide robust infrastructures to handle the coordination of distributed execution of services becomes apparent. Web services are also seen as the conduit and infrastructure for realizing grid computing. In the evolution of sharing in enterprises, XML provides a normalized standard for sharing information. Web services build on XML and support sharing of applications. With grid computing, it becomes possible to share computing resources across extended enterprises. IBM and other large organizations are pursuing grid computing and grid technologies. Grid computing has a number of distributed access and service invocation issues similar to Web services, and in fact, a Web services infrastructure can be used to realize grid computing. In other words, Web services make it possible to have grid-computing sharing solutions to access servers, storage, and other resources across the Web—internally or across individual or organizational resources. The Globus project (http://www.globus.org/), which includes the Argonne National Laboratory, the University of Southern California's Information Science Institute, and the University of Chicago, is leading the way in grid computing research. The project has defined an open-grid services architecture that uses Web services as the foundation of grid computing.

7.7 Web 2.0?

[Web 2.0 principles]: the Web as platform; data as the driving force; network effects created by an "architecture of participation"; innovation in assembly of systems and sites composed by pulling

> together features from distributed, independent developers ...; lightweight business models enabled by content and service syndication; the end of the software adoption cycle ...; software above the level of a single device ....
>
> **Wikipedia**

Throughout, this book has explained the emerging enterprise architecture of service oriented enterprises, with top-tier business performance management driving the objectives of the enterprise, and the underlying service oriented integration that spans internal and external service providers. Sandwiched between these two layers is the BPM layer that brings business and IT together to capture and automate business procedures and policies. However, what is often heard, especially in the technology blogs, is the emergence of what is called the second generation of the Web, or Web 2.0. What is Web 2.0, and how does it relate to the service oriented enterprise? Before providing an overview of some of the salient features of Web 2.0, a word of caution is offered here. There is some confusion as to exactly what constitutes Web 2.0. However, despite the confusion and sometimes conflicting definitions, there are some interesting trends and developments on the Web. Here are a few of them:

- Searching: I cannot remember the last time I was on the Internet and I did not find the need to do a Google search. And I know I am not alone. Google has even become an effective sales and marketing tool. Increasingly, SOE interfaces are accessed via Internet devices; this of course includes browsers, but handheld and other new emerging devices are also becoming popular. Searching is often incorporated on the desktop and the enterprise application as well. Searching is becoming increasingly semantics based: This will provide tremendous advantages for SOE, where best practice processes, business rule sets, and solution frameworks could be discovered through searching.
- Broadband and wireless: The propagation of broadband Internet is beginning to emerge, with close to 50 million subscribers in the United States alone. This number is growing exponentially. Equally important is the propagation and availability of wireless Internet access almost everywhere, in hotels, airports, and cafes. Connectivity is essential for SOEs. With the permeation of broadband and wireless connectivity we are perpetually online. This means we can constantly participate in SOE processes, completing tasks, assigning tasks, and responding to notifications.
- Handheld devices: There was almost a panic when there were rumors of Blackberry blackout due to a potential court injunction. Of course there are other alternative devices. The ability to have e-mail access

and to go online via a handheld device has incredible appeal. This goes hand in hand (no pun intended) with the wireless access: Increasingly, SOE applications will be accessed ubiquitously through many types of devices.

- Blogging: This concept of the blog did not exist a few years ago. Now entire communities in diverse fields of science, arts, politics, and human services are sharing and interacting through blogs. Interestingly, commercial enterprises are also starting to use blogs. Blogs are being used effectively by organizations to communicate not only from the higher ups but also the rank-and-file employees. Blogs provide an opportunity to reflect the enthusiasm, thinking, and vision of the SOE. They are an effective tool that has a flattening effect on the organizational hierarchy.
- Wikis: Another Web application that supports Internet communities. Several users can collaborate on articles and even build entire encyclopedias. Users can become co-authors and work on creating useful content. Wikis can be used within an intranet or on the Internet. Through Wikis, employees can easily build tutorials and share experiences over their intranet. Similar to blogs, Wikis also have a flattening effect on organizational hierarchy and help promote employee contribution and involvement within the enterprise.

Business and IT: Other innovations are having profound cultural effects, especially on the younger generation. iTunes have literally exploded. iPod (http://www.apple.com/itunes/) sales are growing at an annual triple-digit rate. Through iPods, digital jukeboxes can be built to hold in the palm of your hand. Suddenly we are witnessing the incredible proliferation of podcasts, which get downloaded automatically to iPods online. We are in the midst of another revolution where the Internet is becoming the main channel for multimedia content and communication.

So far these are some of the technological innovations and tools on the Web. These trends will continue. The day will come, and in fact it may be already here, where we will take for granted that all our appliances, communication devices, and transportation vehicles are online all the time. But wait, there is more. This is the tip of the iceberg. There are other trends at least equally if not more important with potentially tremendous impacts on service oriented enterprises:

- The Web as the platform to deliver software (discussed in more detail in the next section): This is a significant revolution. The delivery is commonplace now with most organizations having deployed intranet portals and accessing various types of software solutions from human resources to sales force automation over the Web. We are seeing the delivery of sophisticated software with only Web interfaces. This trend will continue. It is difficult to argue with Web-based delivery of software solutions where the solution becomes instantly available via browsers or Web services access without the need or overhead of installing thick client software on potentially thousands of laptops and workstations. Even tools such as word processes are becoming available online.
- The Web as the platform to develop software: Now things get really interesting with the advent of browser-based development. Today large organizations are building entire mission critical applications using browser-based business process and service oriented development and deployment tools. Powerful business process management applications can be built while using only browsers. Among other advantages, Web browsers are ubiquitous. The Web platform has become second nature for both business and IT. This common comfort can be leveraged when bringing IT and business together to build a new BPM solution. Browser-based development is in fact highly conducive to continuous improvement and dynamic life cycles. Change needs to involve the people who know and care most about the solution; a flexible browser-based development and deployment platform can only help.
- Rich internet application interfaces: Until recently the Web had been less graphical and limited in its usability as the platform for enterprise applications. Rich and thick (installed on the desktop) client applications characterized themselves as providing much richer graphical interfaces for the user. That is changing. We are now seeing the emergence of rich client interfaces for applications deployed on the Internet. Asynchronous JavaScript and XML (AJAX) is one technology that became quite popular in 2005, promising richer client interfaces and solving inherent performance limitations of Web interfaces. AJAX Internet applications behave similar to rich client applications, both in terms of the graphical user interface (GUI) and in terms of the ability to asynchronously obtain exactly what is needed for the task at hand—versus redrawing and sending the entire HyperText Markup Language (HTML) screen for each access.
- Proliferation of Web services: Of course the coup de grace of the second Internet revolution is the success of the Web services interactions with Web sites, both within and between enterprises. This is

the second phase of using the same Internet technologies and building on the success of XML to deliver back-end enterprise and trading partner connectivity through Web services technologies. In addition to SOAP, there has also been the emergence of other Web service architecture models, especially REST (Representation State Transfer). REST uses HTTP, URLs, and representations, such as HTML and XML. In fact, typical Web interactions are REST based. The REST model goes directly to the resource (e.g., an order or item) and interacts with it through URLs. Thus, there can be programmatic service access with URLs of resources.

Web 2.0 therefore is providing the overall infrastructure for SOEs. All the advances associated with Web 2.0—broadband wireless communications, participation, sharing, networking, rich Internet applications, multi-channel access, and the Web as the medium to build and to deliver applications—are great enablers of SOE solutions.

7.8 Software as a Service

The previous section described how the Web is becoming a delivery vehicle for communities' applications. Software is being sold as a service over the Web. Most organizations have Web sites (e.g., www.acme.com). The three-letter suffix at the end of the Web site address denotes the type of the organization. Dot-com is the most common, indicating a commercial organization. There are many others: dot-gov for government; dot-edu for education; and, more recently, dot-bus for business. Though most organizations have a Web address, most also use a third party to host their Web site. In other words small, medium-sized, and even large enterprises use another hosting company to host their external Web site content. This is a common practice. Dovetailing the Web site hosting is the emergence of a new deployment model for enterprise software: hosted enterprise software accessed through the Web.

The term *outsourcing* is common. Large and medium-sized companies alike use some sort of outsourcing. The outsourcing can take on many forms and shapes and all types in between. Many IT jobs are now being outsourced to other countries, especially to India and China. Usually outsourced projects are difficult to manage from overseas. Any project—for example, software development, quality assurance, and maintenance—can be outsourced. Software as a service extends this notion of outsourcing to the software itself.

Software as a service focuses on outsourced and hosted enterprise software. This has similarities to Web server and application service provider models.

But there are fundamental differences. Basically the service requestors from a software as a service-hosted application can subscribe to the software, which will be hosted on the premises of the service provider. The software will be maintained and upgraded mostly seamlessly to the service requestor. Any type of software could be outsourced and used as a service. Examples include content management, sales force automation, human resources, and CRM. Software as a service is not limited to horizontal applications. It can be used with any vertical domain as well. In short, any software that can be used in the premises of an enterprise can also potentially be hosted and procured as a service.

The more obvious and pervasive model is to allow the customer access to the software via Web browsers. The service providers will manage and maintain the software and also guarantee the required level of service quality. However, there is no reason why services could not be used via programmatic interfaces. In other words, just as end users could have authentication and authorization access for the hosted software procured as a service, Web services could also be procured and accessed via programmatic interfaces and built into the on-premise client or server applications of the enterprise. For instance, if a Web service provides support for an optimization library accessed with a Web service, then operations or functions within this library could be invoked as a service from within the enterprise. Software still functions as a service, but now instead of a browser-based interface a programmatic invocation is used.

Software as a service is an effective mechanism organizations can use in conjunction with IT outsourcing. A fundamental difference is that the outsourced operation is already available and can be accessed via the Web—potentially with little intervention. The service requestor does not need to worry about procuring servers to install and host the software, or all the headaches that go with enterprise software upgrades and platform support. This is an interesting trend in service orientation that is emerging at least initially through browser-based accesses.

Business and IT: IBM had developed a prototype that was called Web Services Outsourcing Manager (WSOM).[8] This is more a concept than a commercial product at this junction. WSOM allowed customers to provide their requirements via easy-to-use interfaces; then, the underlying outsourcing manager would be able to discover the appropriate service provider. Outsourcing managers could support a more direct and intuitive layer of searching and locating providers that is easier to use than UDDI registries and could potentially access multiple registries. The concept is analogous to having a metasearch engine that accesses and collects results from multiple search engines.

The outsourced Web services should be combined with metering and usage functionality. This means the customer will be charged based on the number of times the system is used and the amount of usage. This is important: Just as today some Web sites allow users to search content based on one-time or access-time usage fees, sites that have outsourced services can provide programmatic access to these services based on a fee. Similar to Web site accounts, the service provider will also support and manage customer accounts for the service accesses. In fact, once BPM standards such as Business Process Execution Language (BPEL) become commonplace, an outsourced Web service can access and pay for other services.

7.9 Dynamic Organization for an On-Demand Age

Those of us who have raised children (and I was blessed to have raised four boys) know how demanding two year olds can be. They need it now and often are not that sensitive to societal protocols. They say when we grow old we become like children. That is true of us, and it is also true of organizations.

Agility is supported when we build to change. Agility also needs dynamic discovery. If a company or organization has a specific need and that need is met by a specific provider, a lot depends on how one discovers the other and starts using the needed service. If we were to extrapolate purely in the Web services arena, the future of Web services is dynamic discovery and dynamic service binding.

Initially Web services were—and continue to be—used to connect and to integrate applications within an organization. This usage of Web services is often characterized as the early adoption. Organizations first try out Web services within their intranets and analyze the practicality of using Web services either to access or to integrate disparate applications. Web services accessed through ESBs are often positioned as an alternative to proprietary EAI, providing more flexibility.

As Web services become more popular within organizations, the next step is using them between trading partners to invoke remote operations from one organization to the other. I view this as an extension and tremendous improvement over the HTML era. Such integration uses XML, which is much richer than HTML and can capture almost any message exchange type. Furthermore, the access is programmatic, even though a Web service result could be retrieved and rendered in a Web page. They can be retrieved and used in any application or context, including business processes.

Thus, within an application, a program or process could decide to go out to a partner's Web service and invoke another remote application. These Web services could be statically bound; in other words, the specific Web service and organization involved is known ahead of time. It is true that a trading partner or requestor could do an initial find or discovery. But still, the service endpoint (i.e., a specific partner) and the service level agreement as well as security and reliability are known ahead of time. The binding can also be dynamic.

The Web evolved from static HTML to dynamic population and generation of Web pages. In a similar fashion, as the underlying infrastructure for Web services matures, it should be possible to dynamically discover or dynamically bind a service. This is the next phase. Business rules could be used to discover the most appropriate service dynamically. Increasingly, Web services development platforms and tools are facilitating this dynamic binding. Many technical and business issues must be addressed before Web services evolve to this point (e.g., service contracts, reliability, service semantics, availability, security), but the potential is tremendous. The dynamic discovery and binding of Web services to specific requests is an ideal goal of emerging SOE solutions.

7.9.1 Intelligent Web Services

One of the recurrent themes of this book has been the operational or programmatic exchange between organizations via Web services. The Web is getting smarter. All indications are that the next phase of Web content is going to be the semantic Web.[9] XML and HTML are syntactic structures. They do not provide inherent semantic representation of information. HTML and XML support the complex and hypermedia representation of information, but without additional constructs they do not provide semantics.

The desire is for machines or software to navigate or to make sense out of the Web—or any data for that matter. However, it will be very difficult for automated agents to process raw HTML or XML content. The semantic Web starts with the notion of global identifiers—uniform resource identifiers (URIs), which are similar to WWW URLs. Each resource (e.g., a Web page or any type of data) will have a URI that is globally unique. Semantic metadata then can be associated using a standard called Resource Data Framework (RDF). For example, a description can be given of the <title>

of the article contained in the resource, the <topic>, the <author>, the <date> it was created, and the <place> where it was created. The key point is that the content and the system processing the metadata tags can agree on the semantics of these tags. In fact, the move can be made beyond mere metadata (or data about the resource), and more complex relationships between resources and terms can be represented. Then rules can be created to draw conclusions and inferences from the resource metadata or resource relationships.

We are enriching the ontological experience of the Web. We are starting to link and share knowledge in ways never before imagined. So the day will come where metadata tags and concepts will be associated with resources on the Web. Automated agents will be able to search not only based on exact matches of words or terms but also on concepts. Categorizing concepts, linking terms, and then using inferencing to conduct searches will soon be commonplace. The result will be a much richer search and knowledge linking as well as extraction mechanism on the Web.

The semantic Web addresses the very challenging problem of associating meaning or semantics to the resources on the Web (e.g., Web pages) through organized concepts. This will allow software agents to process Web sites—not just humans. The semantic Web uses metadata—that is, data about the resource (or the data) contained on the Web. An inference engine or agent can then use this metadata to discover knowledge from the Web, to reason, and to make decisions. Vocabularies in many domains can be machine readable.

The Web is an immense database of hypermedia information. Through associating semantics and metadata to the Web resources, the ability of automated software systems to reason about the content, to discover new relationships, and to help answer even more complex queries can be greatly increased.

The World Wide Web evolved from Web pages to composition via hyperlinks. Now a semantically richer Web is beginning to emerge. In a similar way, we are witnessing the evolution of Web services from individual Web service providers to a composition of Web services in processes and then on to the last frontier: intelligent Web service compositions (Table 7.3).

This is very much a digitization[10] and intelligence trend. There is digitized information and digitized processes (through BPM technologies).

Table 7.3 Three C's for Web Pages and Web Services

	WWW	*Web Services*
Components	Web page	Web service
Composition	Hyperlinking of Web pages	Web service orchestration and choreography
Cleverness	Semantic Web	Intelligent Web services

Now the next frontier is digitization of rules for services. These rules capture reasoning, decision making, dynamic discovery, and service level agreements, which are typically in complex programs, in the minds of decision makers, or in volumes of paper. Rules will enrich the decision making in Web services processes. Rules will be able to reason over the performance of Web service invocations through reasoning over the history of monitored Web service calls. But rules will also be used to search and to discover services, to match service provider and consumer, and to create alignment between enterprises. In short, rules will make Web services intelligent.

Now agility can become possible. Through intelligent Web services, service oriented enterprises can become agile and can respond to increasingly demanding business pressures. Web services have to get smarter—and they are. As the evolution of service oriented enterprises demonstrates, the last phase, Phase 3, starts to provide intelligent Web services through tight integration of business rules and dynamic discovery and binding of Web services (Figure 7.14).

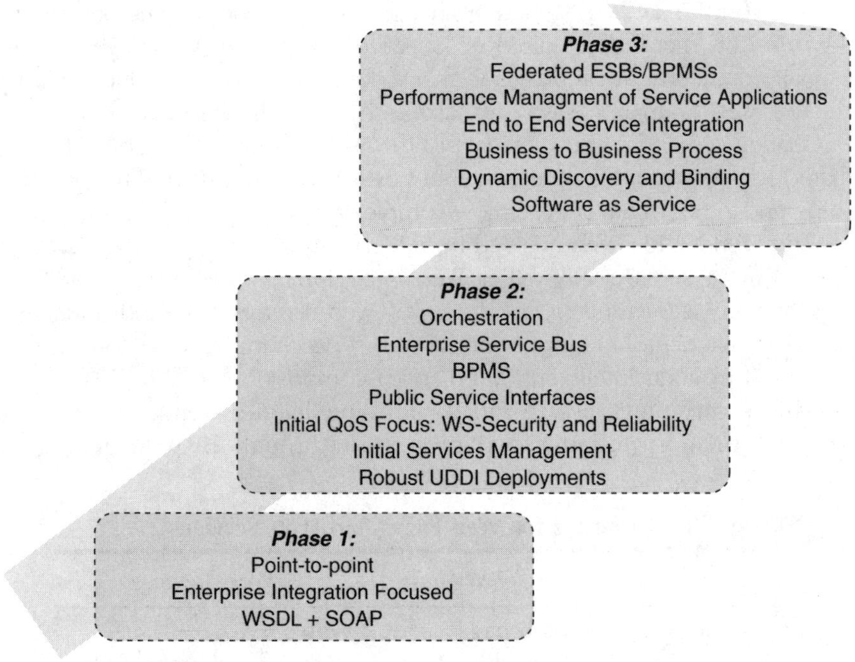

Phase 3:
Federated ESBs/BPMSs
Performance Managment of Service Applications
End to End Service Integration
Business to Business Process
Dynamic Discovery and Binding
Software as Service

Phase 2:
Orchestration
Enterprise Service Bus
BPMS
Public Service Interfaces
Initial QoS Focus: WS-Security and Reliability
Initial Services Management
Robust UDDI Deployments

Phase 1:
Point-to-point
Enterprise Integration Focused
WSDL + SOAP

Figure 7.14 The three phases of service oriented enterprises

7.10 Narrowing the Gap between Business and IT

Throughout this book we dealt with organizational and cultural issues. These are extremely important but often ignored aspects of service orientation. We are dealing with cultures within organizations and cultures between trading partners. We cannot ignore human and organizational dimensions. If we do, we will end up only with technological enablers. These are necessary but not sufficient.

IT and business owners are partners that need to narrow the execution gaps from corporate objectives to operational implementations through IT technologies to realize the desired growth, productivity, and compliance objectives. In fact, there is a difference in perspective between the priorities of IT and the priorities of business owners, as illustrated in Figure 7.15. Considerable gaps exist between the priorities of IT and the priorities of business owners. Understandably, businesses focus on revenue, reduction in operational costs, and compliance. IT, on the other hand, is concerned with the maintenance of existing—and often legacy—systems. IT is also concerned about its backlogs of projects. Businesses focus on sustaining growth. Service orientation, especially through the business process management layer, is the bridge that fills this gap and helps both IT and business owners realize their priorities. Service orientation narrows and attempts to eliminate the business–IT divide.

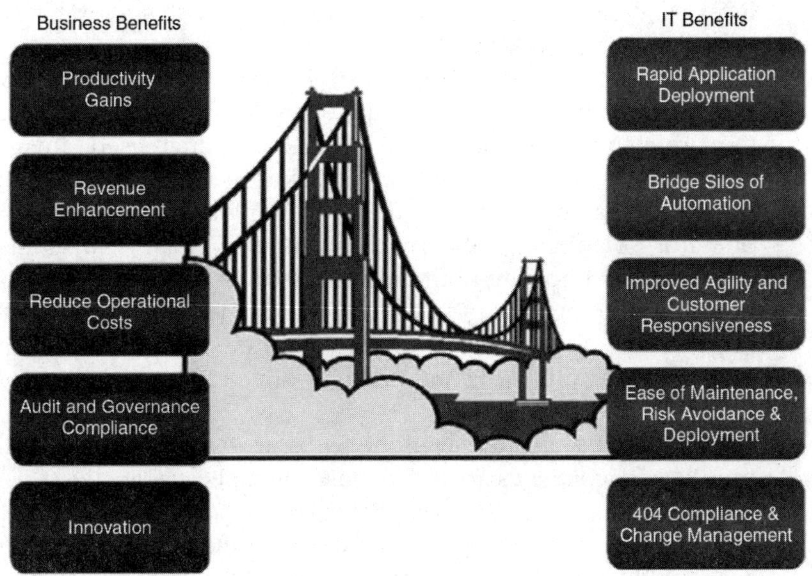

Figure 7.15 Business and IT priorities

7.10.1 More on the Gap

IT projects have had a bad rap. Despite the enormous and commendable efforts of IT staff, often the impression is that IT has not delivered. In fact, there is a troubling and confusing echo in the corridors of many organizations that questions the effectiveness of IT. Publications such as Nicholas G. Carr's "IT Doesn't Matter" paper have not helped. This is how Carr puts it: "As their [IT] availability increased their cost decreased ... they became commodity inputs. From a strategic standpoint, they became invisible; they no longer mattered."[11]

Nothing could be further from the truth. Discussing the merits of Carr's position is beyond the scope of this book.[12] However, it is enough to emphasize that IT's role—especially the strategic role of IT in supporting businesses through BPM—is actually increasing. More specifically, through BPM as the core layer of the SOE architecture, IT and businesses become partners in realizing three essential ingredients for success:

1. Growth: This means new products and services can be created quickly and affordably. It also means existing products and services could be easily specialized. Growth is also tightly related to customer retention and satisfaction. Here BPM helps realize business goals. In fact, through BPM solutions, process innovations can be achieved: Create innovative products that will give the competitive edge. As James Champy states, "This [Process Innovation] is becoming increasingly important. In many industries, how this is executed is the basis of competition."[13]
2. Productivity: This means more can be done with less resources. It means routine tasks can be pushed to the system. It also means the productivity of your employees can be increased. Imagine how much time is spent on manual tasks, on searching, on understanding what needs to be done by a particular employee or operator. A robust rules-driven business process management platform can automate both the processes as well as policies. The resulting automation and digitization can yield unprecedented productivity. As usual, the SOA in these environments becomes the underlying plumbing and the rules-driven BPM the layer above that.
3. Compliance: Compliance with the Sarbanes–Oxley Act of 2002 has caused and continues to cause quite an upheaval in the United States. There are similar compliance regulations in Europe (e.g., Basel II). The Sarbanes–Oxley Act came on the heels of the Enron and Worldcom fiascos. Noncompliance has several serious ramifications for C-level executives, primarily chief executive officers and chief financial officers but also chief information officers. This is where BPM comes into the picture, automating processes and policies

and storing all the transactions, process data, and business rules to support the Sarbanes–Oxley compliance.

IT does matter. Getting business and IT aligned should be a top priority. Through direct collaboration with business stakeholders and the continuous capturing and digitization of business rules and policies, IT becomes the seminal partner in realizing strategic and tactical corporate objectives.

In fact, to achieve growth, productivity, and compliance, chief information officers need to worry about constantly changing conditions, stakeholder pressures, market realities, and changing requirements. The causes for change and agility are many. They include external factors such as changes in the market, demands for new products, production costs, and demands for globalization. Change requests also come from customers. Increasingly there is a high demand for customized products and services. Organizations need to revisit their operations and production processes to make sure they can meet these demands in real-time. There are also internal and technology factors. Supply and value chains are becoming increasingly automated. This implies changes in the overall interoperability between trading partners. Changes are also initiated due to cost overruns. Earlier innovation was alluded to in the context of productivity. Innovation is equally important for growth and compliance.

Innovation means the enterprise has to come up with new processes, new approaches, and new products or services to improve its efficiency and to respond to internal and external challenges through creative approaches.

Process innovations focus on building an adaptive business process management system that increases bottom-line profitability, reduces costs, improves efficiency, raises productivity, and increases employee job satisfaction.[14]

Innovation goes hand in hand with change. To apply innovation and creativity in any business function, the organization needs to be agile in its implementation. Organizations need to adjust and to maneuver as the circumstances change. They need to be able to implement changes quickly and creatively—to innovate. Change is the only constant. And the frequency as well as the magnitude of change is increasing. In this milieu of unprecedented pressures on businesses, the respective roles of IT and businesses are changing. In service oriented enterprises, business and IT are coming together to share and to execute business processes. Businesses are starting to learn how to utilize productive tools involving business rules and business process digitization. In fact, they are managing their businesses through continuous improvements and monitoring. IT is also becoming more business savvy through understanding the language as well as the concerns of businesses. To control the cost and complexity overheads introduced by constant pressures and changes in business rules, IT needs to have an environment that can easily implement, deploy, monitor, and improve. This is easier said than done—but it is essential.

7.11 Service Oriented Enterprises: What Is Most Important

Service orientation is here to stay. Some are skeptical. There have been several decades now of Internet success. The Internet has changed enterprises. It has also changed communities and has created a culture where online connectivity has become second nature. This is especially true of younger generations: The Internet is as common and ubiquitous as radio or television for previous generations. What does it all mean for SOEs?

Service oriented enterprises will be using the robust Internet technologies to connect organizations as never before. Service integration with business processes deployed end to end in the extended enterprises provide a tremendous foundation.

But then again, service orientation is not just about technology; it is about a culture. Technology will help, and the three layers are necessary. They are not sufficient. The revolution starts with a service culture that focuses on the community being served. It is about enterprises and especially the human participants viewing themselves as service providers and service consumers. It is about servicing all the diverse communities of the enterprise (Figure 7.16).

Figure 7.16 The communities served by SOEs

Above all, it starts with the leadership. Servant leaders will be at the helm, leading the enterprise in this brave new world of service computing. The journey has just begun.

Notes

1. "Greed is good" is a famous 1987 movie moment in *Wall Street*. It was uttered as a philosophy of success by the hero, Gordon Gekko, played by Michael Douglas.
2. Page and Wong, "Conceptual Framework for Measuring Servant Leadership," in Senyo B-S.K. Adjibolosso, (Ed.), *The Human Factor in Shaping the Course of History and Development*. New York, NY: University Press of America, 2000. Also Greenleaf Centre servant leadership, http://www.greenleaf.org. au/.
3. From the definition of "servant leadership" at http://www.amca.com/sl/.
4. This book considers business performance measurement and enterprise performance measurement to be synonyms.
5. http://www.juergendaum.com/news/09_30_2004.htm
6. The assumption is made here that the BRE is within the BPM system. There are other options, such as a separate BRE or correlation engine within the event manager.
7. For more details on how BPM systems support Six Sigma, see "Business Process Management for Six Sigma Projects," *Workflow Handbook 2006* http://www.wfmc.org/information/handbook06.htm, Workflow Management Coalition, editor Layna Fischer.
8. http://www.alphaworks.ibm.com/tech/WSOM
9. For an excellent introduction to the semantic Web, see http://www.scientificamerican.com/article.cfm?articleID=00048144-10D2-1C7084A9809EC588EF21&catID=2 by Tim Berners-Lee et al. Also see http://www.w3.org/2001/sw/.
10. Think of digitization as automation or translation into software.
11. Nicholas G. Carr, "IT Doesn't Matter," *Harvard Business Review*, March 2003.
12. In fact for an excellent counter point to Carr's position, see *IT Doesn't Matter Business Processes Do* by Howard Smith and Peter Fingar, Meghan–Kiffer Press, 2003.
13. http://searchcio.techtarget.com/columnItem/0,294698,sid19_gci1098005,00.html
14. http://www.1000ventures.com/products/ss_effective_innovation.html

Selected Bibliography

Throughout the book we provided references to various articles, Web sites, and books. The selected bibliography lists books that are most relevant to *Service Oriented Enterprises*.

Arora, Sandeep (2005). *Business Process Management,* Lightning Source Inc.

Barry, Douglas K. (2003). *Web Services and Service-Oriented Architectures: The Savvy Manager's Guide,* Morgan Kaufmann Publishers.

Cerami, Ethan (2002). *Web Services Essentials,* O'Reilly.

Champy, James (2002). *X-Engineering the Corporation: Reinventing Your Business in the Digital Age,* Warner Books, Inc.

Chappell, David (2004). *Enterprise Service Bus: Theory in Practice,* O'Reilly.

Chowdhury, Subir (2003). *Organization 21C: Someday All Organizations Will Lead This Way,* Prentice Hall.

Christensen, Clayton M., and Raynor, Michael E. (2003). *The Innovator's Solution: Creating and Sustaining Successful Growth*, Harvard Business School Press.

Davidow, William H. and Malone, Michael S. (1993). *The Virtual Corporation,* HarperBusiness.

Debevoise, Tom (2005). *Business Process Management With a Business Rules Approach: Implementing the Service Oriented Architecture,* Arbor Books.

Erl, Thomas (2005). *Service-Oriented Architecture (SOA): Concepts, Technology, and Design,* Prentice Hall.

Fingar, Peter, and Bellini, Joe (2004). *The Real-Time Enterprise,* Meghan-Kiffer Press.

Fingar, Peter (2006). *Extreme Competition: Innovation And the Great 21st Century Business Reformation,* Meghan-Kiffer Press.

Friedman, Thomas L. (2005). *The World Is Flat: A Brief History of the Twenty-First Century,* Farrar, Straus and Giroux.

Greenleaf, Robert K., Spears, Larry C., and Covey, Stephen R. (2002). *Servant Leadership: A Journey into the Nature of Legitimate Power and Greatness,* Paulist Press.

Hammer, Michael, and Champy, James (1993). *Reengineering the Corporation: A Manifesto for Business Revolution*, Harper Business.

Harrison-Broninski, Keith (2005). *Human Interactions: The Heart And Soul Of Business Process Management: How People Really Work And How They Can Be Helped To Work Better,* Meghan-Kiffer Press.

Havey, Michael (2005). *Essential Business Process Modeling*, O'Reilly.

Hunter, James (1998). *The Servant, A Simple Story About the True Essence of Leadership,* Prima Publishing.

Khoshafian, Setrag, and Buckiewicz, Marek (1995). *Introduction Groupware, Workflow, and Workgroup Computing,* John Wiley and Sons.

Koulopoulos, Thomas M, and Palmer. Nathaniel (2001). *The X-Economy: Profiting from Instant Commerce,* Texere.

Krafzig, Dirk, Banke, Karl, and Slama, Dirk (2004). *Enterprise SOA: Service-Oriented Architecture Best Practice,* Prentice Hall.

Morgan, Tony (2002). *Business Rules and Information Systems: Aligning IT with Business Goals,* Addison Wesley.

Newcomer, Eric and Lomow, Greg (2004). *Understanding SOA with Web Services,* Addison Wesley Professional.

Olve, Nils-Göran, Roy, Jan, and Wetter, Magnus (1999). *Performance Drivers: A Practical Guide to Using the Balanced Scorecard,* John Wiley and Sons.

Ould, Martyn A. (2005). *Business Process Management: A Rigorous Approach,* Meghan-Kiffer Press.

Peterson, Eugene H. (1993). *The Message,* Navpress.

Przekop, Penelope (2005). *Six Sigma for Business Excellence,* The McGraw-Hill Companies.

Pyzdek, Thomas (2003). *The Six Sigma Handbook: The Complete Guide for Greenbelts, Blackbelts, and Managers at All Level,* The McGraw-Hill Companies.

Ross, Ron (2005). *Business Rules Concepts,* Business Rule Solutions.

Rumbaugh, James, Jacobson, Ivar, and Booch, Grady (2004). *Unified Modeling Language Reference Manual,* Addison Wesley Professional.

Sadiq, Waqar, and Racca, Felix. *Business Service Orchestration,* Cambridge University Press.

Smith, Howard, and Fingar, Peter (2003). *Business Process Management: The Third Wave,* Meghan-Kiffer Press.

Spanyi, Andrew. *More for Less: The Power of Process Management,* Meghan-Kiffer Press.

von Halle, Barbara (2001). *Business Rules Applied,* John Wiley & Sons.

Weerawarana, Sanjiva, Curbera, Francisco, Leymann, Frank, Storey, Tony, and Ferguson, Donald F. (2005). *Web Services Platform Architecture: SOAP, WSDL, WS-Policy, WS-Addressing, WS-BPEL, WS-Reliable Messaging, and More,* Prentice Hall.

Index

D

Q

R

T

U

X

Y

Z